NEW VOYAGES

TO

NORTH-AMERICA

BY THE

BARON DE LAHONTAN

Reprinted from the English edition of 1703, with facsimiles of original title-pages, maps, and illustrations, and the addition of Introduction, Notes, and Index

By Reuben Gold Thwaites, LL.D.

Editor of "The Jesuit Relations and Allied Documents," Hennepin's "New Discovery," etc.

In Two Volumes
VOLUME II

CHICAGO
A. C. McCLURG & CO.
1905

Copyright
A. C. McCLURG & CO.
1905
Published February 25, 1905

Composition by The Dial Press, Chicago.
Presswork by The University Press, Cambridge.

CONTENTS — VOLUME II

PAGE

LAHONTAN's "NEW VOYAGES TO NORTH-AMERICA"—
Volume II.
   Title-page (facsimile of original) 409
   Discourses —
      Of the Habit, Houſes, Complexion and Temperament of the Savages of North-America . . 411
      Of the Humours and Cuſtoms of the Savages . 420
      The Belief of the Savages, and the Obſtacles of their Converſion 434
      The way of Worſhip, uſed by the Savages . . 446
      Of the Amours and Marriages of the Savages . 451
      Of the Diſeaſes and Remedies of the Savages . 465
      The Diverſions of Hunting and Shooting uſual among the Savages 476
      The Military Art of the Savages 495
      A View of the Heraldry, or the Coats of Arms of the Savages 510
      An Explication of the Savage Hieroglyphicks . 512
   A Conference or Dialogue between the Author and Adario, a Noted Man among the Savages, Containing a Circumſtantial View of the Cuſtoms and Humours of that People 517

Contents

An Appendix, Containing fome New Voyages to Portugal and Denmark; after the Author's Retirement from Canada:

    Letters I (Lisbon, April 20, 1694) – VII (Saragoza, October 8, 1695) 619

A Short Dictionary of the moft Univerfal Language of the Savages 732

INDEX — *The Editor* 751

ILLUSTRATIONS—VOLUME II

(FACSIMILES OF ORIGINALS)

	PAGE
Figure of Indian in an Oval	*Frontispiece*
"A Village of the Savages of Canada"; with figures of men and children	*Facing* 430
Diagram showing "The way of Worſhip"	,, 464
Sketches illustrating "Amours and Marriages"	,, 492
Sketches illustrating remedies, death, and burial	,, 524
"A Beaver Pool," and methods of hunting beavers	,, 556
A beaver hunt	,, 588
"The Military Art" (a)	,, 622
"The Military Art" (b)	,, 654
"Coats of Arms"	,, 686
"Hieroglyphick Symbols"	,, 720

NEW VOYAGES

TO

North-America.

Giving a full Account of the Customs, Commerce, Religion, and strange Opinions of the Savages of that Country.

WITH

POLITICAL REMARKS upon the Courts of *Portugal* and *Denmark*, and the Present State of the Commerce of those Countries.

Never Printed before.

WRITTEN

By the Baron LAHONTAN, Lord Lieutenant of the *French* Colony at *Placentia* in *Newfoundland*: Now in *England*.

VOL. II.

LONDON:

Printed for H. *Bonwicke* in St. *Paul's* Church-yard; T. *Goodwin*, M. *Wotton*, B. *Tooke* in *Fleetstreet*; and S. *Manship* in *Cornhill*, 1703.

A DISCOURSE

OF THE

Habit, Houses, Complexion and Temperament

OF THE

SAVAGES

OF

NORTH-AMERICA.

THE *Grecian* Chronologers who divided the course of Time into three Periods, namely the ἄδηλον, or that which is wrapt up in Obscurity, the μυθιχὸν, alias ἡζωιχὸν, or that which was the season of Fiction and Fables, and the ἰσοειχὸν which affords us true and creditable Actions: These Chronologers, I say, might have sav'd themselves the trouble of writing a Thousand idle Stories relating to the Original of the Inhabitants of the Earth; for the invention of Writing being unknown to them before the Siege of *Troy*, they had no other Standard to consult but the Fabulous Manuscripts of the *Egyptians* and *Chaldeans*, who were a Phanatick Superstitious sort of People. But supposing the

Egyptians and *Chaldeans* to have invented the Art of Writing, what Credit can we give to the accounts of things that are said to have happen'd before the date of that Invention? In all probability they knew no more of the matter than the *Americans*, and upon that score 'twas very hard for them to give a faithful Narrative of the Adventures and Exploits of their Ancestors. I am now fully convinc'd that Tradition is so inconstant, obscure, uncertain and fallacious, that we cann't pretend to rely upon it. And this Notion I owe to the Savages of *Canada*, who being at a loss to trace the truth of what has been transacted in their own Country but 200 Years ago, gave me occasion to call in Question the Purity and Truth of Tradition. Upon this lay you may easily apprehend, that these poor People are as little acquainted with their own History and Origin, as the *Greeks* and *Chaldeans* were with theirs. Let us therefore content our selves, *my good Friend*, in believing that they are descended of honest old *Adam*, as well as you and I.

I have read some Histories of *Canada*, which were writ at several times by the Monks, and must own that they have given some plain and exact Descriptions of such Countries as they knew; but at the same time they are widely mistaken in their Accounts of the Manners and Customs of the Savages.[1]

---

[1] The "monkish histories" of Canada which Lahontan had probably seen, were: *Jesuit Relations*, of which forty volumes had been published yearly in Paris from 1632–73; Du Creux, *Historiæ Canadensis seu Novæ-Franciæ* (Paris, 1664), largely composed from the *Relations;* and Thévenot, *Receuil des Voyages Curieux* (Paris, 1681), containing Marquette's account of his discoveries. The Recollect historians were Sagard-Theodat, *Histoire du Canada et voyages que les frères*

The Recollets brand the Savages for ſtupid, groſs and ruſtick Perſons, uncapable of Thought or Reflection: But the Jeſuits give them other ſort of Language, for they intitle them to good Senſe, to a tenacious Memory, and to a quick Apprehenſion ſeaſon'd [3] with a ſolid Judgment. The former allege that 'tis to no purpoſe to preach the Goſpel to a ſort of People that have leſs Knowledge than the Brutes.[1] On the other hand the latter (I mean the Jeſuits) give it out, that theſe Savages take Pleaſure in hearing the Word of God, and readily apprehend the meaning of the Scriptures. In the mean time, 'tis no difficult matter to point to the Reaſons that influence the one and the other to ſuch Allegations; the Myſtery is eaſily unravell'd by thoſe who know that theſe two Orders cannot ſet their Horſes together in *Canada*.[2]

I have ſeen ſo many impertinent Accounts of this Country, and thoſe written by Authors that paſs'd for Saints; that I now begin to believe, that all Hiſtory is one continued

---

mineurs Récollets y ont faicts (1636); Le Clercq, *Premier établissement de la foy dans la Nouvelle France* (Paris, 1691); Hennepin, *Description de la Louisiane* (Paris, 1683); *New Discovery* (London, 1698). — ED.

[1] See Thwaites (ed.), *Hennepin's New Discovery*, p. 466, for an example of this allegation of the Recollects. — ED.

[2] The rivalry between the two orders was nearly co-extensive with the history of New France, where the Recollects were first upon the field, but after 1632 were supplanted by the Jesuits. Talon re-introduced the Recollects to Canada in 1670, that they might act as a foil to the Jesuits. The former were supported by Frontenac and the governor's party in the colony, and accompanied La Salle upon his explorations. Lahontan means to intimate that the difference in the attitude of the two orders towards the savages, rested upon the varying success of their respective missions — those of the Jesuits being large and flourishing, of the Recollects few and languishing. — ED.

Series of Pyrrhonifm.[1] Had I been unacquainted with the Language of the Savages, I might have credited all that was faid of them; but the opportunity I had of Converfing with that People, ferv'd to undeceive me, and gave me to underftand, that the Recollets and the Jefuits content themfelves with glancing at things, without taking notice of the (almoft) invincible Averfion of the Savages to the Truths of Chriftianity. Both the one and the other had good reafon to be cautious of touching upon that String. In the mean time fuffer me to acquaint you, that upon this Head I only fpeak of the Savages of *Canada*, excluding thofe that live beyond the River of *Miffifipi*, of whofe Manners and Cuftoms I could not acquire a perfect Scheme, by reafon that I was unacquainted with their Languages, not to mention that I had not time to make any long ftay in their Country. In the Journal of my Voyage upon the long River, I acquainted you that they are a very polite People, which you [4] will likewife infer from the Circumftances mention'd in that Difcourfe.

Thofe who have reprefented the Savages to be as rough as Bears, never had the opportunity of feeing them; for they have neither Beard nor Hair in any part of their Body, not fo much as under their Arm-pits.[2] This is true of both Sexes, if I may credit thofe who ought to know better than I.

---

[1] Pyrrho was a Greek philosopher, founder of the school of absolute skepticism. — ED.

[2] The Indians are not altogether beardless; but, disliking the custom of wearing hair upon the face, pluck it out by the roots. See *Jesuit Relations*, i, p. 281; ii, p. 23, where Membertou, the Acadian chief, is spoken of as being bearded like a Frenchman. — ED.

Generally they are proper well made Perfons, and fitter Companions to *American* than to *European* Women. The *Iroquefe* are of a larger Stature, and withal more Valiant and Cunning than the other Nations; but at the fame time they are neither fo Nimble nor fo Dexterous at the Exercifes of War or Hunting, which they never go about but in great Numbers. The *Illinefe*, the *Oumamis*, and the *Outagamins*; with fome other adjacent Nations, are of an indifferent fize, and run like Greyhounds, if the Comparifon be allowable. The *Outaouas*, and moft of the other Savages to the *Northward*, (excepting the *Sauteurs* and the *Cliftinos*) are cowardly, ugly, and ungainly Fellows; but the *Hurons* are a brave, active and daring People, refembling the *Iroquefe* in their Stature and Countenance.

All the Savages are of a Sanguine Conftitution, inclining to an Olive Colour, and generally fpeaking they have good Faces and proper Perfons. 'Tis a great rarity to find any among them that are Lame, Hunch-back'd, One-ey'd, Blind, or Dumb.[1] Their Eyes are large and black as well as their Hair; their Teeth are White like Ivory, and the Breath that fprings from their Mouth in expiration is as pure as the Air that they fuck in in Infpiration, notwithftanding they eat no Bread; which fhews that we are miftaken in *Europe*, in fancying that the eating of Meat [5] without Bread makes one's breath ftink. They are neither fo ftrong nor fo vigorous as moft of the *French* are in raifing of Weights with their Arms,

---
[1] On immunity from disease and deformity, consult *Jes. Rel*, iii, p. 75.—ED.

or carrying of Burdens on their Backs; but to make amends for that, they are indefatigable and inur'd to Hardships, infomuch that the Inconveniences of Cold or Heat have no impression upon them; their whole time being spent in the way of Exercise, whether in running up and down at Hunting and Fishing, or in Dancing and playing at Foot-ball, or such Games as require the Motion of the Legs.

The Women are of an indifferent Stature, and as handsom in the Face as you can well imagine; but then they are so fat, unwieldy and ill-built, that they'l scarce tempt any but Savages. Their Hair is rolled up behind with a sort of Ribband, and that Roller hangs down to their Girdle; they never offer to cut their Hair during the whole Course of their Lives, whereas the Men cut theirs every Month.[1] Twere to be wished, that the same good luck which led them to the observation of this, had thrown them upon the other Advices of St. *Paul*. They are covered from the Neck to under the Knee, and always put their Legs a cross when they sit. The Girls do the same from their *Cradle;* if the Word be not improper, for there is no such thing as a *Cradle* among the Savages. The Mothers make use of certain little Boards stuffed with Cotton, upon which the Children lye as if their Backs were glued to them, being swaddled in Linnen, and kept on with Swathbands run through the sides of the Boards. To these Boards they tye

---

[1] On the various fashions of hair-dressing among the Indians, see *Jes. Rel.*, xliv, pp. 285, 287. A woman's hair was sometimes cut as a punishment for adultery. — ED.

Strings, by which they hang their Children upon the Branches of Trees, when they are about any thing in the Woods.[1]

[6] The old and the married Men have a piece of Stuff which covers them behind, and reaches half way down their Thighs before; whereas the young Men are ſtark naked all over. They alledge that Nakedneſs is no infraction upon the Meaſures of Decency, any otherwiſe than as it is contrary to the Cuſtom of the *Europeans*, and condemn'd by the Notion that they have of it. However, both the young and the old hang upon their Backs in a careleſs way a Covering of Hide or of Scarlet, when they go abroad to Walk or to make Viſits. They have likewiſe a ſort of Cloaks or Coats calculated for the Seaſon, when they go a Hunting or upon Warlike Expeditions, in order to guard off the Cold in Winter, and the Flies in Summer. Upon ſuch occaſions they make uſe of a ſort of Caps made in the form of a Hat, and Shooes of Elk or Hart Skins, which reach up to their mid-Leg.[2]

Their Villages are Fortified with double Paliſſadoes of very hard Wood, which are as thick as one's Thigh, and fifteen Foot high, with little Squares about the middle of the Courtines. Commonly their Huts or Cottages are Eighty Foot long, Twenty five or Thirty Foot deep, and Twenty Foot high. They are cover'd with the Bark of young Elms;

---

[1] For a good description of these Indian cradles, see Thwaites (ed.), *Early Western Travels*, ii, pp. 97, 98; Masson, *Bourgeois de la Compagnie du Nord-Ouest* (Quebec, 1890), ii, pp. 322, 323 — ED

[2] Le Jeune gives in *Jes. Rel.*, vii, pp. 7–19, a good description of the various kinds of dress among the Canadian Indians at different seasons of the year. — ED.

and have two Alcoves, one on the right Hand and the other on the left, being a Foot high and nine Foot broad, between which they make their Fires, there being vents made in the Roof for the Smoak. Upon the fides of the two Alcoves there are little Clofets or Apartments in which the young Women or married Perfons lye upon little Beds rais'd about a Foot from the Ground. To Conclude, one Hut contains three or four Families.[1]

[7] The Savages are very Healthy, and unacquainted with an infinity of Difeafes, that plague the *Europeans*, fuch as the *Palfey*, the *Dropfey*, the *Gout*, the *Phthifick*, the *Afthma*, the *Gravel*, and the *Stone*: But at the fame time they are liable to the *Small-Pox*, and to *Pleurifies*. If a Man dies at the Age of Sixty Years, they think he dies young, for they commonly live to Eighty or an Hundred; nay, I met with two that were turn'd of an Hundred feveral Years.[2] But there are fome among them that do not live fo long, becaufe they voluntarily fhorten their Lives by poyfoning themfelves, as I fhall fhew

---

[1] The domestic architecture of the American aborigines varied with the tribe and their habitat. Lahontan had ranged from Newfoundland to Mackinac, if not farther, and it is a question which of the many classes of huts he had seen he is now describing. Probably he refers to those of the Huron, who then lived in settled villages both in the Mackinac district and near the French fort on Lake St. Clair. See Parkman, *Jesuits in North America*, pp. xxvi–xxviii. Upon the entire subject of Indian dwellings, consult Morgan, "Houses and House-Life of American Aborigines," United States Geological Survey, *Contributions to Ethnology*, 1881. — ED.

[2] Early travellers obtained a mistaken notion of Indian longevity. Older chiefs, like many old men among the whites, took pride in their length of years and delighted in enlarging upon the facts. Modern observation proves that savages are the victims of their unsanitary life, and are subject to peculiar hardships and vicissitudes, hence die rather younger than white men. — ED.

you elsewhere. In this Point they seem to join issue with *Zeno* and the *Stoicks*, who vindicate *Self-Murther;* and from thence I conclude, that the *Americans* are as great Fools as these great Philosophers.

A short View of the Humors and Customs of the
SAVAGES.

THE *Savages* are utter Strangers to distinctions of Property, for what belongs to one is equally anothers. If any one of them be in danger at the Beaver Hunting the rest fly to his Assistance without being so much as ask'd. If his Fusee bursts they are ready to offer him their own. If any of his Children be kill'd or taken by the Enemy, he is presently furnish'd with as many Slaves as he hath occasion for. Money is in use with none of them but those that are Christians, who live in the Suburbs of our Towns. The others will not touch or so much as look upon Silver, but give it the odious Name of the *French Serpent.* They'l tell you that amongst [8] us the People Murther, Plunder, Defame, and betray one another, for Money, that the Husbands make Merchandize of their Wives, and the Mothers of their Daughters, for the Lucre of that Metal. They think it unaccountable that one Man should have more than another, and that the Rich should have more Respect than the Poor. In short, they say, the name of Savages which we bestow upon them would fit our selves better, since there is nothing in our Actions that bears an appearance of Wisdom. Such as have been in *France* were continually teazing us with the Faults and Disorders they obferv'd in our Towns, as being occafion'd by Money. 'Tis in vain to remonftrate to them how ufeful the Diftinction of Property is for the fupport of a Society: They make a Jeft of what's to be faid on that Head. In fine, they neither Quarrel nor Fight, nor Slander one another. They fcoff at Arts and Sciences, and laugh at the difference of Degrees which is obferv'd with us. They brand us for Slaves, and call us miferable Souls, whofe Life is not worth having, alledging, That we degrade our felves in fubjecting our felves to one Man who poffeffes the whole Power, and is bound by no Law but his own Will; That we have continual Jars among our felves; that our Children rebel againft their Parents; that we Imprifon one another, and publickly promote our own Deftruction. Befides, they value themfelves above any thing that you can imagine, and this is the reafon they always give for't, *That one's as much Mafter as another, and fince Men are all made of the fame Clay there fhould be no Diftinction or Superiority among them.* They pretend that their contented way of Living far furpaffes our Riches; That all our Siences are not fo valuable as the Art of leading a peaceful calm Life; [9] That a Man is not a Man with us any farther than Riches will make him; but among them the true Qualifications of a Man are, to run well, to hunt, to bend the Bow and manage the Fuzee, to work a Cannoo, to underftand War, to know Forrefts, to fubfift upon a little, to build Cottages, to fell Trees, and to be able to travel an hundred Leagues in a Wood without any Guide, or other Provifion than his Bow and Arrows. They fay, we are great Cheats in felling them bad Wares four times dearer than they are worth, by way of Exchange for their Beaver-skins: That our Fuzees are continually burſting and laming them, after they havê paid ſufficient Prices for them. I wiſh I had time to recount the innumerable Abſurdities they are guilty of relating to our Cuſtoms, but to be particular upon that Head would be a Work of Ten or Twelve Days.

Their Victuals are either Boild or roaſted, and they lap great quantities of the Broath, both of Meat and of Fiſh: They cannot bear the taſte of Salt or Spices, and wonder that we are able to live ſo long as thirty Years, conſidering our Wines, our Spices, and our Immoderate Uſe of Women. They dine generally Forty or Fifty in a Company, and ſomtimes above Three Hundred: Two Hours before they begin they employ themſelves in Dancing, and each Man ſings his Exploits, and thoſe of his Anceſtors; they dance but one at a time, while the reſt are ſet on the Ground, and mark the Cadence with an odd Tone, *He, He, He, He;* after which every one riſes and dances in his turn.

The Warriers attempt nothing without the Advice of the Council, which is compoſed of the Old Men of the Nation; that is to ſay, ſuch as are above Sixty: Before they are aſſembled a [10] Cryer gives notice of it through all the Streets in the Village: Then theſe old Old Men run to a certain Cottage deſign'd for that purpoſe, where they ſeat themſelves in a Square Figure; and after they have weigh'd what is propos'd for the benefit of the Nation, the Speaker goes out of the Cottage, and the Young Men get about him, and liſten with great attention to the Resolves of the Old ones, crying out at the end of every Sentence *That's Good.*[1]

They have several sorts of Dances. The principal is that of the *Calumet;* the rest are the Chiefs or Commanders Dance, the Warriers Dance, the Marriage Dance, and the Dance of the Sacrifice. They differ from one another both in the Cadence and in the Leaps; but 'tis impossible to describe them, for that they have so little resemblance to ours.

All these Dances may be compared to Minerva's Pyrrhiche. *For while the Savages dance with a Singular Gravity, they humour the Cadences of certain Songs, which* Achilles's *Malitia called* Hyperchematica. *I am at a loss to inform you whether the Savages had these Songs from the* Grecians, *or the* Grecians *from the Savages.*[2]

That of the *Calumet* is the most grave and handsome; but they don't perform that but upon certain Occasions, *viz.* When Strangers pass through their Country, or when their Enemies send Ambassadors to treat of a Peace. If they approach to a Village by Land, when they're ready to enter, they depute one of this Number, who advances, and proclaims, that he brings the *Calumet of Peace;* the rest stopping in the mean time, till he calls to them to come: Then some of the Young Men march out of the

---

[1] The council is the most important institution of tribal life, and of indigenous growth. For a good description of forms of procedure, and the ceremonies connected therewith, see *Jes Rel.*, x, pp. 251–263. — Ed

[2] It is needless to say that there was no historical connection between Greek and North American dances and their accompanying songs, save as the development in these lines has a certain similarity among all primitive peoples. The pyrricha was a war dance of Doric origin, performed by men in armor; while the hyporcheme (hyperchematica), allied to the pæan, was one variety of the song or cadence that accompanied the early Greek dances. — Ed.

Village, at the Gate of which they form an Oval Figure, and when the Strangers are come up to them, they dance all at a time, forming a Second Oval round him that bears the *Calumet:* This [11] Dance continues half an Hour. Then they receive the Travellers with some Ceremony, and conduct them to a Feast. The Ceremonies are the same to those that come by Water, with this difference, that they send a Canoo to the Foot of the Village, with the *Calumet of Peace,* upon its Prow, in the shape of a Mast, and one comes from the Village to meet 'em.[1] The Dance of War is done in a Circle, during which the Savages are seated on the Ground. He that dances moves from the Right Hand to the Left, singing in the mean time the Exploits of himself and his Ancestors. At the end of every Memorable Action, he gives a great Stroke with a Club upon a Stake plac'd in the middle of the Circle, near certain Players, who beat Time upon a sort of a Kettle-Drum; Every one rises in his turn to sing his Song: And this is commonly practis'd when they go to War, or are come from it.

The greatest Passion of the Savages consists in the Implacable Hatred they bear to their Enemies; that is, all Nations with whom they are at Open War: They value themselves mightily upon their Valour; insomuch that they have scarce any regard to any thing else. One may say, That they are wholly govern'd by Temperament, and their Society is perfect Mechanism. They have neither Laws, Judges, nor Priests; they are naturally inclin'd to Gravity, which makes them very

---

[1] The classic description of the calumet dance is that of Marquette; see *Jes. Rel.*, lix, pp. 129-137. — ED.

circumspect in their Words and Actions. They observe a certain Medium between Gayety and Melancholy. The *French* Air they could not away with; and there was none but the younger sort of them that approv'd of our Fashions.

I have seen Savages when they've come a great way, make no other Compliment to the Family than, *I am arriv'd, I wish all of you a great deal of* [12] *Honour*. Then they take their Pipe quietly without asking any Questions: When that's done, they'l say, *Heark'e Friend, I am come from such a Place, I saw such a thing, &c.* When you ask a Question, their Answer is exceeding concise, unless they are Members of the Council; otherwise you'll hear 'em say, *That's Good; That signifies nought; That's admirable; That has Reason in it; That's valiant.*

If you tell a Father of a Family that his Children have signaliz'd themselves against the Enemy, and have took several Slaves, his Answer is short, *That's Good*, without any farther Enquiry. If you tell him his Children are slain, he'll say immediately, *That signifies nought*, without asking how it happen'd? When a Jesuit preaches to them the Truth of the Christian Religion, the Prophecies, Miracles, &c. they return you, a *That's wonderful*, and no more. When the *French* tell them of the Laws of a Kingdom; the Justice, Manners and Customs of the *Europeans*, they'll repeat you a hundred times, *That's reasonable*. If you discourse them upon an Enterprise of great importance, or that's difficult to execute, or which requires much thought, they'll say, *That's Valiant*, without explaining themselves, and will listen to the end of your Difcourfe with great attention: Yet 'tis to be obferved, when they're with their Friends in private, they'll argue with as much boldnefs as thofe of the Council. 'Tis very ftrange, that having no advantage of Education, but being directed only by the Pure Light of Nature, they fhould be able to furnifh Matter for a Conference which often lafts above three Hours, and which turns upon all manner of Things; and fhould acquit themfelves of it fo well, that I never repented the time I fpent with thefe truly Natural Philofophers.

[13] When a Vifit is paid to a Savage, at going in you muft fay, *I am come to fee fuch an one:* Then Fathers, Mothers, Wives, Children go out, or withdraw themfelves to an Apartment at one end of the Cottage, and be who you will, come not near you to interrupt your Converfation. The Fafhion is for him that is vifited, to offer you to eat, drink and fmoak; and one may ufe an entire freedom with them, for they don't much mind Compliments. If one means to vifit a Woman, the Ceremony's the fame; *I am come to fee fuch an one;* then every Body withdraws, and you tarry alone with her you come to fee; but you muft not mention any thing Amorous in the Day time, as I fhall inform you elfe where.

Nothing furpriz'd me more than to obferve the Quarrels between their Children at play: A little after they are warm'd, they'll tell one another, *You have no Soul, You're wicked, You're treacherous:* In the mean time their Companions who make a Ring about them, hear all quietly, without taking one fide or t'other till they fall to play again: If by chance they come to

Blows, the reſt divide themſelves into two Companies, and carry the Quarrellers home.

They are as ignorant of *Geography* as of other *Sciences*, and yet they draw the moſt exact Maps imaginable of the Countries they're acquainted with, for there's nothing wanting in them but the Longitude and Latitude of Places: They ſet down the True *North* according to the *Pole Star;* The Ports, Harbours, Rivers, Creeks and Coaſts, of the Lakes; the Roads, Mountains, Woods, Marſhes, Meadows, &c. counting the diſtances by Journeys and Half-journeys of the Warriers, and allowing to every Journey Five Leagues. Theſe *Chorographical Maps* are drawn upon the Rind of your *Birch Tree;* and when the Old Men hold a Council [14] about War or Hunting, they're always ſure to conſult them.[1]

The Year of the *Outaouas,* the *Outagamis,* the *Hurons,* the *Sauteurs,* the *Ilinois,* the *Oumamis,* and ſeveral other Savages, confiſts of Twelve-Synodical Lunar-Months, with this difference, when Thirty Moons are ſpent, they add one ſupernumerary Month to make it up, which they call the *Loſt Moon,* and from thence begin their Account again, after the former Method. All theſe Months have very ſuitable Names; for Inſtance; What we name *March,* they call the *Worm-Moon,* for then the Worms quit the Hollow Chops of the Trees where they ſhelter'd themſelves in the Winter. *April* is call'd *the Month of Plants;* *May* of *Flowers* and ſo of the others. I

---
[1] For a reproduction of an Indian map drawn by the savage Ochagach see Thwaites, *Rocky Mountain Exploration* (New York, 1904), p. 28. Several others are in the atlas (vol. viii) to *Original Journals of the Lewis and Clark Expedition* (New York, 1904). — ED.

say, at the end of these Thirty Months, the next that follows is supernumerary, and not counted; for Example; We'll suppose the Month of *March* to be the Thirtieth Lunar-Month, and consequently, the Last of the *Epocha*. Next that should be counted the Month of *April;* whereas the *Lost Moon* takes place of it, and must be over before they begin their Account again; and this Month with the others, makes about a Year and an half. Because they have no Weeks, they reckon from the First till the Twenty Sixth of these sort of Months, and that contains just that space of time which is between the first appearance of the Moon at Night, till having finish'd its Course, it becomes almost invisible in the Morning; and this they call the Illumination-Month. For Instance; A Savage will say, *I went away the first of the Month of Sturgeons* (that's *August*), *and returned the Twenty-ninth of the Month of* Indian-Corn (the same with our *September); and next day,* (which is the last) *I rested my self.* As for the remaining three Days and a half of the *Dead-Moon,* during which 'tis [15] impossible to be discern'd, they give them the Name of the *Naked Days.* They make as little use of Hours as Weeks, having never got the way of making Clocks or Watches; by the help of which little Instruments, they might divide the Natural Day into equal parts.[1] For this Reason, They are forc'd to reckon the Natural Day as well as the Night, by Quarters, Half, and Three-quarters, the Rising and the Setting-Sun, the

---

[1] This is a good account of the calendar of the primitive Indians, usually composed of thirteen lunar months. The aborigines of Central America, Mayas and Aztecs, had a more elaborate system. See Thomas, "Maya Calendar," in U. S. Bureau of Ethnology, *Bulletin* No 18. — ED.

Fore-noon and the Evening. As they have a wonderful Idea of any thing that depends upon the Attention of the Mind, and attain to an Exact Knowledge of many Things by Long Experience: To cross a Forest (for Instance) of a Hundred Leagues in a strait Line, without straying either to the Right or Left; to follow the Tract of a Man or Beast upon the Grass or Leaves: So they know the Hour of the Day and Night exactly, even when it is so cloudy, that neither Sun nor Stars appear. I impute this Talent to a steddy command of Mind, which is not natural to any but those whose Thoughts are as little distracted as these Mens are.

They are more surpriz'd to see some little Problemes of *Geometry* put in Practice, than we would be to see Water turn'd into Wine. They took my *Graphometer* for somewhat Divine, being unable to guess how we could know the distance of Places without measuring them by Cords or Rods, without there were some Supernatural Assistance. *Longimetry* pleas'd them far more than *Altimetry*, because they thought it more necessary to know the breadth of a River, than height of a Tree, &c. I remember one Day in a Village of the *Outaouas* at *Missilimakinac* a Slave brought into the Cottage where I was, a sort of Vessel made of a thick piece of soft Wood, which he had borrowed on purpose, in which [16] he pretended to preserve Mapletree-Water. All the Savages which saw this Vessel, fell to arguing how much it would hold, and with that view call'd for a Pot, and for Water to determine the matter by Measuring. The humor took me to lay with them a Wager of a Treat, that I could tell the Quantity of

Water that would fill it better than they. So that finding by my Computation, that it held about 248 Pots, or thereabouts, I went to make the Tryal, and made them not a little wonder that it fail'd but one or two Pots; upon which I perſwaded them, that the Pots that were wanting were ſuck'd up by the new Wood.[1] But what was moſt pleaſant they were continually begging me to teach them *Stereometry*, that they might make uſe of it upon occaſion: 'Twas to no purpoſe to tell them 'twas impoſſible they ſhould underſtand it, tho' there were Reaſons for't that might convince any body but Savages. They preſs'd me ſo much to't that I could not be quiet till I was forc'd to tell them, that no body could do it to Perfection but the Jeſuits.

The Savages prefer your little Convex Glaſſes of two Inches Diemeter to any others, becauſe they give but a faint Repreſentation of the Pimples and Bloches upon their Faces. I remember that while I was at *Miſſilimakinac*, one of the Pedlers call'd *Coureurs de Bois*, brought a Convex Glaſs that was pretty large, and conſequently repreſented the Face with ſome Deformity. All the Savages that ſaw this Piece of Catoptricks, thought it no leſs Miraculous than the awaker of a Clock, or a Magical Lanthern, or the Spring of a Machine. But what was moſt Comical, there was among the reſt of the Spectators a *Huroneſe* Girl who told the Pedlar in a jocoſe way, That *if the Glaſs had the Vertue of Magnifying* [17] *the Objects really, as it did in appearance, all her ſhe Companions would give him in Exchange as many Beaver Skins as would make his Fortune.*

---
[1] The pot is a French liquid measure equal to 3.29 English pints. — Ed.

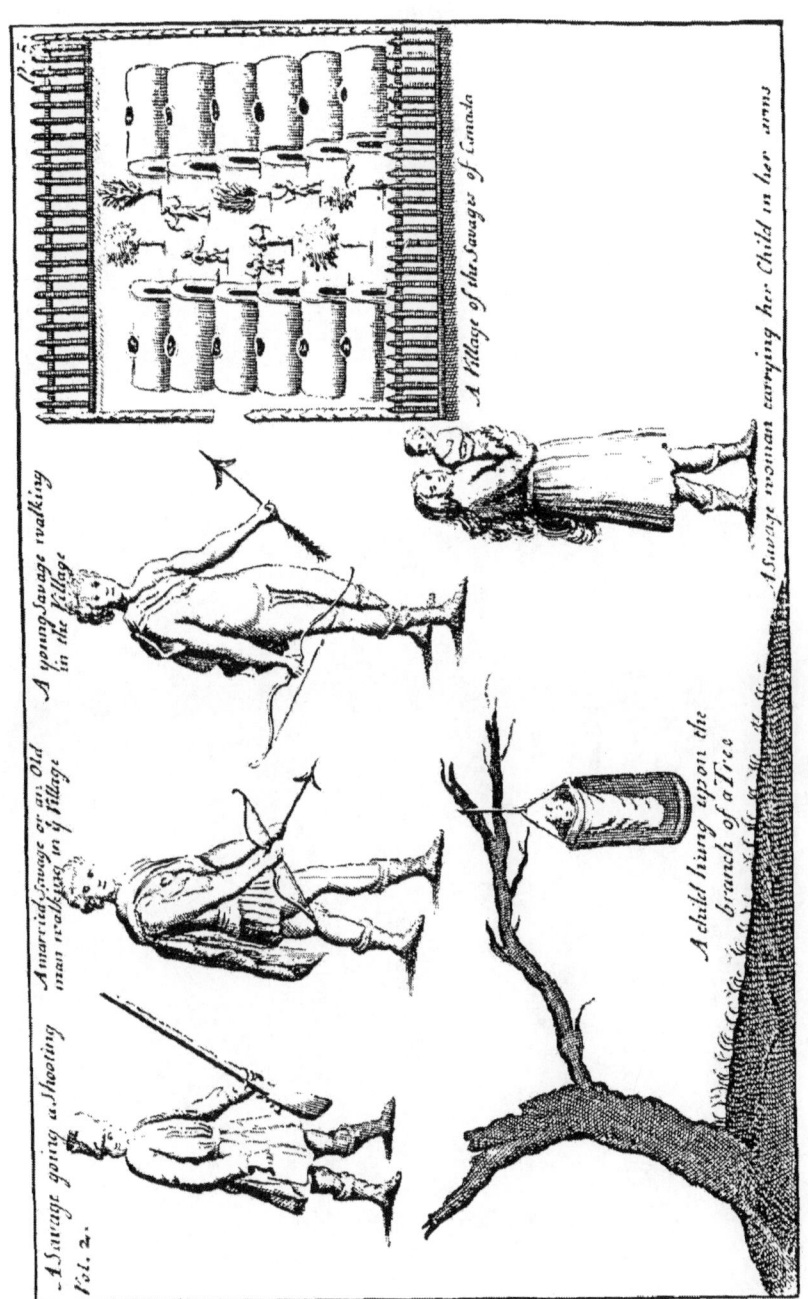

The Savages have the moſt happy Memory in the World. They can carry their Memory ſo far back, that when our Governors or their Deputies treated with them about War, Peace or Trade, and propoſed things contrary to what was offer'd Thirty or Forty Years ago; They reply, That the *French* are falſe, and change their Opinion every Hour, that 'tis ſo many Years ſince they ſaid ſo and ſo; and to confirm it bring you the Porcelain *Colier* that was given them at that time. You remember I acquainted you in my Seventh Letter, that the *Coliers* are the Symbols of Contracts, without which they conclude no Buſineſs of Moment.[1]

They pay an infinite Deverence to Old Age. The Son that Laughs at his Father's Advice ſhall tremble before his Grandfather. In a Word, they take the Ancient Men for Oracles, and follow their Counſel accordingly. If a Man tell his Son 'tis time he ſhould Marry, or go to the War, or the Hunting, or Shooting! he ſhall anſwer careleſsly, *That's Valiant, I thought ſo.* But if his Grandfather tell him ſo, the Anſwer is, *That's good, It ſhall be done.* If by chance they kill a Partrige, a Gooſe, or Duck, or catch any delicate Fiſh, they never fail to preſent it to their oldeſt Relations.[2]

The Savages are wholly free from Care; they do nothing but Eat, Drink, Sleep, and ramble about in the Night when

---

[1] See p. 76, *ante.* — ED.

[2] The evidence upon the deference paid by Indians to old age, is conflicting. The opinions of an elderly chief had especial weight in council; but on the other hand aged people, when infirm, were frequently abandoned or put to death as a useless burden. See *Jes. Rel.*, xx, p 239; also *Original Journals of the Lewis and Clark Expedition*, index. — ED.

they are at their Villages. Having no set Hours for Meals, they Eat when they're hungry; and commonly do it in a large Company, Feasting here and there by turns. The Women and Girls do the same among themselves, and don't admit any Men into [18] their Company at that time. The Women Slaves are employed to Sow and Reap the *Indian-Corn;* and the Men Slaves have for their Business the Hunting and Shooting where there is any Fatigue, tho' their Masters will very often help them. They have three sorts of Games. Their Game of Counters is purely Numerical, and he that can Add, Substract, Multiply and Divide best by these Counters is the Winner. This depends purely upon the Mind. Another Game which is Hazard and Chance, is perform'd with eight little Stones, which are Black on one side and White on the other. They're put on a Plate which they lay on the Ground, throwing the little Stones up in the Air, and if they fall so as to turn up the Black side 'tis good luck. The odd number wins, and eight Whites or Blacks wins double, but that happens but seldom. They have a third Play with a Ball not unlike our Tennis, but the Balls are very large, and the Rackets resemble ours, save that the Handle is at least three Foot long. The Savages, who commonly play at it in large Companies of three or four Hundred at a time, fix two Sticks at five or six Hundred Paces distance from each other; They divide into two equal Parties, and toss up the Ball about half way between the two Sticks. Each Party endeavour to toss the Ball to their side; some run to the Ball, and the rest keep at a little distance on both sides to assist on all Quarters. In fine this Game is fo violent that they tear their Skins, and break their Legs very often in ftriving to raife the Ball. All thefe Games are made only for Feafts or other trifling Entertainments; for 'tis to be obferv'd, that as they hate Money, fo they never put it in the Ballance, and one may fay, *Intereft is never the occafion of Debates among them*.[1]

[19] 'Tis not to be denied but the Savages are a very fenfible People, and are perfectly well acquainted with the Intereft of their Nations. They are great Moralifts, efpecially when they Criticife on the Manners of the *Europeans*, and are mightily upon their Guard in our Company, unlefs it be with fuch as they are intimately acquainted with. In other Matters they are Incredulous and Obftinate to the laft degree, and are not able to diftinguifh between a Chimerical Suppofition and an undoubted Truth, or between a fair and a falfe Confequence, as you'l fee in the infuing Chapter, which treats of their Belief, and in which I affure you you'l meet with very odd Notions.

---

[1] Lahontan appears to intimate that the Indians do not gamble for gain; nevertheless, it is well-known that this is one of their strongest passions. The game of ball here described is that known as lacrosse, a modification of which is the present Canadian national game. For description see Thwaites (ed.), "J. Long's Voyages," in *Early Western Travels*, ii, pp. 89, 90. — ED

The Belief of the Savages, *and the Obstacles of their Converfion.*

ALL the Savages are convinc'd that there muft be a God, becaufe they fee nothing among Material Beings that fubfifts neceffarily and by its own Nature. They prove the Exiftence of a Deity by the Frame of the Univerfe, which naturally leads us to a higher and Omnipotent Being, from whence it follows, fay they, that Man was not made by chance, and that he's the Work of a Being fuperior in Wifdom and Knowledge, which they call the *Great Spirit*, or the *Mafter of Life*, and which they Adore in the moft abftracted and fpiritual manner. They deliver their Thoughts of him thus, without any fatisfactory Definition. The Exiftence of God being infeparable from his Effence, it contains every thing, it appears in every thing, acts in every thing, and gives motion [20] to every thing. In fine, all that you fee, all that you can conceive, is this Divinity which fubfifts without Bounds or Limits, and without Body; and ought not to be reprefented under the Figure of an old Man, nor of any other thing, let it be never fo fine or extenfive. For this Reafon they Adore him in every thing they fee. When they fee any thing that's fine or curious, efpecially when they look upon the Sun or Stars, they cry out, *O Great Spirit, we difcern thee in every thing.* And in like manner when they reflect upon the meaneſt Trifles they acknowledge a Creator under the Name of the *Great Spirit* or *Maſter of Life*.[1]

I forgot to tell you that the Savages liſten to all the Jeſuits Preach to them without the leaſt Contradiction. They content themſelves to rail among one another at the Sermons the Fathers make at Church, and if a *Savage* talks freely to a *French*-man he muſt be fully aſſur'd of his Diſcretion and Friendſhip. I have been frequently much puzzled to anſwer their impertinent Objections, (for they can make no others in relation to Religion) but I ſtill brought my ſelf off by entreating them to give Ear to the Jeſuits. To preſent you with a view of their Opinion relating to the Immortality of the Soul: They all believe it; but not upon the plea that 'tis one ſimple ſubſtance, and that the Deſtruction of any Natural Being is accompliſh'd by the ſeparation of its Parts; they're Strangers to that Argument. All they urge, is, that if the Soul were Mortal, all Men would be equally Happy in this Life; for God being all Perfection and Wiſdom, 'twould be inconſiſtent

---

[1] The religious beliefs and mythologic development of the North American Indian have been much discussed, and but little determined. The evidence of Lahontan is valuable because the Indians with whom he associated were but slightly changed by contact with the European missionaries, and because his own materialistic, skeptical bent of mind divested him of certain preconceptions, and rendered his observation more accurate. His account of the spiritism of the Algonquians corresponds with the latest scientific conclusions as to the mythologic stage attained by the aborigines — that it was neither monotheistic nor pantheistic, but recognized all manifestations of the unseen, yet without sense of personal unity. See Powell, "Mythology of North American Indians," in U. S. Bur. of Eth. *Report*, 1879-80, pp 17-56; Brinton, *Myths of the New World* (3d ed., Phila., 1896); Dorman, *Origin of Primitive Superstitions among the Aborigines of America* (Phila., 1881). — ED.

with his Nature to create some to be Happy and others to be Miserable. So they prove the Immortality of the Soul by the Hardships of Life to which most Men are [21] expos'd, especially the best of People, when they are Kill'd, Tortur'd, made Prisoners, &c. For they pretend, that by a Conduct somewhat strange to our Apprehension, the Almighty orders a certain number of Creatures to suffer in this World, that they may be sav'd in the next; and upon that score they cannot endure to hear the *Christians* say, Such a one has had the misfortune to be Kill'd, Wounded or made a Slave; and look upon what we call a Misfortune to be only such in Fancy and *Idea*, since nothing comes to pass but by the Decrees of that infinitely perfect Being, whose Conduct cannot be Fantastical or Capricious, as they falsely pretend we Christians think it to be. On the contrary they think those Persons have very good Fortune who are Kill'd, Burnt or taken Prisoners. 'Tis the great unhappiness of these Poor, Blind People, that they will not suffer themselves to be instructed: For their Opinions are not in all respects contrary to the Light of the Gospel. They believe that God for Reasons above our reach makes use of the Sufferings of good People to display his Justice; and in this Point we cannot oppose them, for 'tis one of the Principles of our own Religion: But when they alledge that we look upon the Divinity as a whimsical fantastick Being, are they not under the greatest mistake? The first and supreme cause must be suppos'd to make the wisest choice of means conducing to an end. If then 'tis true, as 'tis a Point of our Belief, that God does permit the Sufferings of the Innocent, 'tis our part to

Adore his Wifdom, and not be fo arrogant as to Cenfure it. One of the Savages that argued the Point with me, alledg'd that we reprefented the Divinity like a Man that had but a little Arm of the Sea to crofs, and rather chofe to take a [22] turn of five or fix Hundred Leagues about. This Quibble puzzled me a little: *For why*, fays he, *fince God can bring Men to Eternal Happinefs by rewarding Vertue and Merit, why does not he go that fhorteft way to Work? Why does he conduct a juft Man to the Eternal Beatitude by the path of Sufferings?* Thus 'tis that thefe poor Savages contradict themfelves, and from hence it appears, that *Jefus Chrift*, our Lord and Mafter, is the only Author of fuch Truths as fupport themfelves, and contain not the leaft fhadow of Contradiction. In a Word, the fingular madnefs of this unfortunate People confifts in denying their Affent to any thing but what's vifible and probable. This is the ftanding and true Principle of their Religion, when you confider it abftractedly: But if you ask them in particular why they Adore God in the Sun, rather than in a Tree or a Mountain; their Anfwer is, That they choofe to admire the Deity in publick by pointing to the moft glorious thing that Nature affords.[1]

The Jefuits ufe their utmoft Efforts to make them fenfible of the Importance of Salvation. They explain to them the Holy Scriptures, and fet forth the manner by which the Law of *Chrift Jefus* took place in the World, and the change that it wrought. They lay before them the Prophecies, Revelations

---

[1] This is in accord with modern conclusions, that the North Americans did not worship the sun, save as a symbol. The fashion of a decade or more ago, to explain most myths as solar in origin, is not to-day held sufficient. — ED.

and Miracles, by which our Religion is inforc'd. But the poor Wretches are such obstinate Infidels, that all the Characters of Truth, Sincerity and Divinity that shine throughout the Scriptures, have no impression upon them. The greatest length that the good Fathers can bring them to, is to acquiesce after a Savage manner, contrary to what they think. For Instance, when the Jesuits Preach up the Incarnation of *Jesus Christ*, they'l answer, *That's Wonderful:* When the Question is [23] put to them, whether they'l turn Christians, they reply, that *they'l consider of it.* If the secular *Europeans* sollicit them to come to Church to hear the Word of God, they reply, *'Tis reasonable;* the meaning of which is, that they'l come; but at the bottom they have no other design in approaching to the place of Worship, than to snatch away a Pipe of Tobacco, or to Ridicule the good Fathers, as I intimated above: For they have such happy Memories, that I knew ten of my own Acquaintance that had all the Holy Scriptures by Heart.

'Twill be worth your while to hear the thoughts of Reason that come from those People who pass for Beasts among us. They maintain, That a Man ought never to strip himself of the Privileges of Reason, that being the noblest Faculty with which God hath enrich'd him; and That forasmuch as the Religion of the Christians is not put to the test of their Reason, it cannot be but that God ridicul'd them in enjoyning them to consult their Reason in order to distinguish Good from Evil. Upon this score they affirm that Reason ought not to be controul'd by any Law, or put under a necessity of approving what it doth not comprehend; and in fine, that what we call an Article of Faith is an intoxicating Potion to make Reaſon reel and ſtagger out of its way; forſomuch as the pretended Faith may ſupport Lies as well as the Truth, if we underſtand by it a readineſs to believe without diving to the bottom of things. They pretend that if they had a mind to talk in the Language of the Chriſtians, they might with equal right reject the Arguments propos'd by the Chriſtians againſt their Opinions, and plead that their Opinions are Incomprehenſible Myſteries, and that we muſt not pretend to fathom the Secrets [24] of the Almighty, which are plac'd ſo far above our weak reach.

'Tis in vain to remonſtrate to them, That Reaſon gives only a faint and dazzling Light which leades thoſe to a Precipice that truſt to its Direction and Conduct: That 'tis a ſlave to Faith and ought to obey it blindly without diſputing, juſt as an *Iroqueſe* Captive does his Maſter. 'Tis needleſs to repreſent to them, that the Holy Scriptures can contain nothing that's directly repugnant to right Reaſon. They make a jeſt of all ſuch Remonſtrances, for they imagine ſo great a Contradiction between the Scripture and Reaſon, that they think it impoſſible for the Advocates of the former to avoid the receiving of very dubious Opinions for certain and evident Truths. Their Prejudice proceeds from this, that they can't be convinc'd, that the Infallibility of the Scripture is to be made out by the Light of Reaſon. The Word *Faith* is enough to choak them; they make a Jeſt of it, and alledge that the Writings of paſt Ages are falſe, ſuppoſititious and alter'd, upon the Plea that the Hiſtories of our own times are juſtly liable to the fame Cenfure. They plead, That a Man muft be a Fool who believes that an Omnipotent Being, continued from all Eternity, in a ftate of Inactivity, and did not think of giving being to Creatures till within thefe five or fix Thoufand Years; or that at that time God Created *Adam* on purpofe to have him tempted by an evil Spirit to eat of an Apple, and that he occafion'd all the Mifery of his Pofterity by the pretended tranfmiffion of his Sin. They ridicule the Dialogue between *Eve* and the Serpent, alledging that we affront God in fuppofing that he wrought the Miracle of giving this Animal the ufe of Speech, with intent to deftroy all the Humane Race.

[25] To continue their wild Remonftrances they fay, "'Tis
' a thing unheard of, that for the expiation of *Adam*'s Sin God
' fhould put God to Death to fatisfie himfelf; That the Peace
' of the World fhould be brought about by the Incarnation
' of God and his fhameful Death; That his Difciples fhould
' be ignorant Men that fear'd to dye. This, they fay, is ftill
' the more unaccountable, that the Sin of the firft Father hath
' done more harm than the Death of the latter hath done
' good, the Apple having intail'd Death on all Men, whereas
' the Blood of *Jefus* hath not fav'd one half of them. They
argue, 'That upon the Humanity of this God the Chriftians
' build a Religion without a Foundation, which is fubject to
' the Changes and Viciffitudes of Humane Affairs. That this
' Religion being divided and fubdivided into fo many Sects,
' as thofe of the *French*, the *Englifh*, *&c*. it can be no other
' than an Human Artifice: For had God been the Author of
' it, his Providence had prevented fuch diverfity of Sentiments

'by unambiguous Decisions. That if the Evangelical Law
'had descended from Heaven it had not contain'd those
'obscure Sayings that give rise to the Christian Dissensions;
'for that God who foresees what is in the Womb of Futurity
'would have deliver'd his Precepts in such clear and precise
'terms as would leave no room for Disputes.

'But supposing (continue they) that this Law descended
'from Heaven, which of the Christian Sects must we join with?
'For we understand from an infinite number of Christians, that
'in some Communions we run the risque of Damnation.'
The great Article that they stickle most at is the *Incarnation
of God*. They exclaim against the supposition that the Divine
Word was shut up for nine Months in the Bowels of a
Woman, and that the same God came to take up an Earthly
Body in this World, and carry'd it up to his Seat of Bliss.
Nay, they carry the thing farther, for they rally upon the
unevenness and inconstancy of *Christ*'s Will. Tho' he came
into the World to dye, say they, yet it appears that he had no
mind to it, and that he was affraid to Die. If the Divinity
and Humanity had made but one Person, he would not have
needed to pray or ask for any thing; nay, supposing that his
Divine Nature had not the Ascendant within him, yet he ought
not to have fear'd Death, in regard that the loss of a Temporal Life is nothing to one that is assur'd of reviving for
ever; he knew for certain where he was a going, and consequently ought to have embrac'd Death more chearfully than
we do, when we Poyson our selves in order to accompany our
Relations to the Country of Souls.

They brand St. *Paul* for a Phantaſtical Man, alledging that he contradicts himſelf every Foot, and Reaſons very ſorrily. They Ridicule the Credulity of the Primitive Chriſtians, whom they look upon as ſimple and ſuperſtitious Creatures; and upon that Head take occaſion to ſay, *That the Apoſtle Paul would have found a great deal of difficulty in perſwading the People of* Canada *that he was raviſh'd up to the third Heaven.* There's one place of Scripture above all other that they can't digeſt, viz. *Many are called, but few chosen.* Their Comment upon it is this, *God hath ſaid, that many are call'd but few choſen, and what God ſays muſt needs be true. Now, if of three Men only one be ſav'd, and the other two damn'd, then the Condition of a Stag is preferable to that of a Man; Nay, put it upon an even lay, and let there be but one Man damn'd for one ſav'd, even then the Stag hath the better of* [27] *it.* This Objection was once put to me by the Rat, or the General of the Savages, when I was a Hunting with him. I reply'd, that we ought to indeavour to be in the number of the Choſen by following the Law and the Precepts of *Jeſus Chriſt*. But my Anſwer did not ſatisfie him, for he ſtill ran upon the great riſque of two Men damn'd for one ſav'd, and that by an immutable Decree. Upon that I refer'd him to the Jeſuits, for I durſt not tell him, That 'twas in his own Power to procure his Election: If I had, he had given me leſs Quarter than he did to St. *Paul;* for in Religious Matters they always ſtick to Probability. This General was not ſo void of good Senſe, but that he could think juſtly and make true Reflections upon Religious Matters; but he was ſo prepoſſeſs'd with an Opinion, that the Chriſtian Faith was contrary to Reason, that all the Attempts I made could not convince him of the contrary. When I laid before him the Revelations of *Moses* and the Prophets, the universal Consent of almost all Nations in owning and acknowledging *Jesus Christ*, the Martyrdom of his Disciples and of the Primitive Christians, the perpetual Succession of our Sacred Oracles, the entire Destruction of the *Jewish* Republick, and the Destruction of *Jerusalem* foretold by our Saviour; he ask'd me if my Father or my Grandfather had seen all these Events, and whether I was so credulous as to take our Scriptures for Truth, since the Histories of Countries writ but t'other Day are found to be Fabulous. He added, That the *Faith* which the Jesuits beat their Brains about imported no more than to be perswaded of a thing either by seeing it with their Eyes, or by finding it recommended by clear and solid Proofs; That these Fathers and I were so far from convincing them of the truth of our [28] Mysteries, that we only cover'd their Thoughts with Obscurity and Darkness.

Such, Sir, is the Obstinacy and prepossession of this People. I flatter my self that this short view of their Notions may divert you without Offence. I know that you are too well confirm'd and rivetted in our most Holy Faith, to receive any dangerous Impression from their impious Advances. I assure my self that you will joyn with me in bemoaning the deplorable state of these ignorant Wretches. Let us jointly admire the depth of the Divine Providence, which permits those Nations to entertain such an Aversion to our Divine Truths; and in the mean time let us make the best use of the undeserv'd Advantage we have over them. Give me leave to acquaint you with the Reflections that these same Savages make upon our Conduct when they confine themselves to the Subject of Morality. *The Christians, say they, contemn the Precepts of the Son of God, they make a Jest of his Prohibitions, and doubt of the Sincerity of his Expressions; for they counteract his Orders without intermission, and rob him of the Worship which he claims as his due, by paying it to Silver, to Beavers, and to their own Interest. They murmur against Heaven and him when things go cross with them; they go about their usual Business on such Days as are set apart for Works of Piety and Devotion, and spend both that and the other parts of their time in Gaming, Drinking to excess, Fighting and Scolding. Instead of Comforting their Parents they leave them for a Sacrifice to Hunger and Misery, and not only deride their Counsel, but wish impatiently for their Death. In the Night time, all of them, barring the Jesuits, roll from House to House to debauch the Women Savages. They Murther one another every Day upon the Plea of Theft or Affronts, or upon the score of Women; they Pillage and Rob one another without* [29] *any regard to the tyes of Blood or Friendship, as often as they meet with an opportunity of doing it with impunity. They bespatter and defame one another with outragious Calumnies; and make no scruple to lye when they find 'twill serve their Interest. They are not satisfied with the Company of single Women, but debauch other Mens Wives; and these Adulterous Women bring forth in the abscence of their Husbands a spurious Off-spring, that are at a loss to know their Fathers. In fine,* (continue they) *though the Christians are so docile as to believe the Humanity of God, which is the most unrea-*

sonable Article that can be; yet they seem to doubt of his Precepts, and incessantly transgress them, notwithstanding they are very pure and reasonable. I should never come to an end, if I enter'd into the Particulars of their Savage way of Reasoning; and for that reason 'twill be more proper to take leave of this Subject, and pass directly to the manner of Worship which they offer to their great Spirit or God, call'd *Kitchi Manitou*. A view of that will be more agreeable than the tedious Series of this sort of Philosophy, which at the bottom is but too true, and affords matter of Grief to all good Souls that are perswaded of the Truth of Christianity.

The way of Worſhip, uſed by the Savages.

BEFORE we launch out into the particulars of their Worſhip, 'twill be proper to remark that the Savages give the name of *Genius* or *Spirit* to all that ſurpaſſes their Underſtanding, and proceeds from a cauſe that they cannot trace. Some of theſe Spirits they take to be Good, and ſome Bad; of the former ſort are the Spirit of [30] Dreams, the *Michibichi* mentioned in my liſt of Animals, a *Solar Quadrant*, an *Alarm Watch*, and an infinity of other things that ſeem to them to be inconceivable. Of the latter ſort are *Thunder*, *Hail falling upon their Corn*, a *great Storm*, and in a word every thing that tends to their Prejudice, and proceeds from a cauſe that they are ignorant of. If a *Fuſee* burſt either through the fault of the Metal, or by being over Loaded, and Maims a Man, they'll tell you there was an Evil Spirit lodg'd within it. If by chance the Branch of a Tree put out a Mans Eye, the effect is owing to an Evil Spirit; If a ſudden guſt of Wind ſurpriſes 'em in a *Canow* about the middle of their Paſſage acroſs the Lakes, 'tis an Evil Spirit that diſturbs the Air; if the dregs of any Violent Diſtemper robs a Man of his Reaſon, 'tis an Evil Spirit that Torments him. Theſe Evil Spirits they call *Matchi Manitous*, and *Gold* and *Silver* they liſt into that number.[1] However, 'tis to be obferv'd that they talk of thefe Spirits in a Bantering way, or much after the fame manner that our fhrewd *Europeans* rally upon *Magicians* and *Sorcerers*.

Here I cannot forbear to repeat once more that the Hiftorical Accounts of *Canada*, are as fcarce as the Geographical Maps of that Country; for I never met with a true one but once, and that in the hands of a *Quebec* Gentleman, the Impreffion of which was afterwards Prohibited at *Paris*, but for what reafon I know not. I mention this with regard to their opinion of the *Devil;* for it is alledg'd that the Savages are acquainted with the *Devil*. I have read a thoufand Ridiculous Stories Writ by our Clergymen, who maintain that the Savages have conferences with him, and not only confult him, but pay him a fort of Homage. Now all thefe advances are ridiculous; for in earneft, the *Devil* never appear'd to thefe *Americans*. [31] I ask'd an infinity of Savages whether the *Devil* was ever feen among 'em in the fhape of a Man or any other Animal; I likewife confulted upon this head the ingenioufeft of their Mountebanks or Jugglers, who are a very Comical fort of Fellows (as you fhall hear anon;) and it may be reafonably prefum'd that if ever the *Devil* appear'd to 'em, they had been fure to have told me of it. In fine, after ufing all poffible means for a perfect knowledg of this matter; I concluded that thefe Ecclefiafticks did not underftand the true

---

[1] Brinton considers that the idea of dualism of spirits, so far as ethical qualities were concerned, was borrowed from Europeans; the Indians believed in benevolent and mischievous spirits, not because of a moral natuie, but because of the effect upon their own lives. — ED.

importance of that great word *Matchi Manitou*, (which signifies an *Evil Spirit*, *Matchi* being the word for *Evil* and *Manitou* for *Spirit;*) For by the *Devil* they underſtand ſuch things as are offenſive to 'em, which in our Language comes near to the ſignification of Misfortune, Fate, Unfavourable Deſtiny, &c. So that in ſpeaking of the *Devil* they do not mean that Evil Spirit that in *Europe* is repreſented under the figure of a Man, with a long Tail and great Horns and Claws.[1]

The Savages never Offer Sacrifices of Living Creatures to the *Kitchi Manitou;* for their common Sacrifices upon that occaſion are the Goods that they take from the *French* in exchange for *Beavers.* Several perſons of good Credit have inform'd me, that in one day they Burnt at *Miſſilimakinac*, Fifty Thouſand Crowns worth of ſuch Goods. I never ſaw ſo Expenſive a Ceremony, my ſelf: But let that be as it will, the particular circumſtances of the Sacrifice are theſe. The Air muſt be Clear and Serene, the Weather Fair and Calm; and then every one brings his Offering and laies it upon the Wood-Pile: When the Sun mounts higher the Children make a Ring round the Pile, with pieces of Bark Lighted, in order to ſet it on Fire; and the Warriours Dance and [32] Sing round 'em till the whole is Burnt and Conſumed, while the Old Men make their Harangues addreſs'd to the *Kitchi Man-*

---

[1] Lahontan's skeptical instincts revolted against the prevalent idea that all the gods of the savages were some manifestation of the devil — a conception that vitiates many of the recorded observations of Indian myths in the *Jesuit Relations.* On this subject see Brinton, *Myths of the New World,* pp. 75-82. The Moravian missionaries asserted that the aborigines " seem to have had no idea of the *Devil,* as the Prince of Darkness, before the Europeans came into the country;" — Loskiel, *History of the Mission of the United Brethren* (London, 1794), i, p. 34. — ED.

itou, and prefent him from time to time with Pipes of Tobacco Lighted at the Sun. Thefe Dances, Songs and Harangues laft till Sun fet, only they allow themfelves fome intervals of Reft, in which they fit down and Smoak at their Eafe.

It remains only (before I make an end of this *Chapter*) to repeat the very Words of their Harangues pronounc'd by the Old Fellows, and of the Songs fung by the Warriors: 'Great Spirit, Mafter of our Lives; Great Spirit, Mafter of 'all Things both Vifible and Invifible; Great Spirit, Mafter 'of other Spirits, whether good or Evil; command the Good 'Spirits to favour thy Children, the *Outaouas*, &c. Command 'the Evil Spirits to keep at a diftance from 'em. O Great 'Spirit, keep up the Strength and Courage of our Warriors, 'that they may be able to ftem the fury of our Enemies: Pre-'ferve the Old Perfons, whofe Bodies are not quite wafted, 'that they may give Counfel to the Young. Preferve our 'Children, enlarge their Number, deliver 'em from Evil 'Spirits, to the end that in our old Age they may prove our 'Support and Comfort; preferve our Harveft and our Beafts, 'if thou mean'ft that we fhould not die for Hunger: Take 'care of our Villages, and guard our Huntfmen in their Hunt-'ing Adventures. Deliver us from all Fatal Surprizes, when 'thou ceafeft to vouchfafe us the Light of the Sun, which 'fpeaks thy Grandeur and Power. Acquaint us by the Spirit 'of Dreams, with what thy Pleafure requires of us, or pro-'hibits us to do. When it pleafes thee to put a Period to 'our Lives, fend us to the great Countrey of Souls, where we 'may meet with thofe of our Fathers, our Mothers, our

'Wives, [33] our Children, and our other Relations. O
' Great Spirit, Great Spirit, hear the Voice of the Nation, give
' ear to all thy Children, and remember them at all times.

As for the Songs which the Warriors fing till Sun fet, they
are to this purpofe: 'Take heart, the Great Spirit vouchfafes
' fuch a Glorious Sun; Cheer up my Brethren: How great
' are his Works! How fine is the Day! this Great Spirit is
' all Goodnefs; 'tis he that fets all the Springs in motion;
' he ruleth over all: He is pleas'd to hear us; Let us cheer up
' my Brethren, we fhall fubdue our Enemies: Our Fields fhall
' bear Corn; our Hunting fhall fucceed well; we fhall all of
' us keep our Health; the Old Perfons fhall rejoice, the Chil-
' dren fhall increafe, and the Nation fhall profper. But now
' the Great Spirit leaves us, his Sun withdraws, he has feen the
' *Outaouas, &c.* 'Tis done, ay, 'tis done; the Great Spirit is
' fatisfied; my Brethren let us pluck up a good heart.

We muft remark, that the Women likewife make Addreffes
to him, and that commonly when the Sun rifes; upon which
Occafion they prefent and hold up their Children to that Lu-
minary. When the Sun is almoft down, the Warriors march
out of the Village, to dance the Dance of the Great Spirit.
But after all, there is no Day or Time fix'd for thefe Sacrifices,
no more than for the Particular Dances.[1]

---

[1] The method and manner of sacrifice among the more barbarous North American Indians is a study strewn with difficulties. There are traces of human sacrifice among nearly all the tribes (see Dorman, *Primitive Superstitions*, pp. 208-213; *Jes. Rel.*, x, 159-167), but Lahontan is doubtless correct in asserting that it was not usual. Dogs were frequently sacrificed to the dead or departing spirits; but the more ordinary offerings were food and tobacco, and there does not appear to have been any fixed time for or form of sacrificial ceremonial. — ED.

[34] *An Account of the Amours and Marriages of the Savages.*

I COULD recount a thousand Curious Things relating to the Courtship, and the way of Marrying among the Savages; but the Relation of so many Particulars, would be too tedious; for which Reason I shall only confine my self to what is most essential to that Subject.

It may be justly said, That the Men are as cold and indifferent as the Girls are passionate and warm. The former love nothing but War and Hunting, and their utmost Ambition reaches no farther. When they are at home, and have nothing to do, they run with the Match; that is, they are Nightwalkers. The Young Men do not marry till they are Thirty Years of Age, for they pretend that the Enjoyment of Women does so enervate 'em, that they have not the same measur of Strength to undergo great Fatigues, and that their Hams are too weak for long Marches, or quick Pursuits: In pursuance of this Thought, 'tis alledged, That those who have married, or stroled in the Nights too often, are taken by the *Iroquese*, by reason of the Weakness of their Limbs, and the decay of their Vigour. But after all, we must not imagine that they live chaste till that Age; for they pretend that Excessive Continence occasions Vapours, Disorders of the Kidneys, and a

Suppreffion of Urine; fo that 'tis neceffary for their Health to have a Run once a Week.

If the Savages were capable of being fubjected to the Empire of Love, they muft needs have an Extraordinary Command of themfelves to difguife [35] the Juft Jealoufie they might have of their Miftreffes, and at the fame time to carry it fair with their Rivals. I know the Humour of the Savages better than a great many *French* People that have liv'd among 'em all their Life-time; for I ftudy'd their Cuftoms fo narrowly and exactly, that all their Conduct of Life is as perfectly well known to me, as if I had been among 'em all my Life-time: And 'tis this Exact Knowledge that prompts me to fay, That they are altogether Strangers to that Blind Fury which we call Love. They content themfelves with a Tender Friendfhip, that is not liable to all the Extravagancies that the Paffion of Love raifes in fuch Breafts as harbour it: In a word, they live with fuch Tranquility, that one may call their Love Simple Goodwill, and their Difcretion upon that Head is unimaginable. Their Friendfhip is firm, but free of Tranfport; for they are very careful in preferving the Liberty and Freedom of their Heart, which they look upon as the moft valuable Treafure upon Earth: From whence I conclude that they are not altogether fo favage as we are.

The Savages never quarrel among themfelves, neither do they reproach or affront one another; One man among them is as good as another, for all are upon the fame Level. They have no Diforders occafion'd by a Girl or a Wife, for the Women are Wife, and fo are their Husbands: The Girls indeed are a little foolish, and the Young Men play the fool with them not unfrequently: But then you must consider that a Young Woman is allow'd to do what she pleases; let her Conduct be what it will, neither Father nor Mother, Brother nor Sister can pretend to controul her. A Young Woman, say they, is Master of her own Body, and by her Natural Right of Liberty is free to do what she pleases. But on the other [36] hand the Married Women being allow'd the Priviledge of quitting their Husbands when they please, had as good be dead as be guilty of Adultery. In like manner, the Husbands being entituled to the same Priviledge, would look upon themselves as infamous, if they were faithless to their Wives.

Nothing of Intrigue or Courtship must be mention'd to the Savage Ladies in the Day time, for they will not hear it; they'll tell you the Night-time is the most proper season for that; insomuch that if a Youth should by chance accoast a Girl in the Day-time, after this manner, *I love thee more than the Light of the Sun* (such is their Phrase) *listen to what I say, &c.* she would give him some Affront, and withdraw. This is a general Rule, that whoever designs to win the Affection of a Girl, must speak to her in the Day-time, of things that lie remote from the Intrigues of Love. One may converse with them privately as long as he will, and talk of a thousand Adventures that happen every minute, upon which they make their Replies very pleasantly; for you cannot imagine what a Gay and Jovial Temper they are of; they are very apt to laugh, and that with a very engaging Air. 'Tis at these Private Interviews that the Savages smell out the Young Womens Thoughts; for though the Subject of their Discourse is of an Indifferent Strain, yet they talk over nicer Subjects in the Language of their Eyes. After a Young Man has paid two or three Visits to his Mistress, and fancies that she has look'd upon him with a favourable Eye, he takes the following Course to know the Truth of the Matter.

You must take notice, that forasmuch as the Savages are Strangers to *Meum* and *Tuum*, to Superiority and Subordination; and live in a State of [37] Equality pursuant to the Principles of Nature; they are under no apprehension of Robbers or Secret Enemies, so that their Huts are open Night and Day. You must know farther, that Two Hours after Sun-set, the Old Superannuated Persons, or the Slaves (who never lie in their Masters Huts) take care to cover up the Fire before they go. 'Tis then that the Young Savage comes well wrapt up to his Mistress's Hut, and lights a sort of a Match at the Fire; after which he opens the Door of his Mistresses Apartment, and makes up to her Bed: If she blows out the Light, he lies down by her; but if she pulls her Covering over her Face, he retires; that being a Sign that she will not receive him. The Young Women drink the Juice of certain Roots, which prevents their Conception, or kills the Fruit of the Womb; for if a Girl proves with Child, she'll never get a Husband. They'll suffer any body to sit upon the Foot of their Bed, only to have a little Chat; and if another comes an hour after, that they like, they do not stand to grant him their last Favours. As to this Custom, which indeed is singular, the moſt ſenſible Savages gave this Reaſon for it, That they will not depend upon their Lovers, but remove all ground of Suſpicion both from the one and the other, that ſo they may act as they pleaſe.

The Savage Women like the *French* better than their own Countreymen, by reaſon that the former are more prodigal of their Vigour, and mind a Woman's Buſineſs more cloſely. In the mean time the Jeſuits uſe all Efforts to prevent their keeping Company with the *French:* They have Superannuated Fellows placed in all the Huts, who, like Faithful Spies, give an Account of all that they ſee or hear. The *French* who have the Misfortune to be diſcover'd, are publickly nam'd [38] in the Pulpit, complain'd of to the Biſhop and the Governor General, excommunicated, and treated as Tranſgreſſors of the Law: But after all the Artifices and Oppoſition of the Good Fathers, a great many Intrigues are carried on in the Villages, that they know nothing of. The Jeſuits never offer to check the Young Savages for keeping company with Girls; for if they offer'd to cenſure their Conduct, and uſe 'em with the ſame liberty as they do the *French*, they would tell 'em roundly, that they're ſorry the Fathers have a mind to their Miſtreſſes. This was the Anſwer that a Young *Huron* ſpoke aloud one day in the Church, when a Jeſuit addreſſing himſelf to him, was preaching down the Night-Rambles of the Savages with an Apoſtolical Freedom.

This People cannot conceive that the *Europeans*, who value themſelves upon their Senſe and Knowledge, ſhould be ſo blind and ſo ignorant as not to know that Marriage in their way is a fource of Trouble and Uneafinefs. To be ingag'd for one's Life time, to them is matter of Wonder and Surprife. They look upon it as a monftrous thing to be tied one to another without any hopes of being able to untie or break the Knot. In fine, in fpite of all the Reafons and Arguments that that Subject affords, they lay down this for a firm and unmoveable Truth, that we *Eropeans* are born in Slavery, and deferve no other Condition than that of Servitude.

In our Country, their ftate of Marriage would be juftly look'd upon as a Criminal way of Converfation. A Savage (for Inftance) that has fignalis'd himfelf feveral times in the Field, and acquir'd the Reputation of a brave Warrior, hath a mind to Marry by the means of a Contract, or rather a Leafe of Thirty Years, with the hopes of feeing in his old Age a Family defcended [39] of himfelf, that fhall provide for him. This Hero looks out for an agreeable Girle, and after he and fhe have fettled the matter, they reveal their Defign to their Relations, who at the fame time cannot oppofe it, but are oblig'd to confent, and to affift at the Ceremony. They meet together in the Hut of the ancienteft Relation or Parent, where a Feaft is prepar'd on a Day fix'd for that purpofe. Upon fuch Occafions the Company is very numerous, and the Table is cover'd with all manner of Dainties in a very prodigal manner; and thofe who affift at the Feftival, Dance and Sing, and perform the other Diverfions of the Country. After the Feafting and Merry-making is over, all the Relations of the Bridegroom retire, excepting four of the oldeft, after which the Bride, accompany'd with four of her ancienteft Female Relations, appears at one of the Doors of the Hut, and is receiv'd by the moſt decrepit Man of the Bridegroom's Company, who conducts her to the Bridegroom at a certain place, where the two Parties ſtand upright upon a fine Mat, holding a Rod between them, while the old Men pronounce ſome ſhort Harangues. In this Poſture do the two married Perſons Harangue one after another, and Dance together, ſinging all the while, and holding the Rod in their Hands, which they afterwards break into as many pieces as there are Witneſſes to the Ceremony, in order to be diſtributed among them. This done, the Bride is reconducted out of the Hut, where the young Women ſtay for her to accompany her to her Father's Apartment, and the Bridegroom or married Man is oblig'd to go there to find her when he has a mind to her Company, till ſuch time as ſhe brings forth a Child; then, indeed, ſhe conveys her Cloaths [40] to her Husbands Apartment, and continues with him till the Marriage is diſſolv'd.[1]

'Tis allowable both for the Man and the Woman to part when they pleaſe. Commonly they give one another eight Days Warning; ſometimes they offer Reaſons to juſtifie their Conduct, but for the moſt part the uſual Plea is, that they are ſick and out of order, and that Repoſe is more proper for them than the fatigue of a married Life. Then the little

---

[1] Lahontan's account of courtship, and the ceremony of marriage, is more extended than those of other early travellers; he does not, however, mention a prominent feature of the transaction, the presents given to the father of the bride, constituting a sort of wife-purchase. See *Jes. Rel.*, iii, p. 99, lxviii, pp 141-145 Long and Grant, early English traders among the Chippewa, give interesting details of courtship and marriage in that tribe See Thwaites, *Early Western Travels*, ii, pp. 173-175; Masson, *Bourgeois*, ii, pp 319-321. — ED.

pieces of the Rod that were diftributed among the Relations of the married Perfons, are brought into that Hut in which the Marriage was Solemniz'd, and burnt in their Prefence. You muft obferve that this Separation is accomplifh'd without any Difpute or Quarrel. Both the Men and the Women thus unmarried may be marry'd again to whom they pleafe: But commonly they lie bye three or fix Months before they confummate their fecond Marriage. When this Separation happens the Children are divided equally between them, for the Children are the Treafure of the Savages. If their number be odd the Woman hath the better half.

Though they are at their liberty to change, yet there are feveral Savages that live all their Life time with one Woman. I gave you to know above, that during the whole courfe of their married State they maintain an inviolable Fidelity to one another: But, which is yet more Edifying, as foon as the Woman is declar'd to be with Child, both fhe and her Bedfellow abftain from Enjoyment, and obferve an exact courfe of Continence from thence to the thirtieth Day after her Childbirth. When a Woman is ready to lye in, fhe withdraws to a certain Hut allotted for that ufe, being attended by her fhe Slaves, who ferve and affift her as far as they can. In [41] fine, the Female Sex in this Country deliver themfelves without the affiftance of Midwives; for they bring forth their Children with a facility that the *European* Women can fcarce have any Notion of, and they never lye in above two or three Days. They obferve a fort of Purification for thirty Days if the Child be a Boy, and for forty if it be a Girle, and till that time is expir'd they do not return to their Husband's Apartment.

As foon as their Children come into the World they dip them in warm Water up to the Chin, after which they fwathe them down upon little Boards or Planks ftuffed with Cotton, where they lye upon their Backs, as I infinuated under the Head of the *Habit, Houfes,* &c. *of the Savages*. They never make ufe of Nurfes unlefs it be when the Mothers are out of order, and they never wean their Children, but fuckle them fo long as they have Milk, with which indeed they are very plentifully provided.

The Women have no opportunity of Marriage after the Fiftieth Year of their Age; for the Men of the like Age alledge, that fince they cannot then bear Children, 'twould be a piece of Folly to meddle with them; and the young Sparks affirm, that their wither'd Beauty has not force enough to Charm them, at a time when there is no fcarcity of Buxfome young Girles. In this Diftrefs, when the young Men will not ufe them as Miftreffes, and Men of riper Years refufe them for Wives, if their Complexion be any thing Amorous, they are forc'd to adopt fome Prifoner of War that is prefented them, in order to anfwer their preffing Neceffities.

When the Husband or Wife comes to dye, the Widowhood does not laft above fix Months; and if in that fpace of time the Widow or Widower [42] dreams of their deceas'd Bedfellow, they Poyfon themfelves in cold Blood with all the Contentment imaginable; and at the fame time fing a fort of tune that one may fafely fay proceeds from the Heart. But if the furviving Party dreams but once of the Deceafed, they fay, that the Spirit of Dreams was not fure that the dead Perfon was uneafie in the Country of Souls, forafmuch as he only pafs'd by without returning, and for that reafon they think they are not oblig'd to go keep him Company.[1]

Thefe Savages are uncapable of Jealoufy; that is a Paffion they know nothing of. They jeer the *Europeans* upon that head; and brand a man's diftruft of his Wife, for a piece of manifeft Folly; as if, fay they, we were not certain that 'tis impoffible for fo weak an Animal to be true to its promifes. To purfue their fallacious way of arguing, they alledge that fufpicion is only a doubt, and that to doubt of what one fees is an argument of Blindnefs and Folly; and in fine, that 'tis impoffible, but that the conftraint and perpetuity that attends our Marriages, or the bait of Gold and Silver, fhould oblige a Woman when Cloy'd with one and the fame Husband, to whet her Appetite in the Embraces of another Man. I am fully convinced that a Savage would chufe rather to fuffer Mutilation than to Embrace his Neighbours Wife. Nor is the Chaftity of the fhe Savages lefs nice, for I do not believe that in the fpace of Fifty Years there has been one Inftance among 'em of the Invafion of another Man's Bed.[2] 'Tis true

---

[1] The influence of dreams is one of the most marked superstitions of the Indians They are regarded as divine intimations, whose suggestions must be followed even to the extent of suicide and death The influence of "medicine men" was largely perpetuated by means of this belief in dreams. See *post*. — ED

[2] Among the Western Indians adultery was punished by mutilation, and even by death. Consult *Jes Rel.*, xlv, p. 237, liv, p 187, *Wis. Hist Colls*, xvi, pp 362, 375; Thwaites, *Hennepin's New Discovery*, pp. 482, 483. — ED.

the *French*, being uncapable to diftinguifh between the Married and Unmarried Women, fometimes make their Addrefs to the former, when they find them alone in the Woods, or when they walk out into the Fields; but upon such occafions they always receive this Anfwer; [43] *The Fiend which is before mine Eyes hinders me to fee thee.*

The Savages go always by the Mothers Name. To make this plain by an example: the Leader of the Nation of *Hurons*, who is called *Saftaretfi*,[1] being Married to a Daughter of another *Huron* Family, by whom he has feveral Children, that General's Name is extinct at his Death, for that his Children affume the Name of the Mother. Now, it may be ask'd how the Name of *Saftaretfi* has been kept up for the fpace of Seven or Eight Hundred Years among that People, and is likely to continue to future Ages? But the Queftion is eafily Anfwered, if we confider, that the Sifter of this *Saftaretfi* being Married to another Savage, whom we fhall call *Adario*, the Children Springing from that Marriage, will be called *Saftaretfi* after the Mother, and not *Adario* after this Father. When I asked them the Reafon of the Cuftom, they replyed, that the Children having received their Soul from their Father, and their Body from their Mother, 'twas but

---

[1] The family of Sastaretsi were the hereditary chiefs of the nation of the Tobacco or Petun Hurons (see p. 54, note 2, *ante*). They belonged to the deer clan (or totem) of this tribe, and exercised their authority until 1794, when, at Wayne's battle of Fallen Timbers, this clan was almost annihilated. A chieftain of this name treated with the French in 1682 (*N. Y. Colon. Docs.*, ix, p. 178); another died at Quebec in 1746, and by that means precipitated the Huron revolt under Chief Nicholas (see *Wis. Hist. Colls.*, xvii). The Sastatetsi were commonly faithful to the French alliance. — ED.

reasonable that the Maternial Name should be perpetuated. I represented to them I do not know how often, that God alone was the only Creator of Souls, and that it was more reasonable to derive the original of that Custom from the certainty that they had of the Mother beyond that of the Father; but they possitively affirmed that this reason was absurd, without offering any proof.[1]

When a Woman has lost a Husband that leaves Brothers who are Batchelours, one of these Marries the Widow Six Months after his Death. The same is the Case with the Sisters of a Wife; for when a Married Woman Dies, commonly one of the Sisters supplies her place. But you must take notice that this Custom is only observed by the Savages that pretend to be Wiser than their [44] Neighbours. Some Savages continue Batchelours to their Dying day, and never appear either at Hunting or in Warlike Expeditions, as being either Lunatick or Sickly: But at the same time they are as much esteem'd as the Bravest and Hailest Men in the Country, or at least if they rally upon 'em, 'tis never done where they are present. Among the *Illinese* there are several Hermaphrodites, who go in a Woman's Habit, but frequent the Company of both Sexes.[2] These *Illinese* are strangely given to Sodomy, as well as the other Savages that live near the River *Missisipi*.

---

[1] This custom of naming children was used in support of the theory of mütterrecht as a basis of ancient family institutions. See Morgan, *Ancient Society* (New York, 1877); McLennan, *Patriarchal Theory* (London, 1885) — ED.

[2] See Marquette's description of the class called "berdashes," in *Jes. Rel.*, lix, pp. 129, 309, 310. — ED.

This, Sir, is all that I could learn of the way of Marriage and the Amours of the *Americans;* who are so far from giving a full loose to their Venerial Appetite, that they always act with a command over themselves, being very moderate in their Adventures with Women, whom they make use of only for the Propagation of their Families and the Preservation of their Health. Their Conduct upon this Head may serve for a just Reprimand to the *Europeans.*

I observ'd before, that if once a Girle proves with Child, she never gets a Husband; but I ought to have added that some young Women will not hear of a Husband, through a principle of Debauchery. That sort of Women are call'd *Ickoue ne Kioussa,* i. e. *Hunting Women:* for they commonly accompany the Huntsmen in their Diversions. To justify their Conduct, they alledge that they find themselves to be of too indifferent a temper to brook the Conjugal yoak, to be too careless for the bringing up of Children, and too impatient to bear the passing of the whole Winter in the Villages. Thus it is, that they cover and disguise their Lewdness. Their Parents or Relations dare not censure their Vicious Conduct; on the contrary they seem to approve of it, in [45] declaring, as I said before, that their Daughters have the command of their own Bodies and may dispose of their Persons as they think fit; they being at their liberty to do what they please. In short, the Children of these Common Women are accounted a Lawful Issue, and intitled to all the Privileges of other Children; abateing for one thing, namely, that the noted Warriours or Counsellours will not accept of 'em for their

Sons in Law, and that they cannot enter into Alliance with certain Ancient Families; though at the same time these Families are not possessed of any peculiar Right or Preheminence. The *Jesuits* do their utmost to prevent the Lewd Practices of these Whores, by Preaching to their Parents that their Indulgence is very disagreeable to the Great Spirit, that they must answer before God for not confineing their Children to the measures of Continency and Chastity, and that a Fire is Kindled in the other World to Torment 'em for ever, unless they take more care to correct Vice.

To such Remonstrances the Men reply, *That's Admirable;* and the Women usually tell the Good Fathers in a deriding way, *That if their Threats be well grounded, the Mountains of the other World must consist of the Ashes of souls.*

Vol. 2. Noon Sun p. 29

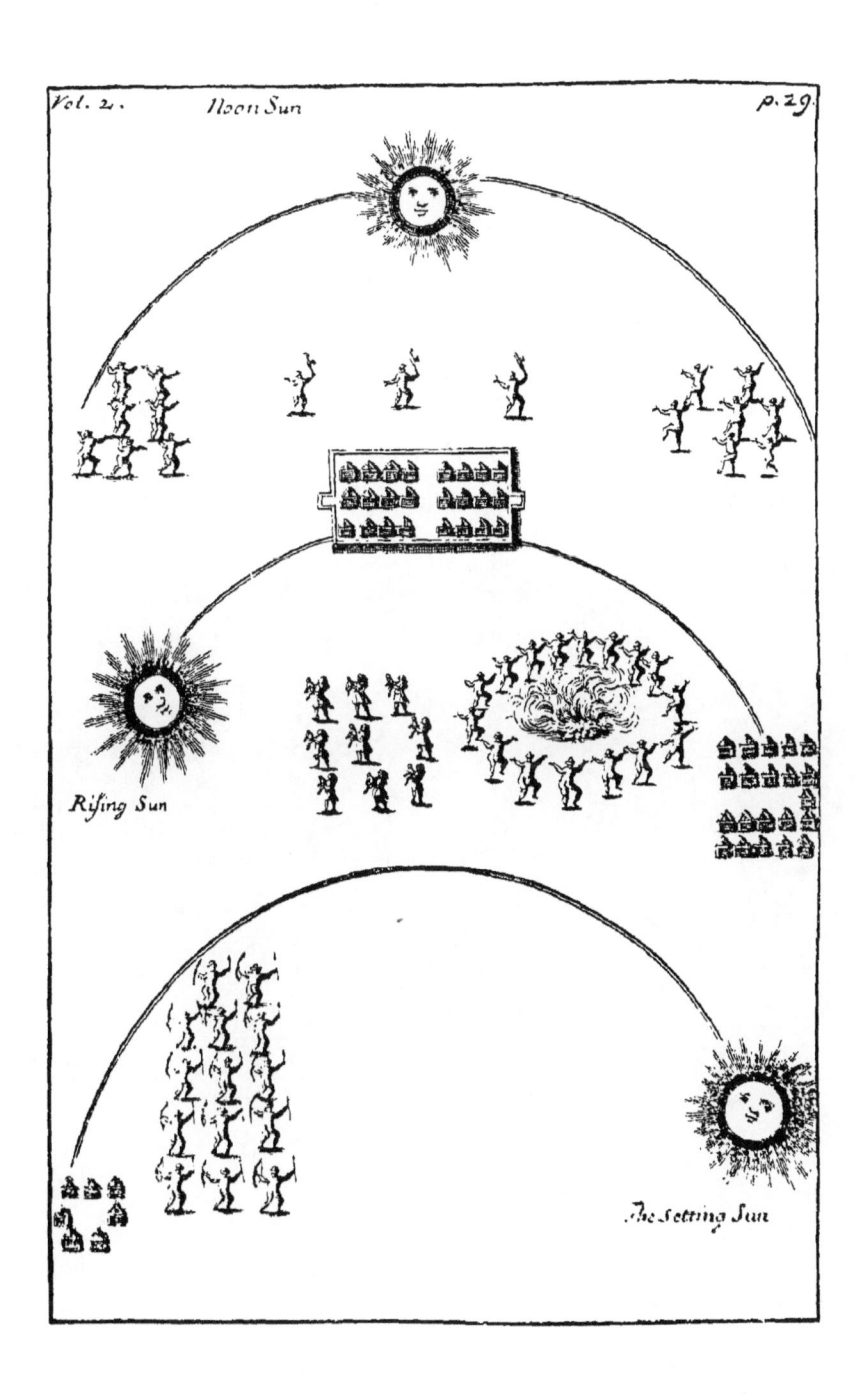

Rising Sun

The Setting Sun

A View of the Diseases and Remedies of the Savages.

THE *Savages* are a robust and vigorous sort of People, of a Sanguine Temperament, and an admirable Complexion. They are unacquainted with a great many Diseases that afflict [46] the *Europeans*, such as the *Gout, Gravel, Dropsy, &c.* Their Health is firm, notwithstanding that they use no precaution to preserve it; for on the contrary one would think that they weaken themselves by the Violent Exercises of Dancing, Hunting, and Warlike-Expeditions, in which they have frequent returns of Heats and Colds in one day, which in *Europe* would occasion a Mortal Distemper. Sometimes indeed they are seiz'd with *Plurisies*, but these are as unfrequent as they are mortal; for this is the only Distemper that all their Remedies cannot conquer. The *Small-Pox* are as common in the *North of Canada*, as the *Great-Pox* are to the *Southward*: in the Winter time the *Small-Pox* is very dangerous, by reason of the difficulty of respiration; but notwithstanding that 'tis mortal, the Savages matter it so little, that when 'tis upon 'em, they walk about from Hut to Hut, if they are able; or if they have not strength to walk, are carried about by their Slaves. In the *Illinese* Country, and near the *Mississipi*, the *Venereal Distemper* is very common. I remember, that in the Interview I had with the *Akansas* upon that great

River, at the Mouth of the *Miffouris* (as I faid in my Sixteenth Letter) I faw a Savage, who uncovering himfelf, fhew'd me part of his Body, that was ready to fall off, through Rottennefs; at that time he was bufy'd in boiling Roots, and after I had ask'd him the ufe of 'em, he gave me to underftand by his Interpreter, that he hop'd to be cur'd in a Months time, by drinking the Juice of thefe Roots, and eating conftantly the Broth or Decoction of Meat and Fifh.

Brandy makes a terrible havock among the People of *Canada*, for thofe who drink it are much more numerous than thofe who have the power to abftain from it. That Liquor, which of it felf is murdering ftuff, and which is brew'd and adulterated [47] before 'tis imported into this Countrey, fweeps off men fo faft, that one who has not feen the fatal effects of it can fcarce credit 'em: It extinguifhes their Natural Heat, and throws almoft all of 'em into that Languifhing Diforder, which we call a *Confumption:* They look pale, livid and ghaftly like Skeletons.[1] Their Feafts are the bane and entire ruine of their Stomacks, as being nothing but plentiful Entertainments, at which they value themfelves upon leaving nothing.[2] They pretend, that by vertue of their drinking great quantities of Water and Broth, they digeft their Victuals

---

[1] The ravages of the liquor habit among the aborigines of North America are well-known. The Indians do not drink for the taste of the liquor itself, but for the effect it produces — intoxication constituting a great enjoyment, for which they will sacrifice much. They do not hold anyone responsible for acts committed in that state — see vol. i, p. 124, *ante*. The early Jesuits opposed the brandy trade with the Indians, but were unable to secure its prohibition — see *ibid.*, p. 94. — ED.

[2] The "eat-all" feasts were among the most marked and disgusting habits of the Indians. See Le Jeune's description in *Jes. Rel.*, vi, pp. 281-293. — ED.

with greater Facility than the *Europeans*, who load their Stomacks with Wine and other Liquors, that produce Crudities.

The Savages are not at all alarm'd by Sickness, for they fear Death much less than the Pain and Duration of their Illness. When they are sick, they only drink Broth, and eat sparingly; and if they have the good luck to fall asleep, they think themselves cur'd: They have told me frequently, that sleeping and sweating would cure the most stubborn Diseases in the World. When they are so weak that they cannot get out of Bed, their Relations come and dance and make merry before 'em, in order to divert 'em. To conclude, when they are ill, they are always visited by a sort of Quacks, *(Jongleurs);* of whom 'twill now be proper to subjoin two or three Words by the bye.

A *Jongleur* is a sort of *Physician*, or rather a *Quack*, who being once cur'd of some dangerous Distemper, has the Presumption and Folly to fancy that he is immortal, and possessed of the Power of curing all Diseases, by speaking to the Good and Evil Spirits. Now though every Body rallies upon these Fellows when they are absent, and looks upon 'em as Fools that have lost their Senses by [48] some violent Distemper, yet they allow 'em to visit the Sick; whether it be to divert 'em with their Idle Stories, or to have an Opportunity of seeing them rave, skip about, cry, houl, and make Grimaces and Wry Faces, as if they were possess'd. When all the Bustle is over, they demand a Feast of a Stag and some large Trouts for the Company, who are thus regal'd at once with Diversion and Good Cheer.

When the Quack comes to visit the Patient, he examines

him very carefully; *If the Evil Spirit be here*, says he, *we shall quickly dislodge him.* This said, he withdraws by himself to a little Tent made on purpose, where he dances and sings houling like an Owl; (which gives the Jesuits Occasion to say, *That the Devil converses with 'em.*) After he has made an end of this Quack Jargon, he comes and rubs the Patient in some part of his Body, and pulling some little Bones out of his Mouth, acquaints the Patient, *That these very Bones came out of his Body; that he ought to pluck up a good heart, in regard that his Distemper is but a Trifle; and in fine, that in order to accelerate the Cure, 'twill be convenient to send his own and his Relations Slaves to shoot Elks, Deer, &c. to the end they may all eat of that sort of Meat, upon which his Cure does absolutely depend.*

Commonly these Quacks bring 'em some Juices of Plants, which are a sort of Purges, and are called *Maskikik*. But the Patients choose to keep them by 'em rather than to drink them; for they think all Purgatives inflame the Mass of the Blood, and weaken the Veins and Arteries by their violent Shocks. All their Cure consists in sweating well, in drinking Broth, in keeping themselves very warm, in sleeping if they can, and in drinking the Lake-water or Spring-water, in the Paroxysms of *Fevers*, as well as in other Distempers.[1]

[1] There is a large literature on the subject of "medicine men" and their therapeutics. There appear to have been two classes of these practitioners: those of the rational school, who depended for their cures upon herbs, baths, etc.; and the mystics or conjurers, who sought by religious ceremonies to expel the unwelcome manitou from the patient. For observations of ethnological students, see *Jes. Rel.*, index; Masson, *Bourgeois*, ii, p. 259-265, 363; Hoffman, "Midewinin of the Ojibwa," in U. S. Bur. of Eth *Report*, 1885-86; Bourke, "Medicine Men of the Apache," *ibid*, 1887-88; also Brinton, *Myths*, pp. 304-328. — ED.

[49] They cannot conceive how we come to be such Fools as to make use of Vomits; for when ever they see a *French-man* take down such a violent Remedy, they cannot forbear saying that he swallows an *Iroquese*. They plead, that this sort of Remedy shakes the whole Machine, and makes terrible Efforts upon all the inward Parts. But they are yet more astonish'd at our custom of Bleeding; *For,* say they, *the Blood being the Taper of Life, we have more occasion to pour it in than to take out, considering that Life sinks when its Principal Cause is mov'd off; from whence 'tis a Natural Consequence, that after loss of Blood Nature acts but feebly and heavily, the Intrails are over-heated, and all the Parts are dry'd, which gives rise to all the Diseases that afflict the* Europeans.

The Savages are never eight Days together without Sweating, whether they be well or bad; only they observe this difference, that when they are perfectly well they throw themselves while the sweating moisture is yet upon them, into the River in Summer, and into the Snow in Winter; whereas when they are out of order they go immediately into a warm Bed. Five or six Savages may sweat conveniently in the place allotted for that use, which is a sort of Oven or Stove cover'd with Mats, Skins, *&c.* In the middle of this Bagnio there stands a Dish or Porringer full of burning Brandy, or of great red hot Stones, which occasions such a piercing heat, that in the twinkling of an Eye they sweat prodigiously.[1] They never

---

[1] The sweat houses of the Indians are familiar to all students of aboriginal life, they were used both in sickness and in health. For a good description see *Jes Rel.*, vi, pp. 189, 191; xxxviii, pp. 253, 255 —ED.

make ufe of hot Baths and Glyfters, unlefs it be when they are over perfwaded by the Jefuits and our Phyficians.

I remember, that in a Conference I had one Day with a Savage, the Barbarian faid with a great deal of Senfe, *That a good Air, good Water, and Contentment of Mind could not indeed keep a* [50] *Man's Life from coming to an end, but that at leaft it muft be own'd, that thefe Advantages contribute in a great meafure to make a Man run through the courfe of his Life without being fenfible of any Diforder or Inconveniecy.* They make a Jeft of the Impatience of the *Europeans*, who would be cur'd as foon as they are fick. They alledge that our fear of Death, occafion'd by the invafion of the leaft Feaver, does fo inflame and fortifie the Difeafe, that oftentimes we fall a Sacrifice to Fear it felf; whereas if we look'd upon our Illnefs as a Triffle as well as Death, and kept our Bed with Patience and a good Heart, without offering Violence to Nature, by cramming down Drugs and Medicines, the good old Dame would not fail to Comfort and Refresh us by degrees.

The Savages are always againft the making ufe of our Surgeons and Phyficians. They affirm, that all mixtures of Drugs are Poyfon that deftroys Natural Heat, and confumes the Breaft; and that Glyfters are only proper for the *Europeans*, though after all they fometimes make ufe of them, when the *French* refort to their Villages. They are of the Opinion, that the obferving of a Diet heats the Blood, and that 'tis of dangerous Confequence to baulk the Appetite as to what it craves, provided the Aliment hath a good Juice. The Meat that they eat is little more than half done; but their Fifh is always over boyl'd. They never touch Sallade, upon the Plea that all cold Herbs oblige the Stomach to hard labour.

There's no Wound or Diflocation that they cannot cure with the Simples or Plants, whofe Vertues they are well acquainted with; and, which indeed is fingular, their Wounds never run to a Gangrene. But after all, this is not to [51] be imputed to thefe Herbs, nor to the Air of the Country, but to their hail Conftitution; for notwithftanding the ufe of thefe very Remedies a Gangrene invades the Wounds of the *French*, who queftionlefs are harder to cure than the Savages. This People attribute our liablenefs to Gangrenes, and indeed all our Difeafes, to the Salt that we eat; for they cannot tafte any falt thing without being fick unto Death, and drinking perpetually. They cannot be perfwaded to drink Ice-water, for they alledge that it infeebles the Stomach, and retards Digeftion. Such, Sir, are their fantaftical Opinions of things, which proceed from their Prepoffeffion and Bigotry with reference to their own Cuftoms and ways of Living. 'Tis in vain to vifit them when they lie at the point of Death, in order to prefs them to Bleed or take a Purge; for they ftill make anfwer, that they cannot confent to the forwarding of their Death by the Remedies of the *French*, which they take to be as bad as the Perfons who exhibit them.

As foon as a Savage dies he is dreft as neatly as can be, and his Relations Slaves come and mourn over him; neither Mother, Sifter nor Brother fhews the leaft mark of Affliction; they fay, Their deceas'd Friend is happy in being thus ex-

empted from farther Sufferings; for this good People believe, and not without Reason, that Death is a paſſage to a better Life.[1] When the Corps are dreſt they ſet them upon a Mat in the ſame Poſture as if the Perſon were alive; and his Relations being ſet round him, every one in his turn addreſſes him with a Harangue, recounting all his Exploits as well as thoſe of his Anceſtors. He that ſpeaks laſt expreſſes himſelf to this purpoſe. 'You ſuch a one, you ſit now along with us, and
'have the ſame Shapes that [52] we have; you want neither
'Arms, nor Head, nor Legs. But at the ſame time you ceaſe
'to be, and begin to evaporate like the ſmoke of a Pipe.
'Who is it that talk'd with us but two Days ago? Sure!
''twas not you; for then you would ſpeak to us ſtill. It muſt
'therefore be your Soul which is now lodg'd in the great
'Country of Souls along with thoſe of our Nation. This
'Body which we now behold will in ſix Months time become
'what it was two Hundred Years ago. Thou feeleſt nothing,
'thou knoweſt nothing, and thou feeſt nothing, becauſe thou
'art nothing. Nevertheleſs out of the Friendſhip we had for
'thy Body while animated by thy Spirit, we thus tender the
'Marks of that Veneration which is due to our Brethren and
'our Friends.

After they have made an end of their Harangues the Male Relations remove to make room for the ſhe Friends, who

---

[1] All tribes of North American Indians appear to have entertained some form of belief in the future life. See Brinton, *Myths*, pp. 271–278. The Jesuits describe the mourning and wailing consequent upon death, but assert that it is largely customary rather than the expression of grief. They likewise mention the funeral orations. See Le Jeune, in *Jes Rel*., x, pp 265–277. — ED.

make him the like Compliment. This done, they ſhut the Corps up twenty four Hours in the Hut for the Dead, and during that time are imploy'd in Dances and Feaſts, which are far from bearing a mournful ſhew. After the twenty four Hours are expir'd the Slaves of the deceas'd Perſon carry his Corps upon their Backs to the Burying-place, where it is laid upon Stakes that are ten Foot high, in a double Coffin of Bark, with his Arms and ſome Pipes with Tobaco and *Indian* Corn put up in the ſame Coffin. When the Slaves are carrying the Corps to the Burying-place, the Male and Female Relations accompany them, Dancing all the while; and the reſt of the Slaves of the deceas'd Perſon carry ſome Baggage, which the Relations preſent to the dead Perſon and lay upon his Coffin. The Savages that live upon the long River burn their Corps, as I inſinuated before; [53] but you muſt know that they keep them in Vaults or Cellars till they have a ſufficient number to burn together, which is perform'd out of the Village, in a place ſet a part for that Ceremony.[1] In fine, the Savages know no ſuch thing as Mourning, and never mention the Dead in particular; I mean, they never repeat their Names.[2] They deride us when they hear us recount the Fate of our Parents, our Kings, our Generals, *&c.*

---

[1] Cremation was seldom practiced by the barbarous nations of the North, but was customary in Central America and among certain California tribes. The scaffolds built for corpses were but temporary resting places; among perhaps most of the wandering tribes the body was taken down at the close of the hunt or raid, when the tribesmen next passed that way, and interred at the village of the deceased; among the Hurons, at the end of a period of from eight to twelve years, all bones were collected and interred. *Jes. Rel.*, 1, p. 267. — Ed

[2] This singular custom of avoiding mention of the name of the dead is frequently

Upon the Death of a Savage his Slaves marry the other Women Slaves, and live by themselves in a diſtinct Hut, as being then free, or ſuch as have no Maſter to ſerve. The Children that ſpring from this ſort of Marriages, are adopted and reputed the Children of the Nation, by reaſon of their being born in the Village and in the Country. *There's no reaſon*, ſay they, *that ſuch Children ſhould bear the Misfortunes of their Parents, or come into the World in Slavery, ſince they contributed nothing towards their Creation.* Theſe Slaves take care to go every Day to the foot of their Maſter's Coffin, and there offer ſome Pipes and Tobaco, as a grateful acknowledgment of their Liberty. But now that I am got upon the Subject of Tobaco, I muſt acquaint you that almoſt all the Savages ſmoak, but they never chew Tobaco, nor take it in Snuff. They ſow and reap a great deal of it, but then it differs from what we have in *Europe*, though our firſt Seed came from *America;* and in regard that 'tis in a manner good for nothing, they are forc'd to buy up *Braſil* Tobacco, which they mix with a certain Leaf of an agreeable Smell, call'd *Sagakomi*.[1]

---

mentioned by the Jesuits. For great men, the custom of resuscitation was practiced, whereby one was appointed to take upon himself the name and responsibilities of the deceased. *Jes. Rel.*, i, p. 267; xvii, p. 242. — ED.

[1] Sagakomi (sacacommis) is the bear berry (*Arctostaphylos uva-ursi*), one of the ingredients of Indian tobacco or kinnikinnik. The Spanish called it manzanita. Lewis and Clark say that this word is derived from the habit of the clerks (commis) of the North West Company who carried this berry in a bag (sac) for smoking;— see Thwaites, *Original Journals of the Lewis and Clark Expedition*, iv, pp. 13, 21, 22; but Coues, *New Light on the Early History of the Greater Northwest* (New York, 1897), p. 581, shrewdly conjectures that the form sacacommis was a pun upon a native word—as is here proven. Brazil tobacco (*Nicotiana tabacum*) is stronger than the northern species (*N. rustica*), hence more desired by the Indians. — ED.

I have nothing more to ſay upon this Head ; for I think I have given you a ſufficient account [54] of their Diſeaſes and of their Remedies, which in my Opinion are as Savage as themſelves. But let that be as it will, 'tis certain they ſeldom die of any other Diſtemper than of a Pleuriſy. As for the other Diſeaſes they get over them with the greateſt danger in the World, for ſetting aſide their Courage and Patience which goes beyond any thing that we can imagine, they take all the ways of the World to burſt themſelves by Eating and Drinking when they have groſs Feavours upon them, and when the fit is over ſmoaking that *Braſil* Tobaco, which without diſpute is the ſtrongeſt ſort that we know of.

The Women of this Country are ſubject to the Natural Diſorders as well as elſewhere, and ſometimes die of them. 'Tis true they have an admirable Remedy for redreſſing the Diſorders that flow from that Source; I mean, a certain Potion; but it hath no Operation unleſs they abſtain from all manner of Exceſs, which they are very unwilling to do. Some *French* Surgeons aſſur'd me, that the *European* Women void a much greater quantity and hold the Flux longer upon them than theſe *Americans*, who ſeldom have thoſe upon them above two Days at a time. Another Inconvenience that frequently annoys them, is an over-bearing quantity of Milk; for which they uſe to put little Puppies to ſuck their Breaſts.

[55] *The Diverſions of Hunting and Shooting uſual among the* Savages.

I HAVE already deſcrib'd the Hunting of the Elks and ſome other Animals of *Canada* in my 10th and 11th Letter, ſo that now it remains only to give you an exact account of the Beavers, which are ſaid to be *Amphibious Animals*, as I obſerv'd in my 16th Letter, with which I ſent you the Figure of theſe Animals. And becauſe theſe Beaſts do ſome things very ſurpriſing by a wonderful Inſtinct, to give you a right Notion wherein their Cunning conſiſts, I ſend you a Draught of thoſe Ponds which they know how to make more Artificially than any Man can do.

The Savages of *Canada* reflecting on the excellent Qualities of the Beavers, are wont to ſay, *That they have ſo much Wit, Capacity and Judgment, that they cannot believe their Souls die with their Bodies.* They add, *That if they were permitted to reaſon about things inviſible, and which fall not under their Senſes, they durſt maintain, that they are Immortal like ours.* But not to inſiſt on this Chimerical Fancy, it muſt be allow'd, that there are an infinite number of Men upon the Earth (without mentioning the *Tartars*, the Peaſants of *Muſcovy*, of *Norway*, and a Hundred other ſorts of People) who have not the Hundredth part of the Underſtanding which theſe Animals have.

The Beavers discover so much Art in their Works, that we cannot without offering violence to our Reason attribute their Skill to mere [56] Instinct, for it is lawful to doubt of some things whereof we cannot discover the Cause, provided they have not any Connexion with Religion; I mean such things as appear so strange to Sence and Reason, that we cannot give credit to them, unless we have seen them our selves. However, I will venture to write to you many Particulars upon this Subject, which perhaps may make you doubt of the truth of my Narrative. I will begin with assuring you, that these Animals join together in a Society consisting of an Hundred, and that they seem to talk and reason with one another by certain bemoaning inarticulate Sounds.[1] The Savages say they have an intelligible Jargon, by means whereof they communicate their Sentiments and Thoughts to one another. I never was an Eye Witness of this kind of Assemblies, but many *Savages* and *Coureurs de Bois*, who are People worthy of Credit, have assur'd me, that there is nothing more true. They add, that they consult among themselves about what things they must do to maintain their Cottages, their Banks and their Lakes, and about every thing that concerns the Preservation of their Commonwealth. These good People would perswade me, that the Beavers set Centries while they are cutting through great Trees, as big as Tuns, with their Teeth, in the Neighbourhood of their little Lakes, and that when these Centinels

---

[1] On the methods of communication between beavers, consult a recent monograph by Dugmore, "The Outlaw; a character study of a Beaver," in Smithsonian Institution *Report*, 1900, pp. 517-522. — ED.

cry out, upon the approach of Men or Beasts, all the Beavers that are at Work throw themselves into the Water and save themselves by diving, till they come at their Cottages.[1] I mention this matter of Fact upon the Report of a Thousand Persons, who could have no Interest to impose upon me with Fables; but what follows I have observ'd my self, in the Country where the *Outagamis* Hunt, [57] which I mention'd in the beginning of my 16th Letter.

The Beavers finding a Rivulet that runs cross a Meadow, set themselves to make Banks and Ramparts, which stopping the course of the Water cause an Inundation over the whole Meadow; that sometimes is no less than two Leagues in Circumference. This Bank is made with Trees which they cut down with their four great sharp Teeth, and then drag them along as they swim in the Water. These Trees being rang'd a cross at the bottom of this Meadow, the Animals load themselves with Grass and fat Earth, which they transport upon their great Tails, and throw in between the Wood with so much Art and Industry, that the most skilful Bricklayer can hardly make a stronger Wall with Lime and Morter. In the Night time they are heard to Work with so much Vigour and Diligence, that one would think them to be Men at Work, if he were not assur'd before hand that they are

---

[1] Apropos of Lahontan's hearsay reports of the sagacity of the beaver, the following should be noted: "Numberless writers upon this fertile and suggestive theme have been too easily betrayed into a fanciful exaggeration of facts, making the beaver a marvel of reflective, purposive, and coöperative intelligence — an imaginary picture, which an appeal to nature does not justify."—*Riverside Natural History*, v, p. 120.—ED.

Beavers. Their Tails ferve them for *Trouels*, and their Teeth for *Axes*, their Paws fupply the place of *Hands*, and their Feet ferve inftead of *Oars:* In fine, they make Banks of 4 or 500 Paces in length, of 20 Feet in heighth, and 7 or 8 in thicknefs, in the fpace of 5 or 6 Months, though there are not above a Hundred at moft that Work upon them.[1] I muft obferve here by the by, that the Savages, out of a fcruple of Confcience, never break thefe Banks, but only bore a hole through them, as I fhall fhow you hereafter. Befides their Talent of cutting down the Trees, their Art of making them fall upon the Water appears to me altogether furprizing; for it requires Judgment and clofe Attention to fucceed in it, and chiefly to nick the time when the Wind can affift them to make the fall of the [58] Tree more eafie, and to make them fall upon their little Lakes. But this is not the fineft Work of thefe Animals, that of their Cottages furpaffes all Imagination; for it requires both Skill and Strength to make holes at the bottom of the Water, for planting their fix Pofts which they take care to place exactly in the middle of the Lake: Upon thefe fix Pofts they fix their little Houfe, which is built in the form of an Oven, and is made up of fat Earth, Herbs and Branches of Trees, having three Stories that they may mount up from one to the other when the Waters rife by Rains or Thaw. The Rafters are of Rufhes, and each Beaver hath an Apartment to himfelf. They enter into their Cabin

---

[1] Upon the subject of beaver dams, consult *Jes Rel.*, i, p. 251; ix, pp. 129, 131; Martin, *Castorologia*, pp. 75, 76; Wells, "The Beaver," in *Harper's Magazine*, January, 1889. — ED.

under Water, thro' a great hole in the first Floor, which is encompass'd with Asp Wood cut in pieces on purpose, that they may the more easily drag it into their Cells when they have a mind to eat; for since it is their common Food, they are always so Provident as to lay up great heaps of it, and chiefly during the *Autumn*, foreseeing that the cold Weather will freeze up their Lakes, and keep them shut up two or three Months in their Cabins.[1]

I should never make an end if I attempted to give an account of all the several Artifices of these Ingenious Animals, the Order settled in their little Commonwealth, and the Precautions they use to secure themselves from the pursuit of other Animals: I shall only observe, that all other Animals upon Earth, however Strong, Active and Vigorous they may be, have other Animals which they are affraid of; but these I now speak of are not apprehensive of any danger but only from Men, for the Wolves, the Foxes, the Bears, &c. care not for offering to attack them in their Cabines, although they have the faculty of Diving; and it is certain it [59] is not their Interest to do it, for the Beavers would defend themselves very easily with their sharp cutting Teeth; so that they cannot be insulted but by Land, and 'tis for that reason they never go farther than twenty Paces from the edge of their Lake, and always set Centinels to watch, who cry out to give them notice when they hear the least noise.

---

[1] It does not appear to be true that beavers can determine the direction a tree will fall; see Martin, *op cit.*, pp 68-72. Nor do they plant posts to build their lodges; see Hearn's account in Martin, p. 226; also *Jes. Rel.*, ix, pp. 127, 129. — ED.

It remains now only that I should give an Account of the Nature of the Countries where the Beavers are hunted, some of which are describ'd in my Map.[1] And first you must know, that you cannot go four or five Leagues in the Woods of *Canada*, but you meet with a little Beaver-Lake: So that one may say, that all this vast Continent is a Country for *Beaver hunting;* but this is not what I mean. The Places for Hunting that I now speak of are a multitude of little Lakes replensh'd with these Animals, the distance of which from one to another is inconsiderable. For Instance, those of *Saguinan*, of *L' ours qui dort*, of the *River of Puants*, are about twenty Leagues in length, and in that whole compass of Ground their are found Sixty little Beaver Lakes more or less, where a certain number of Savages may Hunt in the Winter time.[2] 'Tis commonly about the end of *Autumn* that the Savages set out from their Villages in a Canow to go and post themselves in the places for Hunting, and as they know all the places much better than I do the Streets of *Quebec*, they agree among themselves, as they are Travelling, to allot each Family a certain compass of Ground, so that when they arrive at the place they divide themselves into *Tribes*.[3] Each Hunter fixes his House in the Center of that Ground which is his District, as you may see

---

[1] For a map of beaver habitat and distribution, see Martin, p. 58. The beaver will probably soon become extinct in North America; even the interesting preserved colonies in the Yellowstone National Park, where they can still be studied with comparative ease, suffer a steady depletion at the hands of poachers — ED.

[2] See pp. 143, 168, 208, *ante*. — ED

[3] Martin (*Castorologia*, p. 140) cites instances where the Indians kept with fidelity to the bounds of their beaver reserves. — ED.

describ'd in this Cut. There are eight or ten Hunters in each Cottage, [60] who have four or five Lakes for their share. In each Lake there is at least one House or Kennel of Beavers, and sometimes two or three. After the Huntsmen have built their Huts they employ themselves in laying Traps for *Otters*, *Foxes*, *Bears*, *Land Beavers* and *Martens*, upon the sides of their Lakes; and when they are set go very orderly to look after them every Day: But above all they are so Just, that they would choose rather to die for Hunger than to straggle out of the Bounds allotted them, or to steal the Beasts that are taken in their Neighbours Traps. They feed well and make merry during this Hunting Season, which lasts for four Months; for they find more than they have occasion for, of *Trouts*, *Hares*, *Wood-Foul*, *Bears*, and sometimes they meet with *Deer* and *Roebucks*.

The *Beavers* are seldom catch'd by Traps unless they put in them some pieces of red Asp* which they love extreamly, and is not easie to be found. They are taken in the *Autumn* by making a great hole under their Banks, by which they drain all the Water out of their Lakes, and then the Beavers being left on dry Ground the Savages kill them all, except a dozen of Females, and half a dozen of Males; after which they are very exact in stopping up the hole they had made, which they do in such a manner that the Lake is fill'd with Water as before.

* *A sort of a Willow.*

Their way of Hunting in the Winter time when the Lake is frozen, is by making holes round the Kennels of the

Beavers, upon which they place Nets that reach from one to the other, and when they are extended as they fhould be, they lay open the Kennels of thefe poor Animals with an Ax; upon which they throw themfelves into the Water, and coming to take [61] Breath at thefe Holes, are catch'd in the Nets; at this rate not one of them efcapes, but the Savages having no mind to extirpate 'em throw back into the Holes, the fame number of Beavers, Male and Female, as they ufually do at their Hunting in Autumn, as I have already told you.

They may likewife be kill'd when they Swim upon the Water, or when they come Afhore to cut down Trees; but then you muft be very well hid and not ftir, for upon the leaft noife that they hear, they throw themfelves into the Water, and Dive till they come to their Kennels. This way of Hunting is peculiar to Travellers, who finding themfelves lodg'd near fome Beaver Lake, endeavour to furprize them, by Sculking behind fome Log or fome great Tree till Night comes on.[1]

The Savages take alfo other Animals in thefe Beaver-Hunting-Countries, by running up and down. I have already told you, that they fet Traps, in which *Foxes*, *Wolves*, *Martens* and others are catch'd when they bite at the Bait. I have alfo explain'd to you the way of making this fort of Traps, in my

---

[1] On methods of beaver hunting, see *Jes. Rel.*, vi, pp. 299–303; Masson, *Bourgeois*, ii, pp. 342–344. On modern methods, consult Wells, "Beaver." The use of castoreum as a bait was not adopted until near the close of the eighteenth century, and led to new methods of hunting which rapidly reduced the numbers of this animal. For the method of preparation of this bait, see frequent references in *Original Journals of Lewis and Clark Expedition*.— Ed.

11th Letter. Thefe Engines do not differ from one another, but only in bulk: Thofe for the Bears are the ftrongeft, but they are of no ufe till the beginning of Winter; for then the Bears feek out great Trees which are Hollow, where the Branches begin to fpread, that they may Neftle in them. Many People will hardly believe that thefe Animals can live 3 Months in fuch Prifons, without any other Food but the Juice of their Paws which they fuck continually: And yet the matter of Fact is undeniably true. But I reckon it yet more ftrange, that they are able to climb up to thofe Lurking-Holes, efpecially at a time when they are fo Fat, [62] that 2 Savages conduct them whither they pleafe with Poles, they being fcarce able to walk. This I faw 3 or 4 times during the Winter in 1687, when I Winter'd at *Fort St. Jofeph;* for the *Hurons* of *Gaintfouan* brought fome of them off, which enter'd the Fort without any reluctancy.[1]

The Savages make likewife Traps for the *Land-Beavers,* which for the reafon given in my 16th Letter, neftle on the Land, like *Foxes, Conies* and *Badgers:* And notwithftanding that they are purfu'd by the other Beavers, yet they make their Dens about the Lakes, Brooks and Rivers. They are eafily taken in thefe Traps, efpecially when they are Baited with the Head of an *Otter:* For there is fo great an Antipathy

---

[1] This Huron appellation has not been certainly identified; but consult Coyne (ed.), "Exploration of the Great Lakes, 1669-70," in Ontario Historical Society *Records and Papers,* iv (Toronto, 1903), especially the map; also Jones, "Identification of St. Ignace II and of Ekarenniondi," in Ontario Archæological *Report,* 1902, pp. 92-136, particularly the map of Petun Country, p. 113. — ED.

between thefe 2 forts of Animals, that they are continually at War with one another.[1]

The Savages inform'd me, that they faw a great Company of *Otters* Affembled together about the Month of *May*, who had the boldnefs to attack the *Beavers* in their Huts, but were beaten back and driven from the Lake with lofs. They added, that a Beaver can defend himfelf againft 3 Otters, by the help of his Teeth and Tail. In fine, 'tis certain that the Lake Beavers are feldom taken in Traps, unlefs they be Baited with fome Afpwood, as I have already obferv'd. I acquainted you above that the Savages vifit their Traps every day, and carry into their Cottages the Prey that they find catch'd. Immediately after that, the Slaves Flea the Beafts that are taken, and ftretch out their Skins in the Air, or on the Ice to dry them. This Imployment lafts as long as the time of Hunting, which ends with the great Thaw; and then they put up their Skins in Bundles, and carry them to the place where they left the Canows when they firft came into this Hunting-Country.

[63] Altho the Savages have great reafon to be afraid of their Enemies, while they lye difperfed up and down in a Country, which is no lefs than 20 Leagues in Compafs, as I intimated above; yet they fcarce ever ufe the Precaution of fending out Scouts upon all hands, and for want of it are often Surpriz'd, when they leaft think of it. I could relate 20 fatal Excurfions of the *Iroquefe* into the Hunting-Countries

---

[1] On land beavers, see pp. 170–172, *ante*. — ED.

I have been speaking of, in which they cut the Throats of many of our Friends and Allies. I did all that I could to perfuade our Allies that their Conduct was faulty upon this occafion, fince they could eafily fecure themfelves from fuch Infults, by Building their Cottages at a place where they might poft a Guard of Centinels, to watch and difcover any Enemies, that might advance to the Frontiers of thefe Hunting-Countries. They only made anfwer; *that this indeed was reafonable, and that it was true, they did not fleep in fafety for want of that Precaution.* In fine, they imagine that their Enemies are bufied in Hunting on their own Coafts; and upon that Apprehenfion, are fuch Fools as not to ufe any Precaution. But this I know, that the *Iroquefe* take quite another Method, having their Scouts and advanc'd Guards, which are always in Motion; by which means they are fcarce ever difturb'd in their Hunting. Neverthelefs, I think I ought not to conclude this Chapter, without giving you an account of 2 Attempts wherein the *Iroquefe* mifs'd of their defign to furprize their Enemies, tho they had very good Succefs upon many other occafions.

In the year 1680. The *Oumamis* and *Ilinefe* being at Hunting near the River *Oumamis;* a Party of 400 *Iroquefe* furpriz'd them, kill'd 30 or 40 Hunters, and took 300 Prisoners, including [64] Women and Children.[1] After they had refted a little while, they prepar'd to return Home by fhort Jour-

---

[1] Evidently this was an episode (although probably with exaggerated numbers) occurring in the Illinois-Iroquois war (1680-82). The Miami were at first reluctant allies of the latter, but later complained that they "were daily slaughtered by the Iroquois." See *N. Y. Colon. Docs.*, ix, pp. 162, 177, 192. — ED.

neys, becaufe they had reafon to believe that they fhould reach their own Villages before the *Ilinefe* and *Oumamis* could have time to Rally, and give notice of their Difafter to fuch of the Nations as were Hunting in remoter Places. But they were fo much deceiv'd, that the *Ilinefe* and *Oumamis* Rallied to the number of 200, and refolv'd to die Fighting rather than fuffer their Countrymen to be carried away by the *Iroquefe*. In the mean time, becaufe their Party was not an equal Match for the Enemies, they contriv'd a notable Stratagem: For after they had well confider'd in what manner they fhould Attack them, they concluded that they ought to follow them at a fmall diftance till it began to Rain. Their Project fucceeded, and the Heavens feem'd to favour it: For while it Rain'd continually one whole day from Morning to Night, they fo quicken'd their pace, from the time that the Rain begun to fall, that they pafs'd by on one fide at 2 Leagues diftance from the *Iroquefe*, and fo got before them to lay an Ambufcade in the middle of a Meadow, which the Enemy was to crofs in order to reach a Wood, where they had a mind to make a halt and kindle great Fires. The *Ilinefe* and *Oumamis* lying upon their Belly among the *Fern*, waited till the *Iroquefe* were got into the middle of them before they Shot off their Arrows; and then they Attack'd them fo vigoroufly with their Clubs, that the Enemy finding their Fire-Arms unferviceable, by reafon that their Prime was wet, were forc'd to throw them down on the Ground, and defend themfelves with the fame Arms wherewith they were Attack'd, (I mean with Clubs.) But as I obferv'd before, that the [65] *Ilinese* are something more dextrous and nimble than the *Iroquese*, so the latter were forc'd to yield to the former, and retreated Fighting till Night came on, after they had lost 180 Soldiers. The Fight which lasted but one hour, had continued all Night, if the Conquerors had not been afraid, lest their Countrymen being still Bound and left behind 'em, should be expos'd to some Surprize in the dark: And therefore after they had rejoyn'd them, and seiz'd all the Fire-Arms of their Enemies who were fled and dispers'd up and down, they return'd into their own Country, without taking one *Iroquese*, for fear of weakning themselves.

The 2d Attempt hapned 3 years after this, in the Hunting-Country of the *Outagamis;* where the Governor of that Nation, as I inform'd you in my 16th Letter, gave me 10 Soldiers to accompany me to the Long River. The Blow then given was after this manner. A Body of 1000 *Iroquese* being come in their Canows about the end of Autumn, as far as the Bay of *Missisagues*, in the Lake of the *Hurons*,[1] without being discover'd, Landed at this place; and being very numerous, march'd up the Country with their Nets, in order to Fish in the little Lakes and Rivers, till the Frosty Season should come on, which hapned a few days after. After the Ice was strong enough to bear them, they continued their Course, coasting along the great Lake of the *Hurons*, till they were 5 or 6 Leagues below the Fall call'd *Saut Sainte Marie*, which they would not approach to for fear of meeting with some *Coureurs*

---

[1] "Bay of Missisagues" is the present Georgian Bay, off Lake Huron. The Huronia of the *Jesuit Relations* was bounded on the west by this bay. — ED.

de bois in the Fort of the *Jesuits*. Having cross'd the Bay, they judg'd it convenient to make very short Journies, for fear of being discover'd. And they were so cautious as to march all in a Row upon the Snow; that if [66] by chance any one should discover their Footsteps, it might be thought that they were not above Thirty or Forty at the most. After this manner they Travell'd till the 15th or 20th of *February*, without being perceiv'd, but at last they had the misfortune to be discover'd by four *Sauteurs*, who seeing so great a number pass over a little Lake, run with all speed to the Hunting Country of the *Outagamis* to give them notice, notwithstanding that the *Sauteurs* were then at War with the *Outagamis*. In the mean time the Thaw coming on suddenly contrary to the Expectation of the *Iroquese*, who reckon'd upon Twenty Days of Frost to come, according to the common course of the Season; this made them mend their pace, and look out for the narrowest and least frequented Passes. The *Outagamis* were mightily perplex'd what course to take in this case. It was certain that they might get back again to their Villages in safety, but then they would be forc'd to abandon their Wives and Children, who had not strength to run as the Men. In fine, after they had held a Council among themselves, they resolv'd to advance as far as a certain Pass about half a League in length and Thirty Paces in breadth, between two little Lakes, which way they saw plainly that the *Iroquese* were oblig'd to pass.

The *Outagamis* being no more than four Hundred thought fit to divide themselves into two Bodies, and it was agreed, that two Hundred should be posted at the end of a Pass which they should Fortifie immediately with a Range of Stakes from one Lake to another; and that the other two Hundred should go about a quarter of a League off of the other end of the Pass, thro' which the *Iroquese* were to march, to the end that every one having cut down a Stake they [67] might all run quickly in to stop up that end of the Passage, and that immediately after the *Iroquese* had entred the Defile, the Scouts appointed to observe their March should come and give them notice; all which was punctually put in Execution: For as soon as that great Multitude, who industriously pitch'd upon the narrow Roads, was entred into this Pass, the two Hundred *Outagamis*, who were about a quarter of a League to one side of it, run in with all their Might and carried with them a sufficient number of Pales to enclose that little piece of Land which was bounded by the two little Lakes, so that they had time enough to set them up and fasten them with Earth, before the *Iroquese*, being astonish'd to find their way block'd up at the other end, could return back the same way, to see themselves shut up between two Barricadoes. Now the Savages, as I have often told you, are never so rash as to attack a Redoubt of Fifty Palisadoes, yet these *Iroquese* were resolv'd to venture upon an Attack, and with that view run up with all expedition to force the new Barricado; but they slacken'd their pace after the first discharge which the *Outagamis* made through the intervalls of the Pales, for they had not time to joyn them as they should be. The *Iroquese* seeing themselves thus shut up, took the number of the *Outagamis* to be much greater than realy it was. In the mean time the great Queſtion was, how to get out of this Priſon? For to throw themſelves into the Water and ſwim over one of theſe Lakes, was to run the hazard of ones Life, beſides that one muſt be long-winded and have a good Heart to ſwim over a broad Lake, at a time when the Water was cold, the Ice being not quite melted. This Conſultation gave the *Outagamis* time to fortifie their Barricadoes, and to [68] ſend out Scouts who were plac'd at a diſtance from one another, upon the Banks of theſe two Lakes, to knock all on the Head that offer'd to ſwim to the ſhore.

Notwithſtanding all theſe Precautions the *Iroqueſe* found out a wonderful Expedient, which was to make Floats of the Trees wherewith they were encompaſs'd ; but the blows of the Ax made too great a noiſe, which diſcover'd their Deſign to the *Outagamis*, and therefore they made Canows of Hart-skins to run backward and forward upon the two Lakes in the Night time. Theſe Boats were made in five or ſix Days, during which time the *Iroqueſe* fiſh'd and catch'd abundance of Trouts in the ſight of the *Outagamis*, who could not hinder them. After this no body doubted, but they muſt croſs one of the Lakes, and fight ſtoutly when they came to the Landing place, in caſe their ſecret Navigation was diſcover'd. That they might the better ſucceed in their Deſign they made a Feint, which had infallibly anſwer'd their end if the bottom of the Lake had not been Clay: For about Midnight having Sacrific'd Twenty Slaves upon one of the Lakes, whom they forc'd to puſh a Float along, they made account to paſs the other the fame way, making ufe of Poles inftead of Oars: But in regard that the Poles funk fo deep into the Clay, that the Steerfmen could not pull them out again without great difficulty, they made but flow difpatch; infomuch that the *Outagamis*, that at first were under a miftake in joyning themfelves to the Slaves, had time to run to the other Lake, where they found the *Iroquefe* about a Musket-fhot off the Shore. As foon as the *Iroquefe* came to have but three Foot Water they threw themfelves into the Water with their Guns cock'd, fuffering at [69] the fame time the Fire of the *Outagamis*, who were not above three Hundred, there being Fifty of them left to guard each Barricado. 'Tis a wonder the *Iroquefe* were not all cut off in the Landing, for they funk in the Clay up to their Knees. 'Tis true, 'twas in the Night time, and for that reafon all the Enemy's Fire might not bear upon them. However five Hundred of them fell in the Water, and the reft having gain'd the Shoar notwithftanding all the oppofition of the *Outagamis*, attack'd them with fuch Fury that if the Hundred Men that were left for a Guard to the Barricadoes had not run in to their Affiftance upon the firft noife of the Guns, the poor *Outagamis* were in danger of falling upon the Spot. They fought till the break of Day with wonderful fury, and that in the greateft Confufion imaginable, being difpers'd up and down a Wood, infomuch that feveral were kill'd by their own Men, who could not diftinguifh who was who. The *Iroquefe* were obftinately refolv'd not to yield the Field of Battel, out of regard to their wounded Men, and in confideration that they would not have the *Outagamis* to take the Hair of

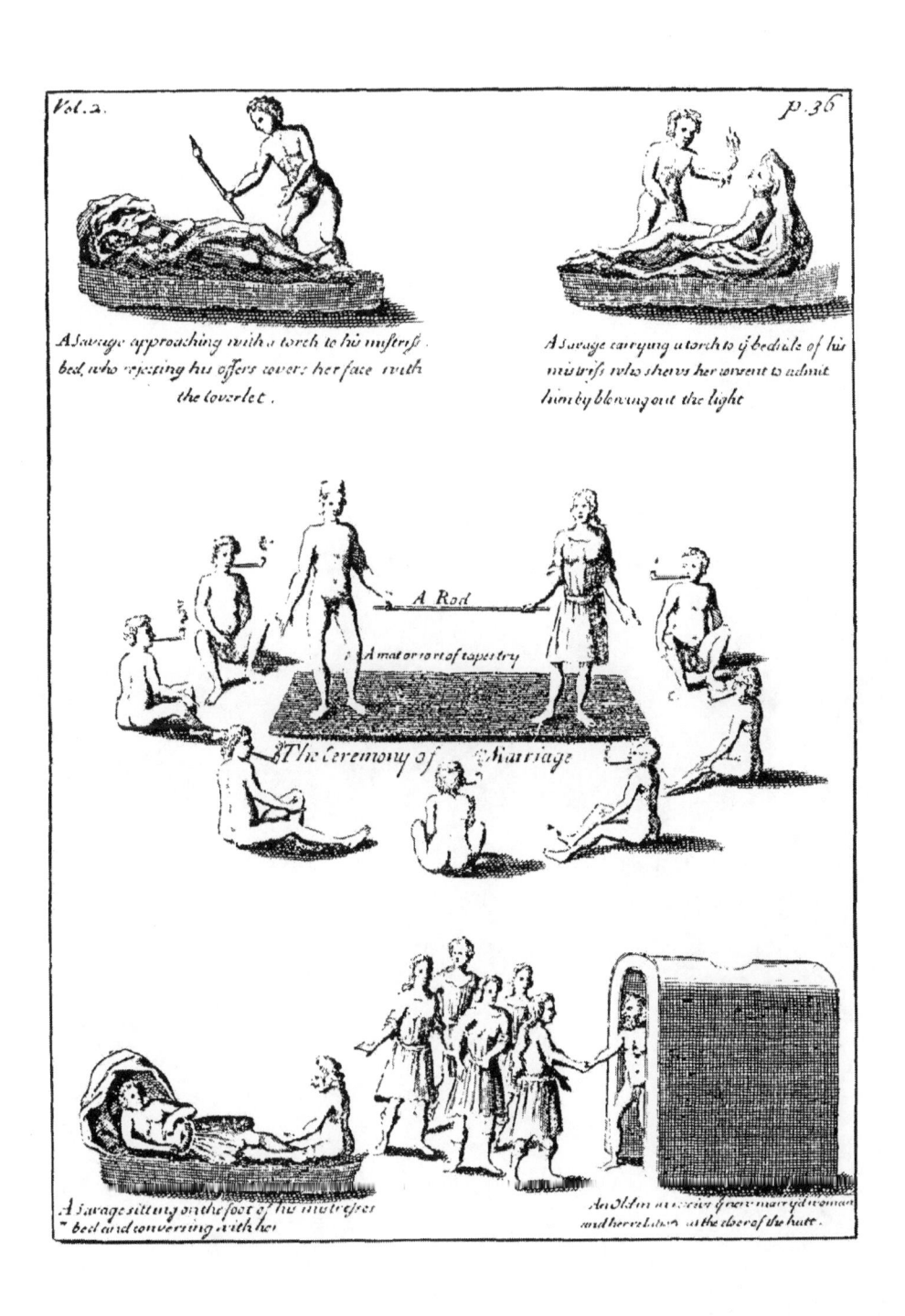

A Savage approaching with a torch to his mistriss. bed, who rejecting his offers covers her face with the coverlet.

A Savage carrying a torch to ye bedside of his mistriss who shews her consent to admit him by blowing out the light.

A Rod
A mat or sort of tapestry
The Ceremony of Marriage

A Savage sitting on the foot of his mistresses bed and conversing with her.

An Old man receives ye new-marryd woman and her relations at the door of the hutt.

their Dead. But at laſt they were oblig'd to give way, without being purſued, and fled half a League off where they rally'd. I was inform'd by ſeveral *Iroqueſe* ſome Years after this Engagement happen'd, that thoſe who ſurviv'd the Engagement were for venturing upon a new Bruſh; but conſidering that they wanted Powder, and that they were oblig'd to return home through the Country of the *Sauteurs*, or thoſe who live on the Confines of the great Water Falls, they chang'd their Reſolution. But after all they were much out in not coming to a freſh Engagement; for being ſtill three Hundred ſtrong they could not but [70] have the better of it, for the *Outagamis* were not ſo numerous by one third, having loſt half their number in that ſharp Engagement, not to mention that of the two Hundred which remain'd there were Thirty Wounded. In ſhort the *Outagamis* having intrench'd themſelves in the ſame place where the Fight was, took care in the firſt place to dreſs the Wounds both of their own Men and of their Priſoners; and after taking the Hair off the Heads of all their dead Enemies, ſent out Scouts to obſerve the Enemy, after which they return'd home in ſafety.

When the *Outagamis* arriv'd at their Villages, the firſt thing they did was a return of Thanks to the four *Sauteurs* that had given them Intelligence of the approach of the *Iroqueſe*. They proclaim'd them to be great Maſters of War, and preſented 'em with one half of what they had got at Hunting, which amounted to Sixty Thouſand Crowns, pretending farther, that theſe four Savages ought to inherit the Beaver and other Skins belonging to thoſe of the *Outagamis* that were kill'd in the Battle. In fine, after entertaining those Intelligencers with good Chear, and all the Marks of Honour that were poffible in their way, they fent them in a Canow to *Saut St. Mary*, by the way of the Bay of *Puantes*, with a Guard of Fifty Warriors. The *Sauteurs* refus'd both their Prefents and their Convoy, upon the account that the two Nations were then at War with one another: But the *Outagamis* forc'd them upon 'em, and 'twas this that procur'd a Peace between them at the end of four Months.[1]

This, Sir, as I take it is fufficient to give you an *Idea* of the Hazards that the Savages run at their Beaver Hunting. In the mean time, tho' I have but juft made an end of two Military Adventures, yet I allot the very next Chapter [71] for an account of their Military Art, in which you'l meet with fomethings that will ferve for Diverfion to your felf and Entertainment to your Friends.

---

[1] Lahontan appears to be the only contemporary author who relates this defeat of the Iroquois by the Foxes (Outagamis). Allouez speaks of a war between them, about 1670; but it is strange that so signal a victory of the French-allied Indians should not have been mentioned in the official documents of the period. The story would therefore appear to be of doubtful authenticity. — ED.

The Military Art of the Savages.

THE Savage call'd *Rat*, whom I have mention'd so often in my Letters, has said to me several times, that the only thing in the World that vex'd and disturb'd his Mind was the seeing Men wage War with Men. *Prithee, my Brother*, said he, *do but look; our Dogs agree perfectly well with the* Iroquese *Dogs, and those of the* Iroquese *bear no Enmity to the Dogs that come from* France. *I do not know any Animal that wages War with others of its own Species, excepting Man, who upon this score is more Unnatural than the Beasts. For my part* (continues he) *I am of the Opinion, that if the Brutes could Think and Reason, and communicate their Thoughts, 'twould be an easie matter for them to extirpate the Human Race: For, in earnest, if the Bears and Wolves were but capable of forming a Republick, who could hinder them to draw together a Body of ten or twelve Thousand, and to fall upon us? If such a thing should happen, what defence can we make? They would scale our Villages with the greatest Facility imaginable, and after the pulling down of our Huts devour our selves. Could we in such a Case undertake a Hunting Expedition, without running the risque of being torn in Pieces? We should then be reduc'd to live upon Accorns and Roots, without Arms and without Cloaths, and to run the perpetual hazard of falling into the Clutches of these*

Animals. Their Strength and Nimbleness would sink all Opposition from us, and command us to yield. [72] *Let us conclude therefore, my dear Brother, that this* Reason *which Man boasts so much of is the greatest Instrument of his Misery; and that if Men were without that Faculty of Thinking, Arguing and Speaking, they would not imbarque in mutual Wars as they now do, without any regard to Humanity or Sacred Promises.*

Such, Sir, are the Moral Thoughts of a Savage, who pretends to Philosophise upon the Custom that we have of killing Men with Justice and Honour. The Jesuits do their utmost to remove this Scruple by such Reasons as they have, as they do upon several other Subjects, and the Savages hear 'em very gravely, but at the same time they tell 'em that they do not understand 'em.

The Wars of the Savages are grounded upon the Right of Hunting, or of a Passage upon such and such Grounds; for their Limits are adjusted, and every Nation is perfectly well acquainted with the Boundaries of their own Country. Now these *Americans* are as Cruel to their Enemies, as they are True to their Allies; for some Nations among them use their Prisoners with the last degree of Inhumanity; as I shall shew you more at large in the Sequel. When the *Europeans* offer to Censure the Savages for their barbarous and cruel Usage, they reply very coldly, *That Life is nothing, that they are not reveng'd on their Enemies by cutting their Throats, but by putting them to a long, tedious, sharp and lasting Torture; and that Women would be as chearful Warriors as Men, if there were nothing to be fear'd but bare Death.* At the Age of Fifteen they begin to bear Arms, and lay 'em down at Fifty. If they happen to bear Arms fooner or later, 'tis only in the way of marauding, for they are not lifted into the number of the Warriors.

[73] The Strength of the *Iroquefe* lies in engaging with Fire-Arms in a Forreft; for they fhoot very dexteroufly; befides that they are very well vers'd in making the beft advantage of every thing, by covering themfelves with Trees, behind which they ftand ftock ftill after they have difcharg'd, though their Enemies be twice their Number. But in regard that they are more clumfy and not fo clever as the more *Southern Americans*, they have no Dexterity in handling a Club; and thus it comes to pafs, that they are always worfted in the open Field, where the Clubs are the only Weapons; for which Reafon they avoid any Engagement in Meadows or open Fields as much as is poffible.

The Savages never court an Engagement but by way of Surprifal, that is, the fide which makes the firft difcovery is almoft always fure of having the better of it; for they have it in their choice to make the Attack either in the open Field, or in the moft dangerous Defiles or Paffes.

In the Day time they take all the Precaution in the World to cover their March, by fending out Scouts on all Hands, unlefs it be that the Party is fo ftrong as to fear nothing; for then, indeed, they March all in a clofe Body. But they are as Negligent in the Night time, as they are Vigilant in the

Day; for they place neither Centries nor Guards at the entry of their Camp, and when they go a Hunting or Shooting of Beavers, they are equally secure or careless. When I enquir'd into the reason of this bad Discipline, I was assur'd that the Savages did it by way of Presumption, as reckoning so much upon the Reputation of their Valour, that they imagine their Enemies will not be so bold as to Attack them: And when they send out Scouts in the Day time, that Precaution proceeds more [74] from an itch to surprise their Enemies, than from the fear of being surpris'd themselves.

There are a great many Savage Nations in *Canada* that tremble at the very Name of the *Iroquese,* for the latter are a brave sort of People; they are expert Warriors, ready upon all Enterprises, and capable to put them in Execution, with all due Dexterity. 'Tis true, they are not so sprightly as most of their Enemies, nor so happy in fighting with Clubs; and 'tis for that Reason that they never march but in numerous Bodies, and that by slower Marches than those of the other Savages. In fine, you'l see in my List of the Nations of *Canada,* which of 'em are Warlike, and which are only qualify'd for Hunting.

The Savages have a wonderful Talent in surprising their Enemies; for they can trace the Footsteps of Men and Beasts upon Grass and Leaves, better than the *Europeans* can upon Snow or wet Sand. Nay, which is more, they can distinguish with a great deal of Facility between fresh Tracts and those of longer standing, and can make a just Estimate of the number and kind that made them. These Tracts they follow whole Days without being miftaken. This I have feen fo often with my own Eyes, that there's no room left for the leaft doubt upon the matter.

The Warriors never undertake any thing without the Advice of the Ancient Men, to whom they propofe their Projects. Upon a Propofal thus made the old Men meet and confult upon it; after which their Speaker walks out of the Council-Hut, and with a loud Voice Proclaims the Refolution of the Council, that all the Village may have due Information of the fame.

[75] You muft obferve that each Village hath its General or Great Head of the Warriors, who in confideration of his Valour, Capacity and Experience is proclaim'd fuch by an unanimous Confent.[1] But after all, this Title invefts him with no Power over the Warriors; for thefe People are Strangers to a Military as well as to a Civil Subordination. Nay, they are fo far from it, that if the great Leader fhould order the fillyeft and moft pittiful Fellow in his Army to do fo and fo, why truly, this fhaddow of a Captain would receive this Anfwer from the Centinel, *That what he orders another to do he ought to do it himfelf.* But 'tis fuch an uncommon thing for the Leader to act fo indifcreetly, that I Queftion if there be one Inftance of it. However this mutual Independance is of no ill Confequence; for though the great Leader is not invefted with Power and Authority, yet they acquiefce entirely in

---

[1] In most tribes the civil and military government is separate, the war chief being from a different clan than the head chief, and usually chosen for ability and valor. See Powell, "Wyandot Government," in U. S. Bur. of Eth. *Report*, 1879-80, pp. 59-69, Dorsey, "Omaha Sociology," *ibid*, 1881-82, pp. 312-333.—ED.

what he Propoſes. He no ſooner opens his Mouth in ſaying, *I think ſuch and ſuch a thing proper, let's detach Ten or Twenty Men*, &c. than 'tis put in Execution, without the leaſt Oppoſition. Beſides the great Leader there are ſome other Leaders that Head a certain number of Warriors who follow them out of Friendſhip and Reſpect; and theſe are not look'd upon as Leaders or Commanders by any other than their own Family or Followers.[1]

When the old Men think it proper that a Party of Warriors ſhould take the Field, the *Great Leader* who always aſſiſts at the Council, hath the privilege of making his choice whether he'll Head them himſelf, or ſtay at home in the Village. If he hath a mind to go himſelf, he orders the Cryer of that Nation to make publick Proclamation in all the Streets of the Village, That on ſuch a Day he gives the Feaſt of War to thoſe who [76] pleaſe to be preſent. Then, thoſe who have a mind to go in that Party, ſend their Diſhes to the General's Houſe on the appointed day, and are ſure to be there themſelves before noon. When the Company is all gather'd, the General walks out to a publick place with his Club in his hand, being followed by the Warriours who ſit down round him. This done, there comes ſix Savages, with as many Kettle Drums, which make a Clutter, rather than a Warlike Sound.[2] Theſe Drummers ſit down ſquat upon their Tails

---

[1] There seem to be some traces among the North American Indians of the institution of fellowship, or "comitatus"—see Powell, *op. cit.*, p. 68. Private war parties were frequently organized, the instigator becoming leader of the band of his selected associates. — ED.

[2] For an account of Indian drums, see Masson, *Bourgeois*, ii, pp. 332, 333. — ED.

by a Poſt fix'd in the Center of the great Ring: And at the ſame time, the General fixes his Eyes upon the Sun, all the Company following his example, and makes his Addreſſes to the Great Spirit; after which a Sacrifice is commonly offer'd up. When this Ceremony is over, he ſings the Song of War, the Drummers beating Time to him after their way; and at the end of every Period, which contains one of his Exploits, he knocks againſt the Poſt with his Club. When he has made an end of his Song, each Warriour ſings in his turn after the ſame faſhion, provided he has made a Campagne before; for if he has not, he's doom'd to Silence. This done, the whole Company returns to the General's Hutt, where they find their Dinner ready for them.

If the General do's not think it fit to Command the Party in Perſon, and chooſes to ſtay at home; the Warriours that deſign to go upon the Party, chooſe one of the *Under-Leaders* that I mention'd but now: And the *Under-Leader* thus choſen, obſerves the ſame Ceremonies of Addreſſing the Great Spirit, Sacrificing, Singing, and Feaſting. The laſt Ceremony is continued every day till they March out.

Some of theſe Parties go half way, or three quarters of their way in Canows; particularly [77] thoſe who live upon the Banks of Lakes, as well as the *Iroqueſe*. The *Iroqueſe* have this advantage over their Enemies, that they are all Arm'd with good Fire-Locks; whereas the others who uſe thoſe Engines only for the Shooting of Beaſts, have not above half their number provided with 'em: And 'tis for this reaſon, that the nearer they come to their Enemies Country, the leſs they spread out in Hunting or Shooting, especially with Fire-Arms, the report of which might Alarm the Enemy. When they come within thirty or forty Leagues of danger, they give over Hunting and Shooting, being afraid to fire their Guns; and content themselves with the *Indian Corn*, of which each of them carries a Bag of ten pound weight; and upon which they feed, after 'tis mix'd with a little Water without Boiling.

When the *Illinese*, the *Outagamis*, the *Hurons*, and the *Sauteurs* wage War with the *Iroquese*, and have a mind to make a bold Attempt; if there be but thirty of them, they'll march directly up to the end of the Village, presuming that in case of a discovery, they can easily save themselves by their good Heels. In the mean time, they have the Precaution to March one after another; and he that comes last takes care to strow the Ground with Leaves, in order to cover their footsteps. After they have past the Village, and are got into the *Iroquese* Country, they run all night; and in the day time lye flat upon their Bellies, in the Copses and Thickets, being sometimes dispers'd, and sometimes all in a Body. Towards the Evening, or as soon as the Sun sets, they Spring out from their Ambuscade, and fall upon every one they meet, without sparing either Age or Sex: For 'tis a customary thing with these Warriours to shew no Mercy, not to Children and Women. After they have finish'd their Massacre, and taken [78] the Hair off the Heads of the Dead, they have the boldness to make a Funeral Cry. If they see any *Iroquese* at a distance, they strain their Voices to acquaint 'em that they have kill'd some of their Folks, whom they may take care to Bury: That the Action was accomplish'd by such a Leader and such a Nation. This done, they all betake themselves to Flight by different Roads, and run with their utmost speed till they come to a general place of Rendezvous, about thirty or forty Leagues off. In the mean time, the *Iroquese* do not give themselves the trouble of pursuing them, as being sensible that they are not so nimble Footed as to overtake 'em.

If these Parties are two or three hundred Men strong, they'll venture to enter the Village in the Night time; making one or two of their Warriours to Scale the Palissadoes and open the Gates, in case they are shut. But you must know, that the *Outaouas*, as well as the other Savages that have not so much Courage and Activity, content themselves with pursuing the *Iroquese* in the Countries where they Hunt or Fish: For they dare not come within forty Leagues of their Villages, unless they know of a place of Refuge, in case of a discovery or pursuit: And there can be no other Refuge than some little Forts kept up by the *French*.

The Savages never take any Prisoners at the Gates of their Enemies Villages; by reason of the Expedition they are oblig'd to make in running Night and Day to save themselves: 'Tis in the Hunting and Fishing Countries, and in the other places that afford them an opportunity of surprizing their Enemy, that they take 'em Prisoners: For upon such occasions, the weaker side being forc'd to give way, and to maintain a running Fight without any Order or Discipline, [79] while every one flies his own way, 'tis not possible but that the Conquerors must take Prisoners. And there's always some strong brawny Savages who know how to throw down the Prisoner dextrously, and to bind him in a moment. But there are some of the defeated Parties, who choose rather to kill themselves than to be took Prisoners; and others are so obstinate that they must be Wounded before they can be catch'd. As soon as a Savage is Fetter'd, he sings his Death Song, after the manner describ'd in my 23d Letter. The *Iroquese* that have the misfortune to be catch'd, have nothing to expect but fearful Torture, if they fall into the hands of the *Oumamis*, the *Outaouas*, the *Algonkins*, and the Savages of *Acadia:* For these People are extream cruel to their Prisoners.[1] The least Punishment they inflict upon 'em, is, that of obliging the poor Wretches to put their Finger into the mouth of a lighted Pipe; which makes an agreeable diversion to the Conqueror in his Journey home. The other Nations use their Prisoners with much more Humanity. From hence we may conclude, that we ought to make a great difference between the several Nations of *Canada;* some of which are Warlike, others Cowardly; some a lively Active People, others Heavy and Dull: In a Word, the Case is the same in *America* as it is in *Europe*, where every Nation has not the Virtues or Vices of another. For the *Iroquese*, and the other Nations that I nam'd along with them, burn all their Prisoners; whereas the other Nations content themselves with the keeping of them in Slavery, without putting any to Death. 'Tis the first sort that I mean to speak of in the three ensuing Paragraphs.

---

[1] The torture of Indian captives, and the barbarities therein committed, are well-known. For early descriptions, see *Jes. Rel.*, i, p. 271; iv, pp. 199, 201; x, p. 227. — ED.

[80] As soon as a party of *Barbarians* approach their own Village, they make as many Dead-Cries as they have lost Men; and when they come within a Musquet-Shot of the Village, they renew the mournful Tune; and repeat it for a certain number of times answerable to the number of the slain among the Enemies. Then the Youths under sixteen, and above twelve years of age, Arm themselves with Sticks, and make a Lane in order to beat the Prisoners, which they put in execution as soon as the Warriours have made their entry, carrying the Hair of those they have slain upon the end of their Bows.

The next day, the old Men meet in Council upon the distribution of the Prisoners, which are commonly presented to such Married Women or Maids as have lost Relations in the Expedition, and to those that want Slaves. After the distribution is adjusted, three or four Young Scoundrels of the Age of fifteen, take the Prisoners and conduct them to these Women or Girles. Now, if the Woman to whom the present is made, means that the poor Wretch should die, she gives him to understand that her Father, her Brother, her Husband, *&c.* having no Slaves to serve them in the Country of the Dead, it behoves him to take a Journey thither out of hand. If evidence be brought that the poor Slave has kill'd either Women or Children in his lifetime, the young Executioners lead him to a Woodpile, where he is forc'd to undergo the dismal Torments mentioned in my 23d Letter; and sometimes somewhat that is yet more terrible. But if the unfortunate Prisoner can make it appear that he only kill'd

Men, they content themselves with the Shooting of him. If the Woman or Girl has a mind to save the Prisoners life (which often happens) she takes him by the hand; and [81] after conducting him into the Hut, cuts his Bonds and orders him Cloaths, Arms, Victuals and Tobacco. This favour is usually accompany'd with these words. *I have given thee thy life, I have knock'd off thy chains, pluck up a good heart, serve me well, be not ill minded, and thou shalt have whereupon to comfort thee for the loss of thy Country and thy Relations.* Sometimes the *Iroquese* Women adopt the Slaves that are presented to 'em, and then they are look'd upon as Members of the Nation. As for the Women Prisoners they are distributed among the Men, who are sure to grant 'em their lives.[1]

You must take notice that the Savages of *Canada* never exchange their Prisoners.[2] As soon as they are put in Chains, their Relations and the whole Nation to which they retain, look upon 'em as dead; unless it be that they were so much Wounded when they were taken, that they could not possibly kill themselves. These indeed they receive when they make their escape; but if the other Prisoners should offer to return, they would be contemn'd by their nearest Relations, and no body would receive 'em. The way of waging War among the Savages is so harsh, that one must have a Body of Steel to

---

[1] This custom of adoption of prisoners was one of great value to the white captives, and saved the lives of many. See Withers, *Chronicles of Border Warfare* (Thwaites's ed., Cincinnati, 1895), for typical instances. — Ed.

[2] The author means that captives are not exchanged while a state of war persists between the tribes. Upon the arrangement of peace, the captives are all returned. See *Wis. Hist. Colls.*, xvi, pp. 447-451, 465-467. — Ed.

bear the Fatigues they are oblig'd to undergo. Now if we joyn to this inconveniency that of their giving but little Quarter to one another; and for the moſt part, without any regard either to Women or Children, we will not think it ſtrange that the number of their Warriours is ſo ſmall, that ſometimes one Nation can ſcarce muſter up a thouſand.

The Savages are never raſh in declaring War; they hold frequent Councils before they reſolve upon it, and muſt be very well aſſur'd of the ſteddineſs of the Neighbouring Nations, whoſe [82] Alliance or Neutrality they require. Beſides, before they come to ſuch a reſolution, they make it their buſineſs to fathom the Minds of ſuch Nations as lye remote; to the end that they may take juſt meaſures, by weighing all the Conſequences ſeriouſly, and endeavouring to foreſee all the accidents that may happen. They uſe the Precaution of ſending Deputies to the People whom they propoſe for their Allies, to make a narrow inquiry whether their Old Men have Heads well turn'd for Government, and for the giving of judicious and ſeaſonable Counſels to their Warriours, whoſe number they want to know as well as their Valour and Experience. The next thing that they have in view, is the carrying on of the Trade of Skins with the *French* without diſadvantage, and the Hunting of Beavers in Winter without expoſing themſelves to danger. After all, they make this propoſal to their Allies; that they ſhall engage not to put an end to the War till their Enemies are intirely deſtroy'd, or elſe oblig'd to abdicate their Country.

Their way of declaring War is this: They ſend back to

the Nation that they have a mind to quarrel with, a Slave of the fame Country; with orders to carry to the Village of his own Nation an Axe, the Handle of which is painted red and black. Sometimes they fend three or four fuch Slaves, obliging them to promife before hand, that they fhall not bear Arms againft them; and commonly this Promife is religioufly obferv'd.[1]

It remains only to acquaint you how they make Peace; you muft know that the Savages never think of an Accommodation till after a long War: But when they are fenfible that 'tis their Intereft to come to it they detach five, or ten, or fifteen, or twenty Warriors, to make a [83] Propofal to the Enemies. Thefe Commiffioners go fometimes by Land, and fometimes in Canows, and always carry the great Calumet of Peace in their Hand, much after the fame manner as a Cornet carries his Standard. I fet forth in my Seventh Letter what a profound Veneration all the Savages of *Canada* have for this famous Pipe. There was not one Inftance of their Violating the Sacred Rights of this Pipe before the Embaffy of *Chevalier Do*, at which time they took occafion to revenge the Bufinefs of the *Rat*, as I gave you to know in my Seventeenth Letter. If the Commiffioners of Peace march by Land, as foon as they arrive within a Musket-fhot of the Village, fome young Men march out and poft themfelves in an oval Figure. This done, the Commiffioner that carries that great fign of Peace, makes up towards them, finging and dancing the Calumet Dance;

---

[1] This is a rare custom, the object being to surprise the enemy before he is prepared for war. — ED.

which he continues to do while the old Men meet in Council. If the Inhabitants of the Village do not think it proper to accept of the Propofal of Peace, their Orator or Speaker makes a Harangue to the Envoy that carries the Calumet, who upon that goes and rejoins his Company. This Pacifick Retinue is regal'd with Prefents of Tents, Corn, Meat and Fifh; but at the fame time they are acquainted that they muft depart their Country the next Day. If on the other Hand, the old Men agree to the conclufion of a Peace, they march out and meet the Commiffioners, and after conducting the whole Company into the Village, provide them with extraordinary good Lodgings and a plentiful Table, during the whole courfe of the Negotiation. When the Commiffioners come by Water they fend out a Canow while the reft lye by; and as foon as this Canow comes near to the Village, the Inhabitants [84] of the Village fend out another to meet it, and conduct the Propofer of Peace to their Habitations, where the Ceremonies are perform'd after the fame manner as before.[1] This great Calumet is likewife made ufe of by the Confederate Savages, that demand Paffage thro' the Country of their Allies, whether by Land or Water, in purfuance of Warlike or Hunting Expeditions.

---

[1] The person of an envoy was sacred among Indian tribes, and to maltreat one was the worst of insults Dorsey describes similar ceremonies as persisting among the Omaha. U. S. Bur. of Eth. *Report*, 1881-82, p. 368. — ED.

A View of the Heraldry, or the Coats of Arms of the Savages.

AFTER a perufal of the former Accounts I fent you of the Ignorance of the Savages with reference to Sciences, you will not think it ftrange that they are unacquainted with Heraldry. The Figures you have reprefented in this Cut will certainly appear ridiculous to you, and indeed they are nothing lefs: But after all you'l content your felf with excufing thefe poor Wretches, without rallying upon their extravagant Fancies. They make ufe of the Blazoning reprefented in the Cut, for the following Purpofes.[1]

When a Party of Savages have routed their Enemies in any Place whatfoever, the Conquerours take care to pull the Bark off the Trees for the height of five or fix Foot in all Places where they ftop in returning to their own Country; and in honour of their Victory paint certain Images with Coal pounded and beat up with Fat and Oyl. Thefe Pictures,

---

[1] Lahontan's somewhat absurd and distorted description of Indian heraldry probably arose from his misconception of the institution of totemism — a primitive superstition by which each gens or clan of a tribe adopted some animal as a totem or mythical protector One of the earliest uses of the term "totemism" was by John Long (see Thwaites, *Early Western Travels*, ii, pp. 123-125), but there is now a large literature upon this subject. See M'Lennan, *Patriarchal Theory;* Lang, *Myth, Ritual, and Religion* (London, 1887); Brinton, *Myths of New World,* and sociological articles in U. S. Bur. of Eth. *Reports,* already cited. — ED.

which are defign'd and explain'd in the infuing Chapter, continue upon the peel'd Tree for ten or twelve [85] Years, as if they were Grav'd, without being defac'd by the Rain.

This they do to give all Paffangers to underftand what Exploits they have done. The Arms for the Nation, and fometimes a particular Mark for the Leader of the Party, are painted in Colours upon thefe ftrip'd Trees; and for that reafon 'twil not be improper to fubjoin a Defcription of 'em.

The five *Outaouafe* Nations have a *Sinople* or Green Field, with four Elks in Sable Canton'd, and looking to the four Corners of the Efcutcheon, there being a heap of Sand in the middle.

The *Illinefe* bear a Beech Leaf with a Butterfly Argent.

The *Nadoueffis* or *Scioux* have a Squirrel *Gules*, gnawing a Citron *Or*.

The *Hurons* bear a Beaver Sable, fet fquat upon a Beaver Kennel Argent, the midft of a Pool or Lake.

The *Outagamis* bear a Meadow Sinople, crofs'd by a winding River Pale, with two Foxes Gules at the two Extremities of the River, in Chief and Point.

The *Pouteoutamis* call'd *Puants* bear a Dog in Argent, fleeping upon a Mat *d' Or*. Thefe People obferve the Rules of Blazoning lefs than the other Nations.

The *Oumamis* have a Bear Sable, pulling down with his two Paws a Tree Sinople moffy, and laid along the Efcutcheon.

The *Oucahipoues*, call'd *Sauteurs*, have an Eagle Sable, pearching upon the top of a Rock Argent, and devouring an Owl *Gules*.

[86] *An Explication of the Hieroglyphicks that ſtand oppoſite to the Letters A B C D E F G H I K, being plac'd at the ſide of a Column repreſenting the Foot of a ſuppos'd Tree.*

IF we take the Word *Hieroglyphick* in its natural Senſe, 'tis only a Repreſentation of Sacred and Divine Objects, Calculated according to the *Ideas* we have of 'em. But without any regard to the Etymology, I chooſe rather to make uſe of the common Priviledge of an infinity of Authors, in beſtowing the Title of Hieroglyphick Symbols upon all theſe Figures that correſpond to the following Letters.[1]

A. Oppoſite to this Letter you ſee the Arms of *France*, with an Ax above. Now the Ax is a Symbol of War among the Savages, as the Calumet is the Bond of Peace: So that this imports, that the *French* have taken up the Ax, or have made a Warlike Expedition with as many tens of Men as there are Marks or Points round the Figure. Theſe Marks you ſee are Eighteen in number, and ſo they ſignifie an Hundred and eighty Warriors.

---

[1] On the subject of picture writing see Mallery, "Picture-Writing of American Indians" in U. S. Bur. of Eth. *Report*, 1888–89; *Jes. Rel*, lxvii, p. 227; Hoffman, "On Native Indian Pictographs," in Catholic University *Bulletin* (Washington), April, 1897. — Ed.

B. Over againſt this Letter you meet with a Mountain that repreſents the City of *Monreal*, (according to the Savages) and the Fowl upon the Wing at the top ſignifies Departure. The Moon upon the Back of the Stag ſignifies the firſt Quarter of the *July* Moon, which is call'd the *Stag-Moon*.

[87] *C.* Oppoſite to this Letter you deſcry a Canow, importing that they have travel'd by Water as many Days as you ſee Huts in the Figure, *i. e.* 21 Days.

D. Upon the ſame parallel with this Letter you ſee a Foot, importing that after their Voyage by Water they march'd on Foot as many Days as there are Huts deſign'd; that is, ſeven Days Journeys for Warriors, each Days Journey being as much as five common *French* Leagues, or five of thoſe which are reckon'd to be twenty in a Degree.

E. By this Letter you perceive a Hand and three Huts, which ſignifie that they are got within three Days Journey of the *Iroqueſe Tſonnontouans*, whoſe Arms are a Hut with two Trees leaning downwards, as you ſee them drawn. The Sun imports that they were juſt to the Eaſtward of the Village: For you muſt obſerve, that if they had march'd to the Weſtward the Arms of theſe Savages had been plac'd where the Hand is, and the Hand had been turn'd and plac'd where you now ſee the Hut with the two Trees.

F. Oppoſite to this Letter you perceive twelve Marks, ſignifying ſo many times ten Men, like thoſe at the Letter *A*. The Hut with the two Trees being the Arms of the *Tſonnontouans* ſhews that they were of that Nation; and the Man in a lying poſture ſpeaks that they were ſurpris'd.

G. In the row which anfwers to this Letter there appears a Club and eleven Heads, importing that they had kill'd eleven *Tfonnontouans,* and the five Men ftanding upright upon the five Marks fignifie, that they took as many times ten Prifoners of War.

[88] *H.* Oppofite to this Letter you fee nine Heads in an Arch, the meaning of which is, that nine of the Aggreffors or of the Victorious fide (which I fuppofed to be *French*) were kill'd; and the twelve Marks underneath fignifie that as many were Wounded.

I. Oppofite to this Letter you fee Arrows flying in the Air, fome to one fide and fome to the other, importing a vigorous Defence on both fides.

K. At this Letter you fee the Arrows all pointed one way, which fpeaks the worfted Party either flying or fighting upon a Retreat in diforder.

The meaning of the whole is in a few Words as follows. An Hundred and eighty *French* Men fet out from *Monreal* in the firft Quarter of the *July* Moon, and fail'd twenty one Days; after which they march'd thirty five Leagues over Land and furpris'd a hundred and twenty *Tfonnontouans* on the Eaft fide of their Village, eleven of whom were Kill'd, and fifty taken Prifoners; the *French* fuftaining the lofs of nine Kill'd and twelve Wounded, after a very obftinate Engagement.[1]

---
[1] The drawings accompanying this description are evidently the work of a European quite unacquainted with Indian pictographs. For correct drawings of Indian representations of expeditions and battles, see illustrations in Mallery, *op. cit.*, pp. 552-556; Thwaites, "Atlas of Maximilien's Voyage," in *Early Western Travels,* xxv. — Ed.

This may ferve to prompt you and me to return thanks to God for vouchfafing to us the means of expreffing our Thoughts by the bare ranking of twenty three Letters, and above all of Writing in lefs than a Minute a Difcourfe that the *Americans* cannot Decypher with their impertinent Hieroglyphicks in the fpace of an Hour. Though the number of thofe dark Symbols is of no large extent, yet 'tis very perplexing to an *European;* for which Reafon I have contented my felf in learning only fuch of 'em as are moft Effential; the knowledge of which [89] I owe to Neceffity more than Curiofity. I could fend you others that are as extravagant as thefe I now fend you; but confidering that they will be of no ufe to you, I choofe to fave my felf the labour of drawing them upon Paper, and you the trouble of looking 'em over.

I am, Sir,

Yours, &c.

A CONFERENCE OR DIALOGUE

BETWEEN THE

AUTHOR and ADARIO,

A Noted Man among the

SAVAGES.

CONTAINING

A Circumstantial View of the Customs and Humours of that People.

Labontan. I AM infinitely well pleas'd, my dear *Adario*, that I have an opportunity of reasoning with you upon a Subject of the greatest Importance; for my business is to unfold to you the great Truths of Christianity.

Adario, I am ready to hear thee, my dear Brother, in order to be inform'd of a great many things that the Jesuits have been Preaching up for a long time; and I would have us to discourse together with all the freedom that may be. If your Belief is the same with that of the Jesuits, 'tis in vain to enter into a Conference; for they have entertain'd me with so many Fabulous and Romantick Stories, that all the credit I can give 'em, is to believe, that they have more Sense than to believe themselves.

Lahontan. I do not know what they have said to you; but I am apt to believe that their Words and mine will agree very well together. The Christian Religion is a Religion that Men ought to profess in order to obtain a place in Heaven. God hath permitted the discovery of *America*, meaning to save all Nations that will follow the Laws of Christianity. 'Twas his Divine Pleasure that the Gospel should be Preach'd to thy Nation, that they may be inform'd of the true way to Paradise, the blessed Mansion of good Souls. 'Tis pity thou wilt not be perswaded to make the best use of the Favours and the Talents that God hath bestow'd upon thee. Life is short; the Hour of our Death is uncertain, and Time is precious. Undeceive thy self therefore, as to the imagin'd Severity of Christianity, and imbrace it without delay, regrating the loss of those Days thou has spent in Ignorance, without a due sense of Religion and Worship, and without the knowlege of the true God.

Adario. How do you mean, *without the Knowledge of the True God?* What! are you mad? Do'st thou believe we are void of Religion, after thou hast dwelt so long amongst us? Do'st not thee know in the first place, that we acknowledge a Creator of the Universe, under the Title of the Great Spirit or Master of Life; whom we believe to be in every thing, and to be unconfin'd to Limits? 2. That we own the Immortality of the Soul.[1] [92] 3. That the Great Spirit has furnish'd us with a Rational Faculty, capable of diftinguifhing Good from Evil, as much as Heaven from Earth; to the end that we might Religioufly obferve the true Meafures of Juftice and Wifdom. 4. That the Tranquility and Serenity of the Soul pleafes the Great Mafter of Life: And on the other hand, that he abhors trouble and anxiety of Mind, becaufe it renders Men Wicked. 5. That Life is a Dream, and Death the Seafon of Awaking, in which the Soul fees and knows the Nature and Quality of all things, whether vifible or invifible. 6. That the utmoft reach of our Minds can't go one Inch above the Surface of the Earth: So that we ought not to corrupt and fpoil it by endeavouring to pry into Invifible and Improbable things. This my dear Friend is Our Belief, and we act up to it with the greateft Exactnefs. We believe that we fhall go to the Country of Souls after death; but we have no fuch apprehenfion as you have, of a good and bad Manfion after this Life, provided for the good and bad Souls; for we cannot tell whether every thing that appears faulty to Men, is fo in the Eyes of God. If your Religion differs from ours, it do's not follow that we have none at all. Thou knoweft that I have been in *France*, *New-York* and *Quebec;* where I Study'd the Cuftoms and Doctrines of the *Englifh* and *French*.[2] The *Jefuits* allege, that out of five or fix hun-

---
[1] On Indian religious beliefs, see pp. 435, note 1, *ante*.—ED.

[2] For a brief biography of Adario see p 149, note 2, *ante*. Lahontan is the only contemporary authority who speaks of the travels of this interesting savage, but a letter of 1691 mentions a Huron who is about to pass into France, and wishes to see the king. Possibly this may have been Adario, the most noted of his tribe See *Canadian Archives*, 1883, p. lvi.—ED.

dred forts of Religions, there's only one that is the good and the true Religion, and that's their own; out of which no Man shall 'scape the Flames of a Fire that will burn his Soul to all Eternity. This is their allegation: But when they have said all, they cannot offer any Proof for it.

[93] *Lahontan.* They have a great deal of reason, *Adario*, to assert that there are bad Souls; for without straggling far for a Proof, they need only to give thine for an Instance. He that is unacquainted with the Truths of the *Christian Religion*, is not capable of receiving a Proof. All that thou hast offer'd in thy own defence is prodigious Madness. The Country of Souls that thou speakest of is only a Chimerical Hunting Country: Whereas our Holy Scriptures inform us of a Paradise, Seated above the remotest Stars, where God does actually reside; being incircled with Glory, and the Souls of all the Faithful Christians. The same very Scriptures make mention of a Hell, which we take to be Situated in the Centre of the Earth: And in which the Souls of all such as reject Christianity, as well as those of bad Christians, will burn for ever without Consumption. This is a Truth that you ought to think of.

Adario. These Holy Scriptures that thou quotest every foot, as well as the *Jesuits*, require that mighty Faith which the Good Fathers are always teazing us with. But this can be nothing but a persuasion: To believe, Imports no more than to be persuaded of a thing: and to be persuaded or convinc'd, is to see a thing with one's eyes, or to have it recommended by clear and solid Truths. Now how can I have that Faith, since thou canst neither prove a tittle of what thou say'st, nor shew it me before my eyes. Believe me, my Friend; do not wrap up thy Mind in obscurity; give over the visionary thoughts of these Holy Scriptures, or else let us make an end of our Conferences upon that Head; for according to our Principles, we must have probability in every thing we admit of. What Ground hast thou for the Destiny of the good Souls, who are [94] lodg'd with the Great Spirit above the Stars, or the Fate of the bad ones that shall burn for ever in the Centre of the Earth? Thou canst not but charge God with Tyranny, if thou believest that he Created but one single Man, with intent to render him eternally Miserable amidst the Flames in the Centre of the Earth. I know you'll pretend, that the Holy Scriptures prove that Great Truth: But granting it to be so, then the Earth must be of eternal Duration; which the *Jesuits* deny. That flaming Place must therefore cease to be, when the Earth comes to be consum'd. Besides, how canst thou imagine, that the Soul which is a pure Spirit, a thousand times subtiler and lighter than Smoak; how canst thou imagine, I say, that this airy Being should move to the Centre of the Earth, contrary to its natural tendency? 'Tis more likely, it should mount upwards and fly to the Sun, where you may fix that fiery place more reasonably; especially considering that this Star is much bigger, and infinitely more hot than the Earth.

Lahontan. Hark ye me, my dear *Adario*, thy Blindness is screw'd up to an extremity, and the hardness of thy Heart makes thee reject this Faith and these Scriptures, the truth of which does eafily appear, if one would but lay afide Prejudices: For you have nothing to do but to caft your Eye upon the Prophecies contain'd in the Sacred Pages; which beyond all difpute were Written before they came to pafs. This Sacred Hiftory is confirm'd by *Heathen* Authors, and by the Monuments of greateft Antiquity, and thofe the moft uncontefted that paft Ages can afford. Believe me, if thou wouldft but reflect upon the manner in which the Religion of *Jefus Chrift* was Eftablifh'd in the World, and the Change that it wrought; if thou hadft but a juft view of the [95] Characters of Truth, Sincerity and Divinity that fhine in the Scriptures: In a word, if thou didft but enter into the particulars of our Religion; thou wouldft fee and be fenfible, that its Doctrines and Precepts, its Promifes and Threats, are not chargeable with any abfurdity; nor with any ill defign, or any thing that runs contrary to our natural Sentiments: And that nothing is more fuitable to right Reafon, and the Principles of Confcience.

Adario. This is the fame Stuff that the *Jefuits* have had up above a hundred times. They will have it, that fome five or fix thoufand years ago, all that is fince come to pafs, was then unchangeably decreed. They lay down the way in which the Heavens and the Earth were Created; and tell you, that Man was made of the Duft of the Earth, and the Woman out of one of his Ribs, as if God had not made her of the fame Stuff; that a Serpent tempted this Man in a Garden of Fruit-Trees to eat of an Apple, which was the occafion that the Great Spirit put his own Son to Death, on purpofe to fave all men. If I should say that these advances have a greater appearance of fabulousness than of truth, you would close upon me with Reasons fetch'd from your Bible: But according to your own words, this Scripture of yours had not always a Being; the invention of it bears the date of some three thousand years ago; and 'twas not Printed till within these four or five Centuries. Now, considering the divers events that come round in the course of several Ages, one must certainly be very credulous in giving credit to so many idle Stories as are huddled up in that great Book that the Christians would have us to believe. I have seen some of the Books that the *Jesuits* Writ of our Country; and those who knew how to read [96] 'em, explain'd to me the sense of 'em in the Language that I speak; but I found they contain'd an infinity of Lyes and Fictions heap'd up one above another. Now, if we see with our eyes that Lyes are in Print, and that things are not represented in Paper as they really are; how can you press me to believe the Sincerity of your Bible that was Writ so many Ages ago, and Translated out of several Languages by ignorant Men that could not reach the just Sense, or by Lyars who have alter'd, interpolated, or pared the Words you now read. I could mention several other Objections, which in the end will perhaps influence thee in some measure, to own that I have some reason to confine my Belief to such things as are visible and probable.

Lahontan. Poor *Adario*, I have laid before thee, the certainty and evidence of the Christian Religion; but instead of being convinc'd, thou look'st upon my Proofs as Chimerical, and offereſt the moſt fooliſh Reaſons in the World. You quote the Falſhoods Written in the Accounts of your Country that you have ſeen; as if the Jeſuits who Writ 'em could not have been impos'd upon by thoſe who ſupplied them with ſuch Memoirs.[1] You muſt conſider, that theſe Deſcriptions of *Canada* are Bawbles that cannot come into the Ballance with the Books that treat of Sacred things; ſuch things as a hundred different Authours have Writ of, without contradicting one another.

Adario. How do you mean, *without contradicting one another?* Why! That Book of Holy Things, is not it full of Contradictions? Theſe Goſpels that the Jeſuits ſpeak of, do not they occaſion diſcord between the *French* and the *Engliſh?* And yet if we take your word for it, every Period of that Book ſprung from the Mouth [97] of the Great Spirit. But if the Great Spirit mean'd that his Words ſhould be underſtood, why did he talk ſo confuſedly, and cloath his Words with an ambiguous Senſe? One or two things muſt follow from this advance. If he was born and died upon the Earth, and made ſpeeches here, why, then his diſcourſes muſt be loſt; for he would certainly have ſpoke ſo diſtinctly and plainly, that the very Children might conceive his meaning. Or, if you will have the Goſpels to be his genuine Words, and contain nothing but what flow'd from him; why, then he muſt have come to raiſe Wars in the World inſtead of Peace; which cannot be. The *Engliſh* have told me that tho' their Goſpels contain the ſame Words with the *French*, yet there's as great

---

[1] Upon the early Jesuit histories of Canada, see p. 412, note 1, *ante*. —ED.

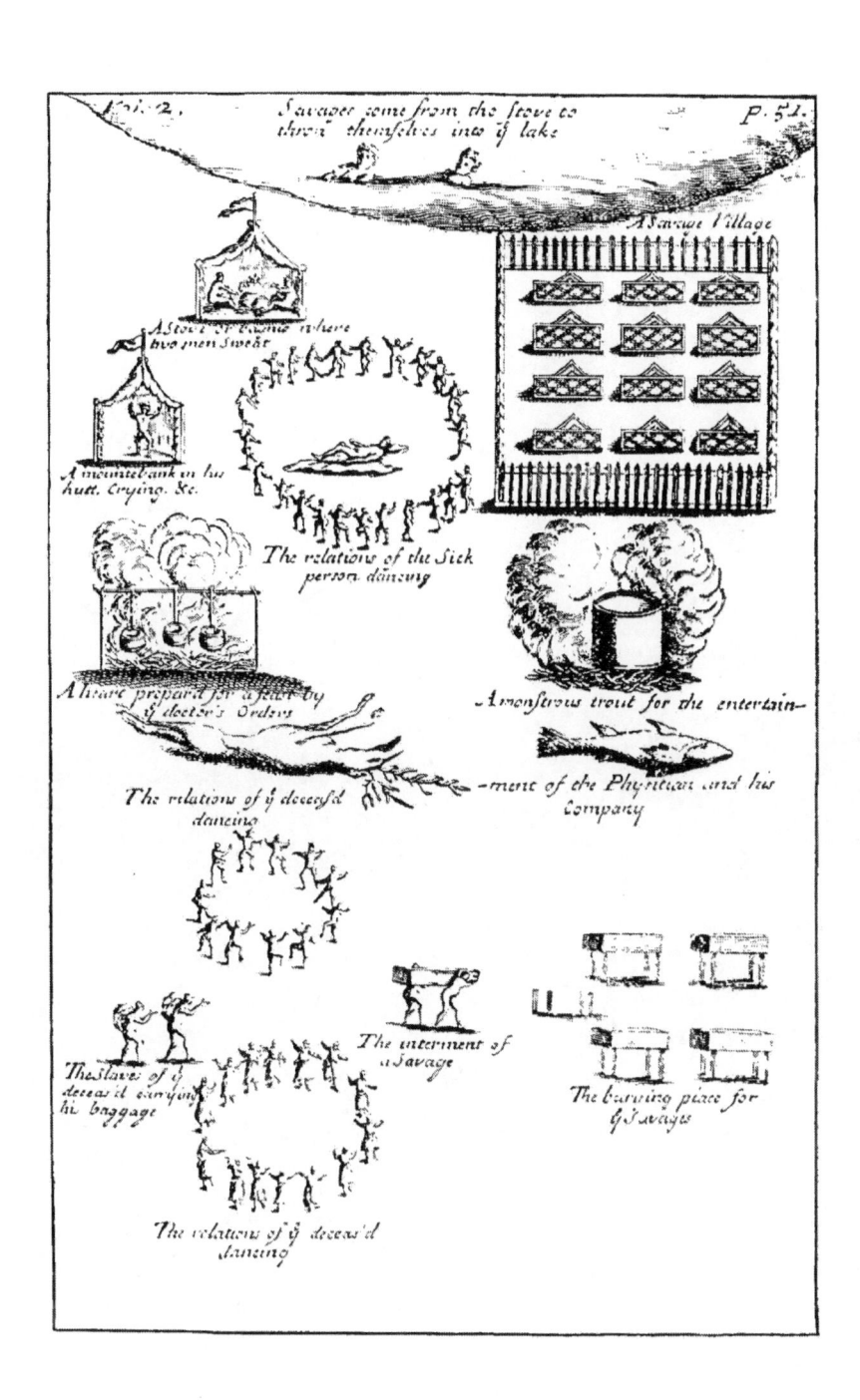

Vol. 2. Savages come from the stove to throw themselves into ye lake. *P. 51.*

A Savage Village

A Stove of beams where two men sweat

A mountebank in his hutt, crying &c.

The relations of the Sick person dancing

A heart prepared for a feast by ye doctor's Orders

A monstrous trout for the entertainment of the Physitian and his Company

The relations of ye deceas'd dancing

The Slaves of ye deceas'd carrying his baggage

The interment of a Savage

The burying place for ye Savages

The relations of ye deceas'd dancing

a difference between their Religion and yours, as between Night and Day. They say positively that their's is the best; and on the other hand, the Jesuits allege, that the Religion of the *English*, and of a thousand Nations besides, is good for nothing. If there be but one true Religion upon Earth, who must I believe in this case? Who is it that do's not take their own Religion to be the most perfect? How can the Capacity of Man be able to single out that Divine Religion from amongst so many more, that lay claim to the same Title? Believe me, my dear Brother, the Great Spirit is Wise, all his Works are perfect; 'tis he that made us, and he knows perfectly well what will become of us. 'Tis our part to act freely, without perplexing our thoughts about future things. He order'd thee to be Born in *France*, with intent that thou shouldest believe what thou neither seest nor conceivest; and me he has caus'd to be Born a *Huron*, to the end that I should give credit to nothing but what I understand, and what my reason teaches me.

[98] *Lahontan*. Reason teaches thee to be a Christian, and yet you refuse to be such. If you would, you might understand the Truths of our Gospel, in which all things are of a piece, and nothing can be found that favours of Contradiction. The *English* are Christians as well as the *French*; and tho' these two Nations have some difference upon the score of Religion, it only relates to some Passages of Scripture, that they understand different ways. The first and principal point that occasions so many disputes, is this. The *French* believe that since the Son of God said, that his Body was in a morsel of Bread;

we are bound to take it for a truth, in regard that he could not lie. He told his Apoſtles that the Bread was truly his Body, and that they ought to eat it, and to perpetuate that Ceremony in Commemoration of him. Accordingly this Precept is obſerv'd; for ſince the death of that God made Man, the Sacrifice of the Maſs is perform'd every day among the *French*, who make no doubt of the real preſence of the Son of God in that bit of Bread. But the *Engliſh* pretend, that the Son of God being in Heaven, cannot be Corporally preſent upon Earth, and that his words inſuing upon that Inſtitution (the repetition of which would be tedious to thee) are evidence that he is only Spiritually preſent in the Bread. This is all the difference between them and us; for as to the other Points, they are ſo trifling, that we could eaſily come to an accommodation upon 'em.

Adario. I perceive then, the words of the Son of the Great Spirit are chargeable with ſelf-contradiction or obſcurity; for as much as you and the *Engliſh* diſpute about his meaning with ſo much heat and animoſity: And this ſeems to be the principal Spring of the hatred that theſe two [99] Nations bear to one another. But that is not what I inſiſt upon. Doſt thou hear, my Brother; both the one and the other muſt needs be fools, in believing the Incarnation of a God; conſidering the ambiguity of thoſe Diſcourſes mention'd in your Goſpel. There you meet with an infinity of things which are too groſs to come from the Mouth of ſo perfect a Being. The Jeſuits aſſure us, that the Son of the Great Spirit declar'd that he ſincerely deſired the Salvation of all Men.

Now, if he defires it, doubtlefs it muft come to pafs; and yet they are not all Sav'd neither, for as much as he has faid; *many are call'd, but few are chofen.* This I take to be a plain Contradiction. The Fathers reply, that God does defire the Salvation of men, but upon the condition that they defire it themfelves. But after all, we do not find that God has added that Claufe, for if he had, he had not fpoke fo pofitively. But the Myftery lies here. The Jefuits have a mind to pry into the Secrets of the Almighty, and to affume what himfelf did not pretend to, for he mention'd no fuch condition. The cafe is the fame, as if the great Captain General of the *French* fhould give notice by his Viceroy, that 'tis his pleafure that all the Slaves of *Canada* fhould be Tranfported to *France*, where they might all grow rich; and thereupon the Slaves fhould make anfwer that they will not go, becaufe that great Captain cannot defire it unlefs they be of the fame mind themfelves. Is not it true, my Brother, that their anfwer would be ridicul'd, and they would be forc'd to go to *France* againft their will? Can you offer anything to the contrary? In a word, the Jefuits have commented to me upon fo many Expreffions in that Book that contradict one another, that I'm amaz'd to find that they ftill call it the [100] Holy Scriptures. 'Tis written there, that the firft man whom the Great Spirit made with his own Hands, did eat of a forbidden Fruit, for which both he and his Wife were punifh'd, as being equally Criminal. Now, let's fuppofe the Punifhment inflicted upon the account of the Apple to be what you will; this poor Man had nothing to complain of, but that the Great Spirit knowing that he would eat of it, fhould have Created him to be Miferable. But let's confider the cafe of his Pofterity, who according to the Jefuits are involv'd in his Overthrow: Are the Children Blame-worthy for the Gluttony of their Father and their Mother? If a man Murder'd one of our Kings, muft the Punifhment reach to his whole Generation; to Fathers, Mothers, Uncles, Coufins, Sifters, Brothers, and all his other Relations? Shall we fuppofe, therefore, that when the Great Spirit gave this Man a Being, he knew not what he might do after his Creation? But that cannot be. But let's fuppofe again that all his Pofterity were accomplices of the Crime, (which at the fame time is an unjuft fuppofition) do's not your Scripture make this Great Spirit to be a Being of fuch Mercy and Clemency, that his Loving-Kindnefs to the Human Race leaves all Conception far behind it? Is not he fo great and fo puiffant, that if all the Spirits of men that either are, or have been, or are to come, were united in one Perfon, 'twould be impoffible for that Mighty one to comprehend the leaft tittle of his Omnipotence? Now, fince his goodnefs and mercy are fo tranfcendent, can't he by one Word vouchfafe a Pardon to that man and all his defcendants? And fince he is fo powerful and great, how improbable is it, that fuch an Incomprehenfible Being fhould turn himfelf into a Man, and not only live a miferable Life, [101] but die an infamous Death; in order to expiate the Sin of fo mean a Creature, that is as much or more beneath him, as a Flie is beneath the Sun and the Stars? Where would that infinite Power be then? What ufe would it be of to him, and what advantage would he make of it? To my mind, to believe the debafing of the Divine Nature, fpeaks a doubt of the Incomprehenfible reach of his Omnipotence, and an extravagant Prefumption with refpect to our felves.

Lahontan. Do'ft not thou perceive, my dear *Adario*, that the Great Spirit being fo powerful, and intitled to the Perfections you have nam'd, the Sin of our Primitive Father muft by confequence be the moft enormous and heinous Crime that imagination it felf can reach? To make the cafe plain by an example; If I beat one of my Soldiers, there's no harm done, but if I offer'd an affront to the King, my Crime would be inflam'd to the laft degree, and be juftly accounted unpardonable. Now, *Adam* having offer'd a piece of Indignity to the King of Kings, we come into the lift of his Accomplices, as being part of his Soul; and confequently the Divine Juftice requires fuch a Satisfaction as the Death of his Son. 'Tis true, God could have Pardon'd us with one Word; but for reafons that I cannot give you eafily to underftand, he was gracioufly pleas'd to live and to die for all Mankind. I own that he is merciful, and that he might have acquitted Adam the fame day that the Crime was committed; for his Mercy is the ground of all the hopes we have of Salvation: But if he had not refented *Adam*'s Difobedience, his Prohibition had been a jeft. Had he overlook'd it, the confequence would have been that he did not fpeak ferioufly; and upon that foot, all the World would have had a juft Plea for doing what they pleas'd.

[102] *Adario.* Hitherto thou proveft nothing; and the

more I sift the pretended Incarnation, I find it the less probable. What! To think that this Great and Incomprehensible Being, the Creator of the Earth, of the Seas, and of this vast Firmament, should be capable of debasing himself so far, as to lye nine Months Prisoner in the Bowels of a Woman, and expose himself to the miserable Life of his Fellow Sinners, that Writ the Books of your Gospel; to be Beaten, Whip'd, and Crucify'd like an unhappy Wretch; this, I say, is what can't enter into my thoughts. 'Tis written, that he came upon the Earth on purpose to die there, and with the same Breath 'tis said that he was afraid to die. This implies a Contradiction two ways. In the first place, if his design was to be Born, in order to die, he ought not to have dreaded death; for, what is the ground of the fear of death? The dread of death proceeds from this, that one do's not know what will become of 'em when they depart this Life. But he was not unacquainted with the place he was bound for, so that he had no reason to be afraid. You know very well that we and our Wives Poyson our selves frequently, in order to keep one another Company in the Regions of the dead, when one or t'other is snatch'd away.[1] So you see plainly the loss of Life does not scare us, tho' at the same time, we are not certain what course our Souls will steer. What answer canst thee give me upon this Head? In a second place; Since the Son of the Great Spirit was invested with a Power equal to that of his Father; he had no occasion to pray his Father to

---

[1] Suicide by poisoning was not infrequent among Indians, although not deemed commendable. See *Jes. Rel.*, index, caption Suicide. — ED.

save his Life, in regard that he was able to guard off Death by his own Power; and that in praying to his Father he pray'd to himself. As for my part, my dear Brother, I can't have any notion [103] of what thou wouldest have me to Conceive.

Lahontan. I find you were in the right of it in telling me but now, that your capacity would not reach an inch above the surface of the Earth. Your way of Reasoning is sufficient Proof of your Assertion. Now that I have heard this, I do not think it strange that the Jesuits have so much trouble in Preaching to you, and giving you to understand the Sacred Truths. I play the fool in reasoning with a Savage, that is not capable of distinguishing a Chimerical Supposition from a certain and a standing Principle, or a Consequence well drawn from a false Inference. To give you an instance. When you spake of this truth, that God was willing to save all men, and at the same time that they are but few who are sav'd; you charg'd a Contradiction upon it, and at the same time there's no such thing in the case: For he desires to save all men that wish their own Salvation, by observing his Law and his Precepts; that is, such as believe his Incarnation, the truth of the Gospels, the rewards provided for the Good, the punishments prepared for the Wicked, and a State of Futurity. But in regard that few such will be found, all the rest are doom'd to the everlasting Flames of that Fire that you make a jest of. Take care you are not one of the latter Class. If it should happen so, 'twould be a great trouble to me, because thou art my Friend. You will not say then, that the Gospel is cramm'd with Contradictions and Chimæra's; you will not then require grofs Proofs for all the Truths I have laid before you; you'll repent in earneft of having branded our Evangelifts for weak and filly Tale-tellers. But, the worft is, 'twill then be too late. Prithee, think of all this, and be not fo very obftinate; [104] for, in earneft, if thou doft not yield to the uncontestable Reafons that I produce for our Myfteries, I will never fpeak to thee as long as I live.

Adario. Ha! my Brother, do not trouble thy head, I do not pretend to provoke thee by offering my Reafons. I do not hinder thee to believe the Gofpels: I only beg the favour that thou'lt fuffer me to doubt the truth of all the Advances thou haft made. Nothing can be more natural to the Chriftians than to believe the Holy Scriptures, upon the account, that from their Infancy they have heard fo much of 'em, that in imitation of fo many People Educated in the fame Faith, they have 'em fo much Imprinted upon their Imagination, that Reafon has no farther influence upon their Minds, they being already prepoffefs'd with a firm belief of the truth of the Gofpels. To People that are void of Prejudice, fuch as the *Hurons*, there's nothing fo reafonable, as to examine things narrowly. Now, after frequent reflexions for the courfe of ten years upon what the Jefuits Preach'd of the Life and Death of the Son of the Great Spirit, I muft tell you, that all my *Hurons* will give thee fourty reafons to the contrary. As for my own part, I have always maintain'd that if 'twere poffible that the Great Spirit had been fo mean, as to defcend to the Earth, he had fhewn himfelf to all the Inhabitants of the Earth; he had defcended in Triumph, and in publick view, with Splendour and Majesty; he had rais'd the dead, restor'd sight to the blind, made the lame to walk upright, cur'd all the diseases upon the Earth: In fine, he had spoke and commanded all that he had a mind to have done, he had gone from Nation to Nation to work these great Miracles, and to give the same Laws to the whole World. Had he done so, we had been all of the same [105] Religion, and that great Uniformity spread over the face of the Earth, would be a lasting Proof to our Posterity for ten thousand years to come, of the truth of a Religion that was known and receiv'd with equal approbation in the four Corners of the Earth. But instead of that Uniformity, we find five or six hundred Religions, among which that Profess'd by the *French*, is according to your Argument the only true one, the only one that is Good and Holy. In fine, after I had reflected a thousand times upon those Riddles that you call Mysteries, I was of the Opinion that a Man must be Born beyond the great Lake[1]; that is, he must be an *English-man* or a *French-man*, that can form any Idea of 'em. For when they allege that God, who can't be represented under any Figure; could produce a Son under the Figure of a Man: I am ready to reply, that a Woman can't bring forth a Beaver; by reason that in the course of Nature, every Species produces its like. Besides, if before the coming of the Son of God all men were devoted to the Devil, what reason have we to think that he would assume the Form of such Creatures as were lifted into the Service of the

---

[1] "Beyond the Great Lake" was a common rendition of the Indian term for the land across the ocean. — ED,

Devil. Could not he take upon him another Form, which might be finer and more pompous than the Humane? That he might, is the more reafonable, fince the third Perfon of that Trinity (which is fo inconfiftent with Unity) affum'd the Form of a Dove.

Lahontan. Thou haft drawn up a Savage fort of a Syftem by inventing Chimæra's that are nothing to the purpofe. Give me leave to tell thee once more, that I fee 'tis in vain for me to attempt to convince thee by folid Reafons, in regard that thou art not capable of underftanding 'em. I muft therefore refer you to the Jefuits. [106] In the mean time, I have a mind to give you to underftand one thing that's very plain, and that will fall within the Verge of your Genius, *viz.* That 'tis not the bare believing of the Great Truths of the Gofpel which you deny, that is fufficient to conduct one to the Manfions of the Great Spirit. Over and above the belief, one muft inviolably obferve the Precepts of the Law that is there deliver'd; that is to fay, one muft not adore any thing but the Great Spirit alone, one muft not work on the days allotted for folemn Prayer, one muft honour their Father and their Mother, and not only avoid the embraces of Girles, but be free from an inclination that way, unlefs it be upon the foot of Marriage. 'Tis requir'd for this end, that we fhould not kill or promote the killing of any one; that we fhould not fpeak ill of our Brethren, or utter Lies, or touch another man's Wife, or incroach upon the property of our Brethren. We muft go to Mafs on the days appointed for that purpofe by the Jefuits, and Faft fome days of the week. For tho' you believ'd the Holy Scriptures as much as we do, unlefs you obferve the Precepts they contain, you'll be doom'd to everlafting Flames after your death.

Adario. So, my dear Brother, this is what I expected. 'Tis a long time fince I knew all that thou haft now fet forth; and indeed I take it to be a very reafonable Article in your Gofpel. Nothing can be jufter and more plaufible than thofe Precepts you fpeak of. You act difingenuoufly in faying that unlefs the Commandments are punctually obferv'd and practis'd, the giving Faith and Credit to the Gofpel will not avail: For, pray, how comes it about that the *French* believe the Gofpel, and yet make a jeft of its Precepts. This I take to be a manifeft Contradiction: [107] For, in the firft place, as to the Adoration of the Great Spirit, I fee no fign of it in your Actions, fo that your Worfhip confifts only in Words, and feems to be Calculated to cheat us. To give you an inftance; do not you fee every day that your Merchants when they bargain with us for Beaver-Skins, do commonly fay, my Goods coft me fo much, 'tis true as I Adore the Almighty; I lofe fo much by you, 'tis as true as that God is in Heaven. But I do not find that they offer him the Sacrifice of their moft valuable Goods, as we do after we have bought 'em from them, when we burn 'em before their Faces. In the next place, as for Working on the days fet apart for Worfhip, I do not find that you make any difference between Holy-Days and Work-Days; for I have frequently feen the *French* bargain for Skins on your Holy-Days, as well as make Nets, Game, Quarrel, beat one another, get Drunk, and commit a hundred extravagant Actions. In a third place, touching the Veneration we have for our Fathers or Anceftours, 'tis but feldom that you follow their Counfel; you fuffer 'em to die for Hunger, you leave 'em and take up feparate Habitations; you are always ready to ask fomething of 'em, but never to give 'em any thing; and if you expect any thing from 'em, you wifh for their death; or at leaft you expect it with impatience. In the fourth place, as for Continence with refpect to the tender Sex; who is it among you (abating for the Jefuits) that has ever acted up to it; do not we fee every day that your Youths purfue our Daughters and our Wives, even to the very Fields, with a defign to inveigle 'em by prefents? Do not they Roll every Night from Hutt to Hutt in our Village, in order to debauch 'em? And doft not thee know how many fuch Adventures [108] there are among thy own Soldiers? In the fifth place, to touch upon the head of Murder; 'tis fuch a common thing among you, that upon the leaft accident, you clap your Hands to your Swords and Butcher one another. I remember when I was at *Paris*, People were run thro' in the Streets every night; and upon the Road between *Paris* and *Rochel*, I was told that I was in danger of my life. Sixthly. Lying and Slandering your Brethren, is a thing that you can as little refrain as Eating and Drinking. I never heard four *French-Men* Converfe together, without fpeaking ill of fome body; and if you knew what I have heard 'em fay publickly of the Viceroy, the Intendant, the Jefuits, and of a thoufand People that you know, not excepting your Self, you would be convinc'd that the *French* are very well vers'd in Defamations. And as to the bufinefs of Lying, I affirm it for a truth, that there is not one Merchant in this Country that will not tell you twenty Lies in felling the worth of a Beaver's Skin in Goods; not to mention the lies they invent in order to defame their Neighbours. In a feventh place, to adjuft the Point of ingaging with Married Women, we need no other Proof than to hear your Difcourfes when you have got a little Drink in your Heads; then you'll entertain us with a great many fine Stories of your Adventures that way. But to go no farther, pray reckon up how many Children are got upon the Wives of the *Coureurs de Bois* during their Husbands abfence. In the eighth place, to come to the Article of not encroaching upon our Neighbours Property, how many Thefts or Robberies have you feen committed among the *Coureurs de Bois* fince you came to this Country? Have not the Thieves been taken in the Fact, and punifh'd accordingly? Is not it fuch a common [109] thing in your Towns, that one can't walk in the Streets in the Night time with fafety, and that you dare not leave your Doors open? In the ninth place, as for going to your Mafs to hear fome Words fpoke in an unknown Language; 'tis true the *French* go commonly to it, but their defign in going is to think of other things than Praying. At *Quebec*, the Men go to Mafs to pick up the Women, and the Women take the fame Method to make Affignments with the Men. I have feen fome of your Women call for Cufhions, for fear of fpoiling their Stockins and Petti-coats; then they fit down upon their Heels, and pull a Book out of a great Bag, which they open and hold in their hands, tho' at the fame time, they look more at the Men they like, than at the Prayers contain'd in the Book. Moſt of your *French* People take Snuff when they're at Maſs; they talk, and laugh; and ſing rather for Diverſion than out of Devotion. And, which is yet worſe; I know that during the time of Maſs, ſeveral Women and Girles take the opportunity of purſuing their Amours, by ſtaying at home all alone. As for your Faſts, I muſt ſay they are very comical: You eat of all ſorts of Fiſh till you burſt again, you cram down Eggs and a thouſand other things, and yet you call this faſting. In fine, my dear Brother, you *French* Folks do all of you make large Pretenſions to Faith, and yet you are downright Infidels; you would fain paſs for wiſe People, and at the ſame time you are fools; you take your ſelves to be Men of Senſe, but at the bottom Ignorance and Preſumption is your true Character.

Lahontan. This concluſion, my dear Brother, favours too ſtrong of the *Hurons*, in being apply'd to all the *French* in general. If your repreſentation were juſt, ne're a one of 'em would go to [110] Paradiſe. But we know that there are Millions of 'em in the State of the Bleſſed, whom we call Saints, and whoſe Images you ſee in our Churches. I own that there are but few of the *French* who have that true Faith that's the only Principle of Piety; ſeveral make a Profeſſion of believing the Truths of our Religion, but this belief is wanting as to its due ſtrength and livelineſs. I own that the greateſt part of thoſe who know the Divine Truths, and make a Profeſſion of believing them, do act quite contrary to what

Faith and Religion injoyns. I cannot deny the juftnefs of your Charge, in alleging a Contradiction upon 'em. But you muft confider, that fometimes Men fin againft the light of their own Confcience, and fome Men lead wicked Lives that have receiv'd good Inftruction. Now this may be owing either to their want of Attention, or to the force of their Paffions, and the tyes they lye under to their Temporal Intereft. Man being full of Corruption is fway'd to evil by fo many various motives, and by fo ftrong an inclination that way, that 'tis hard for him to renounce it, without an abfolute Neceffity.

Adario. When you fpeak of *Man,* you ought to fay *French-Man;* for you know that the Paffions, the Intereft, and the Corruption we fpeak of, are not known among us: But that is not the Point I would be at. Do ye hear, my Brother, I have talk'd frequently to the *French* of all the Vices that reign among them; and when I have made it out that they have no regard to the *Laws* of their *Religion,* they confefs'd that 'twas true, and that they faw it plainly and knew it to be fo; but at the fame time they faid 'twas impoffible for them to obferve thofe Laws: Upon that I ask'd 'em if they did not believe then that their Souls would be doom'd to eternal Flames; and receiv'd this anfwer, [111] *That the Mercy of God is fo great, that whoever trufts in his Goodnefs fhall be Sav'd; that the Gofpel is a Covenant of Grace, in which God condefcends to the Condition and Weaknefs of Man, who is tempted by fo many violent and frequent Attractives, that he is forc'd to give way; and that this World being a place of Corruption, there can be no Purity in Corrupt Man, unlefs it be in the Country where*

God refides. This, I think, is a lefs rigid fort of Morality than that of the Jefuits, who fend us to Hell for a Trifle. Your *French* Men have reafon to fay, *That 'tis impoffible to keep that Law;* fo long as the diftinction of *Meum* and *Tuum* is kept up among you: You need no other proof for this than the Example of all the Savages of *Canada,* who notwithftanding their Poverty are Richer than you, among whom all forts of Crimes are committed upon the fcore of that *Meum* and *Tuum.*

Lahontan. I own, my dear Brother, that thou'rt in the right of it; and I can't but admire the Innocence of all the Savage Nations: And 'tis for that reafon that I earneftly wifh they were acquainted with the Sanctity of our Scriptures, I mean, that Gofpel that thou and I have talk'd fo much of. There's nothing wanting but that to render their Souls Eternally Happy. All of you live fo Morally that you will then have but one Difficulty to furmount before you arrive at Paradife; I mean, that Cuftomary Fornication that prevails amongft the fingle perfons of both Sexes, and the liberty that the Men and the Women take in breaking their Marriage Bonds, in order to a Reciprocal Change, and a frefh Choice. For the Great Spirit has faid, *That Death and Adultery are the only two things that can break that indiffoluble Bond.*

[112] *Adario.* We fhall take another Opportunity of Difcourfing more particularly of that great Obftacle that thou findeft to ftand in the way of our Salvation. In the mean time, I'll content my felf with giving thee one Reafon with refpect to one of the two Points that are mention'd, that is, the

liberty that Batchelors and Girls take with one another. In the first place the young Warrior will not Embarque in a Married State till he has made some Campaigns against the *Iroquese*, and took some Slaves to serve him either in the Village, or at Hunting, Fishing, &c. and till he is perfectly well vers'd in the Exercises of Hunting, Shooting and Fishing. Farther, he will not enervate himself by the frequent Exercise of Venery, at a time when his Strength enables him to serve his Nation in opposing their Enemies; not to mention that he will not expose a Wife and Children to the affliction of seeing him kill'd or taken Prisoner. Now, considering that 'tis impossible for a young Man to abstain from the Embraces of Women altogether, you must not Censure the Youths for keeping Company with young Women once or twice a Month, nor the Girles for receiving their Addresses. Without that Liberty our Batchelors would be liable to great Disorders, as Experience has taught me, with reference to several that observ'd a severe Continence to make 'em run the better; and besides, our Daughters and young Women would be thereby tempted to a mean submission to the Embraces of Slaves.

Lahontan. Believe me, my dear Friend, God will not be satisfied with these Reasons; he orders you either to Marry, or to entertain no Commerce with the Sex: For everlasting Flames are entail'd upon one amorous thought alone, upon one longing wish, one bare desire to satisfie the brutish Passion. When thou fastens upon Continence a Character of Impossibility, thou givest God the lie, for he injoyns nothing but what is possible. 'Tis in our Power to moderate our

Paſſions when we will; there's nothing requir'd towards that but our Good-will and Conſent. All Men that believe in God ought to obſerve his Precepts, and to reſiſt Temptations by the aſſiſtance of his Grace which never fails 'em. To inſtance in the Jeſuits, Doſt not thee think that when they ſee a pretty Girle in thy Village, they feel the Influence of Temptation as well as other Folks? Queſtionleſs they do; but they call in God to their Aſſiſtance; they paſs the whole courſe of their Lives, as well as all our Prieſts, without Marrying, or having any criminal Converſation with the tender Sex. When they put on the black Habit they make ſolemn Promiſes to God to that Effect. They wage an uninterrupted War with all Temptations, during the whole courſe of their Lives, and are oblig'd to reach the Kingdom of Heaven by Violence. When one therefore is apprehenſive of falling into that Sin, he can't avoid it better than by throwing himſelf into a Cloyſter.

Adario. I would not for ten Beaver Skins lye under an obligation of ſilence upon this Head. In the firſt place, that ſet of Men are guilty of a Crime in taking an Oath of Continence, for God having created an equal number of Men and Women, he mean'd that both the one and the other ſhould be imploy'd in the Propagation of Mankind. All things in Nature multiply, whether Trees, Plants, Birds, Beaſts, or Inſects. They repeat this Leſſon to us every Year, and ſuch Perſons as do not follow it are uſeleſs to the World, they do good to none but themſelves, [114] and rob the Earth of the Corn that feeds 'em, in regard that they convert it to no uſe, according to your Principles. A ſecond Crime that they are guilty of confifts in violating their Oath (which they do but too commonly) and making a Jeft of their Word and Promifes to the Great Spirit. This Crime draws on one or two more, whether in Converfing with young Women or with other Men's Wives. If they keep Company with Girles, 'tis manifeft that by Deflowring 'em they rob 'em of what they can never return; I mean, they rob 'em of that Flower, which the *French* have fuch an itch to gather themfelves when they Marry, and which they look upon as fo valuable a Treafure, that a Robbery of that Nature is reckon'd a Crime of the higheft demerit. Another Crime they are guilty of confifts in ufing the abominable precaution of doing things by halves to prevent Impregnation. If they court the Embraces of Married Women, they ftand accountable for the Adultery, and for the Injury that the Woman does to her Husband. Farther; the Children fpringing from thofe Adulterous Embraces are Robbers and Interlopers, that live upon the Means of a pretended Father and half Brethren. In a fifth place, they are chargeable with the unlawful and prophane Methods that they take to ftifle their Brutifh Paffion; for they being the Perfons that Preach your Gofpel, they give a quite different turn to things in private to what they do publickly, or elfe they could never find a Salvo for their Libertinifm which the Vulgar take for a Crime. Thou art fenfible, my Friend, that I fpeak juftly upon the Point, and that in *France* I have feen fome of thefe Black Priefts that would not hide their Talent under their Caps when they came into the Company of Women. [115] Give me leave, my dear Brother, to tell thee once more that 'tis impoffible for thefe Men to be without the Converfation of Women at a certain Age, and far lefs to be free from amorous Thoughts. As for that Refiftance and thofe vigorous Efforts thou fpeak'ft of, that's but a frivolous and poor Plea, as well as their idle pretence of avoiding the Temptation by being mew'd up in a Convent. If Convents are Antidotes againft Temptation, why do you fuffer the young Priefts and Monks to Confefs Maids and Married Women? Is that the way to avoid the Temptation; or is it not rather a plain contrivance for a handfome Opportunity? What Man in the World can hear the Amorous Intrigues of the confeffing Ladies, without being Tranfported, efpecially if he be one of thofe who injoy Health, Youth and Strength, who live without Fatigue or Working, and who encourage Nature with the moft Nourifhing Liquors and Food, feafon'd with I do not know how many Drugs and Spices, that are fufficient to inflame the Blood without any other Provocation? For my part, after a due Confideration of thefe Articles, I fhall not think it ftrange if there be not fo much as one Ecclefiaftick in the Paradife of the Great Spirit. And pray, how have you the Confidence to maintain that this Cattel turn Monks and Priefts in order to avoid Sin, when you know they are addicted to all manner of Vice? I have been inform'd by *French* Men of very good Senfe, that thofe who enter into Priefts or Monks Orders among you, have no other view than to live at their eafe, without the fatigue of Work, and without the difquieting fears of dying for Hunger or being oblig'd to venture their Lives in the

Army. If you would have your Priests good Men, they ought [116] to be all Married, and to live with their respective Families; or else they should be all above Sixty Years of Age. Then indeed they might Confess, Preach and visit Families without Scruple, and Edifie all the World by their Example. Then, I say, 'twould not be in their Power to seduce Maids or married Women; their Age and their Conduct would speak them Wise, Moderate and Considerate; and at the same time the Nation would sustain no loss by their being set apart for Divine Service, in regard that after Sixty Years of Age they are not fit for Warlike Exploits.

Lahontan. I told you before, that you ought not to charge the whole World with the Misdemeanours of a few. 'Tis true there are some who take upon 'em Monks or Priests Orders, with no other design than to subsist handsomely; and unmindful of the devoirs of their Ministry, think of nothing but calling in their yearly Rents. I own that some of 'em are Drunkards, and extravagant in their Actions and Words; that among some of 'em who are wedded to their Interest, Sordid Avarice bears the Ascendant; that some are Proud and Implacable in the way of Resentment; that some of 'em are Whore-masters, Debauchees, Swearers, Hypocrites, Ignorant Fellows, Worldly minded, Backbiters, &c. But their number is but very inconsiderable with respect to the whole; for the Church receives none but the wiser and graver sort of Men, of whom they have some moral Assurances, and whom they try and endeavour to know throughly before they admit 'em: Tho' after all their precaution it can't be otherwise but that they muſt be impos'd upon ſometimes; and indeed this is a great Misfortune, for when the Conduct of Eccleſiaſticks is blacken'd with ſuch [117] Vices, it raiſes the greateſt Scandal that can be; the Sacred Word is polluted in their Mouths, the Laws of God are contemn'd, Divine Things are diſreſpected, the Office of the Miniſtry is debas'd, Religion in general is trampled under Foot, and the People ſhaking off the due regard to Religion give way to an uncontroul'd Licencioufnefs. But in the mean time you ought to conſider, that in ſuch Caſes we take our Meaſures from their Doctrine more than from the Example of ſuch ſcandalous Eccleſiaſticks; we are not upon the ſame lay with you who have not the neceſſary Diſcretion to diſtinguiſh the Doctrine from the Example, and to remain unſhaken by the Scandalous Lives of thoſe you ſaw at *Paris*, whoſe Converſation and Sermons were far from being of a piece. In fine, all that I have to ſay upon this Head, turns upon this, that the Pope having given expreſs Orders to our Biſhops not to confer the Eccleſiaſtical Dignity upon any unworthy Object, they take all the Precaution imaginable, and at the ſame time uſe their utmoſt Efforts to reclaim thoſe who have already gone aſtray.

Adario. I am ſurpris'd to find that you give all along ſuch ſuperficial Anſwers to all the Objections I have offer'd. I perceive that you court Digreſſions, and always depart from the Subject of my Queſtions. But ſince 'tis ſo, I'll come to the Pope then; and with reference to that Point, you muſt know that one Day at *New York* an *Engliſh*-man gave me to know that the Pope was ſuch another Man as he or I was;

but that he fent every body to Hell that he Excommunicated; that he releas'd whom he pleas'd from a fecond place of Torment, that it feems you have forgot, and open'd the Gates of the Great Spirit's Country to fuch Perfons as he lik'd, as being [118] intrufted with the Keys of that upper Region. If all this be true, methinks all his Friends fhould kill themfelves when he expires, that they may croud in along with him when he opens the Gates for himfelf; and if it be in his Power to fend Souls to Hell, 'tis a dangerous thing to be rank'd in the number of his Enemies. At the fame time, I was inform'd by that *Englifh* Gentleman, that this Papal Authority had no footing in *England*, and that the *Englifh* ridicul'd it. Now, prithee, tell me whether this *Englifh* Chriftian fpoke the truth, or not.

Lahontan. The unfolding of this queftion would run me out to fo wide a compafs of things, that I fhould not have done, not in fifteen days. The Jefuits will fatisfie you upon that point better than I can pretend to. However I'll take the liberty to fay one thing, namely: That the *Englifh* Man rally'd and jeer'd while he mention'd fome things that were true. He had a great deal of reafon to perfuade you that thofe of his Religion, did not depend upon the Pope for their Paffage to Heaven, becaufe that lively Faith which you and I fpoke of before, conducts 'em thither without any regard to that holy Man. The Son of God is willing to fave all the *Englifh* by his Blood and Merits. And thus you fee that they are happier than the *French*, of whom God has requir'd good Works that they fcarce ever mind, and who are doom'd to everlasting Flames, if their evil Actions run counter to the above mention'd Commandments of God; tho' at the same time, both they and we are of the same Faith. As to the second flaming place, which we call *Purgatory*, they are exempted from the necessity of passing thro' it; because they'd rather choose to continue upon Earth thro' all the Ages of Eternity without visiting Paradise, than to Burn [119] for some thousands of years by the way. They are so tender upon this point of Honour, that they'll never accept of any Present at the purchase of bearing some Bastinadoes. According to their Notions of things, they do not take a man to be oblig'd by the giving him Mony and hard Usage at the same time: This is rather an affront in their way. But the *French*, who are less nice upon the point; they take it for a mighty favour, that they're allowed to burn for an infinity of Ages in *Purgatory*, upon the apprehension that by that means, they will be better acquainted with the true value of Heaven. Now for as much as the Pope is the Creditor of the *English*, and demands Restitution of his own, they are far from asking his Pardons; that is, his Passports for removing to Heaven without touching at *Purgatory;* for if they did, he would order 'em a Pass to that sort of Hell, which they pretend was never made for 'em. But we *French* Folks that pay him good round Annuities, being acquainted with his Wonder-Working Power, and affected with a sense of our Sins against God; we, I say, that lye under such Circumstances, must of necessity have recourse to the Indulgences of that holy Man, in order to obtain a Pardon that he has Power to grant; for if one of us be Condemn'd to lye forty years in *Purgatory* before he is remov'd to Heaven, why, 'twill coft the Pope but one Word to get the Sentence Revers'd. In fine, to repeat once more what I faid before, the Jefuits will inform you admirably well, of the Authority and Power of the Pope, and of the State of *Purgatory*.

Adario. I am at a lofs to know how to form a diftinct Idea of the difference between you and the *Englifh*, as to the point of Belief; for the more I endeavour to have it fet in a clearer light, [120] the lefs light I find. To my mind, the beft way for all of you is to agree upon this conclufion; That the Great Spirit has beftow'd upon all Men, a Light fufficient to fhew 'em what they ought to do, without running the rifque of being impos'd upon: For I have heard that in each of thefe different Religions, there's an infinite number of Perfons of different Opinions. To inftance in your Religion; every religious Order maintains certain Points that the reft do not, and obferves as great a diverfity in their Inftitutions as in their Habits. This makes me think that in *Europe* every particular Man forms a peculiar Religion to himfelf, which differs from that which he outwardly profeffes. As for my own part, I firmly believe that Men are not capable of knowing what the Great Spirit requires of 'em; and I can't diffuade my felf from believing, that fince the Great Spirit is fo juft and fo good, 'tis impoffible that his Juftice fhould render the Salvation of Mankind fo difficult, as that all of 'em fhould be Damn'd that are not retainers to your Religion, and that even few of the Profeffors of it fhould be admitted into Paradife. Believe me, my Friend; the other World goes upon a lay that's quite different from what we have in this. Few People know what passes there: All *our* knowledge amounts only to this; That we *Hurons* are not the Authours of our own Creation, that the Great Spirit has vouchsaf'd us an honest Mould, while Wickedness nestles in yours; and that he sends you into our Country, in order to have an opportunity of Correcting your Faults, and following our Example. Pursuant to this Principle, my Brother, thou may'st believe as long as thou wilt, and have as much Faith as thou hast a mind to: But after all, thou shalt never see the good Country of Souls, unless thou [121] turn'st *Huron*. The Innocence of our Lives, the Love we tender to our Brethren, and the Tranquility of Mind which we injoy in contemning the measures of Interest: These, I say, are three things that the Great Spirit requires of all Men in General. We practise all these Duties in our Villages, naturally; while the *Europeans* defame, kill, rob, and pull one another to pieces, in their Towns. The *Europeans* have a strong mind to Inherit a Place in the Country of Souls, and yet they never think of their Creator, but when they dispute with the *Hurons*. Fare well, my dear Brother; it grows late: I'll now retire to my Hutt, in order to recollect all the advances thou hast made, that I may call 'em to mind to morrow, when I come to reason the Point with the Jesuits.

Of Laws.

Labon-tan. WELL, my Friend; thou haft heard what the Jefuit had to fay; he has fet matters in a clear light, and made 'em much plainer than I could do. You fee plainly there's a great difference between his Arguments and mine. We Soldiers of Fortune have only a fuperficial knowledge of our Religion, tho' indeed we ought to know it better; but the Jefuits have Study'd it to that degree, that they never fail of converting and convincing the moft obftinate Infidels in the Univerfe.

Adario. To be free with thee, my dear Brother, I could fcarce underftand one tittle of what he meant, and I am much miftaken if he underftands it himfelf. He has repeated the very [122] fame Arguments a hundred times in my Hutt; and you might have obferv'd, that yefterday I anfwer'd above twenty times, that I had heard his Arguments before upon feveral occafions. But, what I take to be moft ridiculous, he teazes me every minute to get me to interpret his Arguments, word for word, to my Countrymen; upon the Plea that a Man of my Senfe may find out in his own Language, more fignificant terms, and render the meaning of his Words more Intelligible, than a Jefuit who is not throughly Mafter of the *Huron* Language. You heard me tell him, that he might Baptife as many Children as he pleas'd, tho' at the fame time he could not give me to know what Baptifm was. He may do what he pleafes in my Village; let him make Chriftians, and Preach, and Baptife if he will; I fhall not hinder him. But now, methinks, we have had enough of Religion, let us therefore talk a little of what you call Laws; for you know that we have no fuch Word in our Language; tho' at the fame time, I apprehend the force and importance of the Word, by vertue of the explication I had from you t'other day, together with the examples you mention'd, to make me conceive what you meant. Prithee tell me, are not Laws the fame as juft and reafonable Things? You fay they are. Why then, to obferve the Law, imports no more than to obferve the meafures of Reafon and Juftice: And at this rate you muft take juft and reafonable things in another fenfe than we do; or if you take 'em in the fame fenfe, 'tis plain you never obferve 'em.

Lahontan. Thefe are fine Diftinctions indeed, you pleafe your felf with idle Flams. Haft not thee the Senfe to perceive, after twenty Years Converfation with the *French*, that what the *Hurons* [123] call Reafon is Reafon among the *French*. 'Tis certain that all Men do not obferve the Laws of Reafon, for if they did there would be no occafion for Punifhments, and thofe Judges thou haft feen at *Paris* and *Quebec* would be oblig'd to look out for another way of Living. But in regard that the good of the Society confifts in doing Juftice and following thefe Laws, there's a neceffity of punifhing the Wicked and rewarding the Good; for without that Precaution Murthers, Robberies and Defamations would fpread every where, and in a Word, we should be the most miserable People upon the Face of the Earth.

Adario. Nay, you are miserable enough already, and indeed I can't see how you can be more such. What sort of Men must the *Europeans* be? What Species of Creatures do they retain to? The *Europeans*, who must be forc'd to do Good, and have no other Prompter for the avoiding of Evil than the fear of Punishment. If I ask'd thee, what a Man is, thou wouldst answer me, *He's a Frenchman*, and yet I'll prove that your *Man* is rather a *Beaver*. For *Man* is not intitled to that Character upon the score of his walking upright upon two Legs, or of Reading and Writing, and shewing a Thousand other Instances of his Industry. I call that Creature a *Man*, that hath a natural inclination to do Good, and never entertains the thoughts of doing Evil. You see we have no Judges; and what's the reason of that? Why? We neither quarrel nor sue one another. And what's the reason that we have no Law Suits? Why? Because we are resolved neither to receive nor to know Silver. But why do we refuse admission to Silver among us? The reason is this: We are resolv'd to have no Laws, for since the World [124] was a World our Ancestors liv'd happily without 'em. In fine, as I intimated before, the Word *Laws* does not signifie just and reasonable things as you use it, for the Rich make a Jest of 'em, and 'tis only the poor Wretches that pay any regard to 'em. But, pray, let's look into these *Laws*, or reasonable things, as you call 'em. For these Fifty Years, the Governors of *Canada* have still alledg'd that we are subject to the Laws of their great Captain. We content our selves in denying all manner of Dependance, excepting that upon the Great Spirit, as being born free and joint Brethren, who are all equally Masters: Whereas you are all Slaves to one Man. We do not put in any such Answer to you, as if the *French* depended upon us; and the reason of our silence upon that Head is, that we have no mind to Quarrel. But, pray tell me, what Authority or Right is the pretended Superiority of your great Captain grounded upon? Did we ever sell our selves to that great Captain? Were we ever in *France* to look after you? 'Tis you that came hither to find out us. Who gave you all the Countries that you now inhabit, by what Right do you possess 'em? They always belong'd to the *Algonkins* before. In earnest, my dear Brother, I'm sorry for thee from the bottom of my Soul. Take my advice, and turn *Huron;* for I see plainly a vast difference between thy Condition and mine. I am Master of my own Body, I have the absolute disposal of my self, I do what I please, I am the first and the last of my Nation, I fear no Man, and I depend only upon the Great Spirit: Whereas thy Body, as well as thy Soul, are doom'd to a dependance upon thy great Captain; thy Vice-Roy disposes of thee; thou hast not the liberty of doing what thou hast a mind to; thou'rt affraid of Robbers, [125] false Witnesses, Assassins, &c. and thou dependest upon an infinity of Persons whose Places have rais'd 'em above thee. Is it true, or not? Are these things either improbable or invisible? Ah! my dear Brother, thou seest plainly that I am in the right of it; and yet thou choosest rather to be a *French* Slave than a free *Huron,* What a fine

Spark does a *Frenchman* make with his fine Laws, who taking himself to be mighty Wise is assuredly a great Fool; for as much as he continues in Slavery and a state of Dependence, while the very Brutes enjoy that adorable Liberty, and like us fear nothing but Foreign Enemies.

Lahontan. Indeed, my Friend, thy way of Reasoning is as Savage as thy self. I did not think that a Man of Sense, who hath been in *France* and *New England*, would speak after that Fashion. What benefit hast thou reap'd by having seen our Cities, Forts and Palaces? When thou talk'st of severe Laws, of Slavery, and a Thousand other idle Whims, questionless thou preachest contrary to thy own Sentiments. Thou takest pleasure in discanting upon the Felicity of the *Hurons*, a set of Men who mind nothing but Eating, Drinking, Sleeping, Hunting, and Fishing; who have not the enjoyment of any one Conveniency of Life, who travel four Hundred Leagues on Foot to knock four *Iroquese* on the Head, in a Word, who have no more than the shape of Men: Whereas we have our Conveniences, our unbending Diversions, and a Thousand other Pleasures, which render the Minutes of our Life supportable. To avoid the lash of those Laws which are severe only upon wicked and criminal Persons, one needs only to live honestly, and offer Injuries to no man.

[126] *Adario.* Ay, my dear Brother, your being an honest Man would not avail you; if two false Witnesses swear against you, you'll presently see whether your Laws are severe or not. Have not the *Coureurs de Bois* quoted me twenty instances of Persons that have been cruelly put to death by the lash of

your Laws, whose Innocence has appear'd after their death? What truth there is in their Relations, I do not pretend to know; but 'tis plain that such a thing may happen. I have heard 'em say farther (and indeed I had heard the same thing in *France* before) that poor innocent Men are Tortur'd in a most horrible manner, in order to force 'em by the violence of their Torment to a Confession of all that is charg'd upon 'em, and of ten times more. What execrable Tyranny must this be! Tho' the *French* pretend to be Men, yet the Women are not exempted from this horrid Cruelty, no more than the Men; both the one and the other choose rather to die once than to die fifty times. And indeed they are in the right of it: For if it should happen that by the influence of extraordinary courage, they were capable of undergoing such Torments without confessing a Crime that they never committed; what health, what manner of life can they enjoy thereafter? No, no, my dear Brother, the black Devils that the Jesuits talk so much of, are not in the Regions where Souls burn in Flames, but in *Quebec* and in *France*, where they keep Company with the Laws, the false Witnesses, the Conveniencies of Life, the Cities, the Fortresses and the Pleasures you spoke of but now.

Lahontan. The *Coureurs de Bois* and the other Sparks who told you such Stories, without acquainting you with the other Circumstances that they knew nothing of, are Block-heads that had [127] better have held their peace. I'll set the whole matter before thee, in its clear and natural colours. Suppose, two false Witnesses depose against a Man; they are

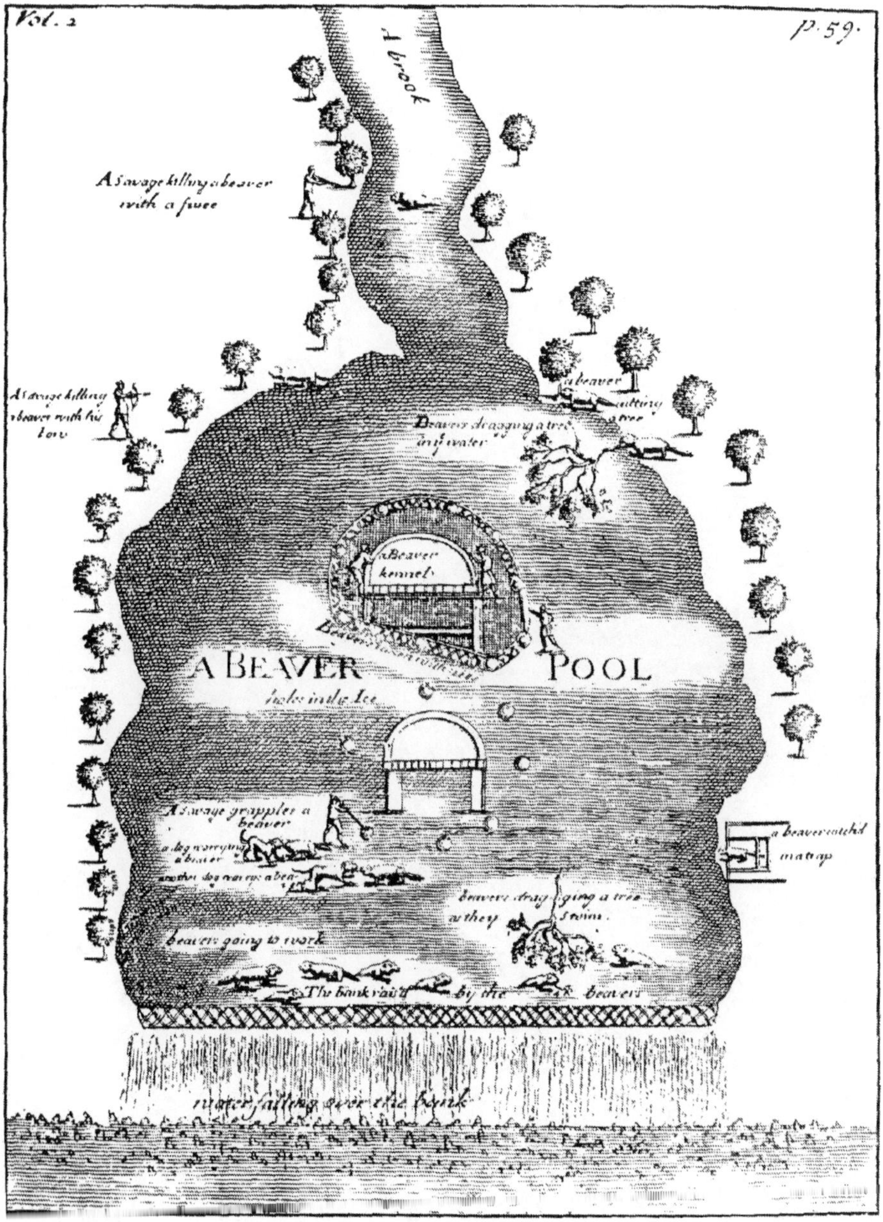
Vol. 2
P. 59.
A brook
A savage killing a beaver with a fusee
A savage killing a beaver with his bow
a beaver cutting a tree
Beavers dragging a tree in ye water
a Beaver kennel
A BEAVER POOL
holes in the Ice
A savage grappler a beaver
a dog worrying a beaver
beavers dragging a tree as they swim.
beavers going to work
The bank rais'd by the beavers
water falling over the bank

presently put into two separate Rooms, where they can't see or converse with one another. Then they are examin'd one after another upon the Articles charg'd against the Person Arraign'd; and the Judges are of such tender Consciences, as to use their utmost efforts to discover whether one or both of 'em vary's, as to the Circumstances. If they happen to perceive any falsity in their depositions, which is easily perceiv'd, they Sentence 'em to die without remission. But if it appears that they are so far from contradicting, that they back one another, they are presented before the Prisoner, to see if he has any Objection to make against 'em, and if he is willing to rely upon their Consciences. If he has nothing to object, and if the two Witnesses Swear by the Great Spirit, that they saw him Murder, Rob, &c. the Judges condemn him out of hand. As for Torture, 'tis never made use of, but when there's only one Witness, whose Oath can't infer Death; for the Law which requires the Testimony of two Men for a sufficient Proof, looks upon the Attestation of one but as half a Proof. But at the same time, you must remark that the Judges take all imaginable Precaution to avoid the passing of an unjust Sentence.

Adario. I'm e'en as wise as I was; for when all comes to all, the two false Witnesses have a perfect good understanding between themselves, before they are brought to the Bar, and they are not to seek for the Answers they are to make: And I find the deposition of one Scoundrel will put a Man to the Rack as well as that of an honest Man; who in my Opinion do's justly forfeit [128] the Character of Honesty by such a deposition, even when he has seen the Crime committed. The *French* are a fine sort of People, who are so far from saving one another's Lives, like Brethren, that they refuse to do it when 'tis in their power. But, prithee, tell me; what dost thou think of these Judges? Is it true that some of 'em are so ignorant as they are said to be; and that others are so Wicked as to pronounce unjust Judgments contrary to their own Consciences; with intent to favour a Friend, or to oblige a Mistress or a great Lord, or to hook in Mony. I foresee thou'lt reply that the Allegation is false, and that Laws are just and reasonable things. But at the same time, I know 'tis as true as that we are here; for a Man that demands his Estate of another who is unjustly possess'd of it, and makes the Innocence of his Cause to appear as clear as the Sunshine; that very Man, I say, shall never make any thing of his Suit; if the great Lord, the Mistress, the Friend, and the Mony business, speak on the Adversary's behalf, to the Judges who are empower'd to decide the Cause. The same is the case of persons Arraign'd for Crimes. Ha! Long live the *Hurons;* who without Laws, without Prisons, and without Torture, pass their Life in a State of Sweetness and Tranquility, and enjoy a pitch of Felicity to which the *French* are utter Strangers. We live quietly under the Laws of Instinct and innocent Conduct, which wise Nature has imprinted upon our Minds from our Cradles. We are all of one Mind; our Wills, Opinions and Sentiments observe an exact Conformity; and thus we spend our Lives with such a perfect good understanding, that no Disputes or Suits can take place amongst us.

But how unhappy are you in being expos'd to the lash of Laws, which your ignorant, [129] unjust, and vicious Judges break in their private Actions, as well as in the Administration of their Offices? These are your just and equitable Judges; who have no regard to Right; who make their Interest the Standard of their Conduct, in the way of their Office; who have nothing in view but the Inriching of themselves; who are not accessible by any but the Dæmon of Silver; who never administer Justice, but thro' a Principle of Avarice or Passion; who give Countenance to Crimes, and set aside Justice and Honesty, in order to give a full range to Cheating, Quarrelling, and the carrying on of tedious Law Suits, to the abuse and violation of Oaths, and to an infinity of other Disorders. This is the practice of these doughty Assertors of the fine Laws of the *French* Nation.

Lahontan. I gave you to know before, that you ought not to give credit to all that every Fool whispers in your Ear. You give Ear to some Blockheads that have not a tincture of Common Sense, and that spread lies under the notion of truths. These bad Judges, that they speak of, are as uncommon as white Beavers; for 'tis a question if there are four such in all *France*. Our Judges are men that love Vertue, and have Souls to be sav'd as well as thee and I; being invested with a publick Capacity, they are to answer for their Conduct before a Judge that has no respect to Persons, and before whom the greatest Monarch is no more than the meanest Slave. There's scarce any of these Men, who would not choose to die, rather than wound their Conscience or violate the Laws. Mony is too bafe a Metal to tempt 'em, and Women warm 'em no more than the Ice. Friends and great Lords make lefs Impreffion upon their Minds, than the Waves upon the Rocks. They curb Libertinifm, [130] they redrefs Diforders, and do Juftice to all that Sue for it; without the leaft regard to what we call Intereft. As for my own part, I have loft my whole Eftate by being caft in three or four Law-Suits at *Paris;* but I would be loth to believe that the Judges are in fault, notwithftanding that my Adverfaries found both Mony and Friends to back bad Caufes. 'Twas the Law that gave it againft me, and I take the Law to be juft and reafonable, imputing my furprize upon the matter, to my unacquaintednefs with that Study.

Adario. I proteft I don't underftand one word of what thou haft faid; for I know the contrary of what thou fayeft to be true, and thofe who inform'd me fo of the Judges are Men of undifputed Honour and Senfe. But if no body had given me any fuch Information, I am not fo dull Pated as not to fee with my own Eyes, the Injuftice of your Laws and your Judges. I'll tell thee one thing my dear Brother; I was a going one day from *Paris* to *Verfailles,* and about half way, I met a Boor that was going to be Whipt for having taken Partridges and Hares with Traps. Between *Rochel* and *Paris,* I faw another that was Condemn'd to the Gally's for having a little Bag of Salt about him. Thefe poor Men were punifh'd by your unjuft Laws, for endeavouring to get Suftenance to their Families; at a time when a Million of Women were got with Child in the abfence of their Husbands, when the Phyficians Murder'd three fourths of the People, and the Gamefters reduc'd their Families to a Starving Condition, by lofing all they had in the World; and all this with Impunity. If things go at this rate, where are your juft and reafonable Laws; where are thofe Judges that have a Soul to be Sav'd as well as you and I? After this, [131] you'll be ready to Brand the *Hurons* for Beafts. In earneft, we fhould have a fine time of it if we offer'd to punifh one of our Brethren for killing a Hare or a Partridge; and a glorious fight 'twould be, to fee our Wives inlarge the number of our Children, while we are ingag'd in Warlike Expeditions againft our Enemies; to fee Phyficians Poifon our Families, and Gamefters lofe the Beaver Skins they've got in Hunting. In *France*, thefe things are look'd upon as trifles, which do not fall within the Verge of their fine Laws. Doubtlefs, they muft needs be very blind, that are acquainted with us, and yet do not imitate our Example.

Lahontan. Very fine, my dear Friend; thou goeft too faft; believe me, thy Knowledge is fo confin'd, as I faid before, that thy Mind can't reach beyond the appearances of things. Wouldft thou but give Ear to Reafon, thou wouldft prefently be fenfible that we act upon good Principles, for the fupport of the Society. You muft know, the Laws Condemn all without exception, that are guilty of the Actions you've mention'd. In the firft place, they prohibit the Peafants to kill Hares or Partridges, efpecially in the Neighbourhood of *Paris;* by reafon that an uncontroul'd liberty of Hunting, would quickly exhauft the whole Stock of thofe Animals. The Boors Farm the Grounds of their Landlords, who referve to themfelves the Priviledge of Hunting, as being Masters. Now, if they happen to kill Hares or Partridges, they not only rob their Masters of their Right, but fall under the Prohibition enacted by the Law: And the same is the Case of those who run Salt, by reason that the Right of Transporting it is solely lodg'd in the King. As to the Women and the Gamesters that you took notice of; you can't think sure that [132] we'd shut 'em up in Prisons and Convents, and Condemn 'em to a perpetual Confinement. The Physicians 'twould be unjust to abuse, for of a hundred Patients they do not kill two; nay, on the contrary, they use their utmost efforts to Cure 'em. There's a necessity that Superannuated Persons, and those who are worn out, should put a Period to their Lives. And after all, tho' all of us have occasion to imploy Doctors, if 'twere prov'd that they had kill'd any Patient, either thro' Ignorance or Malice, the Law would not spare 'em no more than others.

Adario. Were these Laws observ'd, you would stand in need of a great many Prisons; but I see plainly that you do not speak all the truth, and that you're afraid of carrying the Thing farther, least my Reasons should put you to a stand. However, let's now cast our eyes upon those two Men who fled last year to *Quebec*, to avoid the being Burnt in *France*. If we look narrowly into their Crime, we'll find occasion to say, that *Europe* is pester'd with a great many foolish Laws.[1] But, to

---

[1] Sorcery was at this period a statutory crime in France, liable to be punished with death by burning. There was a considerable revival of the fear of witchcraft under Louis XIV, the last law passed upon the subject being the edict of 1682. As late as 1731, a Jesuit was condemned by the parlement of Provence to be burned for sorcery — ED.

speak to the purpofe; thefe two *French* Men were Branded for Jugglers, pretended Magicians, and charg'd with the Crime of playing Magical Tricks. Now, what harm have thefe poor Fellows done; perhaps they have had a fit of Sicknefs, that has brought 'em into that State of Simplicity and Folly, as it happens fometimes among us. Prithee tell me, what harm do our Jugglers do? When a Patient is recommended to 'em, they fhut themfelves up all alone in a little Hutt, where they Sing, Roar, and Dance, and utter fome extravagant Expreffions; then they give the Patient's Relations to know, that they muft prepare a Feaft for Solaceing the Patient; and this Feaft confifts of Flefh or Fifh, according to the Humour of this Juggler, who is only an imaginary [133] Phyfician, whofe Head has been turn'd by fome hot Feaver or other. You fee we rally upon 'em in their abfence, and fee thro' the Impofture; you are fenfible that they are as foolifh in their Actions as in their Words, and that they never go upon Hunting or Warlike Expeditions: And why would you Burn the poor Wretches, that in your Country fall under the fame Misfortune?

Lahontan. There's a great deal of difference between our Jugglers and yours: Thofe of that Profeffion among us, have interviews with the evil Spirit, and feaft with him every Night; by vertue of their Witchcraft, they hinder a Man from Imbracing his own Wife; by putting a certain Charm into the Victuals or Drink of Vertuous and Wife Ladies, they draw 'em to Debauchery; they Poyfon the Cattel, they blaft the Product of the Earth, they caufe Men to die in a languifhing Condition, and a Big-Belly'd Woman to Miscarry: In fine, they do an infinity of mischievous Actions, which I have not nam'd. This set of Men calls themselves Inchanters and Sorcerers; but there's another sort that is yet worse, namely, the Magicians, who converse in a familiar way with the evil Spirit, and get him to appear in what Figure they please, to those who have the curiosity to see him. They have secret Charms that will procure good Luck at Gaming, and Inrich those upon whom they are bestow'd; they foretel Futurities, and have the Power to transform themselves into all sorts of Animals, and the most frightful Figures; they run about to certain Houses, where they make a fearful Howling, interlac'd with Cries and dismal Moans, and appear to be as tall as the loftyest Trees, with Chains on their Feet, and Serpents in their Hands: In fine, they do so terrify [134] the People, that they are forc'd to have recourse to the Priests, for their Exorcisms; upon the apprehension that these Apparitions are Souls come from *Purgatory* to this World, to beg some Masses which are necessary for their Translation into the Presence of the Almighty. Now, take all these Articles together, you will not think it strange, that we Burn 'em without Mercy, pursuant to the Tenor of our Laws.

Adario. Is it possible, that you believe such idle Stories? Sure, you only rally to see what I would answer. These Stories seem to be of a piece with those I have Read in the *Books of speaking Animals. Some of our *Coureurs de Bois* Read these idle Fictions every day; and I'm much mistaken if what you now speak of, is not Writ-

*Æsop's Fables.

ten in thefe Books: For, one muft be a Fool that believes that the evil Spirit is invefted with the Power of coming upon the Earth; fuppofing it to be true that he is fuch as the Jefuits reprefent him. No Creature can fubfift out of its own Element: Fifh die when forc'd upon the Land, and Man expires when under Water. How can you imagine then that the Devil can live out of his Element, which is Fire? Befides, If he could come upon the Earth, he would do mifchief enough by himfelf, without imploying thefe Sorcerers; and if he convers'd with one Man, he would be ready to converfe with many others; for confidering that in your Country the wicked out-number the good, every one of you would then turn Sorcerer, and fo all would go to Deftruction together; the World would be turn'd upfide down; and in a word, a remedylefs Diforder would enfue. Doft not thee know, my Brother, that to credit fuch idle Whims, is an affront offer'd to the Great Spirit; in regard that it charges him with Authorifing [135] Mifchief, and being the direct Authour of all the abovemention'd Diforders, by fuffering the Evil Spirit to turn out of Hell? Since the Great Spirit is fo good, as you and I are fenfible he is, 'tis more credible that he would fend good Souls with agreeable Shapes, to check men for their unwarrantable Actions, and to invite 'em in an amicable way to the practice of Vertue, by fetting forth the Felicity and Blifs of thofe Souls that are poffefs'd of the good Country. As for the Souls that lye in *Purgatory* (if fo be that there's any fuch place) I take it, the Great Spirit has no occafion to be intreated and pray'd to on their behalf, by thofe who have enough to do to pray for themselves: Besides, since he gives 'em leave to come to the Earth, he might as well allow them to mount up to Heaven. Upon the whole, my dear Brother, if I thought you spoke seriously of these things, I should truly be apprehensive that you are Delirious, or have lost your Senses. Certainly, there must be some more inflaming Article against these two Jugglers, or else both your Laws and your Judges are equally unreasonable. If 'twere true that these mischievous Actions were actually committed, the Consequence I should draw from thence, would be this; That since there's no such thing heard of among any of the Nations of *Canada*, it can't be otherwise but that the Evil Spirit has a power over you that he has not over us. Upon this lay, we are a good People, and you on the other hand are perverse, malicious, and addicted to all degrees of Vice and Wickedness. But, prithee, let's make an end of our Conferences upon this Head; and so I'll expect no answer to what has been said. To come back to your Laws, pray inform me how it comes to pass that they suffer Women to be Sold for Mony to those who have [136] a mind to make use of 'em? Why do they suffer those publick Houses where the Whores and Bawds are in readyness all the hours of the day, to oblige all sorts of Persons? Why are some allow'd to wear Swords, in order to kill others that dare not wear 'em? Why do not they prohibit the Selling of Wine above a determin'd quantity, or the adulterating of it with I do not know how many Ingredients, that ruin one's Health? Do not you see the Disorders committed at *Quebec* by Drunkards? You'll answer perhaps, as others have done before you; that the Vintner is allow'd to Sell as much Goods as he can put off, for the maintenance of himself and his Family; and that he who drinks the Wine ought to regulate his own Conduct; and be moderate in that as well as in all other things. But I'll prove that to be impossible, for a Man in drink, loses his Reason before he is aware, or at least his Reason is so drown'd that he is not capable of distinguishing what he ought to do. Why do not your Laws restrain the excessive Gaming, that is the source of a thousand evils? Fathers ruin their Families (as I said before) Children either Rob their Fathers, or run 'em into Debt; the Wives and Daughters prostitute themselves for Mony, when they're reduc'd to extremities, and have plaid away their Cloaths, and their Houshold Furniture. This gives rise to disputes, murders, enmity, and irreconcileable hatred. These prohibitions, my Brother, would be of no use among the *Hurons;* but they are very much wanted among the *French*. If by such methods you would gradually reform the Disorders that Interest has rais'd amongst you, I should hope that one day you might come to live without Laws as we do.

[137] *Lahontan.* I acquainted you before, that our Laws inflict Penalties on Gamesters; and provide Punishments for Whores and Bawds, and above all, for Publick House-Keepers, when disorders happen in their Houses. All the difference lies here, that our Cities are so large and populous that 'tis not easy for the Judges to trace all the Abuses that are committed: But at the same time, they are prohibited by the

Laws, and all possible measures are us'd to prevent 'em: In one word, our Judges indeavour with such care and application to stiffle bad Customs, to establish a good Order in all the Branches of the Society, to punish Vice and reward Vertue; this, I say, they do with such care and application, that if you could but shake off your faulty Prejudices, and weigh narrowly the excellency of our Laws, you would be oblig'd to own that the *French* are a just, judicious and knowing People, who pursue the true measures of Justice and Reason more than you do.

Adario. I would gladly embrace any opportunity of working my self into that Belief before I die, for I have a natural affection for the *French;* but I am very apprehensive that I shall not meet with that Consolation. Upon this foot, your Judges ought to begin first to observe the Laws, that their example may influence others; they ought to discontinue their Oppression of Widows, Orphans, and poor Creatures; to give dispatch to the Suits of Persons that come an hundred Leagues off for a Hearing; and in a word, to form such Judgments of Causes as the Great Spirit shall do. I can never entertain a good thought of your Laws, till they lessen the Taxes and Duties that poor People are constrain'd to pay, at a time when the Rich of all Stations pay nothing in proportion to their Estates; till [138] you put a stop to the course of Drunkenness that spreads thro' our Villages, by prohibiting the *Coureurs de Bois* to import Brandy among us. Then indeed I shall hope that you'll compleat your Reformation by degrees, that a levelling of Estates may gradually creep in among you; and that at last you'll abhor that thing call'd Interest, which occafions all the Mifchief that *Europe* groans under. When you arrive at that pitch, you'll have neither *Meum* nor *Tuum* to difturb you, but live as happily as the *Hurons*. This is enough for one day: I fee my Slave coming to acquaint me that I am wanted in the Village. Farewel, my dear Brother, till to morrow.

Lahontan. I am of the Opinion, my dear Friend, that you would not have come fo foon to my Apartment, if you had not defign'd to purfue our laft Difpute. As for my part, I declare I will not enter the lifts farther with you, upon the confideration that you are not capable to apprehend my Arguments. You are fo prepoffefs'd on the behalf of your own Nation, fo ftrongly byafs'd to the Savage Cuftoms, and fo little fond of a due enquiry into ours; that I fhall not daign to kill both my Body and my Soul, in endeavouring to make you fenfible of the ignorance and mifery that the *Hurons* have always liv'd in. Thou knoweft I am thy Friend; and fo I have no other view, but to fet before thine eyes the Felicity that attends the *French*, to the end that thou and the reft of thy Nation may live as they do. I told you, I do not know how often, that you infift on the Converfation of fome *French* Debauchees, and meafure all the reft by their Bufhel. I acquainted you, that they were punifh'd for their Crimes; but thefe reafons will not go down with you; you obftinately [139] maintain your affertion by throwing in affrontive anfwers, as if the *French* were not Men. Upon the whole, I am downright weary of hearing fuch poor ftuff come from the Mouth of a Man that all the *French* look upon as a Man of excellent

Senfe. The People of thy Nation refpect thee not only for thy Senfe and Spirit, but for thy Experience and Valour. Thou art the Head of the Warriours, and the Prefident of the Council; and without flattery, I have fcarce met with a Man of a quicker apprehenfion than thy felf. 'Tis upon this confideration, that I pity thee with all my heart for not throwing off thy prejudicate Opinions.

Adario. Thou'rt miftaken, my dear Brother, in all thou haft faid; for I have not form'd to my felf any falfe Idea of your Religion, or of your Laws. The Example of all the *French* in General, will ever oblige me to look upon all their Actions as unworthy of a Man. So that my Idea's are juft; the prepoffeffion you talk of is well grounded; and I am ready to make out all my advances. We talk'd of Religion and Laws, and I did not impart to you above a quarter of what I had to fay upon that Head. You infift chiefly upon our way of living, which you take to be Blame-worthy. The *French* in general take us for Beafts; the Jefuits Brand us for impious, foolifh and ignorant Vagabonds. And to be even with you, we have the fame thoughts of you; but with this difference, that *we* pity you without offering invectives. Pray hear me, my dear Brother, I fpeak calmly and without paffion. The more I reflect upon the lives of the *Europeans*, the lefs Wifdom and Happinefs I find among 'em. Thefe fix years I have bent my thoughts upon the State of the *Europeans*: But I can't light on any thing in their Actions that is not [140] beneath a Man; and truly I think 'tis impoffible it fhould be otherwife, fo long as you ftick to the meafures of *Meum* and *Tuum*.

I affirm that what you call Silver is the Devil of Devils; the Tyrant of the *French;* the Source of all Evil; the Bane of Souls, and the Slaughter-House of living Persons. To pretend to live in the Mony Country, and at the same time to save one's Soul, is as great an inconsistency as for a Man to go to the bottom of a Lake to preserve his Life. This Mony is the Father of Luxury, Lasciviousness, Intrigues, Tricks, Lying, Treachery, Falseness, and in a word, of all the mischief in the World. The Father sells his Children, Husbands expose their Wives to Sale, Wives betray their Husbands, Brethren kill one another, Friends are false, and all this proceeds from Mony. Consider this, and then tell me if we are not in the right of it, in refusing to finger, or so much as to look upon that cursed Metal.

Lahontan. What! is it possible that you should always Reason so sorrily! Prithee, do but listen once in thy life time to what I am going to say. Dost not thou see, my dear Friend, that the Nations of *Europe* could not live without Gold and Silver, or some such precious thing. Without that Symbol, the Gentlemen, the Priests, the Merchants, and an infinity of other Persons who have not Strength enough to labour the Earth, would die for Hunger. Upon that lay, our Kings would be no Kings: Nay, what Soldiers should we then have? Who would then Work for Kings or any body else, who would run the hazard of the Sea, who would make Arms unless 'twere for himself? Believe me, this would run us to remediless Ruine, 'twould turn *Europe* into a Chaos, and create the most dismal Confusion that Imagination it self can reach.

[141] *Adario.* You fobb me off very prettily, truly, when you bring in your Gentlemen, your Merchants and your Priests. If you were Strangers to *Meum* and *Tuum*, those distinctions of Men would be sunk; a levelling equality would then take place among you as it now do's among the *Hurons.* For the first thirty years indeed, after the banishing of Interest, you would see a strange Desolation; those who are only qualify'd to eat, drink, sleep and divert themselves, would languish and die; but their Posterity would be fit for our way of living. I have set forth again and again, the qualities that make a Man inwardly such as he ought to be; particularly, Wisdom, Reason, Equity, &c. which are courted by the *Hurons.* I have made it appear that the Notion of separate Interests knocks all these Qualities in the Head, and that a Man sway'd by Interest can't be a Man of Reason. As for the outward Qualifications of a Man; he ought to be expert in Marching, Hunting, Fishing, Waging War, Ranging the Forests, Building Hutts and Canows, Firing of Guns, Shooting of Arrows, Working Canows: He ought to be Indefatigable, and able to live on short Commons upon occasion. In a word, he ought to know how to go about all the Exercises of the *Hurons.* Now in my way, 'tis the Person thus qualify'd that I call a *Man.* Do but consider, how many Millions there are in *Europe*, who, if they were left thirty Leagues off in the Forrests, and provided with Fusees and Arrows, would be equally at a loss, either to Hunt and maintain themselves, or to find their way out: And yet you see we traverse a hundred Leagues of Forrests without losing our way, that we kill Fowl and other Beasts with our Arrows,

that we catch Fish in all the places where they are to be had; that we [142] Dog both Men and Wild Beasts by their Footsteps, whether in Woods or in open Fields, in Summer or in Winter; that we live upon Roots when we lye before the Gates of the *Iroquese*, that we run like Hares, that we know how to use both the Axe and the Knife, and to make a great many useful things. Now since we are capable of such things, what should hinder you to do the same, when Interest is laid aside? Are not your Bodies as large, strong and brawny as ours? Are not your Artisans imploy'd in harder and more difficult Work than ours? If you liv'd after our manner, all of you would be equally Masters; your Riches would be of the same Stamp with ours, and consist in the purchasing of Glory by military Actions, and the taking of Slaves; for the more you took of them the less occasion you would have to Work: In a word, you would live as happily as we do.

Lahontan. Do you place a happy Life, in being oblig'd to lye under a pittiful Hutt of Bark, to Sleep under four sorry Coverlets of Beaver Skins, to Eat nothing but what you Boil and Roast, to be Cloath'd with Skins, to go a Beaver Hunting in the harshest Season of the Year, to run a hundred Leagues on Foot in pursuit of the *Iroquese*, thro' Marshes and thick Woods, the Trees of which are cut down so as to render 'em inaccessible! Do you think your selves happy when you venture out in little Canows, and run the risque of being drown'd every foot in your Voyages upon the Great Lakes; when you lye upon the ground with the Heavens for your Canopy, upon approaching to the Villages of your Enemies; when you run with full Speed, both days and nights without eating or drinking, as being purfued by your Enemies; when you are fure of being reduc'd to the laft extremity, if [143] the *Coureurs de Bois* did not out of Friendfhip, Charity and Commiferation, fupply you with Fire-Arms, Powder, Lead, Thread for Nets, Axes, Knives, Needles, Awls, Fifhing-Hooks, Kettles, and feveral other Commodities?

Adario. Very fine, come, don't let's go fo faft; the day is long, and we may talk one after the other at our own leifure. It feems you take all thefe things to be great hardfhips; and indeed I own they would be fuch to the *French*, who like Beafts, love only to eat and to drink, and have been brought up to Softnefs and Effeminacy. Prithee, tell me what difference there is between lying in a good Hutt, and lying in a Palace; between Sleeping under a Cover of Beaver-Skins, and Sleeping under a Quilt between two Sheets; between Eating Boil'd and Roaft Meat, and feeding upon dirty Pies, Ragou's, &c. drefs'd by your greafy Scullions? Are we liable to more Diforders and Sickneffes than the *French*, who are accommodated with thefe Palaces, Beds and Cooks? But after all, how many are there in *France* that lye upon Straw in Garrets where the Rain comes in on all hands, and that are hard put to't to find Victuals and Drink? I have been in *France*, and fpeak from what I have feen with my Eyes. You rally without reafon, upon our Cloaths made of Skins, for they are warmer, and keep out the Rain better than your Cloth; befides, they are not fo ridiculoufly made as your Garments, which have more Stuff in their Pockets and Skirts, than in the Body of the Garment. As for our Beaver-Hunting, you take it to be a terrible thing; while it affords us all manner of pleasure and diversion; and at the same time, procures us all sorts of Commodities in exchange for the Skins. Besides, our Slaves take all the Drudgery off our hands, (if so be [144] that you will have it to be drudgery.) You know very well that Hunting is the most agreeable Diversion we have; but the Beaver-Hunting being so very pleasant, we prefer it to all the other sorts. You say, we have a troublesome and tedious way of waging War; and indeed I must own that a *French* Man would not be able to bear it, upon the account that you are not accustom'd to such long Voyages on Foot; but these Excursions do not fatigue us in the least, and 'twere to be wish'd for the good of *Canada*, that you were possess'd of the same Talent; for if you were, the *Iroquese* would not Cut your Throats in the midst of your own Habitations, as they do now every day. You insist likewise on the risque we run in our little Canows, as an instance of our Misery; and with reference to that Point, 'tis true that sometimes we cannot dispense with the use of Canows, because we are Strangers to the Art of Building larger Vessels; but after all, your great Vessels are liable to be cast away as well as our Canows. 'Tis likewise true, that we lye flat upon the open ground when we approach to the Villages of our Enemies; but 'tis equally true that the Soldiers in *France* are not so well accommodated as your Men are here, and that they are oftentimes forc'd to lye in Marshes and Ditches, where they are expos'd to the Rain and Wind. You object farther, that we betake our selves to a speedy Flight; and pray what can be more natural than to flye when the number of our Enemies is triple to ours. The Fatigue indeed of running night and day without Eating and Drinking, is terrible; but we had better undergo it than become Slaves. I am apt to believe that such extremities are matter of Horrour to the *Europeans*, but we look upon 'em as in a manner, nothing. [145] You conclude, in pretending that the *French* prevent our Misery by taking pity of us. But pray consider how our Ancestors liv'd an hundred years ago: They liv'd as well without your Commodities as we do with 'em; for instead of your Fire-Locks, Powder and Shot, they made use of Bows and Arrows, as we do to this day: They made Nets of the Thread of the Barks of Trees, Axes of Stone; Knives, Needles and Awls of Stag or Elk-Bones; and supply'd the room of Kettles with Earthen Pots. Now, since our Ancestors liv'd without these Commodities for so many Ages; I am of the Opinion, we could dispense with 'em easyer than the *French* could with our Beaver Skins; for which, by a mighty piece of Friendship, they give us in exchange Fusees, that burst and Lame many of our Warriors, Axes that break in the cutting of a Shrub, Knives that turn Blunt, and lose their Edge in the cutting of a Citron; Thread which is half Rotten, and so very bad that our Nets are worn out as soon as they are made; and Kettles so thin and slight, that the very weight of Water makes the Bottoms fall out. This, my dear Brother, is the anfwer I had to give to your Reflexions upon the Mifery of the *Hurons*.[1]

Lahontan. 'Tis well; I find you would have me to believe that the *Hurons* are infenfible of their Fatigue and Labour; and being bred up to Poverty and Hardfhips, have another notion of 'em than we have. This may do with thofe who have never ftir'd out of their own Country, and confequently have no Idea of a better Life than their own; who having never vifited our Cities and Towns, fancy that we live juft as they do. But as for thee, who haft feen *France, Quebec* and *New-England*, methinks thy judgment and relifh of things are too much of the Savage [146] Strain; whilft thou prefers the Condition of the *Hurons* to that of the *Europeans.* Can there be a more agreeable and delightful Life in the World, than that of an infinity of rich Men, who want for nothing? They have fine Coaches, Stately Houfes adorn'd with Rich Hangings and Magnificent Pictures, Sweet Gardens replenifh'd with all forts of Fruit, Parks Stock'd with all forts of Animals, Horfes and Hounds and good ftore of Mony, which enables 'em to keep a Sumptuous Table, to frequent the Play-Houfes, to Game freely, and to difpofe handfomely of their Children. Thefe happy Men are ador'd by their Dependants; and you

---

[1] As the result of contact with Europeans, there was soon noticeable a great change in Indian customs and mode of living. The introduction from Europe of iron implements, fire-arms, utensils, clothing, and ornaments, profoundly affected our aborigines, and rendered them thenceforth dependent upon traders for the very means of subsistence. Lahontan has here put into the mouth of Adario an illuminating although satirical reference to the process by which the American Indians were quickly converted by the fur-traders from a self-reliant people into a dependent class.— ED.

have seen with your own eyes our Princes, Dukes, Mareſhals of *France*, Prelates, and a Million of perſons of all Stations, who want for nothing, and live like Kings, and who never call to mind that they have liv'd, till ſuch time as Death alarms 'em.

Adario. If I had not been particularly inform'd of the State of *France*, and let into the knowledge of all the Circumſtances of that People, by my Voyage to *Paris;* I might have been Blinded by the outward appearances of Felicity that you ſet forth: But I know that your Prince, your Duke, your Mareſhal, and your Prelate are far from being happy upon the Compaariſon with the *Hurons*, who know no other happineſs than that of Liberty and Tranquility of Mind: For your great Lords hate one another in their Hearts; they forfeit their Sleep, and neglect even Eating and Drinking, in making their Court to the King, and undermining their Enemies; they offer ſuch Violence to Nature in diſſembling, diſguiſing and bearing things, that the Torture of their Soul leaves all Expreſſion far behind it. Is all this nothing in your way? Do you think it ſuch a trifling matter to have fifty [147] Serpents in your Boſom? Had not they better throw their Coaches, their Palaces and their Finery, into the River, than to ſpend their life time in a continued Series of Martyrdom? Were I in their place, I'd rather chooſe to be a *Huron* with a Naked Body and a Serene Mind. The Body is the Apartment in which the Soul is lodg'd; and what ſignifies it, for the Caſe call'd the Body, to be ſet off with Gold Trappings, or ſpread out in a Coach, or planted before a Sumptuous Table, while the Soul Galls and Tortures it? The great Lords, that you call Happy, lie expos'd to Disgrace from the King, to the detraction of a thousand sorts of Persons, to the loss of their Places, to the Contempt of their Fellow Courtiers; and in a word, their soft Life is thwarted by Ambition, Pride, Presumption and Envy. They are Slaves to their Passions, and to their King, who is the only *French* Man that can be call'd Happy, with respect to that adorable Liberty which he alone enjoys. There's a thousand of us in one Village, and you see that we love one another like Brethren; that whatever any one has is at his Neighbour's Service; that our Generals and Presidents of the Council have not more Power than any other *Huron;* that Detraction and Quarreling were never heard of among us; and in fine, that every one is his own Master, and do's what he pleases, without being accountable to another, or censur'd by his Neighbour. This, my dear Brother, is the difference between us and your Princes, Dukes, *&c.* And if those great Men are so Unhappy, by consequence, those of inferiour Stations must have a greater share of Trouble and perplexing Cares.

[148] *Lahontan.* You must know that as your *Hurons* who are brought up in the way of Fatigue and Misery, have no mind to be rid of it; so these great Lords being inur'd from their infancy to ambition, care, *&c.* can't live without it. As Happiness lies in the imagination, so they feed themselves with Vanity, and in their hearts think themselves as good as the King. That Tranquility of mind that the *Hurons* enjoy,

never car'd for crossing over to *France*, for fear of being confin'd to the little Religious Houses. Tranquility of mind passes in *France* for the Character of a Fool, of a senseless, careless Fellow. To be happy, one must always have somewhat in his view that feeds his Wishes. He that confines his Wishes to what he enjoys, must be a *Huron*, which none will desire to be, if he considers that Life would be a Scene of Uneasyness, if our Mind did not direct us every minute to desire somewhat that we are not yet possess'd of; and 'tis this that makes a Life happy, provided the means imploy'd in the prosecution of such Wishes are lawful and warrantable.

Adario. Is not that Burying a Man alive; to rack his Mind without intermission in the acquisition of Riches and Honour, which cloy us as soon as obtain'd; to infeeble and waste his Body, and to expose his Life in the forming of Enterprises, that for the most part prove Abortive? As for your Allegation, that these great Lords are bred from their Infancy to Ambition and Care, as we are to Labour and Fatigue; I must say, 'tis a fine Comparison for a Man that can Read and Write. Tell me, prithee, if the repose of the Mind and the exercise of the Body are not the necessary Instruments of Health, if the tossing of the Mind and the rest of the Body are not the means to destroy it? What have we [149] in the World that's dearer to us than our Lives, and ought not we to take the best measures to preserve 'em? The *French* murder their Health by a thousand different means, and we preserve ours till our Bodies are worn out, our Souls being so far free from Passions, that they can't alter or disturb our Bodies. And after all, you insinuate that the *French* hasten the Moment of their Death by lawful means: A very pretty conclusion indeed, and such as deserves to be took notice of. Believe me, my dear Brother, 'tis thy Interest to turn *Huron*, in order to prolong thy life. Thou shalt drink, eat, sleep, and Hunt with all the ease that can be; thou shalt be free'd from the Passions that Tyrannise over the *French;* thou shalt have no occasion for Gold or Silver to make thee happy; thou shalt not fear Robbers, Assassins or False Witnesses; and if thou hast a mind to be King of all the World, why, thou shalt have nothing to do but to think that thou art so.

Lahontan. You cannot expect I should comply with your demand, without thinking that I have been guilty of such Crimes in *France*, that I can't return without running the risque of being Burnt: For after all, I can't imagine a more unaccountable *Metamorphosis*, than that of a *French* Man into a *Huron*. How d'ye think I could undergo the Fatigues we talk'd of but now? D'ye think I could have the patience to hear the Childish Proposals of your Ancient and your Young Men, without taking them up? Is it feasible that I could live upon Broth, Bread, *Indian* Corn, Roast Meat and Boil'd, without either Pepper or Salt? Could I brook the Larding of my Face like a Fool, with twenty sorts of Colours? What Spirit must I be of, if I drink nothing but Mapple-Water, and go stark Naked all the Summer, [150] and eat out of nothing but Wooden Dishes? Your Meals would never go down with me, since two or three hundred Persons must Dance for two or three hours before and after. I can't live with an uncivilis'd sort of People, who know no other Compliment than, *I honour you.* No, no; my dear *Adario*, 'tis impossible for a *French-Man* to turn *Huron*, but a *Huron* may easily become a *French-Man*.

Adario. At that rate you prefer Slavery to Liberty. But 'tis no Surprisal to me, after what I have heard you maintain: Tho after all, if you happen'd to enter into your own Breast, and to throw off your prepossession with regard to the Customs and Humours of the *French* Nation; I cannot see that the Objections you've now Started, are of such Moment as to keep you from falling into our way of living. What a mighty difficulty you meet with in bringing your self to approve of our old Men's Counsel, and our young Men's Projects! Are not you equally gravell'd, when the Jesuits and your Superiours make impertinent demands? Why would not you choose to live upon the Broth of all sorts of good and substantial Meat? Our Partridges, Turkeys, Hares, Ducks, and Roe-Bucks; do not they eat well when they're Roasted or Boil'd? What signifies your Pepper, your Salt, and a thousand other Spices, unless it be to murder your Health? Try our way of living but one fort-night, and then you'll long for no such doings. What harm can you fear from the Painting of your Face with Colours? You dawb your Hair with Powder and Essence, and even your Cloaths are sprinkled with the same: Nay, I have seen *French* Men that had Mustaches like Cats, cover'd o'er with Wax. As for the Mapple-Water, 'tis sweet, healthy, well-tasted, and friendly to the Stomach: [151] And I've seen you drink of it oftner than once or twice: Whereas Wine and Brandy destroy the natural Heat, pall the Stomach, inflame the Blood, Intoxicate, and create a thousand Disorders. And pray what harm would it do ye, to go Naked in warm Weather? Besides, we are not so stark Naked, but that we are cover'd behind and before. 'Tis better to go Naked, than to toil under an everlasting Sweat, and under a load of Cloaths heap'd up one above another. Where's the uneasyness of Eating, Singing, and Dancing in good Company? Had not you better do so than sit at Table moping by your self, or in the Company of those that you never saw or knew before? All the hardship then, that you can complain of, lies in conversing with an unciviliz'd People, and being robb'd of the Pageantry of Compliments. This you take to be a sad Affliction, tho' at the bottom 'tis far from being such. Tell me, prithee; do's not Civility consist in Decency and an affable Carriage? And what is Decency? Is it not an everlasting Rack, and a tyresome Affectation display'd in Words, Cloaths and Countenance? And why would you Court a Quality that gives you so much trouble? As for Affability; I presume it lyes in giving People to know our readyness to serve 'em, by Caresses and other outward Marks; As when you say every turn, Sir, *I'm your humble Servant, you may dispose of me as you please.* Now, let's but consider to what purpose all these Words are spoke; for what end must we lie upon all occasions, and speak otherwife than we think? Had not you better speak after this fashion; *Ho! art thou there, thou'rt welcome, for I honour thee?* Is not it an ugly show, to bend one's Body half a score times, to lower one's hand to the ground, and to say every moment, *I ask your Pardon?* Be [152] it known to thee, my dear Brother, that this Submission alone would be enough to unhinge me quite, as to your way of living. You've asserted that a *Huron* may easily turn *French;* but believe me, he'll meet with other difficulties in the way of his Conversion than those you speak of. For supposing I were to turn *French* out of hand, I must begin with a complyance to Christianity, which is a Point that you and I talk'd enough of three days ago. In order to the same end, I must get my self Shav'd every three days, for in all appearance I should no sooner profess Gallicism, than I should become rough and hairy like a Beast: And this inconvenience shocks me extreamly: Sure 'tis much better to be Beardless and Hairless; and I'm equally sure you never saw a rough Savage. How d'ye think it would agree with me to spend two hours in Dressing or Shifting my self, to put on a Blue Sute and Red Stockins, with a Black Hat and a White Feather, besides colour'd Ribbands? Such Rigging would make me look upon my self as a Fool. How could I condescend to Sing in the Streets, to Dance before a Looking-Glass, to toss my Wigg sometimes before and sometimes behind me? I could not stoop so as to make my Honours, and fall down before a parcel of Sawcy Fools, that are intitled to no other Merit than that of their Birth and Fortune. D'ye think that I could see the Indigent languish and pine away, without giving 'em all I had? How could I wear a Sword without attacking a Company of Profligate Men who throw into the Gallys an infinity of poor Strangers, (*) that never injur'd any Body, and are carried, in a woful Condition, out of their Native Country, to Curse in the [153] midst of their Chains,

* *The Algerines, Tripolins, Moors, Turks, &c who are taken in the Mediterranean, and are sent to Marseilles to the Galleys.*

their Fathers and Mothers, their Birth, and even the Great Spirit. Thus 'tis that the *Iroquese* languish, who were sent to *France* some two years ago.[1] Can you imagine that I would speak ill of my Friends, caress my Enemies, contemn the Miserable, honour the Wicked, and enter into Dealings with 'em; that I would triumph o'er my Neighbour's Misfortunes, and praise a naughty Man; that I would act the part of the Envious, the Traitours, the Flatterers, the Inconstant, the Liars, the Proud, the Avaricious, the Selfish, the Taletellers, and all your double Minded Folks? D'ye think it possible for me to be so indiscreet as to boast at once of what I have done, and what I have not done; to be so mean as to crawl like an Adder at the feet of a Lord, that orders his Servants to deny him; and to take a Refusal tamely? No, my dear Brother, no; I can't brook the Character of a *French* Man; I had rather continue what I am than pass my Life in these Chains. Is it possible that our Liberty do's not Charm you? Can you live an easier life than what you may have in our way? When thou comest to visit me in my Hutt, do not my Wife and my Daughters withdraw and leave thee alone with me, that

---

[1] For this incident, and its effect upon the colony, see pp. 122-124, *ante*.—ED.

our Converfation may fuffer no Interruption? In like manner, when thou mean'ft to pay a Vifit to my Wife or my Daughters, are not thou left alone with the party that thou comeft to See? Are not you welcome to Command any Hutt in the Village, and to call for any thing of Eatables that you like beft? Did ever a *Huron* refufe another, either the whole or part of what he had catch'd at Hunting or Fifhing? Do not we make dividends of our Beaver-Skins, in order to fupply thofe who have not enough to purchafe fuch Commodities as they have occafion for? [154] Do not we obferve the fame Method in the diftribution of our Corn, to fuch as have not fufficient Crops upon their Fields for the maintenance of their Families? If any one of us have a mind to Build a Canow or a Hutt, we all fend our Slaves to forward the Work, without being ask'd. This is a quite different way of living from that of the *Europeans,* who would Sue their neareft Relations for an Ox or a Horfe. If the *European* Father asks Mony of his Son, or the Son of the Father, he replys he has none. If of two *French* Men who have liv'd twenty years together, and eat and drink at one Table every day; if of thefe two *French* Men, I fay, one fhould ask the other for Mony, the anfwer is, there's none to be had. If a poor Wretch that goes naked in the Streets, and is ready to dye with Hunger and Hardfhips: does but ask a rich Man for a Farthing, his anfwer is, *'Tis not for him.* Now fince all this is true, how can you have the prefumption to claim a free accefs to the Country of the Great Spirit? Sure, there's not a Man upon Earth that does not know, that Evil is contrary to Nature, and that he was not

Created to do Mischief. What hopes then can a Christian have at his Death, that never did a good Action in his Life time. He either must believe that the Soul dies with the Body (tho' there's none of you that owns that Opinion) or else supposing the Immortality of the Soul, and supposing your Tenents of Hell, and of the Sins that waft Sinners to that Region, to be just and true, your Souls will have a hot time of it.

Lahontan. D'ye hear, *Adario?* I find 'tis needless for us to Reason longer upon these Heads; for all the Arguments you offer have nothing of Solidity in 'em. I have told thee a hundred times, that the instance of a handful of wicked [155] Men concludes nothing upon the whole: You fancy that every *European* has his particular Vice, whether known or unknown; and I may preach the contrary to you till to Morrow Morning and not Convince you when I have done. You make no difference between a Scoundrel and a Man of Honour; and so I may talk to you ten Years together and not unhinge you of the bad opinion you have of our Religion, our Laws, and our Customs. I would give a hundred Beaver Skins that you could Read and Write like a *Frenchman*. Had you that Qualification, you would not so shamefully contemn the happy Condition of the *Europeans*. We have had in *France* some *Chinese* and *Siamese* who came from the remotest parts of the World, and were in every respect more averse to our Customs than the *Hurons*, and yet could not but admire our way of Living. For my part, I protest I can't conceive the ground of your Obstinacy.

Adario, All thefe People have as crooked Minds as they have deform'd Bodies. I have feen fome of the Ambaffadors from the Nations you fpeak of, and the Jefuits at *Paris* gave me fome account of their Country. They obferve a divifion of Property as well as the *French;* and forafmuch as they are more brutifh and more wedded to their Intereft than the *French*, we muft not think it ftrange that they approv'd of the Cuftoms and Manners of a People who treated 'em with all the meafures of Frendfhip, and made 'em Prefents. You muft not think that the *Hurons* will take their Meafures from them. You ought not to take Exceptions at any thing that I have prov'd; for I do not defpife the *Europeans*, tho' indeed I can't but pity 'em. You fay well in alledging that I place no difference between a Rogue and what you call a Man of [156] Honour. My Apprehenfion indeed is flat enough; but for a long time I have Convers'd with the *French* on purpofe to know what they mean by their Man of Honour. To be fure the Word can't be apply'd to a *Huron*, who is a Stranger to Silver, fince a moneylefs Man is no Man of Honour in your way. 'Twere an eafie matter to make my Slave a Man of Honour, by carrying him to *Paris*, and furnifhing him with a hundred Packs of Beaver Skins, to anfwer the charge of a Coach and ten or twelve Footmen. As foon as he appears in an Embroider'd Suit with fuch a Retinue, he'l be Saluted by every one, and Introduc'd to the greateft Treats, and the higheft Company: And if he does but regale the Gentlemen, and make Prefents to the Ladies, he paffes in courfe for a Man of Senfe and Merit: He'l be call'd the

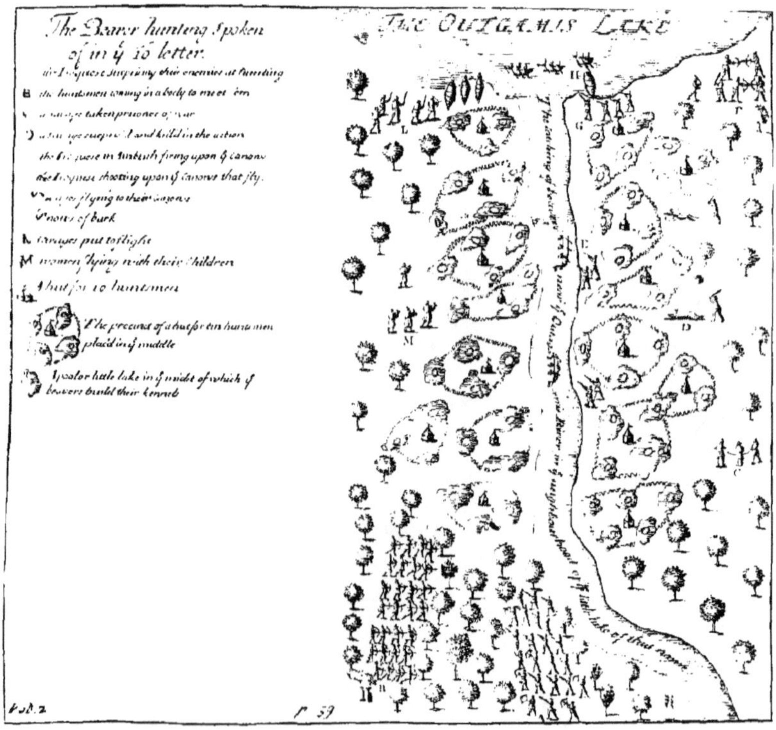

The Beaver hunting spoken of in ye 10 letter.
B the huntsmen coming in a body to meet 'em
the Iroquese shooting upon ye Canows that fly.
L Savages put to flight
M women flying with their Children
A hut for 10 huntsmen
The precinct of a hut for ten huntsmen plac'd in ye middle
beavers build their kennels
THE OUTAGAMIS LAKE
Vol. 2
P. 59

King of the *Hurons*, and every one will give out, that his Country is full of Gold Mines, that himself is the moft Puiffant Prince in *America*, that he is a Man of Senfe and talks moft agreeably in Company; that he is redoubted by all his Neighbours; in fine, he'l be fuch a Man of Honour as moft of your *French* Footmen come to be after they have made fhift, by infamous and deteftable means, to pick up as much Money as will fetch that pompous Equipage. Ha! my dear Brother, if I could but read, I could find out a great many fine things that now I do not know. You fhould not then get off for hearing me mention the few Diforders that I obferv'd among the *Europeans;* for I would then mufter you up a great many more, whether in Wholefale or Retail. I do not believe that there's any one Vocation or Rank of Men that would not be found liable to juft Cenfure, if examin'd by one that can Read and Write. And in my Opinion [157] 'twere better for the *French* that they were Strangers to Reading and Writing: Every Day gives us frefh Inftances of an infinity of Difputes among the *Coureurs de Bois* upon the account of *Writings*, which tend to nothing but Litigiouf- nefs and Law Suits. One bit of Paper is enough to ruin a whole Family. With a flip of a Letter a Woman betrays her Husband, and concerts ways to have her turn ferv'd; a Mother fells her Daughter, and a Forger of Writings cheats whom he pleafes. In your Books which are publifh'd every Day, you write Lies and impertinent Stories; and yet you would fain have me to Read and Write like the *French*. No, my dear Brother, I had rather live without Knowledge, than to Read and Write such things as the *Hurons* abhor. We can do all our Business with reference to our Hunting and our Military Adventures, by the help of our Hieroglyphicks. You know very well that the Characters which we draw upon the peel'd Trees in our Passages, comprehend all the Particulars of a Hunting or Warlike Expedition, and that all who see these Marks know what they signifie.[1] Now, pray, what occasion have we for more? The Communion of Goods among the *Hurons* supersedes the use of Writing. We have no Posts nor no Horses in our Forrests for Couriers to ride upon to *Quebec*. We make Peace and War without Writing, and employ only Ambassadors that carry the Faith and Promise of the Nation. Our Boundaries are adjusted without Writing: And as for the Sciences that you study, they would be of no use to us; for, to instance in *Geography*, we have no mind to puzzle our Brains in the reading of Books of Voyages that contradict one another; and are not in the humour to abdicate our Country, which you know we are [158] so minutely acquainted with, that the least Brook does not scape our Calculation. *Astronomy* would be equally useless; for we reckon the Years by the Moons, and so many Winters stand for an equal number of Years. *Navigation* would be yet less serviceable, for we have no Ships: And *Fortification* can bring us no Advantage, in regard that a Fort of single Palissadoes is to us a sufficient guard from the Arrows and the Surprises of our Enemies, who are Strangers to Artillery. In a Word, consid-

---

[1] See pp. 512-515, *ante*.—ED.

ering our way of living, Writing can do us no good. All that I value in the whole Circle of your Sciences, is *Arithmetick:* I can't but own that that Science pleases me infinitely well, tho' at the same time I am sensible that those who are vers'd in it are not free from great Errors. There is no Trade or Profession among the *French* that I like, excepting that which runs in the way of *Commerce;* that indeed I look upon as a Lawful Calling, and that which is most necessary for our Welfare. The Merchants are welcome to us; sometimes they bring us good Commodities, and some of 'em being Men of Justice and Probity are satisfied with a moderate Gain: They run great hazards, they advance beforehand, they lend, they stay for their due; in fine, I know many Dealers that have a just and reasonable Soul, and have oblig'd our Nation very much. But at the same time there are others who act with no other view than to make an exorbitant Profit upon Goods that have a good shew and are worth but little, particularly Axes, Kettles, Powder, Guns, &c. which we are not qualified to know. This makes it to appear, that in all the Ranks and Degrees of the *Europeans* there's something that ought to be dislik'd. This is a certain truth, that if a Merchant has not an upright Heart, and a [159] sufficient stock of Vertue to withstand the various Temptations to which his Business lays him open, he violates every foot the measures of Justice, Equity, Charity, Sincerity, and true Faith. Are not they chargeable with flaming Wickedness, when they give us sorry Commodities in exchange for our Beaver Skins, which a blind

Man may deal in without being cheated? I have done, my dear Brother, I muft now return to the Village, where I'll ftay for you to Morrow after Dinner.

Lahontan. I am come, *Adario*, to thy Apartment, to pay my Refpects to thy Grandfather, who I hear lies very ill. 'Tis to be fear'd that the good old Gentleman may be long afflicted with the uneafinefs he now complains of; one would think that a Man of his Age, who reckons upon Seventy Years, might refrain the fhooting of Turtle-Doves. I've obferv'd for a long time, that your old Folks are always in Motion and Action, which is the ready way to exhauft fpeedily the little Strength that's left 'em. I'll tell thee, *Adario*, thou muft fend one of thy Slaves for my Surgeon, who underftands Phyfick well enough; for I'm morally affur'd that he'l give him eafe in a Minute: This Feaver is fo inconfiderable that it can't reach his Life, unlefs it reaches to a greater height.

Adario. Thou knoweft very well, my dear Brother, that I have been a mortal Enemy to your Phyficians, ever fince I faw ten or twelve Perfons die in their Hands, through the tyranny of their Remedies. My Grandfather that you take to be Seventy Years old is full Ninety eight. He Marry'd at Thirty Years of Age; my Father was Marry'd at Thirty two, and I am now Thirty five Years old. 'Tis true he is of a [160] ftrong Conftitution, and that this Age could not be attain'd in *Europe*, where People die earlier. One of thefe Days I'll fhew you fourteen or fifteen old Men that are turn'd of a Hundred, nay one of 'em a Hundred and twenty four. I knew another that dy'd fix Years ago at the Age of a Hundred and forty.[1] As for the reftlefs Life that you find fault with in our old Men, I can affure you on the contrary, that if they lay loytering upon their Mats in the Huts, and did nothing but Eat, Drink and Sleep, they would become heavy and dull and unfit for Action; and for as much as their continuall reft would hinder the infenfible Tranfpiration, the Humours then recoyling would rejoin the Blood, and thus by a natural effect their Limbs and Kidneys would be fo infeebled and wafted, that a mortal Phthifick would enfue. This is an Obfervation of long ftanding, that proves true in all the Nations of *Canada*. The Jugglers are to be here prefently to try their Skill, and to find out what Meat or Fifh is requifite for the cure of this Diftemper. My Slaves are now ready to go either a Hunting or Fifhing, and if you'l tarry an Hour or two with me, you fhall fee the apifh tricks of thefe Mountebanks, whom we know to be fuch when we are well, and yet fend for 'em with great impatience when any dangerous Diftemper feizes us.

Lahontan. You muft confider, my dear *Adario*, that in fuch cafes our Mind is fick as well as the Body. We in *Europe* do the fame thing by our Phyficians. When a Man enjoys his Health he hates and avoids the Phyficians; but when he apprehends himfelf out of order, notwithftanding that he knows the uncertainty of their Art, he calls a Confultation of a Dozen: Some who have no other Illnefs than what Fancy fuggefts, [161] do melt down their Bodies by fuch Remedies

---

[1] On the subject of Indian longevity, see p. 431, note 2, *ante*.— ED.

as would kill a Horſe. I own, indeed, that you have no ſuch Fools among you; but to make the Parallel even, you take no care of your Health; for you run at the Hunting ſtark naked from Morning to Night; you dance three or four Hours an end till you ſweat again, and the playing at the Ball in a Company of ſix or ſeven Hundred Perſons on a ſide, to toſs it half a League one way or t'other, is an infinite Fatigue to your Bodies; it infeebles the Parts, diſperſes the Spirits, ſowers the maſs of Blood and Humours, and breaks the union of their Principles. At this rate a Man that might otherwiſe have liv'd a Hundred Years is ſweep'd off at Eighty.

Adario. Suppoſing all you ſay to be true, what ſignifies it for a Man to live ſo long, ſince Life is a ſort of Death after that Age? Perhaps your Reaſons may bear as to the *French*, the generality of whom being lazy and ſlothful, have an averſion to all manner of violent Exerciſes. They are of the ſame temper with our ſuperannuated Perſons, that live in ſuch a ſtupid inſenſible way; that they never ſtir out of their Huts but when they take Fire. Our Temperaments and Complexions are as widely different from yours as Night from Day: And that remarkable difference that I obſerve between the *Europeans* and the People of *Canada*, upon all things in general, is to me an Argument that we are not deſcended of your pretended *Adam*. Among us you ſhan't hear in an Age, of one that is Hunch-back'd, or Lame, or Dwarfiſh, or Deaf, or Dumb, or Blind from their Infancy, and far leſs any that is One-ey'd; for when a one-ey'd Creature comes into the World among us, we look upon it as a Preſage of the enſuing

Calamity [162] of the Nation, and have frequently experienc'd the truth of the Prophecy. A one-ey'd Creature is equally deftitute of Senfe and of an upright Heart; he is Malicious, Goatifh and Slothful to the laft degree; he is more cowardly than a Hare, and never goes a Hunting for fear of running his one Eye againft the Branch of a Tree. As for our Difeafes, we know no fuch thing as your *Dropfies*, *Afthmas*, *Palfy's*, *Gout* and *Pox*. The *Leprofy*, the *Lethargy*, *External Swellings*, the *Suppreffion of Urine*, the *Stone* and the *Gravel*, are Diftempers that we are not acquainted with; to the great Aftonifhment of the *French*, who are fo liable to 'em. *Fevers* indeed reign among us, efpecially upon our return from any Warlike Expedition, and proceed from our lying in the open Air, our croffing of Marfhes, wading over Rivers, our fafting two or three Days at a time, eating cold Victuals, *&c.* Sometimes *Pleurifies* prove mortal to us, when we heat our felves with running, whether in Military or Hunting Adventures, and then drink fuch Water as we are unacquainted with: And *Colicks* attack us now and then upon the fame occafion. We are fubject to the *Meazles* and the *Small Pox*, and that we owe to one of two Reafons. Either we eat fo much Fifh, that the Blood it produces is of a different temper from that proceeding from Meat, and thereupon boils in the Veffels with greater Violence, and throws out its thick and coarfe Particles upon the infenfible Pores of the Skin. Or elfe the bad Air pen'd up in our Villages for want of Windows to our Huts, makes fo much Fire and Smoak, that the difproportion between the Particles of the confin'd Air and thofe of our Blood and

Humours, gives rife to such Infirmities. Now these are the only Distempers that visit us.

[163] *Lahontan*. This, my dear *Adario*, is the first time I have heard thee reason justly since the Commencement of our Conferences. I acknowledge, you are exempted from an infinity of Evils that lie heavy upon us, and the reason of this Happiness may be gather'd from what you offer'd t'other Day, namely, *That the repose of one's Mind is the greatest Ingredient of Health*. The *Hurons* being confin'd to the bare knowledge of Hunting, do not fatigue their Spirits, and impair their Healths, in the pursuit of an infinity of fine Sciences, in watching unseasonably, breaking their rest and toiling hard at the studious Anvil. With us, a Man bred to the Sword makes it his business to read and know the History of the Wars that have happen'd in the World, and to make himself acquainted with the Art of Fortifying, Attacking and Defending Places: This ingrosses his whole time, which after all is too little to procure him the Accomplishments he desires. A Man that takes to the Church plyes the Study of *Theology* Night and Day, for the good and interest of Religion; he writes Books to instruct People in the concerns of their Salvation, and Dedicating to God the Hours, the Days, the Months, and the Years of his Life, receives after this Life an Eternal Inheritance by way of Recompence. Our Judges apply themselves to the knowledge of the Laws Night and Day, they examin Bills and Processes; they give continual Audience to an infinity of Plaintiffs that teaze 'em without Intermission; in fine they can scarce spare leisure to Eat or Drink. Our

Phyficians purfue the Science of rendring Men Immortal, they run about from Patient to Patient, from Hofpital to Hofpital, in order to learn the Nature and the Caufe of different Diftempers: They rack [164] their Brains in unlocking the Qualities of Drugs, Herbs and Simples, by a thoufand uncommon and curious Experiments. The *Cofmographers* and *Aftronomers* bend all their thoughts upon the difcovery of the Figure, Magnitude and Compofition of Heaven and Earth. The former can trace the leaft Star in the Firmament, they meafure its courfe, its diftance from the Ecliptick, its afcenfion and declination: The latter know how to diftinguifh Climates, and the various Pofitions of the Globe of the Earth; they are acquainted with the Seas, Lakes, Rivers, Ifles, Gulfs; they compute the diftances of one Country from another; and in fine, all the Nations of the World are known to them, as well as their Religions, their Laws, their Languages, their Cuftoms, and their various Forms of Government. To wind up all into one Word, all the Profeffors of Sciences are very fenfible that they purfue their Studies with too much Application, and thereby murder their Health. For the animal Spirits are not ftrain'd out in the Brain, but in proportion to the fupplies of fine Blood that it receives from the Heart; and the Heart being a Mufcle can't fquirt out the Blood into all the parts of the Body without the Influence of the animal Spirits. Now, when the Soul is Serene and all Tranquility as thine is, the Brain fupplies all the parts of the Body with as much as they have occafion for in order to perform the Offices allotted 'em by Nature: Whereas in the cafe of a profound

Application to Sciences, the Soul being tofs'd and perplex'd with a croud of Thoughts, the Spirits are much exhaufted and difpers'd, both by long watchings and by the racking of the Imagination. In this cafe all the Spirits that the Brain can form are fcarce fufficient to recruit the parts employ'd by the Soul [165] in the precipitant Motions it calls for; and there being but a fmall Stock of Spirits in the Nerves, which convey 'em to the parts that minifter to the Digeftion of what we eat, their Fibres have a languid drooping motion: And thus it comes to pafs that the Actions of the Body are lamely perform'd, the Digeftion is imperfect, the Serum flies off from the Blood, and by falling upon the Head, the Limbs, the Nerves, the Breaft and other parts, gives rife to the Dropfy, Gout, and Palfy; and to all the other Difeafes you took notice of but now.

Adario. At that rate, my dear Brother, it muft be only the Learned Men that fall into fuch Diforders: And upon that foot, I hope you'll own that one had better be a *Huron* than a *Science-Hunter*, confidering that Health is the moft valuable of all good things. But at the fame time, I know very well that thefe Diftempers have no refpect of Perfons, but fall upon the Ignorant as well as thofe of a greater Character. Not that I deny what thou fayeft, for I am fully convinc'd that *Brain-Work* infeebles the Body extreamly; and I have often wonder'd how your Conftitution comes to be fo ftrong, as to keep up againft the violent Shocks of Difcontent and Fret, that you feel when things go crofs with you. I have feen fome *French*

Men tear their Hair, others cry and weep bitterly like Women Burning at a Stake, others again abstain from eating or drinking for two days, and suffer such violent Sallies of Passion as to dash every thing in pieces that came in their way: And when all came to all, their Health did not appear to be affected. Questionless, their Nature must be different from ours; for there's never a *Huron* in the World that would not die in a days time upon incountring the hundredth part of such Transports. Ay, most certainly, [166] you are of a different Mould from us; for your Wines, your Brandy, and your Spices, make us Sick unto death; whereas you can't live forsooth without such Drugs: Besides, your Blood is Salt and ours is not; you have got Beards, and we have none. Nay farther; I have observ'd that before you pass the Age of thirty five or forty, you are Stronger and more Robust than we; for we can't carry such heavy Loads as you do till that Age; but after that your Strength dwindles and visibly declines, whereas ours keeps to its wonted pitch till we count fifty five or sixty years of Age. This is a truth that our young Women can vouch for. They tell you that when a young *French-man* obliges 'em six times a night, a young *Huron* do's not rise to above half the number; and with the same Breath they declare, that the *French* are older in that Trade at thirty five, than the *Hurons* are at fifty years of Age. This intelligence given in by our good Girles, who are better pleas'd with your young Men's over-doing, than with the Moderation of our Youths; This intelligence, I say, led me to think that your Gout, Dropfy, Phthifick, Palfy, Stone, and Gravel, and the other Diftempers above mention'd, are certainly occafion'd, not only by the immoderatenefs of thefe Pleafures, but by the unfeafonablenefs of the time, and the inconveniency of the way in which you purfue 'em; for when you have but juft done eating, or are newly come off a fatiguing bout, you lie with your Women as often as ever you can, and that either upon Chairs, or in a Standing Pofture, without confidering the Damage that accrues from fuch indifcretion: Witnefs the common practice of thefe young Sparks in the Village of *Doffenra*, who make their Table ferve for a Bed. For the purpofe; you are fubject to two Difeafes more, [167] that we are free from. The firft is that call'd by the *Illinefe, the hot Diftemper*, for that People are liable to it as well as thofe who live upon the *Miffifipi*. This Malady goes by the Name of the *Venereal Diftemper* in your Country. The other is that you call the *Scurvy*, which we Style, the *cold evil*, with regard to the Symptoms and Caufes of that Diftemper, that we have obferv'd fince the Arrival of the *French* in *Canada*. You fee therefore that you are liable to a great many Difeafes, and thofe fuch as are not eafily Cur'd. Inftead of retrieving your Health, your Phyficians murder you, by exhibiting Remedies calculated for their own Intereft, which fpin out the Diftemper and kill you at laft. A Phyfician would be ftill Poor if he cur'd his Patients fpeedily. The men of that Profeffion are cautious of approving of our way of Sweating; for they know the confequence of it too well, and when their Advice is ask'd upon the matter, their Anfwer is to this purpofe. *None but fools are capable of imitating fools; the Savages have not the name of Savages for nothing; and their Remedies are as Savage as themfelves. If 'tis true that after Sweating, they throw themfelves into cold Water or into Snow, without prefent death; their good luck is owing to the Air of the Climate, and to their way of Feeding, which differs from ours. But notwithftanding this favourable Circumftance, fuch and fuch a Savage, that would otherwife have outliv'd a hundred years of age, was cut off at eighty by the ufe of that terrible Remedy.* Such is the Language of your Phyficians, by which they mean to fcare the *Europeans* from the ufe of our Remedies: Tho' at the fame time, 'tis certain that if you had a mind to Sweat after our way now and then, you might do it with the greateft eafe and fafety in the World, and by that means all the evil Humours engendred in [168] your Blood by your Wine, your Spices, your intemperate Venery, your Unfeafonable Watching and your other Fatigues, would be evacuated by the Pores of the Skin. Were this Method follow'd, you might bid an eternal Adieu to Phyfick, and all its Poifonous Ingredients. This, my dear Brother, is as manifeft as the Sun-Shine; tho' 'twill not go down with the Ignorant, who talk of nothing but Pleurifies and Rheumatifms, as the Confequents of this Cure. 'Tis ftrange, methinks, they will not give Ear to the Anfwer we make to the Objection Started by your Phyficians againft our way of Sweating. 'Tis an undifputed Truth that Nature is a good kind Mother, which defires to eternife our Lives; and yet we plague and torment her fo violently, that fometimes she's brought to a low and weak condition, and is scarce able to Succour us. Our Debauches and Fatigues create deprav'd Humours, which Nature would throw out of the Body, if She had but Strength enough to open the Gates, *viz.* the Pores of the Skin. 'Tis true she expells as much as she can, by Urine and Stool, by the Mouth, Nose, and insensible Transpiration: But sometimes the quantity of the Serosities is so overbearing that they overflow all the parts of the Body between the Skin and the Flesh: And in that case 'tis our business to procure their egress the speedyest and shortest way, for fear their longer stay should give rise to this Gout, Rheumatism, Dropsy, Palsy, and all the other Distempers that sink a healthy State. Now, to compass this end, we must unlock the Pores by the means of Sweating; and withal take care to shut 'em soon after, lest the nutritive juice should glide out by the same passage; which can be no otherwise prevented than by throwing our selves into cold Water, as we usually do. [169] 'Tis the same case as if Wolves were got into your Sheep Folds; for then you would open the Doors that the mischievous Animals might turn out; but after they're once out of Doors, you would not fail to shut 'em again for fear your Sheep should run after 'em. I own indeed that your Physicians say well, when they plead that a Man who has over-heated himself by Hunting or any violent Exercise, indangers his Life by throwing himself immediately into cold Water. That I take to be an uncontested truth; for the Blood which in that Case is agitated and boils as it were in the Veins, would certainly congeal; just as boiling Water congeals sooner than cold Water, when expos'd to the Froft or put into a cold Fountain. This is the Sum of my Thoughts upon that Head. As to what remains, I grant we are liable to Difeafes, that equally invade both us and the *French;* namely, the Small-Pox, Fevers, Pleurifies, and fometimes to what you call the Hypochondriac Illnefs: For we have fome Fools among us who fancy they are poffefs'd by a little *Manitou* or Spirit of the bignefs of one's Fift; which in our Language we call *Aoutaerobi;* and affirm that this Spirit is lodg'd in their Body, and particularly in a certain Member that ails never fo little. This imaginary Diftemper proceeds from their Simplicity and weaknefs of Mind: For in fhort, we are not without ignorant foolifh Fellows among us, no more than you. You may fee every day fome *Hurons,* above fifty years of Age, who have lefs Senfe and Difcretion than a young Girl; fome who are as Superftitious as your felves, in believing that the Spirit of Dreams is the Ambaffadour and Meffenger whom the Great Spirit imploys to acquaint Men with their Duty. As for our Jugglers, they are Mountebanks and Cheats of the fame form with your Phyficians; [170] only they content themfelves with the having of good Chear at their Patient's coft, without fending 'em to the other World in acknowledgment of their Feafts and Prefents.[1]

Lahontan. My deareft *Adario,* I honour thee beyond all expreffion, for now thou argueft juftly. You never fpoke more to the purpofe in your life time. Every word you have faid

---

[1] The feaft was one of the chief ceremonies connected with the efforts of the medicine men to expel difeafe; in this, the conjurer played the part of hoft. See *Jes. Rel*, x, pp 179, 183, 197; l, p. 295 — ED

of Sweating is absolutely true; and I know it to be so by experience, insomuch that while I live, I will never use any other Remedy than your way of Sweating. But at the same time, I would not have you run down Bleeding, so much as you did t'other day, when you endeavour'd by a multiplicity of Arguments to make out the necessity of saving our Blood, as being the Treasure of Life. I do not dispute its being the Treasure of Life; but I must needs say that your Remedies against Pleuresies and Inflamations, take effect only by chance, for out of twenty Sick People commonly fifteen die; whereas Bleeding in such a case might Cure 'em all. I own that this method of Cure shortens their lives, and that a man that has Bled often can't hold out so long as another that has done it but seldom; but a Man lying on a Sick Bed, wants to be cur'd at any rate, and thinks of nothing else but the present recovery of his Health; tho' it should cost him the Substraction of some years from his life, together with the loss of his Blood. In fine, all the Remarks I have made on the Subject in hand, center in this; that the People of *Canada* have a better Complexion than the *Europeans*, that they are more Indefatigable and Robust, more inur'd to Watching, Fasting and other hardships, more insensible of Cold and Heat; insomuch that they are not only exempted from the Passions that tumble and disturb *our* Souls, but likewise shelter'd from the Infirmities that *we* groan under. You are [171] poor and miserable, but at the same time you have the benefit of perfect health: But we who enjoy the Conveniences of Life and the Instruments of Ease, are forc'd either thro' Complaisance or by the occafional Adventures of life, to Murder our felves by an infinity of Debauches, to which you are never expos'd.

Adario. My Brother, I come to Vifit thee, and am accompany'd by my Daughter, who is about to Marry, againft my Will, a young Man that's as good a Warriour as he's a forry Huntfman. She has a mind to't; and that is enough in our Country: But 'tis not fo in *France*, where the Parents muft confent to the Marrying of their Children. I am oblig'd to comply with my Daughter's demands: For if I pretend to Marry her again, fhe'd quickly return upon me; *What do you think Father! Am I your Slave? Shall not I enjoy my Liberty? Muft I for your fancy, Marry a Man I do not care for? How can I endure a Husband that buys my Corps of my Father, and what value fhall I have for fuch a Father as makes Brokerage of his Daughter to a Brute? And how can I have an affection for the Children of a Man I cannot love? If I fhould Marry him in obedience to you, and go from him in fifteen days time, as the Priviledges and natural Liberties of the Nation would allow; you'll tell me 'tis not well done; and 'twould trouble you, all the World would laugh at it, and perhaps I might prove with Child.* Thus, dear Brother, would my Girl anfwer me, and it may be a great deal worfe, as it happened fome years ago to one of our old Men, who pretended to Marry his Daughter to a Man fhe did not love, for in my Prefence fhe faid a great many harfh things by way of Reproach: Infinuating that a Man of Spirit ought not to expofe himfelf, in offering to advife a Perfon from whom he may [172] receive fuch affronts; neither ought he to require such respects from his Children as he knows to be impracticable. She added then, *'twas true she was his Daughter, and he might be satisfied. He got her upon a Woman he loved as much as she hated the Husband her Father had provided for her.* You must know, we never have a Marriage contracted between Relations, let the degree be never so remote.[1] Our Women never Marry again after they're forty years of Age, because the Children they have after that Age are generally of a weakly Constitution. Not that they are the more Continent for this: On the contrary, you'll find them more passionately inclin'd than a Girl of twenty. And 'tis for this reason that they entertain the *French* so kindly; nay, and sometimes give themselves the trouble to follow them. However you know that our Women are not so Fruitful as the *French*, tho' they admit of more frequent Embraces; which to me is very strange, for 'tis quite contrary to what might be expected.

Lahontan. 'Tis for the same reason, my poor *Adario*, that they Conceive not so easily as ours. If they did not indulge themselves too much in the frequency of Embraces, and receive 'em with an over-bearing Keenness, the Matter calculated for the production of Children, would have time to assume the necessary qualities for the business of Generation. It's the same case with a Field that is Sowed continually without being suffered to ly Fallow, for at last it will produce nothing (as Experience plainly shews;) on the other side, if you forbear the Ground, the Earth regains its force, the

---

[1] Marriage between members of the same gens was forbidden among many of the Indian tribes, as such persons were assumed to be consanguine.—ED.

Serene Air, the Rain and the Sun give it a new Sap, which makes the Seed to Sprout. But prithee, my dear Friend, suffer me to ask thee one Question. What is the reason that the Women-Savages, being so rarely [173] Fruitful, have the Increase of their Nation so little in view, that a Woman shall make her self Miscarry when the Father of the Child dies, or is kill'd, before she is brought to Bed? You'll tell me, she do's it to save her Reputation; because, without that Precaution she would never have another Husband. But it would seem the Interest of the Nation, which lies in its Increase and Multiplication, is but little regarded by your Women. Now, it is not so with ours, for, as you said t'other day, our *Coureurs de Bois* and many others, find very often new Children in their Houses, at their return from their Journeys: But they are not much dissatisfied, upon the consideration, that this adds so many Bodys for the Nation, and so many Souls for Heaven: Tho' after all, their Women undergo as much disgrace upon such occasions as yours do, and sometimes are Imprisoned for Life, while yours are allow'd to entertain as many Gallants as they please afterwards. 'Tis a most abominable piece of Cruelty for a Woman to make away with her Child: A Crime which the Author of Life will never pardon: And this is one of the greatest Abuses to be reformed among you. You ought to discountenance Nakedness too; for the liberty which your Boys have of going Naked, makes a terrible Hurricane in the Minds of your young Girls; as they are not made of Brass, so the view of those parts which decency forbids me to name, can't but call up the Amorous Fire, especially when the young Wantons shew that Nature is neither dead nor untrue to the Adventures of Love.

Adario. I take it, you account for the Barrenness of our Women admirably; for I perceive how that may come to pass: And as for the Criminal Practice of our young Women in taking [174] Potions to make themselves Miscarry; I find your Reflections upon it are very just. But what you say of Nakedness do's not stand to Reason. I allow that in a Nation where distinctions of Property are acknowledg'd, you are very much in the right of it, to cover not only such parts as ought not to be nam'd, but even all the parts of the Body. What use would the *French* make of their Gold and their Silver, if they did not imploy it in providing themselves with fine Cloaths? Since in your Country Men are valued according to their Dress, is it not a great advantage to be able to cover any Defect in Nature with a handsome Habit? In earnest, Nakedness ought not to offend any but such as allow Property. A deform'd or decrepit Man among you has found the Secret of appearing Handsome or well Dress'd, in a Beau Perriwig and fine Cloaths; under which 'tis impossible to distinguish Artificial Shapes from such as are Natural. Besides, 'twould be a great inconveniency for the *Europeans* to go Naked; for those who are well provided would then find so much Imployment, and earn so much Mony for good Services, that they would not dream of Marrying as long as they liv'd; not to mention that the promising Aspect would tempt the Married Women to violate their Conjugal Vows. Now, these reasons can have no place among us, where every thing must fit, whether great or little, for the young Women taking a view of the Naked parts, make their choice by the Eye: And for as much as Nature has obferv'd the meafures of Proportion in both Sexes, any Woman may be well affur'd what fhe has to expect from a Husband. Our Women are as Fickle as yours, and [175] for that reafon the moft defpicable Man here never defpairs of having a Wife; for as every thing appears naked and open to fight, fo every Girl choofes according to her Fancy, without regarding the meafures of Proportion. Some love a well fhaped Man let a certain matter about him be never fo little. Others make choice of an ill fhap'd forry like Fellow, by reafon of the goodly fize of I know not what; and others again pick out a Man of Spirit and Vigour tho' he be neither well fhap'd nor well provided in [the] namelefs Quarter.

This, my dear Brother, is all the Anfwer I have to give to your Charge upon the fcore of Nudity; which you know lies only againft the Youths; for our married Men and Widows cover themfelves both before and behind with a great deal of Nicety. And, befides, to make fome Compenfation for the Nudity of our Boys, our Girls are Modefter than yours, for they expofe nothing to open view but the Calf of their Leg, whereas yours lay their Breafts open in fuch a Fafhion that our young Men run their Nofes into 'em when they bargain about the Beaver Skins with your handfom She-merchants. Is not this a Grievance among the *French* that wants to be Redrefs'd? For I have it from very good Hands, that fcarce any *French* Woman can refift the temptation of an object that's mov'd by her naked Breasts. A due reformation of this indecent Custom would be a means to preserve their Husbands from the Chimerical Distemper of Horns, which you plant upon their Foreheads without ever touching or seeing them, and that by a Miracle I can't fathom: For if I plant an Apple-tree in a Garden it does not grow upon the top of a Rock; and in like manner one would think your invisible Horns should take root only [176] in the place where their Seed is sown, and appear in the Foreheads of the Women, as being a just representation of the Husbands and the Spark's Tools. In fine, this whim of the Horns is a horrid piece of Indiscretion; for why should you affront the Husband because his Wife takes her Pleasure? If in Marriage a Man marries a Woman's Vices, then the *French* way of Marriage is an Oath that runs counter to right Reason, or else a Man must keep his Wife under Lock and Key to avoid the dishonour of her Vices. The Husbands that retain to the horned List must needs be very numerous; for I can't imagine that a Woman can brook the severity of an eternal Chain, without having recourse to some good Friend to soften her Affliction. I should pardon the *French* if they made the Marriage to stand only upon certain Conditions, that is upon the *Proviso* that the Woman have Children, and that both she and her Husband keep their Health, so as to be able to discharge the Marriage Duties as they ought to do. This is all the Regulation that can be made in a Nation that stands to *Meum* and *Tuum*.——You *Christians* have another impertinent Custom, which I can't but take notice of. Your Men glory in the

Debauching of Women, as if yielding to the Temptations of Love were not equally Criminal in either Sex. Your young Sparks use their utmost Efforts to tempt the Maids and married Women; they set all means at work to compass their end; and when Masters of their Wishes talk publickly of the Adventure; upon which every body Censures the Lady, and cries up the Cavalier, whereas the former merits a Pardon, and the latter deserves to be Punish'd. How d'ye think your Women should be Faithful to you, if you are Faithless to them? If the [177] married Men keep their Cracks, will not their Wives keep Company with other Lovers? And if a Husband prefers Gaming and Drinking to his Wive's Company, will not his Wife Solace her self in the Company of a Friend? Would you have your Wives to be Wise and Discreet, and like ours, you must Love 'em as your selves, and take care not to sell 'em; for I know some Husbands among you, that consent as shamefully to the Debauching of their Wives, as some Mothers do to the Prostituting of their Daughters, and in such cases Necessity obliges 'em to it. From hence it appears, that 'tis a great Happiness for the *Hurons* that they are not reduc'd to the practice of such mean Actions, as Misery occasions among those who are not inur'd to it. We are at all times neither rich nor poor, and our Happiness upon this score goes far beyond all your Riches; for we are not forc'd to expose our Wives and Daughters to sale, in order to live upon their Drudgery in the way of Love. You'l say our Wives and Daughters are foolish and simple; and indeed I grant the Allegation, for they can't write *Billet dou's* to their Acquaintances as yours do; nay, if they could write they have not the fenfe to fingle out by the Rules of Phyfiognomy a faithful old Woman that fhall carry their Love-letters, and obferve a profound Silence. O! that curfed Writing; that pernicious Invention of the *Europeans* who tremble at the fight of their own *Chimera's*, which they draw themfelves, by the ranking and difpofal of three and twenty fmall Figures, that are Calculated, not for the Inftruction but for the Perplexing of Men's Minds. According to your Notions of things, the *Hurons* are likewife foolifh in not minding the lofs of a Maiden-head in the Girls they take in Marriage, and in [178] condefcending to marry the very Women that their own Companions have turn'd off: But prithee tell me, Brother, are the *French* the wifer for fancying that a Girl is a Maid becaufe fhe cries and fwears 'tis fo? Nay, fuppofing her to be a true Maid, is the Conqueft the greater? No, fure, on the contrary the Husband is oblig'd to teach her a Trade that fhe'll practife with others at a time when he is not in a condition to continue the daily Exercife. As for our marrying Women feparated from former Husbands, is not that the fame thing as marrying a Widow, with this difference only, that our Women have all reafon to be perfwaded that we Love 'em, whereas your Widows have reafon to believe that you marry their Riches rather than their Perfons. How many Families are reduc'd to diforder or Ruin by fuch Marriages with Widows? But after all you do not pretend to redrefs fuch diforders, becaufe the evil is incurable as long as the Conjugal Tye lafts for Life. Once more,

I'll take the liberty to mention another piece of Madnefs practis'd among you, which indeed is down right Cruelty to my Mind. Your Marriages are indiffolvable, and yet a Youth and a Girl that burn in the mutual flames of Love, can't marry without the confent of their Parents. Both the one and the other muft marry who their Fathers pleafe, in oppofition to their own Inclination, tho' their Averfion to the Perfon propos'd be fo great, that they hate him mortally. The inequality of Age, Eftate and Birth is the fource of all thefe Inconveniences; they overrule the mutual Love of the two Parties that like one another. What Cruelty! What Tyranny! and that practis'd by a Father upon his own Children. Do you meet with fuch things among the *Hurons*? Among them [179] every one's as Rich and as Noble as his Neighbour; the Women are entitled to the fame Liberty with the Men, and the Children enjoy the fame Privileges with their Fathers. A young *Huron* may marry one of his Mother's Slaves, and neither Father nor Mother are impower'd to hinder him. This Slave by fo doing becomes a free Woman; and fince her Beauty pleafes, why fhould not the Youth prefer her to the great General's Daughter that is not fo handfome? To continue the faults of your Conftitution: Is it not a piece of Injuftice among you who abhor a community of Goods, that a Nobleman or Gentleman fhould give his eldeft Son almoft all that he has, and force the other Brethren and Sifters to reft fatisfied with a Trifle, tho' perhaps that eldeft Son is not a Lawful Child, and all the reft are? The Confequence of this is, that they throw their Daughters into perpetual

Prisons, with a sort of Barbarity which is not suitable to the Christian Charity that the Jesuits preach up. As for the other Sons, they are forc'd to turn Priests and Monks, in order to live by the fine Trade of praying to God against their will, of preaching what they do not practise, and of persuading others into the belief of what they disbelieve themselves. If any of 'em take up a Military Profession, they design the pillaging the Nation more than the guarding off her Enemies. The *French* do not fight for the Interest of their Country as we do; 'tis their own Interest and preferment to higher Posts that they have in view. The Love of their Country and of their Fellow-Citizens does not prevail so much with them as Vanity, Ambition and Riches. In fine, my dear Brother, I conclude this Discourse in assuring thee, That the Christians Self-love is a piece of Folly that [180] the *Hurons* will ever condemn; and that Folly which tinctures all your Actions is remarkable in a distinguishing manner in the way of your Amours and Marriages; which, I must say, is as unaccountable as the People are who suffer themselves to be catch'd in that Noose.

Lahontan. Adario, you remember I set forth before, that the Actions of Rogues are no Standard for those of honourable Men. I own the Justness of your Censure as to some Actions, which we also disallow of. I acknowledge that the distinction of Property is the source of an infinity of Passions, of which you are clear'd. But if you take things by the right handle, especially our way of making Love and Marrying, the good order of our Families, and the Education of our Children,

to North-America. 615

you'l find a wonderful Conduct in all our Constitutions. That Liberty which the *Hurons* preach up occasions dismal Disorders. In their way the Children are Masters as well as the Fathers; and Wives who ought naturally to be subject to their Husbands are invested with an equal Authority. The Daughters scorn the Advice of their Mothers when there's a Lover in the case. In a Word, all this scene of Liberty reduces the way of Life to a continued course of Debauchery, by granting to Nature, in Imitation of the Brutes, an unlimited satisfaction to all its Demands. Your single Women place their Wisdom in concerting and concealing their lewd Adventures. To run with *a Match in your Villages, is the same thing as strolling after a Whore in ours. All your young Men roll from Hut to Hut upon such Adventures while the Night lasts.

*i. e. *to enter into a Woman's Apartment in the Night time with a Light.*

The Doors of every Girls Chambers are open to all Guests, [181] and if a young Man comes that she does not like she pulls the covering over her Head, the meaning of which is, that she is Proof against his Temptation: But if another comes, perhaps she suffers him to sit down on the Foot of her Bed, in order to a dry Conference, without going farther; that is to say, she has a mind to make a setter of this poor Fellow, that she may have several Strings to her Bow. In comes a third, whom she jilts with more refined Politicks, and allows to lye near her upon the Coverings of the Bed. But when this Spark is gone, in comes a fourth, to whose Embraces she readily grants her Bed, and her spreading Arms, for two or three Hours together; and tho' he is far from triffling away the time in empty Words, yet the World takes it to be so. Behold, my dear *Adario*, the Lewdness of the *Hurons*, disguis'd with a Pretext of honest Conversation, and that so much the more that how indiscreet so ever any of their Gallants may be to their Mistresses (which rarely happens) the World is so far from giving Credit to 'em, that they brand 'em with Jealousie, which amongst you is a defamatory Affront. This being premis'd, 'tis no wonder that the *Americans* won't hear any thing of Amours in the Day time, upon the Plea that the Night was made for that purpose. In *France* this way of Intreguing is term'd *Cacher adroitment Son jeu*, dexterously to conceal ones Designs. If there's any thing of Wantonness and Debauchery amongst our Wenches, there is at least this difference, that the Rule is not General, as it is amongst yours; and besides they don't go so brutishly to work with it. The Amours of the *European* Women are Charming, they are Constant and Faithful to Death, and when they are so weak as to yield to a Lover the last Favours, they have a greater [182] regard to their inward Merit than to an outward Apperance; and 'tis not the gratifying of their own Passion that they have so much in view, as the desire of giving their Lovers sensible Proofs of their Affection. The *French* Gallants seek to please their Mistresses by Methods that are altogether agreeable, as by Respect, Attendance, and Complaisance; they are Patient, Passionate, and always ready to Sacrifice their Lives and Fortunes for 'em. They lye sighing a long time before they dare to attempt any thing, for they are resolv'd to merit the laſt Favour by long Services; they are ſeen upon their Knees at their Miſtreſſes Feet, to beg the priviledge of kiſſing the Hand; and as a Dog follows his Maſter, watching over him when he Sleeps, ſo 'mongſt us, a true Lover ne'er quits his Miſtreſs, nor ſhuts his Eyes, but that he may dream of her in his Sleep. If any one is found ſo hot upon't as bluntly to Embrace his Miſtreſs upon the very firſt occaſion, without any regard to her Weakneſs, he paſſes with us under the Character of a *Savage*, that is to ſay, a meer *Clown*, that begins where others leave off.

Adario. Ho, ho, my dear Brother; are the *French* e're a whit the wiſer for calling this ſort of People *Savage?* In truth, I did not believe that Word ſignify'd with you, a Prudent thinking Man. I'm glad with all my Heart at this piece of News, not doubting but one Day you may give the name of *Savage* to all the *French*, who will be wiſe enough to follow exactly the true Rules of Juſtice and Reaſon. Now the Myſtery is unriddled that prompts the cunning *French* Women to have ſuch a Love for Savage Creatures; they're not ſo much to blame for't, for in my mind, Time is too precious to loſe, and Youth too ſhort not to make the beſt of the Advantages [183] it throws in our Laps. If your Wenches are Conſtant in a continual change of Lovers, that may bear ſome reſemblance to the Humour of our Girls; but when they faithfully yield themſelves to be Careſs'd by three or four at a time, that's altogether different from the Temper of the *Hurons*. May the *French* Gallants ſpend their Lives in the Fooleries you ſpoke of but now, to conquer their

Miftreffes; may they fpend their time and their Eftates in purchafing a fmall Pleafure, ufher'd in by a thoufand Troubles and Cares. I fhan't offer to blame them, becaufe I have play'd the fool my felf, in running the rifque of Traverfing, in fuch foolifh Veffels, the rough Seas that feparate *France* from this Continent, to have the pleafure of feeing the Country of the *French*. This obliges me to hold my Peace; but reafonable People will fay, That your Amorous Crew are as foolifh as I, but with this difference, that their Love paffes blindly from one Miftrefs to another, and expofes 'em to the repetition of the fame Torments; whereas I fhall never take another Trip from *America* to *France*.

AN APPENDIX.

Containing Some New

VOYAGES

TO

Portugal and *Denmark*.

LETTER I.

Dated at *Lisbon, April* 20. 1694.

Containing a Defcription of *Viana, Porto a Porto, Aveiro, Coimbra, Lisbon;* together with a View of the Court of *Portugal;* and an Account of the Government, Laws, Cuftoms, Commerce and Humours of the *Portuguefe*.

SIR,

I BEGIN my letter with that ancient faying; *Una falus victis nullam fperare falutem;* my meaning is, that after the receipt of fome bad News relating to my bufinefs, I find I have Spirit enough to brave all the Jolts of Fortune. The Univerfe which Swallows and Jefuits take for their Country, muft likewife be mine; till fuch time as it pleafes God to fend to the other World, fome Perfons that do him very little Service here.

I am glad my Memoirs of *Canada* pleafe you, and that my Savage Style did not turn your Affection: Tho' after all, *you* have no reafon to criticife upon my Jargon, for both you and I are of a Country, where no body can fpeak *French* but when they are not able to open their Mouths: Befides, 'twas not poffible for me who went fo young to *America*, to find out in that Country, the Myftery of Writing Politely. That's a Science that is not to be learn'd among the Savages, whofe Clownifh Society is enough to faften a brutifh twang upon the Politeft Man in the World. Since you prefs me to continue my Accounts of what new things I meet with, I willingly comply with your defire; but you muft not expect thofe nice Defcriptions you fpeak of, for if I pretended to any fuch thing, I fhould expofe my felf to the Derifion of thofe to whom you may fhew my Letters. I am not fufficiently qualify'd to outdo the curious Remarks that an infinity of Travellers have publifh'd. 'Tis enough for me if I furnifh you with fome private Memoirs of fome things that other Travellers have Wav'd, as being beneath their regard: And for as much as thefe Memoirs treat of fuch Subjects as were never yet handled in Print, you will meet with fome Satisfaction upon the fcore of their Novelty. With this View, I fhall be very punctual in Writing to you from time to time, from whatever corner of the World my Misfortunes may lead me to; but upon this condition, that you fhall take an exact care to let me have your Anfwers. In the mean time, I muft acquaint you that I can't undertake to Frenchify [187] the

to Portugal and Denmark. 621

Foreign Names; and therefore shall Write 'em as the People of the Country do, leaving it to you to pronounce 'em as you please.

You remember I Writ to you about ten Weeks ago, that upon laying down three hundred Pistoles to the Captain of the Ship that brought me from *Placentia* to *Viana*, I had the good luck to get a Shoar there; and so I shall resume the thread of my Journal, from that place where I last took leave of it. I had no sooner jump'd out of the Sloop, than a *French* Gentleman, who has serv'd the King of *Portugal* these four and thirty years † in the quality of a Captain of Horse, came and offer'd me the use of his House, for in that place there's no publick Houses but such as are Calculated for common Seamen. The next day this old Officer advis'd me to go and wait upon *Don John of Souza*, Governour General of the Province between the *Douro* and the *Minho*. He acquainted me farther, that every body gave him the Title of *L' Excellentia*; and that he gave the Title of *Senoria* only to the Gentlemen of the first Rank, and *Merced to all the rest. When I heard this, I chose instead of speaking *Spanish* to him, to make use of an Interpreter, who Metamorphos'd all the *You*'s of my Compliment into a *Portuguese Excellentia*.

† *Since Monsieur de* Schomberg*'s time.*

**A Title somewhat higher than* You.

Viana lies five Leagues to the Westward of *Braga*, and is inclos'd in a Right-Angle made by the Sea and the River *Lima*. Here I saw two Monasteries of *Benedictine Nuns*, which were so ill provided that they would Starve for Hunger, if their Relations and ‖ Devoto's did not assist 'em. Upon the Sea Side there stands a very good Castle, Fortified after Count *Pagan*'s way: 'Tis covered [188] with several large Culverines, which guard off the Sallymen from Attacking the Vessels that lye at Anchor in the Road. In this Road, the Ships are Shelter'd from the fourteen Points of the Wind, that lye between North and South, in by East. The River is a *havre de barre*, or * *Bar-Haven*, which no Ship ventures upon without calling out Pilots, by a Signal of a Gun or a Flag twisted round. The Ships come all in at High Water, and when the Tide runs out are left dry, unless they Ride upon the Pit, which has always eight or ten Fathom at low Water.

‖ i. e. *those who have a respect for the* Nuns.

* i. e. *A Port that a Ship can't enter but at full Sea; for fear of touching the Sands or Flats.* Bayonne, Bilbao, Stona, Viana, Porto, Aveirco, Mondego, *and* Lisbon, *are all* Havres de Barre.

Febr. 4. I hir'd two Mules, one for my self and another for my Man, at the rate of three *Spanish* Piasters or Cobs; and put on so briskly that I arriv'd that Night at *Porto a Porto*, which was twelve Leagues off. These Creatures Amble both fast and smoothly, without Stumbling or tyring the Rider. Your Cavaliers have the conveniency of resting themselves when they will upon the Portmantles which are fasten'd to two Iron Rings at the Pummel of the Saddle. The Saddles of that Country are too hard for such a Lean Man as me. The Road between *Viana* and *Porto a Porto* is Stony, but pretty good; the Ground lies upon a Level, the Prospect is

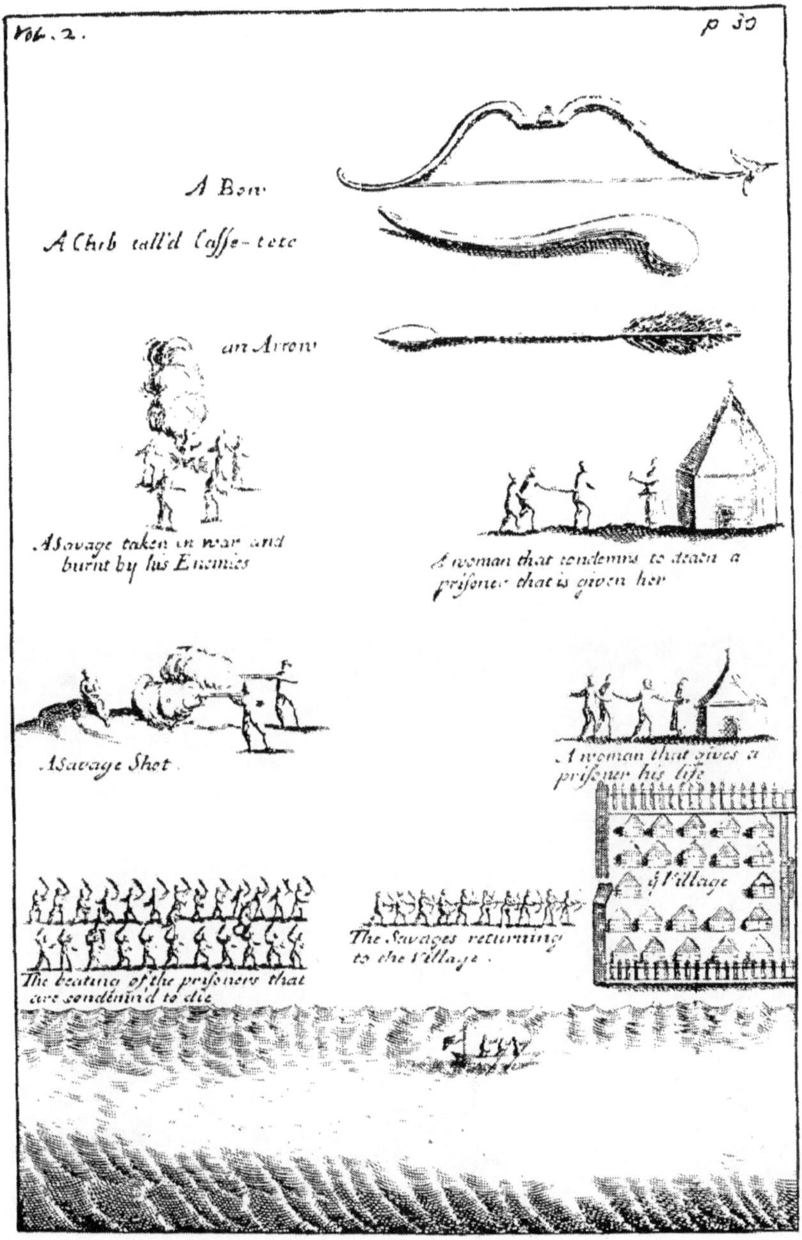
Vol. 2.
p 30
A Bow
A Club call'd Casse-tete
an Arrow
A Savage taken in war and burnt by his Enemies
A woman that condemns to death a prisoner that is given her
A Savage Shot
A woman that gives a prisoner his life
ye Village
The Savages returning to the Village
The beating of the prisoners that are condemn'd to die

pleafant, and the Sea Side is adorn'd with feveral large Villages, the chief of which are *Expofende*, *Faons*, and *Villa de Conde*. When I arriv'd at *Porto*, my Guide carry'd me to an *Englifh* Inn, the only one that was fit to entertain Gentlemen. This City is cramm'd with *French*, *Englifh* and *Dutch* Merchants, [189] who croud thither upon the account of the Commerce; tho' the latter have fuffer'd by't fufficiently, fince the beginning of the War, by vertue of the Civility of our Privateers, who make no fcruple to take their Ships. *Porto* ftands upon the declivity of a Steep Hill, the Foot of which is Wafh'd by the River *Douro*, that falls into the Sea a League lower upon a † *Barr*. This Bar which lies in the Mouth of the *Douro*, is fo fufpected by Sailors, that they never approach to it, but when the Weather is good, and when they have fome of the Pilots of the Country on Board; for upon the Sand of the Bar there are Rocks, fome hidden and fome feen, which render it inacceffible to Strangers. A Ship of four hundred Tun may come over exactly at high Water; which is punctually the time that any Ship ought to make this River. Here we fee a fine Key reaching from one end of the Town to the other, upon which every Veffel is Lafh'd over againft the owners Doors.

**A Bar, *properly fpeaking, is a Bank of Sand, which commonly runs acrofs the Mouth of the Rivers that have not a fufficient Rapidity to throw back into the Sea the Sands that are caft in upon 'em, when the Winds blow hard from the Main. All* Bars *may be call'd Banks of Sand; for I never heard of a* Bar *confifting of a ridge of Rocks. Now this Sand rifes nearer to the Surface of the Water, like a little Hill in a Plain, fo that Ships can't get over it but at high Water.*

In this River, I had

the opportunity of viewing the *Brasil* Fleet, consisting of thirty two *Portuguese* Merchantmen, the least of which carry'd two and twenty Guns. I saw likewise several Foreign Ships, and particularly five or six *French* Privateers, that put in there to Buy Provisions and Ammunition.

Porto is a Stately fine City, and well Pav'd; but its Scituation upon a Mountain is inconvenient, [190] in regard that it obliges one to be always upon the Ascent or Descent. The Gallery of the Regular Canons of St. *Austin*'s is as curious a piece of Architecture for its uncommon length, as their Church is with respect to the roundness of its Figure, and the Riches of the inside. In this City they have a Parliament, a Bishoprick, Academies for the Exercises of young Gentlemen, and an Arsenal for the fitting out of the Men of War, that are Built every year near the Mouth of the River. I wonder that this Town is not better Fortified, especially considering 'tis the Second City in *Portugal*. Its Walls are six Foot thick, and at certain distances shew us the Ruines of old Towers that time has levell'd with the Ground. They were built by the *Moors*, and are the most irregular piece of Work that those times produc'd: So that you may easily guess whether 'twould be any hard matter to take this Town at the first Attack.

'Tis well for the *Portuguese* that this Province, which is one of the best in *Portugal*, is almost inaccessible to their Enemies whether by Sea or Land; the Sea Side being guarded by Barrs, and the Land by impracticable Mountains. 'Tis very

Populous, and all its Valleys which are full of Towns and Villages, afford great quantities of Wine and Olives, and feed numerous Flocks of Cattel, the Wool of which is pretty fine. This I Write upon the Information of some *French* Merchants, who are perfectly well acquainted with this Province. I am told that 'tis impossible to make the *Douro* Navigable, by reason of the Water-Falls and Currents that run between the prodigious Rocks. This, Sir, is all I know of the matter; so I hope you'll content your self with it.

[191] The 10*th* I set out for *Lisbon* in a Sedan, which I Hir'd for eighteen thousand six hundred *Reys*, a number of pieces that are enough to frighten those who do not know that they are but *Deniers*. Since the *Portuguese* State all their Accounts in this fashion; I must acquaint you that a *Rey* is nothing else but a *Denier*, or the 12*th* part of a Penny; and that this numerous quantity of Pieces amounts to no more than twenty five *Piastres*. My Litter-Man ingag'd for this Fare to set me down at *Lisbon*, on the ninth day of *March;* tho' at the same time, he was oblig'd to go two or three Leagues out of his way, to satisfie the Curiosity I had to pass by the way of *Aveiro*, where I arriv'd the next day.

Aveiro is a paltry little Town Seated on the Sea Side, and upon the Banks of a little River, Guarded by a Bar, which the Ships that draw under nine or ten foot Water, cross at High Water by the direction of the Coasting Pilots. 'Tis Fortified after the *Moorish* way, as well as *Porto*. In this place, there's as much Salt made as will serve two or three Provinces. 'Tis adorn'd with a pretty Monaſtrey of Nuns, who give proof of their ancient Nobility and Origin from the † *Chriſtiaon Veilho.* The Country gives a moſt pleaſant Proſpect for three Leagues to the Eaſtward; that is, to the great *Lisbon* Road, which is Hemm'd in by a ridge of Mountains from *Porto* to *Coimbra.*

† i. e. Ancient Chriſtians, *a great Title of Honour in that Country, by reaſon of its being uncommon.*

The 14*th* I arriv'd at *Coimbra;* and when I talk'd of Seeing the Univerſity, my Sedan Man told me that this piece of Curioſity would ſtop me for a whole day: So that I can only tell you that this Univerſity you find mention'd in ſome Travels, is render'd Famous by the King of *Portugal*'s [192] Efforts, ever ſince his Acceſſion to the Throne, to make all Sciences flouriſh within its Walls. The Town affords nothing that's very remarkable, unleſs it be a double Stone Bridge, one above another, between which one may croſs the River without being ſeen; and two fine Convents, one for Monks, and another for Nuns, lying at the diſtance of fourty or fifty Paces from one another. *Coimbra* bears the Title of a Dutchy, and is Intitled to ſeveral conſiderable Prerogatives. It ſtands ſix Leagues off the Sea, at the Foot of a Steep Hill, upon which you may ſee the Churches and Monaſtries, and two or three fine Houſes. The Biſhoprick of this place which is Suffragran to *Braga*, is one of the beſt Biſhopricks in *Portugal.* The Road from *Coimbra* to *Lisbon* is Pleaſant, and affords a pretty Proſpect; the Country is pretty well Peopled.

I arriv'd at *Lisbon* the *Metropolis* of this Country on the 18*th*, and was not near ſo tyr'd as I was uneaſy in making uſe of that flow way of Travelling which can fuit none but Ladies and old Fellows. I had better have hir'd Mules, for then I might have gone through in five days time, and that for a very fmall Charge; *viz.* thirteen *Piafters* for me and my Servant. In the mean time, give me leave to tell you by the bye, that your tender Sparks would never be able to bear the inconveniency of the *Pofada*'s (or Inns) upon the Road: They have fuch forry pitiful Accommodation, that the very Defcription of 'em would be enough to fcare you from going to *Lisbon*, tho' you had never fo much bufinefs there. However I was as well fatisfied, as if they had been the beft Inns in *France;* for having fpent the whole courfe of my Life in Scouring the Sea, the Lakes, and the Rivers of *Canada*, and having liv'd for the moft part upon Roots and Water, [193] with a Bark Tent for my Canopy; I eat heartily of all that they fet before me. You muft know, Sir, the Landlord conducts the Paffengers to a bye place that looks more like a Dungeon than a Chamber; and there you muft ftay with a great deal of patience, till he fends you fome Ragou's Seafon'd with Garlick, Pepper, Chibbols, and a hundred Medicinal Herbs, the fmell of which would turn an *Iroquefe*'s Stomach. To compleat the nicety of your Entertainment, you muft lye down upon Quilts or Mattreffes fpread out on Planks, without either Straw or Coverlets; and thefe Mattreffes are no thicker than this Letter, fo that 'twould require two or three hundred of 'em to make your Bed fofter than Stones. 'Tis true, the Landlord finds you as many Quilts as you pleafe for a Penny a piece, and takes the pains to fhake 'em down, and beat off the Flea's,

Bugs, &c. But thank God, I had no occasion to make use of 'em, for I still kept my Hammock, which was easily hung up in any place I came to, by two large Iron Hooks. But after all, the account I now give you of the *Portuguese* Inns, is all a Jest in comparison with the *Spanish*, if we may credit Men of Reputation: And *that* I take to be the reason that Travellers pay little or nothing for their Fare either in the one or the other.

 The next day after my Arrival at *Lisbon*, I waited upon the Abbot *d'Estrees;* whom the K. of *Portugal* has a great respect for, and who is so much esteem'd by every body, that they justly give him the Title of *'O Mais Perfeito dos Perfeitos Cavalheiros,* i. e. *The most Accomplish'd of the most Accomplish'd Gentlemen.* His Equipage is Magnificent enough, tho' he has not yet made his publick Entry. His Family is kept in excellent Order; his House is very well Furnish'd, and his [194] Table is nice and well serv'd. Oftentimes he entertains the Persons of Note, who would not visit him, if he did not give 'em the Precedency. This piece of deference would have seem'd ridiculous, if the King his Master had not order'd it to be so in Mr. *D'Opede's* * time: For it looks very odd to see the meanest Ensign in the Army take the Right hand of an Ambassadour, who denys that Precedency to all the Ministers of the Second Rate. The *Portuguese* Noblemen and Gentlemen are Men of Honour and Honesty, but they are so full of themselves that they fancy themselves the Purest and Ancientest Stock of Nobility and Gentry in the World.

* *He was formerly Ambassadour at this Court.*

Thofe of diftinguifhing Titles expect your *Excellency* for their Compellation; and they are fo tender of their Dignity, that they never vifit any one that lodges in a publick Houfe. None but Perfons of an Illuftrious Birth are dignify'd with the Title of † *Don;* for the moft honourable Pofts can't Intitle 'em to that Venerable Character; infomuch that the Secretary of State, who is poffefs'd of one of the greateft Pofts in the Kingdom, do's not pretend to affume it.

† *The Word is exactly of the fame Importance with* Meffire, *and with the* Spanifh, Sire *or* Sieur, *which the* Coblers, &c. *claim as their due.*

The King of *Portugal* is of a large Stature, and well Made; he has a very good Meen, tho' his Complexion is fomewhat Brown.[1] 'Tis faid, he is as conftant in his Refolutions, as in his Friendfhip. He is perfectly well acquainted with the State of his Country. He is fo Liberal and full of Bounty, that he can fcarce refufe his Subjects the Favours they ask. The Duke of *Cadaval* his firft Minifter and Favourite has potent Enemies; [195] upon the account that he appears more Zealous for his Mafter than the other Courtiers; and at the fame time, more hearty for the *French* Intereft.

The Situation and various Profpects of *Lisbon* would Entitle it to the Character of one of the fineft Cities in *Europe*, if it were not fo very nafty. It ftands upon feven Mountains, from whence you have a View of the fineft Land-Skip in the World, as well as of the Sea, the River *Taio*, and the Forts that guard the Mouth of the River. This Mountainous City puts the

---

[1] The king of Portugal was Pedro II of the house of Braganza; born in 1648, he succeeded his brother as king in 1683, and reigned until his death in 1706. — ED.

People to a great inconvenience, that are forced to walk on foot; but this inconvenience affects Strangers and Travellers most, whose Curiosity is in some measure thwarted by the trouble of rambling still upon ascents and descents; for you can't have the accommodation of Hackny-Coaches, that are common elsewhere. Here we meet with Stately and Magnificent Churches; the most considerable of which are *La Ceu*, *Notre Dame de Loreto*, *San Vicente*, *San Roch*, *San Pablo*, and *Santo Domingo*. The *Benedictin* Monastery of St. *Bento* is the finest and best Indow'd Monastery that the Town affords; But last Month part of its fine Fabrick was Burnt down by an unfortunate Fire; and upon that occasion I saw more Silver Plate carried out of it than six great Mules could carry.

If the King's Palace were finish'd, 'twould be one of the noblest Edifices in *Europe;* but the compleating of it would cost at least two Millions of Crowns. Strangers lodge for the most part in the Houses that Front the *Taio*. I know several *French* Merchants, some Popish and some Protestants, who are very considerable Traders in this Country. The Popish *French* Merchants are protected by *France*, and the Protestants take Shelter under the *English* and *Dutch*. Here we [196] reckon almost Fifty *English* Families, and as many *Dutch*, besides some other Forreigners, who do all of 'em get Estates in a very little time, by the great vent of the Commodities of the Country. The *English Baetas*, or the *Colchester* light Stuffs sell admirably well in this Place; and there's great Profit got upon the *French* Linnen, the *Tours* and *Lions* Silk Stuffs,

French Ribbands, Lace and Iron Ware; which are ballanc'd by Sugar, Tobacco, Indigo, Cacao Nuts, &c.

The *Alfandigua* or Duty of Sugar and Tobacco is one of the beſt Branches of the Royal Revenue, as well as that on Silk, Linnen and Woollen Cloath, which the Merchants are oblig'd to get Stamp'd upon the payment of a certain Duty proportionable to the value and quality of the Effects. Your dry'd Cod pays almoſt Thirty *per Cent* Cuſtom; ſo that there's ſcarce any thing got by Importing of them, unleſs it be when the firſt Ships come in from *Newfoundland.* Tobacco, whether in Snuſh or in Rolls, is ſold by Retail at the ſame price as in *France;* for Snuſh is worth two Crowns a Pound, and the other Tobacco is ſold for about Fifty Pence. 'Tis eaſie to evade the Cuſtoms, if one has a right underſtanding with the Guards, who are a parcel of Knaves that the ſound of a Piſtole will make as flexible as you can wiſh. No Portmanteau or Cloakbag can be carried into the City without being ſearch'd by theſe doughty Gentlemen. Galloons, Fringes, Brocado's, and Gold or Silver Ribbands are Confiscated as Contreband Goods; for no Perſon, of what Station ſoever, is allow'd to have Silver or Gold Thread either in his Cloaths or the Furniture of his Houſe.

All Books, in what Language ſoever, are immediately laid before the Inquiſition, and burnt [197] if they do not pleaſe the Inquiſitors. This Tribunal, of which a *French* Phyſician gives us a Pathetick Deſcription, from the ſad experiences of the Evils he underwent at *Goa;* this Tribunal, I ſay, which belches out more Fire and Flames than *Mount Gibel*, is so hot upon the Point that if this Letter came before 'em, both it and the Author would be in equal danger of being burn'd; and 'tis upon this Consideration that I take care to hold my Peace, especially since the very Grandees of the Kingdom are affraid to speak of this Sanctified Office. Some Days ago I had an Interview with a sensible wise *Portugese*, who after informing me of the Manners and Customs of the People of *Angola* and *Brasil*, where he had liv'd several Years, took pleasure to hear me recount the Fashions and Humours of the Savages of *Canada;* but when I came to the broiling of the Prisoners of War that fall into the Hands of the *Iroquese*, he cry'd out with a furious Accent, That the *Iroquese* of *Portugal* were yet more cruel than those of *America*, in burning without Mercy their Relations and Friends, whereas the latter inflicted that Punishment only upon the cruel Enemies of their Nation.

In former Times the *Portuguese* had such a Veneration for the Monks, that they scrupl'd to enter into their Wives Chambers, at a time when the good Fathers were exhorting them to something else than Repentance; but now a days they are not allow'd so much Liberty: And indeed I must own, that the greatest part of 'em live such lewd and irregular Lives, that their extravagant Debauches have shock'd me a hundred times. They have Indulgences from the Pope's Nuncio to follow all manner of Libertinism; for that Papal Minister, whose Power is unlimited as to Ecclesiasticks, gives 'em leave, [198] notwithstanding the Remonstrances of their Superiors, to wear a Hat in the City, (*i.e.* to go about without a Companion) to lie out of the Convent, and even to take a Country Journey now and then. Perhaps they would be wifer, and their number would be fmaller, if they were not oblig'd (as well as the Nuns) to make their Vows at 14 Years of Age.

Moft of the *Portuguefe* Coaches are Chariots Imported from *France*. None but the King and Ambaffadors are drawn by fix Horfes or Mules within the City Walls; out of the City, indeed, your Perfons of Quality may have a hundred if they will; but within the Walls they dare not have more than four. The Ladies and the old Gentlemen are carried in Sedans or Chairs, fo that Chariots are only made ufe of by the younger Noblemen; none are allow'd to make ufe of Coaches and Sedans but the Nobility, Envoys, Refidents, Confuls, and Ecclefiafticks; fo that the richeft Citizens and Merchants muft content themfelves with a fort of Calafh with two Wheels, drawn by one Horfe, and driven by themfelves. The Mules that carry the Litters or Sedans are larger, finer and not fo broad Chefted as thofe of *Auvergne*. A Brace of 'em, generally fpeaking, is worth Eight hundred Crowns; nay fome of 'em will fetch Twelve hundred, efpecially if they come from the Country of the famous *Don Quixot*, which lies at a great diftance from *Lisbon*. The Coach Mules come from *Eftremadura*, and are worth about a hundred Piftoles a Pair. The Saddle and Carriage Mules, and the *Spanifh* Horfes, are *Cent per Cent* dearer than in *Caftile*. When 'tis fair Weather the young Sparks ride up and down the City on Horfe-back, on purpofe to fhew themfelves to the Ladies, who like Birds in a Cage [199] have no other Privilege than that of viewing through the * Chinks of Jealoufie the Creatures whofe Company they wifh for in their Prifons. The Monks who are provided for by Indowments make no Vifits on Foot, for their Convent keeps a certain number of Saddle Mules, which they make ufe of by turns: And 'tis wonderful Comical to fee the good Fathers patrol and wheel about the Streets with great long crown'd Hats like Sugar-loafs, and Spectacles that cover three fourths of their Face.

* *Windows with Grates, the Intervals of which are no larger than one's little Finger.*

Tho' *Lisbon* is a very large City, and a place of great Trade, yet there's but two good *French* Inns or Ordinaries in the whole Town, where one may eat tolerably well for five and thirty *Sous* a Meal. Queftionlefs the number of good Ordinaries would be enlarg'd in courfe, if the *Portuguefe* took pleafure in Eating and Drinking; for then they would not contemn thofe who are follicitous to find out good Cheer. They are not contented with difdaining the Trade of an Innkeeper; but the very name of a Publick Houfe is fo odious to them, that they fcorn to vifit any Gentleman that Lodges in thofe charming Quarters. For this reafon, Sir, you would do well to advife any Friend of yours, that has the Curiofity to Travel into *Portugal*, and means to make any ftay in this Town, to go into a Penfion at fome *French* Merchants Houfe. One may feed very well in this Town, only 'tis fomewhat dear. The *Alemteio* Poultry, the St. *Ubal* Hares and Partridges, and the *Algarva* Butchers Meat eat admirably well. The *Lamego*

Bacon and Hams are nicer Food than those of *Mayence* and *Bayonne;* and yet that sort of Meat sits so uneasie upon the Stomach of a *Portuguese*, that, [200] if 'twere not for the Consumption in the Monks and Inquisitors House, there would scarce be any Hogs in all *Portugal*. The *Portuguese* Wines are strong and have a good Body, especially the Red Wines which run very near to a Black Colour. The *Aleguete* and *Barra a Barra* Wines are the finest and those of the thinest Body.

The King never tasts Wine, and the Persons of Quality drink of it but very seldom, no more than the Women. To fathom the reason of this Abstinence we must consider that *Venus* has such an Interest in *Portugal*, that the Face of her Charms hath always kept *Bacchus* from any Footing in this Country. Here that Goddess causes so much Idolatry, that she seems to dispute with the true God for a right to the Worship and Adoration of the *Portuguese*, and that in the most Sacred Places; for the Churches and Processions make the common Randezvous where the Amorous Assignments are made. 'Tis there that the * *Bandarro's*, the Ladies of Pleasure and the Women of Intrigue, take their Posts; for they never fail to assist at the Festivals that are Celebrated at least three or four times a Week, sometimes in one Church and sometimes in another.

* *A sort of Braggadocio Bully's, of Don Quixot's Temper, who have no other Employment than that of hunting after Adventures.*

The swaggering Adventurers have a wonderful Talent of discovering their Amorous Desires with one glance of the Eye to the Ladies who return 'em an Answer by the same Signal; and this they call *Corresponding*. This done, they have nothing to do but to find out their Houses, by following 'em Foot for Foot from the Church Door to their respective Apartments. The conclusion of the Intrigue lies in marching straight on to the corner of the Street without looking about [201] for fear the Husband or Rivals should smell a Rat. At the end of the Street they have so much occasion for a large stock of Patience that they must stand there two or three hours till a Servant Maid comes, whom they must follow till she finds a handsome opportunity of delivering her †*Recado* safely. The Adventurers must trust these goodly Confidents, and sometimes run the risque of their Lives upon their Word and Directions; for they are as cunning as they are true to their Mistresses, from whom they receive Presents as well as from the Suitors, and sometimes from the Husbands.

† i. e. *A Message or a watch Word in order to an Interview.*

In former times the *Portuguese* Women cover'd their Faces with their ‖ *Manto's*, and expos'd nothing to view but one Eye, as the *Spanish* Women do to this Day; but as soon as they perceiv'd that the Sea Towns were replenish'd with as fair Children as any are in *France* or *England*, the poor *Manto's* were discarded, and forbid to approach the Face of a Lady. The *Portuguese* have such an Antipathy and Horror for *Acteon*'s Arms, that they had rather cut their own Fingers than take Tobacco out of an Horn-Box; tho' after all the Horn Commodity begins to take here, notwithstanding the repeated Discouragements of Poyson and the Sword. Almost every Month brings us fresh

‖ *Veils of Taffitas which cover'd both the Face and the Body, and at the same time cloak'd their Intrigues.*

Instances of some Tragical Adventure of that Nature, especially when the *Angola* or *Brasil* Fleets are just come in; for the greatest part of the Seamen that go upon these Voyages are so unfortunate, that when they return home they find their Wives lock'd up in [202] Monasteries instead of their own Houses. The reason of their voluntary Confinement is this; that they choose thus to expiate and atone for the Sins they committed in their Husbands absence, rather than be stabb'd at their return. Upon this score we ought not to Censure those who represented the Ocean with a Bull's Horns, for in good earnest almost all that expose themselves to the brunts of the Sea make much such another Figure. In fine, Gallantry in the way of Amours is too ticklish a Trade in this Place, for it runs a Man in danger of his Life. Here we find plenty of Whores, whose Company ought by all means to be avoided; for besides the danger of ruining one's Health, a Man runs the risque of being knock'd on the Head if he frequents their Company. The handsomest Whores are commonly *Amezada'd* or hir'd by the Month by some *kind Keepers*, that have a watchful Eye over 'em; but notwithstanding all the Keepers Precaution, they enjoy the Diversion of some wise Companions at the expence of such Fools. The Fools I now speak of lye under an indispensible Necessity of keeping up and feeding with Presents the pretended Love and Fidelity of the said *Lais's*, the Enjoyment of whom is unconceivably Chargeable. The Nuns receive frequent Visits from their *Devoto's*, who have a warmer Passion for them than for the Women of this World, as it appears from the Jealousies,

Quarrels, and a Thousand other Disorders that arise among the Rivals upon the score of Intrigue. Formerly the Parlours of the Monasteries were guarded only with a single Grate, but since my Lord *Grafton* and some of the Captains of his Squadron had the Curiosity to touch the Hands, &c. of the Nuns of *Odiveta;* the King ordered all the Convents in the Kingdom to [203] have double Grates upon their Parlours. At the same time he almost stiffled the Pretention of the *Devoto's*, by prohibiting any one to approach to a Convent without a lawful Occasion, tho' to frame an occasion is easie to one that has the folly to be in Love with these poor Girls.

The *Portuguese* are a People of a quick Apprehension; they think freely, and their Expressions come up to the justness of their Thoughts: They have able Physicians and learned Casuists among 'em. The Celebrated *Camoens* was without dispute one of the most Illustrious Citizens of *Parnassus*. The teeming variety of his excellent Thoughts, his choice of Words, and the politeness and easie freedom of his Stile, charm'd all who were sufficiently acquainted with the *Portuguese* Language.[1] 'Tis true he had the Misfortune of being rally'd upon by *Moreri*, and by some *Spanish* Authors; who, when they could not avoid owning, that 'tis impossible to surpass the Genius of this unfortunate Poet, blacken'd his Character with the imputation of Infidelity and Profanity. A *Catalan* Monk falls foul upon a hundred Places of his

---

[1] Lahontan here shows his familiarity with Portuguese literature, and its greatest poet, Luiz de Camoëns, who died in 1579. His genius went largely unrecognized during his lifetime, and, as our author indicates, he was subjected to petty persecutions. — ED.

Laziadas Endechas Eftrivillas, &c. and brands him for an Impious Rattle-brain'd Fellow. To quote two Places that he Cenfures; the firft is the Cadence of a Sonnet entituled *Soneto Nuo Impreffo;* where after fome Reflections the Poet fays, *Mais O Melhor de tudo e crer en Chrifto;* i. e. *After all, the fureft way is to believe in Chrift.* The Second is the Conclufion of a *Gloza*, viz. *Si Deus fe Bufca no Mundo neffes ollos fe achara.* That is to fay, in fpeaking to a Lady, *If we look for God in this World we'll find him in your Eyes.*

The *Portuguefe* Pulpit-men cry up their Saints almoft above God himfelf; and to exaggerate their Sufferings lodge 'em in Stables rather than [204] in Paradife. They conclude their Sermons with fuch Pathetick Cries and Exclamations, that the Women figh and cry as if they were in defpair. In this Country the Title of a Heretick is accounted highly infamous; and indeed it bears a very odious Signification. The Priefts and Friars hate *Calvin* for Curtailing the bufinefs of Confeffion, as much as the Nuns efteem *Luther* for his Monaftical Marriage. In the City they make Proceffions from one end of the Town to the other, every *Friday* in *Lent*. I have feen above a hundred difcipline themfelves in the Streets, in an odd manner. They were clad in White, with their Face cover'd and their Back naked; which they lafh fo handfomely, that the Blood fpurts in the Face of the Women who are fet upon the fides of the Streets, on purpofe to ridicule and vilify the leaft Bloody. Thefe were follow'd by others in Masks, who carried Croffes, Chains, and bundles of Swords of an incredible weight.

The Foreigners of this place are almoſt as Jealous as the *Portugueſe;* inſomuch that their Wives are afraid to ſhew themſelves to their Husband's beſt Friends. They affect the *Portugueſe* Severity with ſo much exactneſs, that theſe poor Captives dare not lift up their Eyes in the Preſence of a Man. But notwithſtanding all their precaution, they ſometimes meet with the Miſchief that they take ſuch care to avoid. The City is Peopled with perſons of all Colours, ſome Black, ſome Mulatto's, ſome Swarthy, and ſome of an Olive Complexion: But the Greateſt part are *Trigenho's,* i. e. of the Colour of Corn. The medley of ſo many different hues, do's ſo mingle the Blood of the Nation, that the true Whites make but a very ſcanty number; and 'tis for this reaſon, that if one were to ſay in *Portugueſe, I am a Man (or* [205] *a Woman) of Honour;* the nobleſt expreſſion he can find, is, *Eu ſou Branco,* or *Branca,* i. e. *I am a White.*

You may walk up and down *Lisbon* night and day without fearing Pickpockets. Till three or four a Clock in the Morning, you have Muſicians that play in the Streets on *Guitars,* and joyn to the Sweetneſs of that Inſtrument, the moſt moanful Songs that can be imagin'd. The way of Dancing among the ordinary ſort of People is very indecent, by reaſon of the impertinent Motions of their Head and Belly. The Inſtrumental Muſick of the *Portugueſe* is diſagreeable at firſt to the Ears of a Foreigner; but at the bottom it has ſomewhat in it that's ſweet, and pleaſes, when one is accuſtom'd to it. Their Vocal Muſick is ſo coarſe, and its diſcordant Notes are ſo unhappily link'd together; that the chattering of a Crow is more Melodious. Their Church Mufical Compofures are all in the *Caftilian* Language, as well as their Paftorals and moft of their Songs. They endeavour to imitate the *Spanifh* Cuftoms as much as poffible; nay, they are fo nice in obferving the Ceremonies of the *Spanifh* Court, that the *Portuguefe* Minifters would be very much difoblig'd if the leaft Formality were lop'd off. The King and the Grandees wear much fuch another Habit as our Financiers or Receivers of the Royal Revenue. They have a clofe Coat with a Cloak of the fame colour; a great Band of *Venice* Point, with a long Perriwig, a Sword, and a Dagger. They give the Title of *Excellentia* to Ambaffadours, and that of *Senhoria* to Envoys and Refidents.

The Port of *Lisbon* is large, fafe and convenient; tho' the Entry is very difficult. The Ships Ride at Anchor between the City and the Caftle of *Almada*, at eighteen Fathom Water on a good [206] ftrong Ground. The *Lisbon* River is call'd by the *Portuguefe*, O Rey dos Rios, i. e. *The King of Rivers*. 'Tis almoft a League broad where the Ships Ride; at which place the Tide rifes twelve foot perpendicular, and runs above ten Leagues farther up towards its fource. All Captains of Ships, whether Men of War or Merchant Men, Foreigners or Natives, are exprefsly prohibited to Salute the City with a Difcharge of Cannon, or fire a Ship Gun before it, upon any pretence whatfoever. The Confuls of *France*, *England* and *Holland*, have five or fix thoufand Livres a piece allow'd 'em yearly; befides which, they make a fhift to get as much more by Trading.

This, Sir, is all the account I can give you at prefent of this charming Country; which to my mind would be a Paradife upon Earth, if 'twere Inhabited by Peafants that had lefs of the Gentleman in their Conduct. The Climate is admirably fweet and agreeable; the Air is clear and ferene, the Water of the Country is wonderful good, and the Winter is fo mild that I have felt no cold as yet. In this Country, the People may live for an Age without any inconveniency from advancing Years. The old Perfons are not loaded with the Infirmities that plague thofe of other Countries; their Appetite do's not fail 'em, and their Blood is not fo difpirited, but that their Wives can vouch for their perfect health. Ardent Fevers make a terrible Havock in *Portugal*, and the Venereal Diforders are fo civil, that no body troubles his head for a cure. The *Pox*, which is very frequent in the Country, gives fo little uneafynefs, that the very Phyficians who have it, are loth to carry it off, for fear of going to the charge of repeated Cures. The Juftices and Peace-Officers are fawcy and unfufferably [207] arrogant, as being authoris'd by a King that obferves the Laws with the utmoft Severity; for this incourages 'em to pick quarrels with the People, from whom they frequently receive very cruel Reprimands. Some time ago, the *Count de Prado* Son in Law to the Marfhal *de Villeroy*, took the pains to fend into the other World an infolent * *Corrigidor*, that would willingly have difpenfed with the Voyage.

* i. e. *An Intendant and Civil Judge.*

While that Gentleman was Riding in Coach with his Coufin, at the corner of a Street he met the *Corrigidor*, who was

Mounted like a St. *George*, and to his Misfortune so proud of his Office, that he did not daign to give the two Gentlemen a Salute. I've acquainted you already that the *Portuguese* Gentlemen are the vainest Men in the World; and upon that score, you will not think it strange that these two Gentlemen alighted from the Coach, and made the *Corrigidor* spring from his Horse and Jump into the other World. A *French Man* will be ready to say that the Intendant's Indiscretion did not deserve such rude usage; but the *Portuguese* Persons of Quality that cover their Heads in the presence of their King, will be of another mind. However, the two Chavalier's took Shelter in the House of the Abbot *d'Estrees*, who sent 'em to *France* in a *Brest* Frigot.

It now remains to give you a List of the King of *Portugal*'s Standing Forces. He has eighteen thousand Foot, eight thousand Horse, and twenty two Men of War; namely,

    4 Ships from 60 to 70 Guns.
    6 Ships from 50 to 60 Guns.
    6 Ships from 40 to 50 Guns.
    6 Frigats from 30 to 40 Guns.

[208] You must know that the King's Ships are light Timber'd, well Built and handsomely Model'd; their Caulking, Iron Work and Roundings is all very neat. Their Arsenals and Naval Stores are in great disorder, and good Sailors are as scarce in *Portugal* as good Sea Officers, for the Government has neglected the Forming of Marine Nurseries and Navigation Schools, and a thousand other necessary things; the discussion of which would lead me too far out of

my way. The *Portuguese* are charg'd with being somewhat dull and slow in Working their Ships, and less brave by Sea than by Land.

The Captains of the King's Ships have commonly twenty two *Patacas* a Month; and a free Table while they are at Sea; besides some Perquesites.

A Lieutenant's Pay is sixteen *Patacas* a Month.

An Ensign of Marines has ten *Patacas* a Month.

An Able Sailor has four *Patacas* a Month.

A Captain of a Company of Foot has about five and twenty *Patacas* a Month, in Pay and Perquisites both in Peace and War.

The *Alusieres*, who are a sort of Lieutenants, have eight *Patacas*.

A Common Soldier's Pay is about two pence half-penny a day of our Mony.

A Captain of Horse has in Pay and Perquisites, in time of Peace, about a hundred *Pataca's* a Month.

A Lieutenant of Horse has near thirty *Pataca's* a Month.

A Quartermaster fifteen *Pataca's* a Month.

A Trooper four *Sous* a day, and his Forrage.

As for the General Land and Sea Officers, 'tis hard to tell exactly what their Incomes amount to: For the King grants Pensions to some, and Commandries to others, as he sees occasion. The [209] Collonels, Lieutenant-Collonels and Majors of Foot, as well as the Maîtres de Camp and the Commissarys, have no fix'd Allowance: For some have more and some less, in proportion to the advantage of the Place where their Troops are Quarter'd, and the number of their Men.

The *Portuguese* Troops are ill Disciplin'd. Neither Horse nor Foot are Cloath'd after the same manner; for some have a Brown Livery, some Red, some Black, some Blew, some Green, *&c.* Their Arms are very good; and the Officers do not mind their brightness, provided they are in a good Condition. One would scarce believe that these are the Troops that did such mighty Feats against the *Spaniards* in the last Wars. In all appearance they were better Disciplin'd in those days than they are now, and were not so much taken up with their *Guitars*.

To shew you the Species and Value of the Mony that's Current in this Country:

A *Spanish Piastre* or piece of Eight, which the *Portuguese* call a *Pataca*, is worth a *French* Crown; and contains 750 *Reys*.

The half pieces and quarter pieces are of a proportionable Value.

A *Rey* is a *Denier*, as I intimated above.

The lowest Silver Coin they have is a *Vintaine* or twenty penny piece, being 20 *Reys*.

A *Testoon* is worth 5 *Vintaines*.

A *Demi-Testoon* goes in a half proportion.

An old *Cruzada* is near 4 *Testoons*.

The *Mæda d' ouro*, a Gold Coin, is worth 6 *Pataca*'s and 3 *Testoons*.

The half and quarter *Mæda*'s have a proportionable Value.

A *Lowis d'or*, whether Old or New, goes for four *Piaſtres* wanting two *Teſtoons*.

[210] The half and quarter *Piſtoles* go upon the ſame proportion.

A *Spaniſh Piſtole*, full Weight, goes at the ſame rate for 4 *Piaſtres*, wanting two *Teſtoons;* ſo that there's Mony got by ſending 'em to *Spain*, where they're worth 4 *Piaſtres* neat.

No Species of Mony bears the King of *Portugal*'s Effigies; and there's no diſtinction made in *Portugal*, between the *Seville Piaſtres* and thoſe of *Mexico*, or of *Peru*, as they do elſewhere.

No *French* Coin paſſes in this Country, excepting Crowns, half Crowns and quarter Crowns.

The *Portugueſe* 128 *pound* is equal to the *Paris* 100 Weight. Their *Calido* is a Meaſure that exceeds the *Paris* half Ell by three inches and a line; ſo that its juſt extent is two *French* foot, one inch and one line. Their *Bara* is another Meaſure, ſix of which makes ten *Calido's*. The *Portugueſe* League is 4200 Geometrical Paces, allowing five Foot to every Pace.

As for the Intereſt of the *Portugueſe* Court, I wave it on purpoſe becauſe I have no mind to enter into Politicks. Beſides, I have already acquainted you that I pretend to Write nothing elſe but ſuch trifles as have not been yet took notice of in Print. If it were not that I had laid my ſelf under that Reſtriction, I could ſend you a circumſtantial account of their different Tribunals or Courts of Juſtice, and ſome Scraps of their Laws: I could give you to underſtand that the Parliament and Arch-Biſhoprick of *Lisbon*, make one of the greateſt Ornaments of this *Metropolis;* that the Eccleſiaſtical Benefices are extream large; that there are no Commendatory Abbeys in the Country, that the Friars are neither so well indow'd nor so well entertain'd as one might expect. I could inform you that the King's Royal Order is call'd *L'habito de Cristo*, If [211] Madam *d' Aunoy* had not taught you so much in Describing the admirable Institution of that Order; and therefore shall content my self in adding that the number of the Knights Companions of this Order runs far beyond that of its Commandries, which are worth very little. Here I must make a halt and take leave of this Royal City, which 'tis possible I may see once more hereafter. I set out immediately for the Northern Kingdoms of *Europe;* waiting patiently till it pleases God that Monsieur *Ponchartrain* should either remove to Paradise, or do Justice to him who shall always be yours more than his own.

Your Humble, &c.

LETTER II.

Dated at *Travemunde*, 1694.

Containing an Account of the Author's Voyage from *Lisbon* to *Garnſey;* his Adventure with an *Engliſh* Man of War and a Privateer: A Defcription of *Rotterdam* and *Amſterdam;* the Author's Voyage to *Hamburg;* the Dimenſions of a *Flemiſh* Sloop; a Defcription of the City of *Hamburg;* the Author's Journy from thence to *Lubeck;* and a Defcription of that City.

I SET out from *Lisbon* on the 4th of *April*, having bargain'd with a Mafter of a Ship to Land me at *Amſterdam* for thirty *Piaſtres*. At the [212] fame time, I had the precaution of taking a Pafs from the *Dutch* Refident, for fear of being ftop'd in that Country. I went in a Boat to a place call'd *Belin*, which lies about two Leagues below *Lisbon*. At this little Town all the Merchant Ships that go and come, are oblig'd to fhew their Cockets, *Invoice*, and Bills of Lading, and to pay the Duty for their Cargo. The 6th we got out of the *Taio*, and follow'd the Rake of a Fleet Bound for the *Baltick* Sea, and Convoy'd by a *Swediſh* Man of War of 60 Guns, Commanded by a *Lubecker* whofe Name was *Crenger;* and whom the King of *Sweden* had prefer'd to a Noble Dignity, notwithſtanding that Originally he had been a Common

Sailor. We crofs'd the *Barr* by the way of the Great Channel or Pafs, between Fort *Bougio*, and the *Cachopas;* the laft being a great Bank of Sand and Rocks, extending to three quarters of a League in length, and half a League in breadth, which Ships are apt to fall foul of in a Calm, by reafon of the Tides that bear that way. You muft know that if we had had Pilots that knew the Coaft, we would have pafs'd between that Bank and the Fort of St. *Julian*, which lies to the North or the *Lisbon* fide, oppofite to *Bougio;* but we had no occafion to employ 'em, fince our *Portuguefe* Captain took the opportunity of following the run of the *Baltick* Fleet. As foon as we came into the Main, and fell into the middle of that North Country Fleet, the Brutifh *Commodore* made down upon us with all Sails aloft, and fir'd a Cannon with Ball in Head of our Ship; after which he fent out his Lieutenant to acquaint our poor Mafter, that it behov'd him to pay two *Pifloles* immediately for the Shot, and to Sheer off from his Fleet, unlefs he had a mind to pay a hundred *Piaftres* for his Convoy, which the Mafter of our Veffel refus'd very Gracefully.

[213] But to drop this Subject; I muft acquaint you that the *Barr* of *Lisbon* is inacceffible while the Wind blows hard from the Weft and South-Weft; which commonly happens in Winter. Add to this, that for eight Months of the Year the North and North-Eaft Winds prevail, and that moderately: By which means it came about, that our Paffage from the Mouth of the *Taio* to Cape *Finifterre* was longer than an ordinary Voyage from the Ifle of *Newfound-Land* to *France*. I never faw fuch conftant Winds as thefe; however we got

clear of 'em, by Traverfing and Sweeping along the Coaft, which our *Portuguefe* Captain durft not leave for fear of the Sally-Rovers, whom they dread more than Hell it felf. At laft, after 18 or 20 days Sailing, we Weather'd Cape *Finifterre;* and then the Wind Veering to the South-Weft, we made fuch way that in ten or twelve days we came in fight of the Ifle of *Guernfey.* I muft fay, that if it had not been for a *French* Pilot that conn'd the Ship, we had frequently fallen Foul on the Coaft of the *Britifh* Channel: For you muft know, the *Portuguefe* have but little acquaintance with the Northern Seas, and the Lands that jut out into 'em; and for that reafon are oblig'd to make ufe of Foreign Pilots when they are Bound for *England* or *Holland.* The fame day that we defcry'd *Guernfey,* two great *Englifh* Ships gave us Chafe with full Sail, and in three or four hours came up with us: One of 'em was a King's Ship of fixty Guns; and the other was a Privateer of fourty Guns, Commanded by one *Cowper,* who was naturally very well calculated for a Pickpocket, as you'll fee in the Sequel. As foon as they came up with us, we were forc'd to Strike and put out our Long Boat, into which I went in order to fhew the Captain, whofe name was *Townfend,* the Pafs I had receiv'd from the [214] *Dutch* Refident at *Lisbon.* This Captain treated me with all poffible Civility, in fo much that he affur'd me all my Baggage fhould be fecur'd from the Rapine of Captain *Cowper,* who purfuant to the Principles of his profeffion, pretended to Pillage me with as little Scruple as Mercy. However, our Ship could not be Search'd till we got into *Guernfey* Road, and for that reafon we were carry'd thither the fame day; and after dropping Anchor the two *Englifh* Captains went a Shoar, and fent two Searchers on Board of us, to try if they could prove that the Wine and Brandy with which our Ship was Fraughted, was of the growth of *France* or Exported by Commiffion from *French* Merchants; which they could not poffibly make out, notwithftanding that they fpent fifteen days in fearching and rummaging, as I heard afterwards at *Lubec*. This troublefome Accident oblig'd me in five or fix days after, to Imbarque in a *Dutch* Frigat of * *Circzee;* having firft prefented Captain *Townfend* with fome Casks of *Allegrete* Wine, a Cheft of Oranges, and fome Difhes Carv'd at † *Eftremos;* and that in acknowledgment of the kind Ufage and good Entertainment that he gave me both a Shoar, and on Board of his Ship.

* *A Place in* Holland.

† *A* Portuguefe City *that ftands almoft on the Frontiers towards* Extremadura.

My Second Voyage prov'd more favourable than the former; for in three days Sailing I arriv'd at *Circzee;* at which place I went on Board of a Paffage Smack, which fteer'd between the Iflands, and by vertue of the Winds and Tydes wafted me to *Rotterdam*.

Rotterdam is a very large fine City, and a place of very great Trade. Here I had the Pleafure of viewing in two days time, the *Maes* College, the [215] Arfenal for Naval Stores, and the great Tower, which by the induftry of a Carpenter was Reinftated in its perpendicular Pofture, at a time when it bended and fhelv'd in fuch a monftrous manner, as to threaten the City with the Load of its Ruines. I had likewife the Satisfaction of seeing the House of the Famous *Erasmus*, as well as the Beauty of the Port or the *Maes*, the Mouth of which is very dangerous, by reason of some Shelves and Banks of Sand that shoot out a pretty way into the Sea. The Trade of *Rotterdam* is very considerable, and the Merchants of that place enjoy the conveniency of bringing their Ships up to the Doors of their Ware-Houses, by the help of the Canals or Ditches, that intersect this great City. Two days after my Arrival, I Imbarqu'd at five a Clock in the Morning in a Travelling Boat or *Tract Scuyt* for *Amsterdam*. This sort of Boats is cover'd with Ribs, being flat, long and broad; and has a Bench or Form on each side, that reaches from the Prow to the Poop. In this Conveniency, which one Horse will draw, we travel a League an hour, for three *Sous* and a half *per* League. In all the Principal Cities of *Holland* the *Scuyts* set out every hour, whether full or empty: But you must know that you frequently shift Boats, and for that end must walk on foot thro' several Cities. In this small Voyage I walk'd thro' *Delft*, *Leyden* and *Harlem*, which appear'd to be large, neat and fine Cities. After I had Travel'd in these Boats twelve Leagues upon Ditches lin'd with Trees, Meads, Gardens, and most pleasant Houses, I arriv'd at *Amsterdam* in the Evening.

When I came to my Inn, my Landlord order'd me a Guide, who in seven or eight days time shew'd me all the Curiosities of this Flourishing City; but I could have done it in three [216] or four days, if the City had afforded the Conveniency of Hackney-Coaches, such as they have at *Paris* and other Places. The City is large, neat and fine; most of its Canals or *Graafs* are deck'd with very pretty Houses: But the Water Stagnating in these large Cisterns smells very strong in Hot Weather. The Edifices are for the most part Uniform, and the Streets are drawn as if 'twere by a Line. The *Guild-Hall* or *Stadt-House* stands upon Wooden Piles or Stakes; tho' that vast Mass of Stone is extream heavy. This Noble Edifice is inrich'd with several fine Pieces of Sculpture and Painting, and adorn'd with rich Tapestry. Here you may see the finest Marble, Jasper and Porphyry that can be: But this is nothing in Comparison with the Mouldy Crowns that are hoarded up under the Vaults of this monstrous Edifice. The Admiralty-House is likewise very fine, as well as the Arsenal. The Port which is little less than a large quarter of a League in Front, was covered all over with Ships, in so much that one might easily Jump from one to another.

In this City I saw some neat Churches, not to speak of a Synagogue of the true Jews, who out of regard to their Antiquity are allow'd the publick Exercise of their Venerable Religion. The *Roman Catholicks, Lutherans*, &c. are tolerated to Worship God in their way, without laying the Doors of their Meeting-Houses open, or ringing Bells or Chimes. I was likewise entertain'd with a Sight of the Houses for Widows and Orphans, and their Bridewells whether for the Punishment of Rogues, or Female Sinners, who are forc'd to Work very hard to expiate their Peccadillo's. The Exchange is a piece of Architecture, large enough to contain eight thousand Men: But the Stateliest thing I saw was [217] ten or twelve *Musick-Houses*, so call'd from certain Musical Instruments sorrily Scrap'd upon, by the Sound of which a Gang of nasty Punks insnare such as have the courage to look upon 'em without Spitting in their Faces. This gracious Tribe assembles in the *Seraglio* as soon as Night approaches. In some of these *Musick-Houses* you are entertain'd with the Sound of an *Organ;* in others with a *Harpsicord* or some other lame Instrument. You enter into a large Room where the frightful Vestal Ladies sit, rigg'd with all sorts of Colours and Stuffs, by the kind assistance of the Jews who let out the Head-Dresses and Suits of Cloaths, that have been kept for that use, from Father to Son, ever since the Destruction of *Jerusalem*. In these *Seraglio*'s every body's Welcome for the Spending of ten or twelve *Stivers*, which he must lay down at his first entry, for a Glass of Wine that's enough to Poison an Elephant. Here you'll see a Swinging Raw-Bon'd Sailor pop in with his Pipe in his Jaws, his Hair all glittering with Sweat, and his Tar Breeches Glew'd to his Thighs; in which Pickle he makes SS's till he falls flat at his Mistrisses Feet. Next comes a Foot-Man half Muddled, that Sings and Dances, and Swills down Brandy to make himself Sober. After him the Stage is Trod by a Soldier that Swaggers and Storms, and makes the whole Palace tremble; or else by a Company of Adventurers muffled up in their Cloaks, who come to play the Devil with three or four Rogues, and get themselves knock'd on the Head by fifty that out-do Asses in Brutishness. In fine, Sir, the whole *Chorus* is a Collection of nasty Miscreants, who in spite of the unsufferable Funk of

The Calumet of peace, being a great pipe &c.

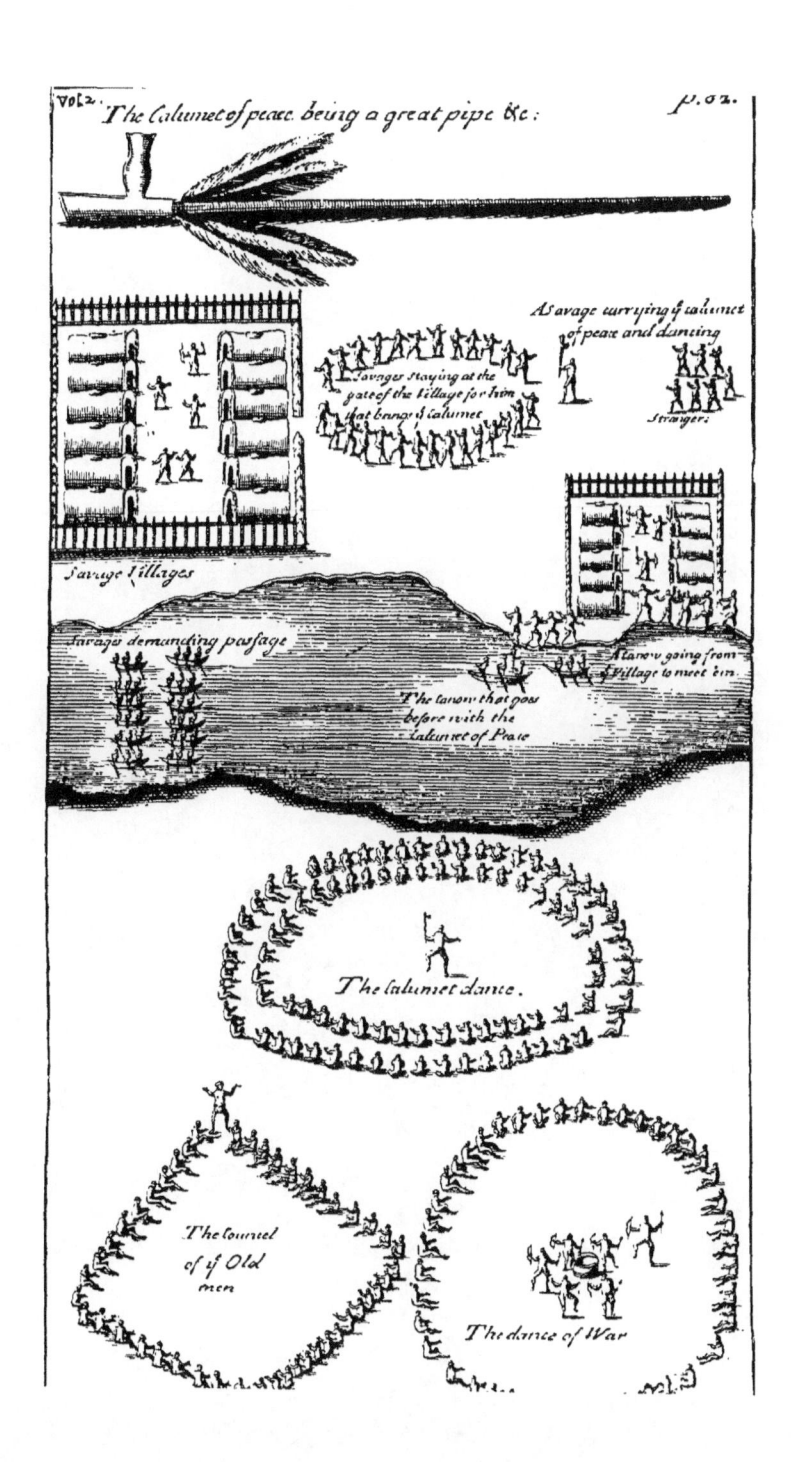

Savage Villages

Savages staying at the gate of the village for him that brings the calumet

A savage carrying the calumet of peace and dancing

Stranger

Savage demanding passage

The canow that goes before with the calumet of Peace

A canow going from the Village to meet 'em

The calumet dance.

The Councel of the Old men

The dance of War

Tobacco and Smell of nasty Feet, continue in that Common Shore of Ordure and Nusance till two a Clock in the Morning, without ever disobliging their Stomachs. [218] This Sir, is the whole of what I know in the matter.

As I pafs'd thro' this famous City, I met with some *French* Merchants of the *Catholick Religion*, the most considerable of which are the Sieurs *d' Moracin*, and *d' Arreche;* both *Bayonne* Men, and persons of Merit and Probity, who have already purchas'd a great Estate, and a very reputable Character. I was inform'd that there were a great many *French* Refugees in this City, who have set up Manufactures that inrich'd some and ruin'd others. This is to me a convincing Proof that the Refugee Trade has been favourable to some and fatal to others; nay, 'tis really true, that some Refugees who brought Mony into *Holland* are now in want, and others who had not a Groat in *France*, are become *Cræsus*'s in that Republick.

There's no Country in the World in which good Inns are so chargeable, as they are in *Holland*. There you must pay for Bed and Fire, in proportion to your Meals, which cost you half a *Ducatoon*, or two and nine pence a time: So that a Gentleman and his Servant must lie at the Charge of eight *French Livres* a day, for Supper, Dinner, Bed and Fire.

As for the *Dutch* Mony, the Value of it is as follows.

A *Ducatoon* is worth three *Guelders*, three *Stuivers*.

A *Rix Dollar* passes for fifty *Stuivers*.

A *Crown* for 40 *Stuivers*.

A *Dollar* for 30 *Stuivers*.

An eight and twenty *Stuck* or Piece, 28 *Stuivers*.

A *Guelder* piece 20 *Stuivers*.

A Stamp'd *Schelling* 6 *Stuivers*.

An Unstamp'd *Schelling*, 5 *Stuivers* 4 *Doits*.

[219] A *Dubbelkie* 2 *Stuivers*.

A *Stuiver* 8 *Doits;* which makes a *French Sol* and a *Liard;* for five *French Sous* make but four *Dutch Stuivers;* and a *French* Crown of 60 *Sous* value is no more than 48 *Stuivers*.

A Gold *Ducat* is worth 5 *Guelders* 5 *Stuivers*.

A *Lowis D'or* passes for 9 *Guelders* 9 *Stuivers*.

As for the Measures of *Holland*, I can tell you with reference to some, that a League is near 3800 Geometrical Paces.

An Ell is a *French* Foot ten Inches and a Line.

A Pound is equal to our *Paris* Pound.

A Pint holds much the same quantity of Liquor with a *Paris* Chopine.

This is all the account I can give you of *Holland*.

When I set out from *Amsterdam* to *Hamburg*, I chose the easyest and cheapest way of Travelling, (I mean by Water.) I had resolv'd indeed to Travel by Post Waggons or Coaches; but that resolution was presently drop'd, when I was advis'd that in Travelling by Land, I might run the risque of being stop'd in the Territories of some of the *German* Princes, who require Passports of all Travellers. This wholesome Advice spar'd both my Corps and my Purse: For to have gone Post, it would have cost me for my self and my Servant fourty Crowns, whereas it cost me but five by Water. There goes two *Dutch* Sloops from *Amsterdam* to *Hamburg* every Week, on purpose to carry Passengers, who may hire little seperate

Cabins, such being made in the Ship for the Accommodation of those who have a mind to be private. These Sloops would be admirably well Calculated for Sailing up the South side of the River of St. *Laurence*, from its Mouth to *Quebec;* and above all, from *Quebec* to *Monreal*. They are preferable to our Barques for that Service; [220] which I'll make out by five or six Reasons. In the first place, they do not draw half so much Water as our Barks of the same Burden. In the next place, they'll tack to the four Quarters of the Wind; they require less Rigging and a smaller compliment of Hands than our Barques, and are Work'd with less Charge; they'll turn their Head where their Stern was before in the twinkling of an Eye, whereas our Barques can't get about under five or six Minutes, and sometimes will not tack at all; they may rub upon Sand or Gravel without danger, as being Built of half flat Ribs, whereas our Barks being round, would split in pieces upon the least touch. Such, Sir, are the Advantages of these *Flemish* Vessels beyond ours; and so you may safely Write to the *Rochel* Merchants who Trade to *Canada*, that they would find 'em very serviceable in that Country: At the same time, you may oblige 'em with the following dimensions of that sort of Shipping, which I took from the Vessel I was on Board of, that was one of the least Size. It was forty two Foot long from the Stern-post to the Head; the Hold was about eight Foot broad and about five Foot deep: The Cabin in the Fore-Castle was six Foot long, and had a Chimney with a Funnel and Vent at the bottom of the Cape-Stane. The Cabin Abaft was of the same length, and its Deck was rais'd three Foot higher than the Fore-Castle. The Helm of the frightful Rudder run along the Roof of the last Cabin. The Ribs of this little Vessel, were, in good earnest, as flat as the Boats in the *Seine*. The Side was about a Foot and a half high; the Mast was 16 Inches diameter, and 30 Foot high; the Sail resembled a Rectangle Triangle in its Form. The Vessel was provided with lee-boards, or a sort of Wings which the Carpenters [221] know very well how to use. In fine, to inform your self more particularly of the matter, you may Write to *Holland* for a Model of that sort of Shipping in Wood; for a *French* Carpenter will never make any thing of the best Verbal Description I can give. The case is the same as with some *Mathematical* Instruments, of which the acutest men can never form a just Idea without seeing 'em.

In Sailing from *Amsterdam* to *Hamburg*, we Steer thro' the *Wat*, that is, between the Continent and a string of Islands that lye about two or three hours off the *Terra Firma;* and round which the Tide ebbs and flows, as in other places. Between the Continent and these Islands there are certain Channels, which are deeper than the other places on the right and left, for these are dry every Tide. These Channels are easily distinguish'd by the help of some Buoys and Masts Planted upon the Flats. At half Flood you may weigh Anchor and Steer along the Channels, which make strange Windings and Elbows; and if the Wind be contrary, you may easily Board along by the help of the Current, till it is low Water, at which time you run a Ground upon the Sand, and are left quite dry. I saw above three hundred of these

Flemiſh Veſſels during the courſe of this Navigation, which I take to be as ſafe as that of a River, abating for ten Leagues Sailing when we croſs over from the laſt Iſland to the Mouth of the *Elbe*. The Tide riſes three Fathom perpendicular from the Mouth of this River to *Aurenbourg*, which lies ten or twelve Leagues above *Hamburg;* ſo that great Ships and Men of War may eaſily Sail up to *Hamburg*.

The Paſſage from *Amſterdam* to *Hamburg* is commonly accompliſh'd in ſeven or eight days; for in thoſe Seas the Weſterly Winds prevail for [222] three Quarters of the Year. But we were not above ſix days in our Paſſage, notwithſtanding that the Maſter of our Ship was oblig'd to loſe a Tide in producing his Invoys and Bills of Lading at the Town of *Stade*, which lies a League off the *Elbe*, and where all Ships are oblig'd to pay Toll to the King of *Sweden*, excepting the *Danes*, who might have an equal Right to claim ſuch a Toll, if they made uſe of the opportunity of Commanding the Paſſage of this River with the Cannon of *Glucſtat*.

The *Elbe* is a large League over at its Mouth, and at Spring-Tides it has Water enough in the Channel for Ships of fifty or ſixty Guns. The Entry of the River is very difficult and dangerous, by reaſon of an infinity of moving Sands, which render it almoſt inacceſſible in a Fogg, as well as in the Night time; notwithſtanding the precaution of Light Houſes Built pretty far out at Sea.

Hamburg is a large City, Fortified irregularly with Ramparts of Earth. I paſs over in Silence the Democratical Government of this *Hans* Town and its Dependancies, presuming you are not ignorant of such things, since the *Geographers* have given ample Descriptions of 'em: And shall content my self with informing you that the Trade of *Hamburg* makes it a considerable place; and considering the advantage of its Situation, one might readily guess so much. It supplies almost all *Germany* with all sorts of Foreign Commodities, by the conveniency of the *Elbe*, which carries flat bottom'd Vessels of two hundred Tun above *Dresden:* And one may justly say that this City is very Serviceable to the Elector of *Brandenburg*, in regard that these Vessels go up to the *Aspree*, and some other Rivers in his Territories. The *Hamburg* Merchants Trade to all parts of the [223] World, bateing *America*. They send but few Ships to the *East-Indies*, or the upper end of the *Mediterranean;* but they fit out an infinity of Ships for *Africa, Muscovy, Spain, France, Portugal, Holland* and *England;* and two Fleets every Year for *Archangel*, where they arrive at the latter end of *June*, and the latter end of *September*.

This little Republick keeps four Men of War of fifty Guns, and some light Frigats that serve for Convoys to their Merchantmen, Bound for the *Streights*, or for the Coast of *Portugal* or *Spain;* where the Sally-Rovers would be sure to pick 'em up if they went without Convoys. The City is neither pretty nor ugly; but most of the Streets are so narrow, that the Coaches must stop or put back every foot. It affords good Diversion enough; for commonly you have Plays Acted by *French* or *Italian* Actors, and a *German* Opera; which for *House, Theatre* and *Scenes*, may vye with the best in *Europe*. 'Tis true, the Habits of the Actours are as irregular as their Air and Meen; but then you must consider that these two Suit one another. The Neighbourhood of *Hamburg* is truly very pretty in the Summer time, by reason of an infinity of Country Houses, adorn'd with excellent Gardens, and great numbers of Fruit-Trees, which by the assistance of Art produce pretty good Fruit. But now that I am speaking of the Country round *Hamburg*, I can't dismiss the Subject without acquainting you with one thing that is uncommon. In the Neighbourhood of *Hamburg* there are Fields of Battel, retaining to the Territories of *Denmark* and *Lubeck;* in which private Quarrels are adjusted before an infinite number of Spectators, notice being given by the Sound of a Trumpet some days before the Champions enter the Lists. One remarkable Circumstance [224] is, that the Combatants, whether on Foot or on Horse-Back, implore the Mediation of two Seconds, only in order to be Judges of the thrusts, and to part 'em when four drops of Blood are spilt; so that the Adventurers retire upon the least scratch. If one of 'em falls upon the Ground, the Conqueror returns to the Territories of *Hamburg*, and makes a Triumphal Procession to that City, while the Air rings with acclamations of Joy from the Spectators. These Tragedies are not unfrequent; for *Hamburg* being resorted to by an infinite number of Foreigners and Strangers, some disorder or other always happens, which is redress'd that way. In former times, the *Danes*, *Swedes* and *Germans*, us'd to repair to the above mention'd Fields to adjust the Quarrels they had in their own Countries, where Duelling was prohibited under severe Penalties. But the Soveraigns of those Countries have since Stiffled such Practices, by declaring that upon their return they should be as severely punish'd, as if the Action had been in their own Territories.

After staying five or six days at *Hamburg*, I took leave of that City and set out for *Lubec* in a Post Waggon, that goes thither every day. Each place in the Coach is a Crown and a half. We arriv'd that same day at *Lubec*, and when we came to the Gates, were ask'd who we were; upon which every one gave a true account of their Country and Profession; but the fear of being stop'd dissuaded me from being so sincere. To be free with you, Sir, I plaid the Jesuit a little; for having guarded my Conscience with a good meaning, I roundly told 'em I was a *Portuguese* Merchant, and so got clear by suffering the affront of being hooted at for a *Jew*. In fine, we were all suffer'd to pass without opening our Portmanteau's.

[225] The City of *Lubec* is neither so great nor so populous as *Hamburg;* but its Streets are broader and straighter, and its Houses are much finer. The Ships that arrive in this Port are rang'd all in a row, upon a very pretty Key that extends from one end of the Town to the other; and that in a River, that in my Opinion is deeper than 'tis broad. The greatest Commerce of this Place retains to the *Baltick* Sea, which is not above two Leagues distant. The place from whence I now Write, is Seated exactly at the Mouth of this little River; which your great Ships can't enter, by reason of a *Bar* that has not above fourteen or fifteen Foot Water;

even when the Wind Springing from the Main swells this River after the same manner as the Tides of the Ocean. To morrow I think to Imbarque in a Frigat that carries Passengers from hence to *Copenhagen*, provided the Southerly Winds continue. I have taken the great Cabin for two *Ducatoons*, which is not above four *French* Crowns. *Ducats* are the most current and convenient Coin in all the Northern Countries; for they pass in *Holland*, *Denmark* and *Sweden*, and in all the Principalities of *Germany:* But a Traveller must take care that they are full Weight, for otherwise the People will scruple to take 'em, or at least cut off some *Sous* in the Change.

To conclude; I have met with good Inns hitherto in all the Towns I pass'd thro'; and drank good *Bourdeaux* Wine both in *Hamburg* and *Lubec*. The People of the Country drink likewise *Rhenish* and *Moselle* Wines; but to my mind they are better to Boil Carp in than for any thing else. Adieu, Sir, I am now call'd upon to pack up my Baggage: I hope to see *Copenhagen* the day after to morrow, if so be that this Southerly Wind stands our Friend, as much as I am,

Sir, Yours, &c.

[226] LETTER III.

Dated at Copenhagen, *Sep.* 12 1694.

Containing a Defcription of the Port *and* City *of* Copenhagen, *a View of the* Danifh Court; *and of the* Humours, Cuftoms, Commerce, Forces, *&c. of the* Danes.

SIR,

THE South-Eaft Wind that blew when I Wrote laft, wafted me into the Port of this good City of *Copenhagen;* after which it took leave of us, and purfued its courfe to the Northern Countries of *Sweden*, where its thawing influence had been expected for fome days. This little Voyage, which was over in eight and fourty hours, afforded me diverfion enough; for I had the pleafure of viewing to the Lar Board, or on the left hand, fome *Danifh* Ifles, which feem'd to be pretty Populous, if we may judge of that from the great number of Villages that I defcry'd upon 'em, when we Sweep'd along their Coaft in clear Weather with a frefh Gale. I take it, the croffing of this Sea muft be fomewhat dangerous in Winter, by reafon of the Banks of Sand that are met with in fome places: For the Nights being long, and the Winds high in that Seafon, no Precaution whatfoever would rid me of the fears of running upon the Sands, till I arriv'd at this City.

As foon as I fet my foot on Shoar, the Waiters came and view'd my Portmanteau's, in which they found more Sheets of Paper than Piftoles. [227] The next day after my Arrival, I waited upon Monfieur *de Bonrepaux*, who was then in the Country for the recovery of his Health: And for want of whom the Navy of *France* has fuftain'd an irreparable lofs.[1] This done, I return'd to this City, which may juftly be lifted in the number of thofe that we in *Europe* call great and pretty. 'Tis well and regularly Fortified, and 'tis pity 'tis not Wall'd with Stone, which is likewife a defect in the Cittadel that commands the Mouth of the Harbour. *Copenhagen* has one of the beft Harbours in the World, for both Nature and Art have confpir'd to fhelter it from all Infults. The City ftands upon a fmooth level Ground, the Streets are broad, and almoft all the Houfes are three Story high, and built of Brick. Here you may fee three very fine places; and amongft the reft, the King's Market, fo call'd from his Statue on Horfe-Back, which is there erected. This Place is furrounded with fome fine Houfes, and Monfieur *de Bonrepaux* Lodges in one of 'em, which is very large; and indeed that Ambaffadour has occafion for fo great a Houfe, confidering the numeroufnefs of his Retinue. The Magnificence of his Table is fuitable

---

[1] Like Lahontan, François Dusson, Sieur de Bonrepaux, was of Gascon birth. By sheer ability he had raised himself from a humble position in the office of the marine to be chief of the French naval squadron. He was also a diplomatist of ability, and had been sent on important missions to England (1685-87); from 1693-97 he was French ambassador to Holland. As a patron of letters, he became interested in Lahontan, and endeavored to reëstablish his credit at the French court. See Macaulay's brilliant characterization, in his *History of England* — ED

to the Grandeur of his Equipage: And every body pays him the honours and efteem that his Character merits. But I'll infift no longer upon that Head.

The City of *Copenhagen* is very advantageoufly Seated, as you may fee in the Map of the Ifle of *Zealand;* and lies very conveniently for Merchantmen which come without any difficulty up to the Canals or Ditches that are cut thro' it. It contains very fine Edifices; particularly the Churches of *Notredame* and St. *Nicholas*, which are both great and fine. The round Tower paffes for an admirable piece of Architecture, and has [228] a Stair-Cafe upon which a Coach may drive up to the top. The Library which ftands in the middle of the round Tower is well Stock'd with Books and valuable Manufcripts. The Exchange is an admirable Fabrick, in regard both to its length, and its Situation in the pleafanteft part of the Town. As for the Royal Palace, its Antiquity recommends it as much to me, as if it had been Built after the Modern way: For in the Maffy Fabrick of a Caftle, 'tis enough if the due Symmetry of Proportion be obferv'd. The Furniture and Pictures in this Caftle are admirably fine; and the Royal Clofet is fill'd with an infinity of very curious Rarities. In the King's Stables there is now but a hundred Coach-Horfes, that is, thirteen or fourteen Set of different forts and fizes; and a hundred and fifty Saddle-Horfes: But both the one and the other are equally fine. *Chriftians-Fawe*, the Second City, is fever'd from *Copenhagen* by a great Canal of running Water. The Royal Palace of *Rozemburg*, which ftands at one end of the City, is adorn'd with a charming Garden.

I come now to give you the Characters of the Princes and Princesses at the Court of *Denmark*. 'Tis needless to take notice of the Valour and Vigilancy of the King, for the two chief Qualities of that Monarch are sufficiently known to all the World.[1] I shall therefore only acquaint you that he is a Person of great Judgment and Capacity, and intirely Wrap'd up in the Interests of his Subjects, who look upon him as their Father and Deliverer. He has all the Qualities of a good General, and is affable and generous to the last degree. He speaks with equal facility, the *Danish*, *Swedish*, *Latin*, *German*, *English* and *French* Languages. The Queen is the most Accomplish'd Princess in the World; and so I have [229] said all in all. The Royal Prince is a Son worthy of so great a King for his Father, and such a good and vertuous Queen for his Mother; as you have heard it proclaim'd by as many Tongues as there are Heads in *France*. He is a Master of Learning, and has a quick Apprehension joyn'd to a sweet Temper. His Manners are as Royal as his Person, and all that see him wish him that Prosperity and Happiness that his Physiognomy promises. Prince *Christian* is a sweet lovely Prince, as well as Prince *Charles* his younger Brother: A certain Air of Affability sits upon their Foreheads and charms Mankind. Prince *William* the youngest Brother is a very pretty Child. Princess *Sophia*, who is commonly call'd the Royal Princess, has truly a Royal Air: She is Handsome, Young, well Shap'd and Witty as an Angel: Which is enough to entitle her to a Preference before all the Princesses upon

---

[1] For the king of Denmark, see p. 3, note 2, *ante*. — ED.

Earth, not to mention a thousand other good qualities, the Relation of which would prove too bulky for a *Missive*. Let's therefore call another Subject.

One may live in this Country for almost nothing, notwithstanding that good Fish is somewhat dear: In the best Ordinaries about Town you pay but fifteen or sixteen *Sous* a Meal. The Butchers Meat of this place is neither so juicy nor so nourishing as that in *France;* but their Poultry, their fresh Water-Fowl, their Hares and their Partridges are exceeding good. The best Claret costs but fifteen *Sous* a Bottle. A Hackney-Coach may be hir'd for a Crown a day, and sixty *Livres* a Month. The Water of this place is muddy and heavy, and for that reason we have recourse to the Beer, which is clear and wholesome, and very cheap. The *French* Refugees in *Copenhagen* are allow'd the free exercise of their Religion, under the direction of Monsieur [230] *de la Placette* a Minister of *Bearn*, who has a very good Pension from the Queen, for Preaching in a publick Church, of which her Self is Protectress.

Commonly the King passes the Summer at his Country Seats, sometimes at *Yegresburg*, sometimes at *Fredericsburg*, and sometimes at *Cronenburg*. There's scarce any Prince in the World that has better Accommodation for Dear-Hunting, than the King of *Denmark:* For all his Parks are full of broad Roads for pursuing the Chace; besides that, the *Danish* Horse have a long stretch of a Gallop, which is very convenient for Hunters; and the Dogs of that Country are scarce ever faulty. The King's Table is as nobly Served up, as you can well imagine: So that when he returns from Hunting he finds a fresh Pleasure in feeding on Angelical Fare. He is frequently imploy'd in reviewing his Troops, and visiting his Forts, Magazines and Arsenals; and sometimes he goes a Fowling with his Courtiers. About two Months ago I saw him Shoot about a quarter of a League out of Town: Upon which occasion a Wood Fowl as big as a Cock was plac'd upon the top of a Mast, and the King Shot at it first and took away a piece of its Neck with his Ball; after which his Courtiers Shot so dexterously that there was nothing left but a little bit of the Fowl, which the King hit at last, after a great many Sports-Men had attempted it in vain.

Most of the People in this place understand *French;* and perhaps the Gentlemen of the Royal Academy are not better Skill'd in the Purity and Delicacy of that Language, than the Countess *de Frizs;* who by her Wit, Birth and Beauty is justly accounted the Pearl and Ornament of the Court. The *Danes* are a proper sort of People; they are civil, honourable, brave and active. They have somewhat that's very ingaging [231] in their Carriage, and bears an Air of affability and complaisance. I take 'em to be a sensible thinking sort of People, and free of that unsufferable affectiation and vanity that gives a disrelish to the Actions of other Nations: At least 'tis apparent that a disengag'd genteel Air shines thro' all their Actions. The *Danish* Ladies are very handsome and lively; generally they are very witty and brisk, and a sparkling gayety hangs very agreeably about 'em, notwithstanding that the nature of their Climate do's not promise it. The *Danish*

Men complain that they are too haughty and nice in their *Conduct;* and indeed they have reason to charge 'em with a scrupulous nicety; but as for their Pride I know nothing of it. They receive almost no visits, and 'tis alleg'd that the reason of this reserv'dness proceeds not so much from the design of avoiding the occasion of Temptation, as from the fear of being Scandalis'd; for Slander reigns in this Country as much as elsewhere. In fine, they have more Vertue and Wisdom than they should have, in bearing the Sighs of Lovers without being mov'd. One may see 'em often enough at the House of Mr. *de Guldenlew,* the King's natural Brother and Viceroy of *Norway.* That Gentleman, who indeed is one of the Stateliest Men in *Europe,* takes pleasure in keeping a Table every day for eighteen persons, and regaling the Ladies and Persons of Quality. After Dinner the Gentlemen make Matches to Game or Walk out with the Ladies. The same Entertainment, and the same sort of Company is to be met with at the Count *de Revenclaw*'s, who is look'd upon as one of the most Zealous and Capable Ministers that the King has. These Dinners or Entertainments are somewhat too long for me, who am accustom'd to Dine Post, I mean, to fill my Belly in five or six [232] Minutes; for commonly they last above two hours. The excellent Messes which are then Serv'd up in great plenty, Feast at once the taste, the sight and the smell. For; in fine, there's no difference between those Tables and the best about the *French* Court, unless it be that the former have great pieces of Salt Beef set upon 'em; and I truly think the *Danes* would be Guilty of an indiscreet Action in eating of it fo heartily, if they did not take care to wafh the Salt out of their Throat with good Liquor.

Among the different forts of Wine that are commonly drank at *Copenhagen*, the *Cahers* and the *Pontac* are the only Wines that fuit a *French Man*'s Palate. It feems to be an inviolable Cuftom in all the Northern Countries, to fwill down two or three good Draughts of Beer, before they turn to Wine, which they value too much to fpoil it with Water. I am told that in former times they us'd to fit four or five hours at Meals, and drink briskly all the while, in fpite of the threats of the Gout. But now adays that cuftom is in difufe; befides, the Glaffes are fo fmall and the number of the Healths fo moderate, that they rife from Table in very good order: Not but that fometimes upon extraordinary Solemnities, the Guefts lye under an indifpenfible Obligation to drink huge Bumpers in certain *Wellcomes;* which in ancient times were in ufe among the *Grecians* under the name of ἀγαθῦ δαίμονος. I tremble when I call to mind thefe Bumpers, ever fince a fatal accident befell me about two Months ago in Mr. *de Guldenlew*'s Houfe: That Gentleman regal'd fome eighteen or twenty Perfons of both Sexes, in Solemnifing the Birth of his Children; and Fate would have it fo that I had the honour to be one of the Male Guefts, who were all oblig'd, excepting Mr. *de Bonrepos*, to drink two dozen of Bumpers to the Health of the prefent and abfent [233] Children. I proteft, I was very much out of Countenance, and would have almoft chofe to drink up the River of St. *Laurence*, rather than thefe Fountains of Wine; for there was no poffibility of baulking a Glafs. 'Twas then too late to reflect upon the ftrange Pofture I was in; for as the Proverb goes, the Wine was drawn, and I was oblig'd to drink it; I mean, I was oblig'd to do as the reft did. However, towards the conclufion of Dinner they put round a great *Wellcome* that held two Bottles; and all the Gentlemen were oblig'd to drink it brim-ful, as a Health to the Royal Family; God knows, the defpairing Mariner never trembled more gracefully upon the difmal Profpect of a Ship-Wrack, than I did upon the approach of the Bumper. In fine, I confefs to you, I drank it, but for the latter part of the Story I beg your Pardon; for I have no mind to glory in the Heroick Action that I did in imitation of three or four more, who difcharg'd their Confcience juft under the Table as gracefully as I. After that fatal blow, I was fo mortified that I durft not appear; nay, I had a ftrong fancy to leave the Country out of hand, and would certainly have done it, if my Pot Companions and thofe who fhar'd the difgrace, had not diffuaded me by an infinity of *German* Proverbs that feem'd to applaud the generous Exploit; among which the following had the greateft influence, viz. *If we are afham'd in taking too much, we ought to place our Glory in giving it up again.*

The *Danifh* Gentry live very handfomely upon their LandRents, and the Peafants want for nothing, no more than ours, unlefs it be for Mony. They have a fufficient Stock of Grain and Cattel, which ferves to maintain 'em in a grofs way, and to pay the Landlord's Rents. Is not it enough that they are well clad and well fed? [234] I would fain know what advantage the *Dutch* Boors reap from their Crowns, while they feed upon nothing but Cheese and Butter-spread upon *Pompernick. If their Crowns and Dollars serve only to pay the Taxes of the Republick, they must be very Blind in hugging a Shadow of Liberty, which they purchase at the expence of the Substance that maintains both Life and Health.

* Pompernick *is a sort of Bread, as black as a Chimney, as heavy as Lead, and as hard as Horn.*

The best thing the *Danes* ever did, was that of setting their Kings upon the same Foot as they now are. The Prince that sways the Scepter at present, exercises an Arbitrary Power with as much Equity as his Predecessor. Before their Government was reduc'd to this happy lay, the Kingdom was overrun with factious Clubs and Civil Wars; the State and Society it self was all in disorder; the Grandees crush'd the inferiour Subjects, and even the Kings themselves were oblig'd to stoop (if I may so speak) to the Laws of their Subjects. In a word, their Eyes being dazled with that Phantasm of Liberty, which by a treacherous lustre imposes upon several other Nations; they were thereby render'd Slaves to so many petty Kings, who acted like absolute Soveraigns without fearing the limited Power of their Monarchs.

At present, the King of *Denmark*'s Revenue amounts to five Millions of Crowns. This I know to be a just and true State of his Treasury: He maintains near thirty thousand Men of regular Troops, in good order, well disciplin'd and well pay'd; besides the Militia who are always ready to March upon a call. Nay farther, he may raife fourty thoufand Men more, upon occafion, without difpeopling his Country. His Officers are provided for at a reafonable rate, efpecially the Marine Officers who are not allotted, (as ours are in *France*,) any greater Pay than what bears a juft proportion to the poor Captains of Foot and Horfe, who are oblig'd to pinch hard to anfwer the Charges that the Sea Captains are exempted from. 'Tis faid, the King of *Denmark* finds his account in letting out his Troops to his Allies, not with regard to the Mony pay'd on that account, but in regard that by this means he keeps his Troops in exercife, inures 'em to the hardfhips of War, and makes 'em compleat Mafters of the Military Art; in order to make ufe of 'em upon occafion. You muft know, Sir, his *Danifh* Majefty is above that ridiculous Scruple that moft other Princes make to imploy Foreigners or thofe of another Religion in their Service. The *Meffieurs de Cormaillon*, *Dumeni*, *L'Abat*, and feveral others have confiderable Pofts in his Army, notwithftanding that they are *French Men* and *Papifts*. From hence it appears that this Monarch is convinc'd that Men of Honour will rather differve their Religion than act counter to the Fidelity due to their Mafter: And to be plain with you, I believe the King is in the right of it: For fince the Foundation of all Religion confifts in the Fidelity we owe to God, to our Friend and to our Benefactor; nothing will be able to unhinge a Man of Honour, or to tempt him to act contrary to his Duty. I will not pretend to meafure the actions of others by my own Standard; but for my own part, I affure you if I had lifted my felf in the

Service of the *Turks*, with the liberty of continuing Popish; and if Orders were issued forth for laying *Rome* in Ashes, I would be the first Man to set fire to it, in obedience to the *Grand Seignior*'s Orders. But we have enough of that.

[236] The *Danish* Laws, contain'd in the *Latin* Book I now send you, will appear to you so clear, so distinct, and so wisely Concerted, that they'll seem to have proceeded from the Mouth of St. *Paul:* You'll find by them that this Country do's not countenance Solicitors, Barristers, and the rest of the litigious Tribe. I own indeed that the Law relating to Man-Slaughter is unreasonable; for you'll find that by the Penalty therein enacted, a Man that kills his Enemy runs much the same risque as if he had suffer'd himself to be kill'd.

The Court of *Denmark* makes as good a Figure in proportion to its Greatness, as any other Court in *Europe*. The Lords and Courtiers have very magnificent Equipages; and which is singular, none but those of the Royal Family are allow'd to give a Red Livery. The time of appearing at Court is from Noon to half an hour after one, or thereabouts; during which time the King appears in a Hall fill'd with very fine Gentlemen. Here you'll see nothing but Imbroidery and Lace after the newest Fashion. The Foreign Ministers make their appearance at the same time, for the King do's 'em the honour of hearing them Talk with a great deal of Pleasure. There are but few Knights of the Order of the *Elephant* to be seen at Court, by reason that the Dignity is bestow'd only upon Persons of the first Rank. This Order may justly be call'd the noblest in *Europe*, and less degenerate than the rest;

insomuch, that of thirty four Knights Companions, which make up the Compliment of the Order, three fourths are Soveraign Princes. The Order of *Dane-brouk is more common, and confequently lefs confiderable; tho' after all, the Knights invefted with that Collar, [237] are intitled to feveral great Prerogatives and marks of Preheminence.

* Danebrouk *fignifies the White Order.*

The natural Sons of the Kings of Denmark, bear the Title of † Guldenlew and High Excellence, * and their Ladies are diftinguifh'd by the Compellation of High Grace. The prefent King has two natural Sons, whofe Merit leaves all Expreffion far behind it. The eldeft Serves in France with all imaginable Applaufe. The Second who is but fifteen years of Age and continues here, is a very promifing Youth: He has a wonderful deal of Senfe and Wit; his Perfon is Handfome and well Shap'd; he is poffefs'd of all the Qualities that ingage the tender Sex; his Meen is perfectly charming; in a word, he is one of the compleateft young Gentlemen I ever faw. He is nominated High Admiral of Denmark; and, which is very furprifing, he is better vers'd in the Mathematicks and the Art of Building Ships, than the ableft Mafters. In the King of Denmark's Dominions there are two Popifh Churches publickly Tolerated; one at Glucftat and the other at Altena.

† Guldenlew *fignifies a Golden Lion.*

* *Which is equivalent to the* German Highnefs.

The Air of this Country is very wholfome for thofe who live foberly; but it has a contrary effect upon difcontented Perfons. The only Difeafe they complain of is the Scurvy;

which the Physicians impute to a foul nasty Air loaded with an infinity of thick and condensated Vapours, which joyn their Forces upon the Surface of the Earth, and insinuate themselves into the Lungs along with the Air: They plead that their Air thus polluted, joyns in with the Blood, and retards its Motion in so much that it congeals, and so gives rise to the *Scurvy*. But with the leave of [238] the good Doctors, I'll take the liberty to Vindicate the Air of this agreeable City, and beg 'em to consider that the impressions of the Air upon the Mass of Blood are less forcible than those of the Aliment. If the *Scurvy* took its rise from the unfavourable Qualities of the Air; by consequence every body would be equally liable to it; but this we find to be false, for that three quarters of the *Danish* Nation are clear of that Distemper. The Argument I now offer is grounded on the Observations I made upon all the Soldiers that dy'd of that Disease at the Forts of *Frontenac* and *Niagara* in the year 1687 (which I imparted to you in my * Letters Dated the next year.) In those Forts we have the purest and wholsomest Air in the World; *See my Letters in the first Volume, dated in 1688.* and for that reason it stands more to reason to attribute the Invasion of the *Scurvy* (which then reign'd) to the nature of the Aliment; I mean, to the Salt Meat, Butter and Cheese, as well as to immoderate Sleep and want of Exercise. This account of the matter will be back'd by all who have made long Voyages, when they consider the terrible havock that the *Scurvy* makes upon the Ship's Crews. I conclude therefore that the frequency of the *Scurvy* is owing to bad Victuals, purfuant to the Opinion of a very fenfible Gentleman whom I credit very much. This Gentleman reprefented one day, that fuch acid Food increafes the acidity of the Blood; and fo it comes to pafs that the Blood of Scorbutick Perfons is deftitute of Spirits; or at leaft, its Spirits are fo thin and fcanty that they are eafily abforbed and invelop'd by the prevailing acids, and by that means put under an impoffibility of exciting Fermentations. As for the influence of immoderate Sleep and [239] long Reft, all the World knows that they have a great tendency to the obftruction of the Inteftines, and promote the Generation of Crude Juices, in cramping the Senfible and wonted Evacuations, partly by the flower Motion of the Spirits, and partly by the Infenfible Tranfpiration of the Sublimer Particles. From thefe Remarks I conclude, that frefh Meat, good Porridge, regular Sleep, and moderate Exercife *(ad ruborem non ad fudorem)* are Antidotes againft the *Scurvy*, and the beft Correctives of the Mafs of Blood, whether by Sea or Land.

If this digreffion, Sir, feems too long; I would have you to impute it to my earneft defire, of directing you how to ward off that ugly Diftemper, when you come to undertake any long Voyage. I would not have you think that I have thus interrupted the thread of my Difcourfe, with intent to prove that the Air of this Ifland is better than that of *Portugal:* That's a thing I know nothing of; for whatever Air I breath in, I am ftill equally well. 'Tis true, the inconftancy of the Weather might affect me in fome meafure, if I were oblig'd to pafs the remainder of my life in *Copenhagen;* for here we have frequent inftances of the Weather's changing three or four times a day, and fhifting from cold to hot, from dry to wet, and from clear to cloudy.

I had the honour to pay my profound refpects to the King of *Denmark* at his Caftle of *Fredericksbourg*, upon the occafion of his Inftalling fome *German* Princes by Proxy in the Order of the Elephant. That Ceremony which indeed was very pretty, drew thither a great confluence of perfons of a diftinguifhing Character; particularly all the Foreign Minifters who were proud of affifting at the Solemnity. Some days after that Prince went to take the Air at *Cronengbourg*, [240] which ftands directly upon the fide of the ftreight call'd the *Sund*. This Caftle has a regular Fortification, being Wall'd with Brick, and cover'd with a great number of wide bore'd and long Culverines, which command the entry of the Streight, that I take to be the breadth of Three thoufand five hundred Geometrical Paces, that is to fay, a large *French* League. Here you have the pleafure of Seeing an infinity of Foreign Ships pafs to and again between the Ocean and the *Baltick-Sea*: And in regard that the Guns of *Cronengbourg* are the Keys of this Port, all Foreign Ships lye under an indifpenfable neceffity of coming to an Anchor at *Elfenor*, to pay the Toll before they go farther. You may allege, perhaps, that a Numerous Fleet of Men of War might force their Paffage at the expence of a little Cannonading: and indeed I own the allegation to be juft; but if the King of *Denmark*'s Navy were at Anchor in the Streight, I am perfwaded they would be able to fecure the Pafs: and for that reafon you ought not to think it ſtrange that his *Daniſh* Majeſty exacts a moderate Toll from the Merchantmen of all Nations, except the *Swedes*: At leaſt I think he has a better Title to demand it, than the *Grandſignior* has in the *Dardanelles*. For moſt of the Ships that ſail to the *Baltick*, go to Trade with *Lubeck*, *Brandenbourg*, *Dantzick*, *Pruſſia*, *Courland*, *Livonia* and *Sweden*; whereas thoſe which paſs the *Dardanelles* are bound for the *Grandſignior*'s Ports, and Trade with none but his own Subjects. I would fain know whether the King of *Spain* would not make the like pretenſions to a Toll upon the Streight of *Gibraltar*, if ſo be that *Europe* and *Africa* were ſo friendly as to ſit a little nearer together. Nay, put the impoſſible ſuppoſition out of the caſe, who knows but that Prince may make ſuch a [241] demand, when he comes to have a Puiſſant Naval Force? This Queſtion is not ſo Problematick as you think for. However, a great many people are of the opinion that they might eaſily avoid the Toll of the *Sund*, if they did but ſteer obſtinately through one of the two *Belts*: But they are miſtaken. 'Tis true indeed, the thing might take, if the Sands in the Sea were as fixt as they are in the Charts; but that they are not; for the former ſhift in every Storm, whereas the latter ſtand for ever in the ſame Paper-ſtation. Beſides there's an infinity of cover'd Rocks, and irregular Currents, unknown to the experteſt Pilots, notwithſtanding the aſſiſtance of their Maps and *Sea-Charts.

* *Books of Hydrographical Charts.*

To call up another Subject; Suffer me to acquaint you that *Denmark* produces a great many Commodities which are sold with great Advantage to the *English* and *Dutch;* particularly *Rye, Corn, Cyder, Mead, Apples, Oxen, Cows, Fat Hogs, Horses, Iron, Copper,* and all sorts of Timber, especially Masts from *Norway,* which affords some of one piece that are big enough for *Noah's Ark.* In *Norway* there are some Silver Mines, which, 'tis said, the King might get by, if he would be at the charge of Digging. The *Norwegians* sell likewise the Skins of *Bears, Foxes, Martins, Otters* and *Elks;* but they are not so fine as those of *Canada.*

To come to the King of *Denmark*'s Naval Force; his Fleet which is always kept in good order, as well as his Magazines and Arsenals, consists of Twenty Eight Ships in the Line of Battle, Twenty Six Fregats and Four or Five Fireships; particularly

    8 Ships from 80 to 100 Guns.
    10 Ships from 60 to 80 Guns.
    10 Ships from 50 to 60 Guns.
    [242] 16 Fregats from 10 to 26 Guns.
    3 Bomb Vessels.

He maintains 1800 Carpenters and 400 Gunners. The Sea Captains Pay is not always the same. Some have Three Hundred, some Four Hundred Crowns a Year. The Captain Commodores have five hundred, and the Commodores six hundred: Besides these, there are twelve Marine Volunteers, call'd Apprentices, who have a hundred Crowns a Year. But after all, you'll be pleas'd to consider that these Allowances are not so sorry as you may think for; for in *Denmark* a Man may live for thirty Crowns, better than for a hundred Crowns in *France.*

Besides the above mention'd Fleet, his Majesty may, upon occasion, call for twenty four Ships from 40 to 60 Guns, which his Subjects are oblig'd to fit out at his Pleasure, and which are otherwise imploy'd in Trading to *Portugal*, *Spain*, and the *Mediterranean*. 'Tis to be observ'd by the bye, that a *Danish* Ship of fifty Guns may safely venture a Broad-Side with a *French* or *English* Ship of sixty, by reason that their Timber is very strong, and their Guns of a wide Bore. All the *Danish* Men of War are Built with half-flat Ribs, which occasions their heavy Sailing. Their Masts are very thick and short; Short that they may not bend under the Sails when they Weather Capes, Islands, Rocks and Banks in a Storm; and thick that they may bear the Sails tight, in doubling these Capes, Islands, *&c.* when the Boisterous Winds furrow the Surface of the *Baltick*. The King of *Denmark*'s Sea Men are well entertain'd, and well pay'd, and have twelve Crowns Bounty-Mony over and above their Wages, as soon as the Fleet is laid up. But at the same time, you must know that three thousand Sea Men are kept in constant Pay, and lodg'd in [243] an uniform Row of Barracks in the Streets of this City.

I shall conclude this Letter with a View of the Coin and Current Mony of the Kingdom.

A *Bank* Rix Dollar is worth 50 *Lubec* Pence.
A *Danish* Rix Dollar goes for 48 *Lubec* Pence.
A *Shet Dal* is worth 32 *Lubec* Sous.
A Marc-lubs passes for 16 Stuivers of *Lubec*.
A Marc *Danish* is worth 8 *Lubec* Stuivers.
A half Mark *Danish* is worth 4 *Lubec* Pence.

One *Lubec* Penny is worth two *Danish* Pence, and two *Danish* Pence are of the same value with fourteen *French* Deniers, which is much the same with an *English* Penny; and by this Standard you may reduce all the above mention'd Denominations.

A Gold Ducat is worth two *Danish* Rix Dollars and fourteen Pence; sometimes 'tis two Pence under or over. A Rose-Noble is two Ducats. A Silver *Lowis* or a *French* Crown passes in *Denmark* for a *Danish* Rix Dollar; and the half and quarter Crowns observe the same proportion, as well as the *Louis d' Ores*.

In the Island of *Zealand* the Leagues consist of 4200 Geometrical Paces; the *Norway* Leagues are longer, and those of *Holstein* are of less extent. The *Copenhagen* Ell is an Inch and a half bigger than the *French* half Ell.

I am,
 SIR,
  Yours, &c.

[244] LETTER IV.
Dated at *Paris, Dec.* 29. 1694.
Containing a Journal of the Author's Travels from Copenhagen *to* Paris.

SIR,

I LEFT *Copenhagen* three days after the Date of my last; being accommodated with Mr. *de Bonrepeau*'s Coaches, who to avoid the fatigue of passing between the two *Belts*, had gone before to Wait upon the King of *Denmark* at *Coldinck*. You must know, that Prince goes thither Post every Year, notwithstanding that his Retinue amounts to a thousand or twelve hundred Persons. Upon that occasion, the Boors of the Villages adjacent to the Road, are oblig'd to bring their Horses to certain Places at an appointed hour, in order to draw the Coaches and Waggons that contain that numerous Retinue, with their Baggage. Tho' these Horses are little, yet they are strong, vigorous, tidy, insensible of cold, and so very light, that they'll go you a good Trott as fast as a Gallop. The Stages for shifting the Horses are two or three Leagues, as well as those for the Horse-Guards which conduct the King from place to place, and are reliev'd every Stage.

We set out from *Copenhagen Sept.* 15. and after three hours Travelling, arriv'd at *Roskild*, which makes six of those Leagues of which twenty goe to a degree. We pafs'd fo fpeedily that we had only time to view the Tombs of the Kings of *Denmark*, while the Boors put frefh Horfes in the [245] Coaches. These *Marble Maufoleums* are a finifh'd piece of Architecture, and adorn'd with *Baffe Releivo's* and *Latin Infcriptions*. The fine Marble of which they are Built, is very well Polifh'd, being that of *Paros*, and *Africa*, and that call'd *Brocatelle*, *Serpentine* and *Cipellino*. The Tombs are plac'd in the Chappel of an ancient Church, that belong'd to the *Benedictins* before *Luther's* Remonftrances. The fame very day we came to take up our night's Lodging in a Village near the great *Belt;* having enjoy'd the pleafure of viewing by the way, fome admirable Land-Skips. Next day at eight a Clock in the Morning, we arriv'd at the Town of *Cortos*, which ftands upon the Chops of the above mention'd Streight; and is Fortified with Earth.

As foon as we Imbarqu'd in the Yacht that lay ready for Mr. *de Bonrepau*, we fet Sail; but in croffing thefe four Leagues of Sea, the Wind was fo low and the Sea fo calm, that one might have drank Bumpers upon the Deck without-fpilling. We no fooner landed at *Nibourg*, a little paltry place regularly Fortified, than we took Coach, and fet out for *Odenzee*, the Capital City of *Fionia*, where we lay that Night. *Odenzee* ftands in the middle of that Ifland, which is one of the moft fertile Territories of *Denmark*. The Cathedral Church is as handfome as 'tis large. In former times this City was the Refidence of the Kings of *Denmark*, and the Inhabitants were fo Barbarous as to murder one of their

Princes. The Nobility of the Island vye with those of *Venice* for Antiquity; especially the Family of *Trool*, which signifies *Sorcerer*, and which bears a Devil *Sable* upon a Field *Gules* for their Arms: From whence I conclude that this *Leo Rugiens* was more tractable and illustrious in the Primitive [246] times, than in those of the * Author of the *Seven Trumpets*, or else the Ancient Nobility would not have glory'd in placing him in their Coats of Arms.

* *An old Dotard that advances a thousand idle Whims, which are enough to turn a Woman's Brains.*

The 18*th* we set out for *Midelford*, where we found a Barque that wafted us over from the farther side of the little *Belt*, after halting two or three hours in vain, for the coming up of the Waggons with Mr. *de Bourepau*'s Domesticks and Provisions. As soon as we crofs'd over, we receiv'd Advice that they had miss'd their way; but we were so pinch'd with Hunger that we were forc'd to go to a Farmer's House, and dress with our own Hands some Broil'd Meat and Pan-Cakes, that we eat without drinking; for our Landlords Beer was as Wretched as his Water. Some time after the Ambassadour's Equipage Arriv'd; but 'twas then so very late that we were forc'd to tarry all night in that House of Martyrdom. The next day we arriv'd at *Coldinck*, where the Magistrate took care to provide Lodgings for the Ambassador in one of the best Houses in Town. Three or four days after, the King arriv'd at the same place.

This little Town is Seated in the Country of *Jutland*, upon the Banks of a shallow Gulf that is Navigable only by Barques: But at the same time, 'tis very considerable upon

The arms of the Outagamis call'd foxes

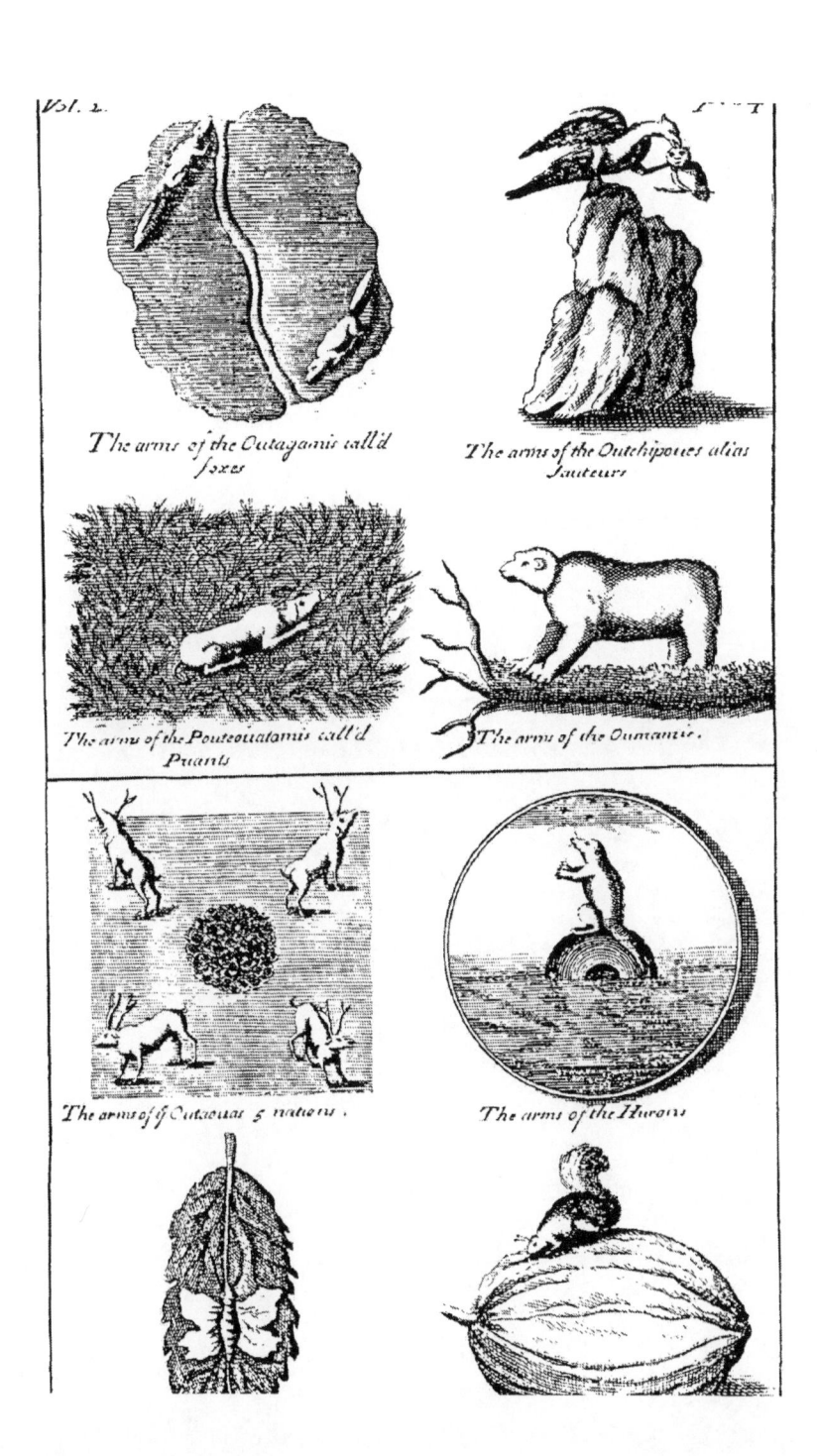

The arms of the Outchipoues alias Sauteurs

The arms of the Poutcouatamis call'd Puants

The arms of the Oumamis.

The arms of ye Outaouas 5 nations.

The arms of the Hurons

the account of the Toll for Cattel that's pay'd at that place, and brings into the Royal Treasury near two hundred thousand Rix Dollars. The Castle is an ancient Pile of Stone, that contains a great many Rooms: But 'tis Situated to great advantage, for it stands on an Eminence that affords you a View of all the Country round. The *Danes* would have us believe upon their Word, [247] that an Angel was sent from Heaven to the great Hall of this Castle, to acquaint *Christian* III. King of *Denmark*, that God was ready to receive him after three days. They add, that in order to perpetuate the Memory of this miraculous Vision, the very place where this Heavenly Ambassadour had Audience of the Prince, was took notice of, and a great Post was fix'd in it, which I saw every time I went to Court; for 'twas in that very Hall that the King made his publick Appearance all the time he was at *Coldinck*.

We took leave of *Coldinck* on the 24th, and Arriv'd on the 25th at *Rensbourg*, after passing by several little Towns and Royal Seats, the Description of which would be too tedious. I shall only tell you by the bye, we have a great deal more pleasure than fatigue in Riding Post in this Country, whether in Coach or Waggon, by reason of the evenness of the Ground, which affords as few Stones as Mountains. As soon as the King Arriv'd at *Rensbourg*, he review'd the Fortifications of the Place, which may easily be made one of the best Forts in *Europe*. Then he review'd a Body of Foot and Horse, and had a great deal of reason to be satisfied with their appearance. After some days he set out for *Glucstat*, a little Town upon the *Elbe;* almoſt as regularly Fortified as the laſt I ſpoke of. In the mean time Mr. *de Bonrepau*, who could not follow that Monarch, by reaſon of ſome Buſineſs he had to adjuſt with the Abbot *Bidal* at *Renſbourg*, gave me recommendatory Letters to ſeveral Perſons, who he thought would be able to influence Mr. *de Ponchartrain:* But he was miſtaken in his Conjecture, as you'll ſee preſently.

After taking leave of the Ambaſſadour, I went to *Hamburg,* where I was inform'd that Count *Caniſſec,* the Emperor's Envoy extraordinary to [248] the Court of *Denmark,* ſollicited the *Burgomaſters* to Arreſt me. The Surmiſe ſeem'd to be not improbable, for I knew that ſome time before he had taken up a Prejudice againſt me at *Fredericſbourg*, upon the account of ſome Illuminations that were made in that place; which oblig'd me to flie with all expedition to *Altena*, and tarry there for a Paſſport from the Duke of *Bavaria*, without which I had certainly been taken up in the *Spaniſh Flanders*.[1] I had no ſooner receiv'd this intelligence, than I met with the favourable opportunity of a return Coach bound for *Amſterdam,* where I found a place at an eaſy rate, without being incommoded with a Croud of Paſſengers, for there was but four of us, *viz.* An old *Engliſh* Merchant, a *German* Lady with her Chamber-Maid, and I. The Journey laſted eight days, and would have ſeem'd eight courſes of Eternity to me, if it had not been for the agreeable Converſation of that lovely Lady, who ſpoke ſuch good *French,* as to expreſs her ſelf

---

[1] Maximilien II was Duke of Bavaria (1679-1726). A firm ally of the Spanish monarch, his passport would secure a traveller in the realms of that ruler. — ED.

very handsomely. You must consider, Sir, that the Ways of *Arabia Deserta* are not so bad as the Roads of *Westphalia;* at least 'tis certain they are not so dirty. But the chief inconveniency lies in the Inns; for you must know, all the publick Houses upon the Road are downright Hospitals; the Landlords of which would Starve for hunger, if Foreigners had not the Charity to give 'em a Share of their Provisions, which they are forc'd to gather in from the Rich Farmers that live at a distance one from another. In these wretched Retreats you must rest satisfied in lying upon Straw; and all the Comfort a poor Traveller has, consists in this, that he may command his Landlord and Landlady, and their Children, to go and run where he pleases. If you find a Frying-Pan and a Kettle to dress your Meat withal, you're a happy [249] Man. Wood indeed there's good Store of; and their Chimneys being Built square, and standing by themselves, a hundred Persons may sit and Warm themselves at the Fire.

In the mean time, I admir'd the Patience of the *German* Lady, who was so far from complaining of the Hardships of the Journy, that she took pleasure in rallying upon the *English* Merchant, her Maid and my self, who were all mightily out of humour. I conjectur'd from her air and carriage, that she was a Person of Quality; and I found afterwards I was not mistaken, for since we parted, I heard she was a Countess of the Empire. She was so well acquainted with the *French* humours, that I did not doubt but that she had been at *Paris:* But the thing that confirm'd me in that Opinion, was her talking so accurately of the Persons of the first Quality about

Court; not to mention that she had an old *French* Servant, a *Roman Catholick*, that could scarce speak a Word of High *Dutch*. The Lady was of a large Stature and well Made; she look'd brisk enough, and her Beauty was so affecting that she us'd all her efforts in vain, to make me believe she was five and fifty years of Age. She could not endure to be answer'd, that her fresh and lively Complexion gave the lie to her Arithmetick; this she took for an affront, alledging that the Charms of a Woman beyond fifty, are too much Shrivel'd to cause Admiration. This, I take it, is a very singular and uncommon thing, for the rest of her Sex are scarce accustom'd to that sort of Language, in regard that they'd rather their Vertue were attack'd than their Beauty: But whatever be in that matter, she seem'd to be mightily prepossess'd against the *French*, in branding 'em for a light, giddy brain'd, indiscreet People, and still reflecting upon 'em for [250] thinking meanly of the *Germans*. " How comes it to pass, said she, that the *French*
" have the impudence to deny the *Germans* the Character of
" *Witty*, and to take 'em for a gross heavy People; instead of
" acknowledging their just Title to solid Sense and Reflection,
" by vertue of which they dive judiciously to the bottom of
" things? What is it, continued she, that the *French* require
" as essential to the Character of *avoir de l'esprit?* Must we
" value our selves upon a livelyness, and a false sparkling Wit
" that dazzles with a vain Splendor? Must we mak't our
" business to procure a ready and subtle imagination, in order
" to dress idle Flams in Gilded Words? No, no; that nicety
" of expression is but Whip'd Cream: And to speak the jus-

" tice of the matter, we ought to allow the *French* a preferable
" Title to the Science of fpeaking well, and to the *Germans* a
" juft claim of going beyond 'em in juft thoughts. But this
was not all: For fhe attack'd the *French* Pride fo vigoroufly,
that fhe made Prefumption and Vanity their ordinary and
leffer Crimes. This fhews, fhe had been in *France;* to which
for a farther proof fhe added, that the *French* infulted the
Germans with thefe ridiculous Proverbs; *viz. This Fellow's as
foolish as a German; He pick'd a German Quarrel with me; he
takes me for a German. Such a Woman would make a good German Woman*, i. e. She is fimple and foolifh. At the fame time,
I endeavour'd to diffuade her from fuch unfavourable thoughts,
by remonftrating that fhe ought to make a wide diftinction
between the fenfible People of *France*, and thofe who are fuch
fools as to imagine themfelves a Standard for all other Nations. I intreated her to throw off her prejudicate Apprehenfions, and to believe that the knowing part of our World have
a profound [251] efteem for the *Germans*, and cry up their
Merit, their Probity, their ftrong Senfe, and their inviolable
Fidelity. In earneft, Sir, the Perfons of any Note in *Germany*,
have a juft Title to all thefe good qualities; nay, the Etymology of the Word, *(Alleman,* i. e. a *German)* gives us fome
light as to their Character: For *All* and *Man* imports that
they are a People capable of any thing, like the *Jefuits* to whom
fome give the Title of *Jefuifta Omnis Homo*, and who are therefore faid to be *Germans*, by a Sophiftical way of Punning. But
this is not all that may be offer'd on their behalf; there are a
thoufand things that fpeak the Merit of the *Germans*. We

are indebted to 'em for the difcovery of the property of the *Load-Stone*, without which the New World had never reach'd our knowledg; for the Invention of *Printing*, which has taught us to diftinguifh Fabulous Manufcripts from Divine Writings; for the Invention of *Clocks*, of the Cafting of *Guns, Bells,* &c. This gives plain evidence of their diftinguifhing Induftry and Capacity. Add to all this that *Germany* has produc'd Soldiers, who by their Valour and Bravery made the *Capitol* to tremble, after defeating the *Roman Confuls*, and ftanding the Brunts of all the Courage and Puiffance of the *Roman Legions;* That it has been equally fertile in great Men, in the way of Learning, particularly *Juftus Lipfius, Furftemberg,* Mr. *Spanheim,* and *Melancthon.*[1] All this I reprefented to the Lady; but when I mention'd *Melancthon,* fhe interrupted me, and faid, fhe was furpris'd to find that the *French* twitted the *Germans* with the Vice of hard Drinking, fince themfelves ftood chargeable with *Plato*'s Crime. I had almoft made anfwer, that if the *French* had the fame relifh of things with that Philofopher, their only view was to love Superannuated Ladies with as much Paffion [252] as he did his old *Archeanaffa:* But I contented my felf in replying, that the *Germans* being difoblig'd by having the Character of *Hard Drinkers* thrown upon 'em, made their reprifals upon the *French*, by faftening upon *them* the imputation

---

[1] A group of German savants, of whom Justus Lipsius (1547-1606) was a great authority upon Roman antiquities; the Prince von Furstemberg (1625-82) was archbishop of Strassburg, and a satellite of Louis XIV; Ezekiel Spanheim (1629-1710) was a Latin scholar, author of a *History of the Cæsars*, and a diplomat of the court of the Elector of Brandenburg; Melancthon (1497-1560), the friend of Luther, was the principal scholar of the Reformation — ED.

of *Hanetonic* Love *(Sodomy)* with intent to render 'em odious to the fair Sex. I had no occasion to make any farther offers in justification of the *French*, for the Lady seem'd to be satisfied with what I said. In fine, this Lady was so comely and agreeable in such advanc'd Years, that if *Balzac* had seen her, he would not have offer'd to say that he never saw a handsome old Woman in his life-time.[1] Questionless, that *Gascogne Oracle* understood, by an old Woman, one of Seventy years of Age; for I have seen three or four that were perfect Beauties at Sixty, without ever a Wrinkle on their Faces, or a grey Hair on their Heads; and whose Eyes made still a retreat for *Cupid*.

As soon as I arriv'd at *Amsterdam*, I hir'd the Roof of the *Night-Boat* for *Rotterdam*; which sets out every day at three a Clock at both places, in order to convey Passengers to and again between these two Cities. It cost me a Crown, which I did not grudge; for I had the conveniency of Sleeping very quietly all Night upon the Quilts that the Waterman is oblig'd to furnish to all Passengers, who take the Stern-Room, call'd the Roof. The next day after my Arrival at *Rotterdam*, I took Shipping for *Antwerp* on Board of a *Hoy*, which is a Vessel with flat Ribs, and Lee-boards or Wings. The passage from *Rotterdam* to *Antwerp* is both safe and easy, and runs between the *Terra Firma* and the *Dutch* Islands; being favour'd by the Tydes. From *Antwerp* to *Brussels* I made use of the

---

[1] Lahontan here refers to the litterateur Jean Louis Guez de Balzac (1597-1654), whose *Letters* and *Dissertations* did much to fix the forms of French prose. On his father's side he also was a Gascon, being descended from a good family of Languedoc. — ED.

common Paſſage-Boat, which is only a great Boat drawn by a Horſe. At *Bruſſels* I was advis'd to Ride Poſt [253] to *Liſle;* becauſe the High-way-men us'd to Rob moſt of the Coaches and Waggons upon that Road. I comply'd with the Seaſonably Advice, and am now convinc'd that if I had not done ſo I had certainly been Rob'd. Two days after my arrival at *Liſle*, I took a place in the Coach which goes twice a Week to this good City of *Paris;* and arriv'd here laſt Week, after being ſufficiently Fleec'd by the Mercyleſs Inn-Keepers upon the Road. Theſe impoſing Dogs give as little quarter to a Traveller, that do's not bargain before hand for what he eats; as the Waiters of *Peronne* do to thoſe who indeavour to run Goods. At *Peronne*, you muſt know, they ſearch ſo narrowly, that they not only turn every thing out of a Cheſt or a Portmanteau, but examine every body from top to toe. They ſuſpect your Big-Belly'd Women moſt; and examine 'em ſo narrowly, that ſometimes they ſlide their Hand into a place that was appointed for ſomewhat elſe. If any Traveller has either *Snuſh*, *Tea*, *Indian Stuffs* or *Dutch* Books among his Baggage, the whole Cargo is Confiſcated.

Immediately upon my Arrival in this place, I repair'd to *Verſailles* to deliver Mr. *de Bonrepau*'s Letters: But the Perſons to whom they were addreſs'd, us'd their utmoſt Efforts to no purpoſe, in folliciting Mr. *de Ponchartrain* to allow me to juſtify my Conduct at *Placentia*. He anſwer'd 'em very coldly, that his Majeſty's ſtiff and inflexible Temper would never admit of any Juſtification from an Inferiour in oppoſition to his Superiour. This anſwer, which in ſome meaſure tarniſhes the Shining Merit and Judicious Conduct of so Wise a Prince; gave me to know that the Severity of Mr. *de Ponchartrain* did not proceed so much from a Principle of Equity, as from a Stiff *Iroquese* Temper. In the mean time I [254] was like to die for Grief, nothwithstanding that all my Friends endeavour'd to solace me, in advising me to raise my Mind above the Shocks of bad Fortune, till a change of Government happen'd. They did not scruple to counsel me to look out for some Refuge, where I might be shelter'd from the Fury of that Minister, so long as it pleases God to vouchsafe him the benefit of life, in order to allow him time to be Converted. *I delight not in the death of a Sinner, but would have him to be Converted*, &c. This Passage affords a fine Speculation, but I must own it has but little influence on one who is oblig'd to wait so long without any other relief than the Treasure at the bottom of *Pandora*'s Box. Adieu, Sir; I am to set out immediately for my Province, where I shall only pass thro' like Lightning. Not to trouble you with what's behind, I conclude with my plain Compliment, that

I am,
SIR,
Yours, &c.

[255] LETTER V.

*Near *Lahontan* in *Basse Navarre*. Dated at * *Erleich, July,* 4. 1695.

Giving a View of the Superstition and Ignorance of the People of Bearn; their addictedness to the Notions of Witchcraft, Apparitions, &c. And the Author's Arguments against that Delusion.

SIR,

DOUBTLESS you'l be mightily surpriz'd when you hear I am now in sight of a Country of which I retain no more than the bare Name; but your surprizal will be yet greater when you're inform'd that all the recommendations of Persons of the first Quality about Court could not influence Mr. *de Pouchartrain*, whose Prepossession against me is invincible. I left *Paris* with a melancholy Mind, and went to Solace my self for some Months in a certain Province of the Kingdom that you will easily guess at. From thence I made a trip streight to *Rochel*, where I went on board of a Vessel that commonly carries Passengers to *Tremblade*. In that Passage I fell into the Company of a White Friar, the History of whom is so very uncommon that I can't pass him in silence.

He calls himself *Don Carlos Baltasar de Mendoza*, and is the Son of a rich Gentleman at *Brussels*. He is about three and thirty or four and thirty Years of Age, and is at least as tall and as meagre as I am. He serv'd the King of *Spain* three or four Years in the quality of a Captain of Horſe; and for as much as he ſtudy'd the purſuit of Sciences, more than the humouring of the Governour of the *Neitherlands*, his Catholick Majeſty refus'd him a Regiment that his Father offer'd to raiſe at his own Charge. This denial oblig'd him to quit the Service: and ſoon after, being preſs'd by his Parents to Marry, he went to *Germany* and put on a Monks Habit, which he threw away ſome time after. Thoſe who gave me an account of him, aſſur'd me that he had taken up and laid down the Habit ſeveral times. But whatever be in that matter, he is certainly one of the moſt Accompliſh'd Men of this Age. He is at once perfectly well acquainted with the fineſt Sciences, and with the principal Languages of *Europe*. This Character was given him by the greateſt Men in *Bourdeaux*, who pay'd him ſeveral Viſits that I was witneſs to, for we lodg'd together in that City. But the beſt of the Story is, that the next Day after our arrival two Merchants of his own Country paid him a round ſum of dry *Louiſd'ors*, part of which he beſtow'd upon the Soldiers in the *Trompet*-Caſtle, who would otherwiſe never have thought that an Eccleſiaſtick would be ſo Liberal to Perſons of a Military Capacity. All the Divines, Mathematicians and Philoſophers that viſited him, were ſo charm'd with the extent of his Knowledge, that they affirm'd that the quickeſt and ſharpeſt Man in the World could not acquire an equal ſtock of Learning in a courſe of ſixty Years Study. We ſtaid fifteen Days at *Bourdeaux*, and during that time he had the Curioſity to ſee nothing but a little Church in the Neighbourhood of his Lodgings, and the

Trompet-Caſtle. He Read and Wrote inceſſantly; and as for the Breviary I believe he had none about him, for he was neither Deacon nor Prieſt. I never could [257] learn what Order he was of; for when I ask'd him, his Anſwer was, *I am a White Monk, and nothing more.*

Both of us took Places in the *Bayonne* Coach (for the Friar was bound for *Spain;*) when we came to *Eſperon* we parted, and I took the *Dax* and *Bayonne* Road. I had no ſooner arrived at the Country Houſe where I now am, than I receiv'd an infinity of Viſits that I could eaſily have diſpens'd with; for within theſe four Days they have ſo fill'd my Head with Stories of Gardening, dreſſing of Vines, Hunting and Fiſhing, that I have ſcarce a ſufficient freedom of thought to diſpatch this Expreſs, and to acquaint you with the Affairs that oblige me to deſire an Interview with you. But that which troubled me moſt, was the impertinent Folly of our wiſer ſort of Country-men: For all of 'em, whether Prieſts, Gentlemen or Peaſants, do nothing but teaze me from Morning to Night with Stories of Wizards and Witches; and Inſtance particularly in you, as being the only Man in the World that has ſuſtain'd moſt harm from that ſort of Cattle; in fine, they ply me ſo hot with their Chimera's, that I'm affrai'd I ſhall turn Magician. The whimſical Souls aſſure me in good earneſt, that ſuch and ſuch a one is a Wizard; nay, ſome ſwear the ſame thing of themſelves, and others declare in Conſcience that they once were of that Society, but had afterwards quited the Devils Sabbath. I ask'd ſeveral of 'em the Charms of that Sabbath, and receiv'd this Anſwer, *That the Sabbath was a*

Palace accommodated with the best Wines, the nicest Food, the handsomest Women, and the most agreeable Musick in the World; That in this Palace they Drink, Eat and Dance, and do with the fine Ladies, what they might do elsewhere without being Wizards. In fine, I verily believe, that [258] Beasts are not allow'd to be so Brutish as these Fools. Imagination can't reach their Folly; for 'tis as usual here to call one another Wizard, as to use the compellation of a Friend elsewhere. Every body believes the Wizards are so numerous, that 'tis a Scandal for a Man not to pass for one of the Gang; and so every one glories in the venerable Title of a Wizard or Conjurer.

Since I came to this place I am taken for an Atheist, because I tire my self in inculcating to the Priests and Gentlemen, that none but shallow Brains will entertain such idle Whims. But that which throws me into Dispair is the News that a Man of your Sense should gulp down such monstrous Flams, notwithstanding all the Arguments that guard off such an Opinion. Be it known to you, Sir, you must absolutely deny the Omnipotence of God, if you establish in this World, Sorcerers, Magicians, Soothsayers, Inchanters, Apparitions, Phantasms, Familiars, Hobgoblins, and a visible Devil that brings up the rear of all these Chimera's. To believe that God makes use of Wizards and Magicians to afflict Men, or blast the Product of the Earth, speaks a want of Religion, Sense and Wisdom. None but *Europeans* are capable to credit such Phantastical Stories. In this Country every body takes pleasure in recounting his Visions, and there's none but who has seen or heard some Spirit or other in his Life-time. Few dive to the bottom of these popular Errors; and most People would scruple to believe that these Errors are the Inventions of Idolatrous and Christian Priests. The World entertains too favourable an Opinion of the Clergy to charge 'em with that Crime; and if by chance one were found who being convinc'd of the Cheats of [259] the Priests makes the Oracles promote the spunging of Mens Pockets and Womens Thighs, an infinity of ignorant Souls would still disbelieve him. Believe me, Sir, I confine my Discourse to these Ancient Priests, that I may not give you Offence by reflecting on the Industry of the Modern; I have the Pope's Kettle too much in view to hinder it to Boil, for one Day it may come to be my last Refuge; and so I ought to hold my Peace. This Subject would require a clear and distinct Dissertation, and perhaps I may present you with some such thing one of these Days.

In the mean time be pleas'd to know that a * strong Genius will never suffer it self to believe the existence of Sorcerers, &c. especially considering that they are all as poor as Church Rats; for how can we imagine that these pretended Miscreants should have the Courage to trust themselves to a Master who is so far from discovering to 'em hidden Treasures, and a thousand other things in the Commerce of the World which might inrich 'em, that he suffers 'em to be Hang'd and Burnt? Prithee, how can

* *By a strong Genius (esprit Fort) I understand a Man that Fathoms the Nature of Things; that believes nothing but what is maturely weigh'd by his Reason; and without any regard to Prejudice makes wise Decisions upon such Heads as he has clearly canvass'd.*

we believe that God impowers thefe poor Wretches to raife Storms and overturn the Elements? 'Tis alledged that the Devil inveigles 'em by Promifes, and makes Contracts with 'em under a private Seal; but from thence 'twould follow that God invefted the Devil with a Power to feduce thofe poor Mortals; which at the fame time he could not do without Authorizing Lies. To pretend that God Arms the Enemy of [260] Mankind againft Humane Creatures, is a downright infulting of his Wifdom. None but airy Fools can entertain the Wickednefs of Sorcerers, the Cunning of Magicians, the Power of Conjurers, the Apparitions of Spirits, and the Soveraignty of the Devil, for Articles of Faith: For fuch Thoughts are only harbour'd by Fools and Bigots. The Vulgar feed themfelves with fuch Chimera's; and the Parfons that preach 'em up find their account in all Countries. Do but mind what I fay, and you'l find I'm in the right of it. In former Times the Character of a Philofopher or Mathematician was a fufficient Qualification for a Sorcerer. The Savages believe that a Watch, a Compafs, and a thoufand other Machines are moved by Spirits; for your ignorant and clownifh People form extravagant Ideas of every thing that furpaffes their Imagination. The *Laplanders* and the *Tartarian Kalmouks* ador'd Strangers for playing *Legerdemain* Tricks. The *Fire-eater* at *Paris* pafs'd a long while for a Magician. The *Portuguefe* burnt a Horfe that did wonderful things, and his Owner had enough to do to make his efcape, becaufe they took him for a Conjurer. In *Afia* the *Chymifts* are look'd upon as Poyfoners. In *Africa* the Mathematicians bear the name of Wizards. In

America the Physicians are branded for Magicians; and in some parts of *Europe* those who are well vers'd in the *Hebrew* Tongue are deem'd for *Jews*.

But to return to the Cunning Men of our Country; What reason have we to think that Men would bequeath their Souls for the imaginary *Sabbatic* Pleasure of poysoning Cattle, blasting Corn with Storms and Hail, and raising such boisterous Winds as overturn Trees, and strip the Earth of its Fruits. One would think these [261] Disciples would rather ask Riches of him; for if the Devil is capable of turning the Elements topsy turvy, and interrupting the Course of Nature, why does not his Power extend to the pumping of Gold from the Mines of *Perou*, or engrossing the Treasures of *Europe*, in order to give Pensions to his Magical Votaries, who are as poor as Church Mice? I know you'l answer, *That pieces of Silver will turn into Oak-leaves in the Hands of the Devil:* But that Allegation sinks his Power of working so many Miracles, and particularly that which he imparts to the Wizards. But supposing that he is not allow'd to work in Silver; might not so wise a Creature as he is represented to be, teach 'em the means to acquire it in the way of Commerce or Gaming? What should hinder him to conduct 'em to hidden Treasures, or to such as are lost in Shipwrack, or at least to teach 'em the Secret that enabled the *Passetes* Magician to recal into his Pocket all the Money he spent? You'l meet with some who maintain, that the Devil us'd such Methods long before the Deluge, to precipitate Men into a Magical Idolatry: But if you trace such Doctors from Consequence to Consequence, 'twill follow that God was guilty of a flaming piece of Malice, which cannot be. I would not have you to be furpriz'd in finding that I deny Magicians as well as Sorcerers or Wizards; for if we allow of the one, the other muft be acknowledg'd in Courfe. All the World takes *Agrippa* for the Prince of Magicians; but at the fame time he was no more fuch than you. His Magick lay here.[1] Being one of the greateft Philofophers of his Age, and having given proof of his Knowledge before the Mob of *Lions*, the Women were fo charm'd with it, that almoft all of 'em employ'd him to cuckold their [262] Husbands, and at the fame time fome Rival Monks who pretended to defcribe the Devil's Art, plac'd him at the Head of the five Popes, that *Berno* the Schifmatick Cardinal had the Infolence to brand for Magicians. But *Agrippa*'s Book made the fame Impreffion upon the Minds of Fools with the Conjuring Book and *Heptameron* of *Appono*. All thefe Chimera's fpring from the impertinent Writers of Conjuring, who have fill'd the World with their Illufions, either thro' Malice or Ignorance. I can't look upon the Books of *John Nider de Vujer*, of *Niger*, *Sprenger*, *Platina*, *Toflat*, and the two Jefuits *Delrio* and *Maldonat*, without curfing 'em for ever; for they advance Pofitions fo contrary to Reafon, and inconfiftent with the Wifdom of God, that all Chriftian Princes would do well to call in all fuch Books and have 'em burn'd by the Hand of the publick Executioner,

---

[1] Cornelius Agrippa, of Nettesheim, who attempted in the fourteenth century to mitigate the horrors of witchcraft superstition, and defended an accused witch. Lahontan refers to his book, *Occulta Philosophia.* — ED.

without fpairing *Bodinus*'s *Demonomania*, the *Mallet of Sorcerers*, and the *Seven Trumpets*.[1] What reafon have we to believe that *Eric* King of the *Goths* was firnam'd *Windy Hat*, becaufe he becken'd to the Winds with his Hat, and made 'em fhift as he pleas'd; That *Paracelfus* had an Army of Devils under his Command; that *Santaberenus* fhew'd to *Bafil* the Emperor his Son alive after his Death; That *Michael* the *Scot* foretold the Death of the Emperor *Frederic* II. That *Pythagoras* kill'd a Serpent in *Italy* by Vertue of fome Magical Words? And yet thefe Authors vent a thoufand Lies of that nature for uncontefted Truths: But what *Gervais* fays of *Virgil*'s Brafs Fly Crowns the whole Work. 'Tis a Miracle to me that the Chancellor of the Emperor *Otho* fhould have thus expos'd himfelf in advancing a Falfhood accompany'd with many other Lies. From hence we may learn, the Dignity of a Chancellor has not the vertue to entail [263] Wifdom upon the Fools that brook it. Is it not commonly given out that the Devil run away with Prefident *Pichon?* Who has not heard of Marfhal *Luxemburg*'s Compact with the Devil? And does not the World blindly believe that the poor Curate of *Loudun*,

---

[1] Lahontan here cites a group of authors on the subject of magic. Nider, an inquisitor of the fourteenth century, published the *Formicarius*, a treatise on heresy. Sprenger, a German inquisitor, was the author of the manual *Malleus Maleficarium* (Mallet of Sorcerers), which was "the most portentous monument of superstition the world has produced." Platina, the learned author of *Vitæ Pontificium* (Lives of the Popes), relates many tales of witchcraft. Tostatus was a Spanish theologian of the fifteenth century, and Delrio, a Jesuit, whose *Disquisitiones Magicæ* went through frequent editions in the seventeenth century. Jean Bodin's *Demonomanie des Sorciers* was a compilation on witchcraft. For the entire subject consult Lea, *History of the Inquisition in the Middle Ages* (New York, 1888); White, *History of Warfare of Science with Theology* (New York, 1896). — ED.

who was burnt by the Tyranny of Cardinal *Richelieu*, without any other Crime than that of incurring his Displeasure; Does not every one believe, I say, that this poor Curate rais'd a hundred young Devils out of Hell to possess the Bodies of the Nuns of *Loudun?* What impertinent and childish Stories does *John Schefer* offer in his History of *Lapland?* Is not it very strange that the People should be allow'd to read such Books? Are not some so foolish as to credit these Chimera's as Articles of Faith? And is it possible for you to disabuse 'em, or to perswade 'em that no Man can cure Wounds by the speaking of a few Words, or that the Men who deal in Characters do not perform all sorts of Miracles by vertue of certain Phials, Garters, &c.? No truly, Sir, you would never compass your end if you offer'd to teach 'em a Doctrine contrary to these receiv'd Opinions; they would hang you for a Heretick, or at least take you for a Magician that by such a cunning fetch mean'd to screen the whole Magical Fraternity from Prosecution.

Believe me, Sir, all that I now write is positively true. The Devil has not the Power to appear visibly before our Eyes, and by consequence he can't engage us in his Interests by a Magical or Witchcraft Contract. Such a Supposition is inconsistent with the Goodness of God, who does not lay Snares for Men that are already apt to go astray. You see I do not deny the Existence of the Devil; for I believe he is in Hell: But I deny that he ever remov'd from [264] the Regions below, to do mischief upon the Earth. As for the Passages of *Scripture*, which you may take for an Objection, I answer; That if all the Places of *Scripture* were to be understood in a Literal Sense, God would be suppos'd to have Hands and Feet, and the *Holy Ghost* to talk like an *Iroquese*. You must know, that before the coming of the *Messias*, Dæmons were the tutelar and benign Gods; and the Word δαιμοὺνιον signifies nothing else but Good Genius; but the *Evangelists* have stamp'd upon them an Infernal Character, by adding the Epithet, Κακο, *i. e.* Evil: And for that Reason the good Devils have been ever since reputed Evil Spirits, according to the Literal Sense. Sir, you may perceive, I only insist against the Existence of Sorcerers, Magicians, Inchanters, *&c.* which I am the more encourag'd to do, upon the Consideration, that the Interpreters of Holy Writ have given 'em Titles of *Astronomers, Chiromancers, Astrologers, &c.* and in giving the Explication of these synonimous Words, never alledg'd, that they were the Devil's Scholars.

This Subject would require a large Dissertation; for 'tis truly a very nice Point, which I only pretend to glance upon by the Bye, without spending more time in justifying the Arraigned Criminals from the guilt of an Imaginary Crime, that 'tis impossible for them to put in execution. Believe me, Sir, the Magicians are Rogues that cut a Purse dexterously and unhinge a Door nimbly: Your Apparitions, Phantomes, Hobgoblins and Spirits are Rascally Varlets, that in the Night time steal Corn and Fruit, and kiss not only the Servant-Maids, but sometimes their Masters Wives: Your Inchanters are roving Fellows, and Lovers by Trade, who inveigle poor Girls under a Promise of Marriage. Your [265] Soothsayers are the Cunning Ecclesiasticks, who knowing the *Foible* of some Rich men, extort pious Legacies from 'em, with their wonted Dexterity. The Sorcerers are those False Coiners, who abound so much in our Country, and the Clippers, who pare the Piastres and the *Spanish* Pistoles so cleverly; for these Sabbatic Works are always performed in the Night-time, and in the obscurest Places. All this I offer for your information; and so shall leave you to believe what you please.

I know the *Bearnese* are too much inclined to Superstition, and owe their Byas to the Ancient Members of their *Parliament, who by a stretch of Cruelty beyond that of *Nero*, burnt so many Innocent Wretches.

* *Held at* Pau, *the Capital of the Province of* Bearn.

If these Bigotted Counsellers are now in Paradise, most certainly neither you nor I will ever be sent to Hell: Believe me, Sir, the Man that's capable of giving credit to the *Chimæra's* I now speak of, will not stand to swallow a thousand other Fables that your Men of Sense make a Jest of. I do not pretend to undeceive the Ignorant Vulgar, for I know 'tis impossible; 'tis you only that I want to instruct; for I'm told, you declare, that all the Cats in the Province have the honour to be animated by the Souls of the Ancient Wizards, whose Ashes have serv'd for Lye to the Washer-women of *Pau* these many Years. Our Salvation does not depend upon the belief of that Article, for I'm sure 'tis no Article of Faith. Some People are very ingenious in frightning themselves, by conceiving that the Devil transforms himself into a Mastiff, a Sorcerer into a Cat, and a Magician into a Wolf; that a Soul way, for that Cattel is not so easy to deal with as Wizards and Phantoms.

I desire an interview at *Ortez:* The Papers I now send along with this Letter, will inform you of the Business I want to discourse. The Country I am now in is a very good Country, [268] but I do not find Mony stirring among us, which in my troth I do not like, for among the *Europeans* one can't live without Money, as they do among the *Hurons* of *Canada*. I always think of that Countrey with regret, when my Pocket is at low water, and my Mind disquieted with Care and Anxiety, in contriving how to fill it with that precious Metal, that gives life and spirit to the sorriest sort of Men, and inspires 'em with all Good Qualities.

I am,
    SIR,
        Yours, &c.

LETTER VI.
Dated at *Huefca, July* 11. 1695.

Containing an Account of the Author's wonderful Escape; his being taken up for a Huguenot, *and examin'd by the Ignorant Curates.*

I'VE 'fcap'd for once, but 'twas a very narrow Efcape, as you may guefs by the Story of my Flight, which was in fhort thus. I was upon the point of meeting you according to agreement at *Ortez*, and for that Reafon had been at *Dax* to receive fome Papers which feem'd to be of ufe to me; when by a matchlefs piece of Good Luck, [269] I met with a Letter from a certain perfon at *Verfailles*. I had no fooner read my Letter, than I march'd ftraight to my Lodging, to contrive within my felf fome way to get fafe out of the Kingdom. You may be fure my Council was foon affembled, for fuch a Head-piece as mine does not ufe to fpend much time in Confultations. I determined to delude my Landlord, by defiring him to give me an Account in Writing of the Road to *Agen*, where I pretended to have fome Bufinefs. The beft of the matter is, that I had already got of my Farmers near two hundred Piftoles, and a fine Horfe, which I was oblig'd to for my lucky deliverance. I got up by the break of day, and defir'd a Guide to conduct me out of one of the Gates of the City, that leads a quite different way from that I had in my Eye.

As soon as I got out of Town, I took the Road of *Ortez*, and avoiding all Villages, steer'd upon Heaths, Fields, Vineyards and Woods, following all By-paths, and lodging in the remotest Houses; I had no other Guide but the Sun, and the sight of the *Pyrenees*, and ask'd every one I met upon the Road, which was the way to *Pau*. But not to detain you too long with the Particulars of my Journey, you must know, I arrived at last at *Laruns*, the last Village of *Bearn*, scituated as you know, in the Valley of *Ozao*. I had scarce entred this foolish Village, when a Company of Peasants surrounded me on all sides: Judge you if I had not reason to fear that the Grand Provost was not far behind; but I was mistaken, for the Rascals stop'd me for no other Reason, but because they fancied there was somewhat in my Countenance that looked like *Huguenotism;* they gave me leave however to alight at a Tavern, which was so dark and full of Smoak, that you would have took't [270] for the Antichamber to Hell; and here, you must know the Parson was to come to examine me in Matters of Religion; and that in a Country where the Priests understand as little what they believe as their Parishioners: For after I had answer'd him upon all the Points he thought fit to mention, he swore I was a *Huguenot;* and upon this, Sir, I was like to have lost all patience. But considering I had Beasts to deal with, I thought my best way was to use 'em as Beasts; so I offer'd to satisfie 'em by reciting the *Litany*, and the *Sunday Vespers*, but this Stratagem fail'd me, for they still continued obstinate, in proposing to carry me to *Pau*. Judge what a perplexity I was in, when the Infamous Rabble said,

The Pſalms *and the* Litanies *were the firſt Prayers the* Huguenots *learn'd to cover their Deſign of getting out of the Kingdom.* It ſignify'd nought to tell 'em, I was Maſter of the Horſe to *Monſieur L' Abbee d' Eſtrees*, and that I was going to that Ambaſſador in *Portugal;* that was *Clamare in deſerto.* 'Twas to as little purpoſe to threaten to ſend immediately to the Intendant at *Pau*, to demand Juſtice for the Affront, and for my being ſtopt: All this did not move 'em. At laſt, after a melancholly Reflection on the danger I was in, I reſolv'd to try all ways to delude theſe Ignorant Creatures; though this was no eaſy task, for they are wholly govern'd by their Doctors. And here I think I ought to pray to God to bleſs the firſt Inventer of Snuff, for after I had fretted my ſelf two or three Hours in talking to theſe Varlets, I accidentally pull'd out my Snuff-box, without thinking of it, and as ſoon as I open'd it, one of the moſt Civiliz'd Men of the Company deſir'd to ſee the Picture on the Inſide, which repreſented a Court-Lady upon a Couch, all naked, with her Hair hanging looſe. As ſoon as he [271] had looked upon it, he ſhow'd it to the reſt, who ſaid to one another in their *Bernoiſe* Language, That it was a *Mary Magdalene.* At this Lucky Word, I rouz'd my Spirits, when all on a ſudden the Parſon ask'd me, What the Meaning of the Picture was? I made anſwer, *'Twas a Saint that would take Vengeance of them for an Affront offer'd to one of her Devouteſt Worſhippers:* And ſo fixing my Eyes upon the Naked Figure, I made a Prayer to that Saint with an Elogy; in which I attributed more Miracles to her than to all the Saints in Paradiſe. This, together with the

Exclamations I made, did so blind the Company, that they all kiss'd the Head of the Pretended Saint with a wonderful Zeal, and from that time I was no *Huguenot*, for I still continued to invoke the Saint that in *Bearn* is known to be a worker of Miracles, with the same fury and disposition that I then feign'd. Every one strove to get my Prayers down in Writing, and all the Peasants now were at Emulation one with another who should guide me over the Mountains, or who should furnish me with Mules. Such, Sir, is the diverting History of the strange Effects of Snuff: If it is of use to others, to hammer out an Argument by gaining the time which is spent in conveying it from the Fingers to the Nose, 'twas of great use to me another way, without so much as expecting it. What a Misfortune it is for an Honest Man to be under a Necessity of prophaning the Saints for the preservation of his Life! 'Tis true, my Meaning was good, and I have asked Pardon of God for it. This shews that a well manag'd Lye can produce among Ignorant People even such Effects as the Naked Truth cannot compass. What pity is it that a Parson should not so much as understand his *Catechism*, and at the same time [272] swallow down Idle Stories for Miracles! But this is the Bishop's Business, not mine.

And indeed our Bishops are much like our Officers, who are prefer'd more by Favour and Interest than by Merit. The greatest part of them are more industrious to please their Sovereign than their God. But a man had as good pretend to drink the Ocean dry, as to attempt a Reformation of these Abuses.

To continue the Thread of my Adventure, you muſt know, I hired two Mules, one for my Guide, another for my ſelf. My Horſe was ſo tired with ſtrugling to ſave me, that Gratitude obliged me to uſe him with all manner of civility and mildneſs; for 'twas no more than what he deſerved by his fatiguing Services. In the mean time the Night, which ſeem'd as long to me as an Age, (ſo much I dreaded the Provoſt's Crew) gave me more leiſure than enough to beg pardon of God for the Contrivance by which I ſaved my ſelf, in making uſe of the Names of his Saints. In this Condition I was continually peeping at the Window to look for the dawning of the Day, but this Village is ſo ſhut up among the *Pyrenees*, that 'tis a hard matter to diſcern the Sun in his Meridian, or the tenth part of the Arch of the Heavens. At laſt wearied with that uneaſineſs, and quite ſpent with the Fatigues both of Body and Mind, I tried to indulge Nature with one Hours ſleep as a recompence for three Days waking, when all on a ſudden I was alarm'd with a great Noiſe of Men and Horſes at the Inn-Gate; the Knocks they gave, and their ſtrange Hollowing, freez'd all the Blood in my Veins, for I thought all the Conſtables in the Kingdom were upon my Back; but my Fears prov'd abortive, for it was only ſome Muliteers going to traffick in *Spain*. [273] By this time Day-light appear'd, and my Guide called upon me, upon which we ſet out, and join'd in with theſe Travellers: That Day we went as far as *Sallent*, the firſt Town in *Spain*, ſeven Leagues diſtant from *Laruns;* having paſs'd a Houſe which the *Spaniards* call *Aigues Caudes*, that is, the Hot-waters, or a Bath which cures a world of Difeafes. When we were got to *Sallent*, they fhewed us to an Inn, fo dark, that it feem'd fitter for a Vault to lodge Dead-Carcafes in, than to entertain Paffengers; my Spirits were then fo exhaufted for want of reft, that I fell afleep immediately, and flept ftanding in a manner; the Beds looking like a Magazine of Lice, I made them fpread me fome Straw upon the Boards, where I laid my felf down, after having order'd my Guide to provide for himfelf what Cheer he lik'd beft, upon the Provifo that he fhould not wake me. I flept in this Pofture from Nine a Clock at Night till Noon next Day without waking; after which we fpent the reft of the Day in finding out a forry Meal of Meat: The next Day after we put on very fmartly, and came to an Inn where we found good ftore of Fouls and Pigeons, and upon thefe we made reprifals for our former Ill Fare. In fhort, we arriv'd laft Night at this City, which ftands upon a flat low Ground, at the diftance of Two Leagues from the Mountains. All I can tell you of the Country, is; That from *Laruns* to this Place, we have two and twenty Leagues diftance; and upon that Road we do nothing but climb up and defcend narrow Paths, upon which, if the Mule did but ftumble, there's an unavoidable neceffity of tumbling down a Difmal Precipice. My Guide [274] told me, That the Road through the Valley of *Afpe*, is the pleafanteft, fhorteft and moft convenient; but the way which leads by St. *John de Pied de Port* has this advantage, that there's only Eight Leagues of Mountains between *Roncevaux* and the Plains of *Navarre*. Upon the whole, I wonder much that *Hercules* did not fplit thefe

Mountains for the Accommodation of Travellers, as well as thofe of *Calpe* and *Abila* for the Conveniency of Sailers. I fet out to morrow by the break of Day, in order to reach *Saragoza* at Night.

I am,
SIR,
Yours, &c.

LETTER VII.

Dated at *Saragoza*, Octob. 8. 1695.

Containing a Description of Saragoza; *a View of the Government of* Arragon, *and an account of the Customs of the People.*

SIR,

I HAVE been three Months in this good Town of *Saragoza*, during which time, I've receiv'd seven or eight Letters, charging me with Carelessness in not satisfying your Curiosity: But the fault lies at your own Door and not at mine; [275] for if you had not been so negligent as to delay the sending of what I receiv'd this very day, my Pen had not trac'd the uneasyness of my Mind, instead of pursuing the following Relation.

Saragoza is the Capital City of the Kingdom of *Arragon*: And I can't tell whether I ought to call it only *pretty*, or *very pretty*. However, I'm sure 'tis a very great City; the Streets are broad and well pav'd; the Houses are for the most part three Story high, tho' some of 'em have five or six; and all of 'em are Built after the old Fashion. The Market and publick Places are not worth speaking of. In the City there are a great many Convents, which are generally very pretty; as well as their Gardens and Churches. The Cathedral Church call'd *La Ceu* is a huge and very Stately Edifice. The Church of

Nueſtra Seniora de l' Pilar is but very ordinary as to its Architecture. The Chappel indeed where that *Seniora* ſtands is Curious, upon the account that 'tis under Ground. The *Spaniards* pretend that the Subſtance of which 'tis Built is unknown to all Mankind; but if 'twere not for their aſſertion, I ſhould have took it for *Walnut-Tree*. This Chappel is thirty ſix Foot long, and twenty ſix Foot broad. 'Tis fill'd with Lamps, Baniſters and Silver Candle-Sticks; and beſides a great Altar, contains a great quantity of Feet, Hands, Hearts and Heads, which the Miracles of that *Virgin* drew to the Sacred Place: For you know the *Virgin* Works Miracles every day that ſurpaſs imagination. But the moſt ſolid thing about her, is an infinity of precious Stones of ineſtimable value, with which her Gown, Crown and Niche are Garniſh'd. Beſides theſe, there are two Churches here which were Built by the *Goths*, and are both Strong and Beautiful; having very pretty Vaults, which ſhew [276] that *that* People were perfectly well acquainted with *Stereometry*.

Saragoza is Seated on the River *Ebro*, which is as broad as the *Seyne* at *Paris*. It ſtands upon ſmooth level Ground, and incompaſs'd with a Wall that's Ruinous in ſeveral places. The People of *Arragon* put a mighty value upon a Stone-Bridge that's over that River; becauſe they never ſaw many better: But they have more reaſon to value the Wooden-Bridge that lyes a little lower, for indeed 'tis one of the fineſt in *Europe*. This City affords *Academies* for the exerciſe both of the Body and the Mind; and above all, a fine *Univerſity* that may be call'd the beſt in *Spain* next to *Salamanca* and *Alcala des He-*

nares. The *Students* are generally Cloath'd like *Priests*, that is, with a long Cloak.

The Duke *de Jovenazo* is Viceroy of this Kingdom; and as I take it, that triennial Dignity is more Honourable than Beneficial, for it does not bring in above six thousand Crowns a Year. The Arch-Bishoprick is worth twenty thousand Crowns; but the present Arch-Bishop being a very good Man, distributes one third of his Revenue among the Poor. Tho' his Birth was obscure, yet he was *President* of one of the Councils of *Spain*, which perhaps occasion'd that natural Antipathy to the *French*, that he shews upon all occasions. The Canons of his Cathedral and those of *Notre dame de Pilier*, make a hundred Crowns a Month of their Canonships. The Minister call'd * *Ell justicia*, receives Appeals from all the Courts of *Arragon*. 'Tis from his Hands that the Kings of *Spain* receive a drawn Sword, when they take the Oath to maintain the Privileges of the Kingdom, upon their Accession to the [277] Throne. This Ceremony is perform'd in the *Deputation-House*, which indeed is a wonderful Edifice. The *Salmedina* is a sort of Lieutenant-General, both Civil and Military. This Office, which bears both the Gown and the Sword, is Triennial as well as that of his Deputy. The † *Audiencia* consists of several Counsellours, who are as nice a sort of Men as our own. Besides these, there are five Sheriffs or *Jurates*, who hold their troublesome Posts but two years, and are properly the Civil Judges that take care of the Government of the City. In fine, I should never

* *His place is much like that of a* Chancellour.

† *Parliament.*

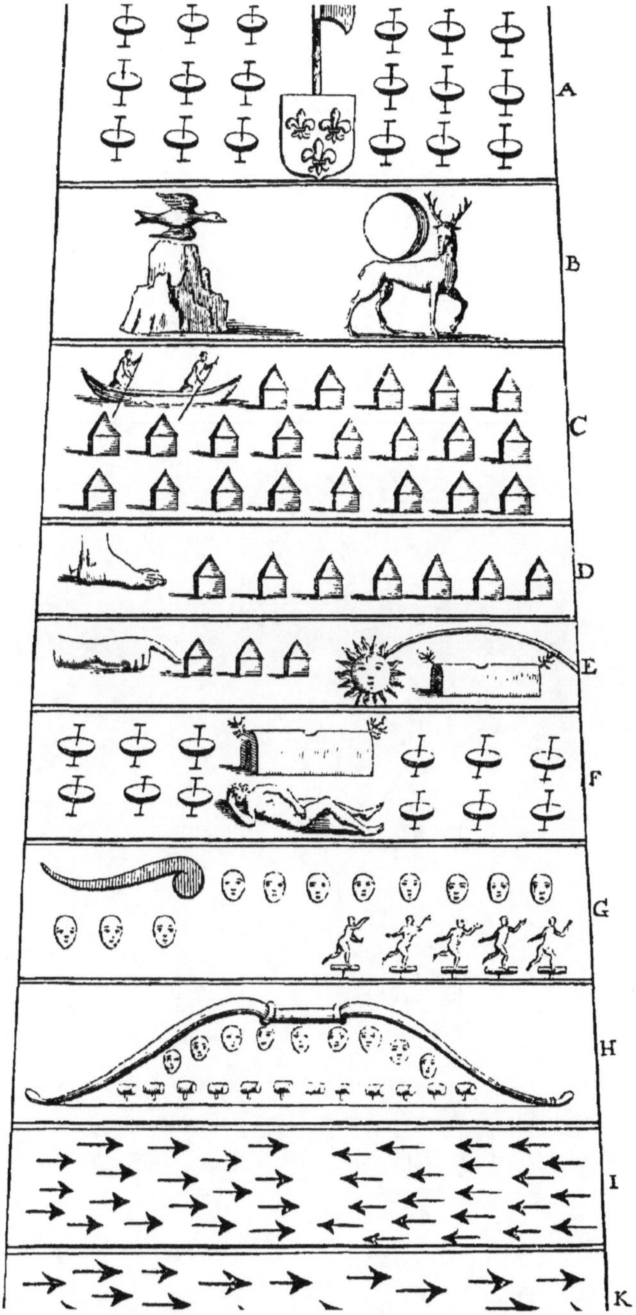
A
B
C
D
E
F
G
H
I
K

to Portugal and Denmark.

have done, if I offer'd to give a particular List of all the Offices in this Kingdom.

Bread, Wine, Fowl, Partridges and Hares are very cheap in this place; but Butchers Meat is very dear, and good Fish is a rarity. The Strangers that Travel this way, are oblig'd to Lodge in certain Inns call'd by the *Spaniards, Meson;* in which the Inn-Keeper furnishes nothing to his Guests but a Chamber, a Bed, a Stable, || Straw and Barley. 'Tis true, the Servants buy what you please for you, and dress it as you order 'em, provided you require nothing but plain Boiling and Rosting. The *Arragon* Wines are sweet and strong, especially the Black sort, for the White is neither so strong nor so sweet. In the Summer time they have no other Diversion but Walking, and that towards the Evening, when the Gentlemen walk out of Town, as well as the Ladies, apart: But 'tis not the fresh Air so much as the warm breathing that they have in view. In Winter, they are entertain'd with Plays, which the *Priests* and *Friars* frequent without any Scruple. Every Night there's an Assembly or Meeting at the House of the Duke [278] of *Jovenazo*, where they Game, and Discourse and drink Chocolate or other Liquors: And the Persons of the first Rank are almost always there. They are honest and affable to the last degree. As for my own part, I have receiv'd very sensible Marks of their Friendship, particularly that of being regal'd in their Houses; which discovers to me that they are not so unsociable as they are represented to be. 'Tis true, that in publick the Smile never

|| *There's nether Hay nor Corn in Spain.*

unfurles their Brow, and no familiarity of Joy can oblige 'em to relent in their affected Gravity: But in private Converfation they are the heartieſt People in the World; I mean, they are the briskeſt and merryeſt Companions that can be.

Almoſt all the People of *Arragon* are as lean as I am, and fo, Sir, you may eafily judge what a fort of Meen they have. They allege for the caufe of their Leannefs, that their Tranfpiration is great, that they Eat and Sleep but little, that their Paffions are fprightly and violent; and in fine, that they diffipate their Spirits by exercifes which the *French* do not follow fo often. Their Complexion is as pale as mine; which perhaps is owing to thefe very exercifes; at leaftwife, 'tis *Ovid*'s Opinion in faying [*Palleat ommis amor; Color hic eſt aptus amanti*.] Their Stature goes fomewhat beyond the middling Standard. Their Hair is of a dark Chefnut colour, and their Complexion is as fair as that of the *Bearneſe*.

All I have faid of the People of *Arragon*, may be apply'd in particular to the Women as well as the Men; tho' indeed the former are not quite fo lean as the latter. They can't be call'd handfome, but at the fame time one can't avoid owning that they are agreeable and lovely. If Nature has been ſtingy and penurious in Forming their Throat and Fore-Head, fhe has been prodigal [276, *i.e.* 279] of her Gifts in giving 'em great fparkling Eyes, fo full of Fire that they burn without mercy from top to toe all that approach to 'em. They are very much oblig'd to *Theano*, *Pythagoras*'s Wife, for teaching 'em that their Sex was Born for no other end than for the agreeable Trade of loving and being lov'd. This foft Moral suits their Complexion perfectly well; and accordingly they practise it to a Miracle: For in the Morning they run to Church, with intent to purchase Hearts rather than Paradise; and Dinner is no sooner over, than they go to Visit their She-Friends, who do mutual Services to one another in the way of Intrigue, by favouring the entry of their Lovers into one another's Houses, and that with a great deal of artifice and cunning. Contrivance is all in all in this Country; for the vertue of the Women lies in playing their Cards handsomely and dextrously, disguising the Intrigue, more than elsewhere. Their Husbands are plaguy Sharp-sighted, and if their Intrigues take but the least Air, they run the risque of taking a Journey to the other World, unless they flie to a Convent. 'Tis not above a Month and a half since I saw a Girl Stabb'd by her own Brother at Church, at the very foot of the Altar, for having entertain'd an amorous Correspondence. He had made a Journey from *Madrid* on purpose to do this mighty Exploit; for which he was Punish'd with two Months Imprisonment.

There has not been above eighteen or twenty design'd Murders and Assassinations committed since I came hither; by reason that the Nights are as yet too short: But I am told that in Winter there never passes a Night without two or three such instances. 'Tis true, 'tis only the poor miserable Wretches of two Parishes in the City, who insult [280] one another at that rate; and are drove to that extremity by Feuds of ancient standing. The frequency of such disorders is owing to this, that a Man can't be condemn'd to die without great Evidence upon the matter, and that the Condemn'd Criminals make ufe of the privileges of the Kingdom, to put off the Execution from Term to Term: By which means they get off at laft for being turn'd over to the Galleys, which there are a thoufand ways to get clear of: So that unlefs the Judge is Sollicited againft them by a ftrong Party, they always 'fcape the Gallows.

As for Robbing in the Streets, they know nothing of it; and the Murders that happen have no relation to any intention of that Nature. I have frequently Walk'd home all alone at Midnight from the *Viceroy*'s Houfe, without meeting with any affront. 'Tis true, I difcontinued that practice after the Perfons of Quality advis'd me to go always in Company, left the Affaffins fhould miftake me for another. However, Perfons of Note or Character have nothing to fear, unlefs they be imbarqu'd in fome Amorous Intrigue; then indeed they run the rifque of being Stabb'd in the Streets at Noon: So that a Man muft either have his Wits about him, or elfe have recourfe to common Whores, if he means to avoid fuch a fatal Exit. Now of thefe two Expedients the firft is the beft, becaufe it preferves at once his Pocket and his Health.

The Nobility of *Arragon* is tolerably Rich; but they might be Richer if the Peafants of *Arragon* Work'd as hard as *ours* do. Thefe idle Fellows imploy the † *Gavachos* (with whom *Spain* is plagued) to Manure their Grounds, and to Sow and Reap. The Vulgar People [281] are of the Opinion that *France* is the worft Country in the World, becaufe the *French* exchange it

† *An Epithet they give to the* French, *which at the bottom fignifies nothing at all*.

for theirs: And indeed 'tis true, that the Labourers, the Reapers, the Fellers of Wood, and all sorts of Tradesmen, without mentioning the Coach-men, Foot-men and Water-bearers, come for the most part from *Bearn*, *Languedock*, and *Auvergne*. Here we meet with some *Bearn* Merchants who have inrich'd themselves by Trading to *France:* For notwithstanding the War, an open Commerce is still maintain'd. If the People of *Arragon* had their Wits about 'em, and had a mind to inrich their Country, they might easily compass their end.

The River of *Ebro* is Navigable from *Tortoza* to *Miranda d' Ebro*, by great flat bottom'd Boats, such as we have in the *Seyne*. A great many Persons who have come down the *Ebro*, have assur'd me that 'tis three Foot deep in the Shallowest places, and that its Current is very gentle: So that the only difficulty lies in finding a Road upon the Banks of the River, in order to drag up the Boats when they want to stem the Stream. The *French* bring hither a great many Mules and little Nags, upon which they gain *Cent per Cent*, all Charges discounted. These Mules are made use of to draw the Coaches and * *Galeras:* For the *Estramadura* Mules are very dear, and do not thrive in this Country so well as in the Southern Countries of *Spain*. As for the little Galloway's, they commonly sell best in the Kingdom of *Valencia*, where the Peasants imploy 'em for different uses. The Coaches of that Country are much of the same Form with our Travelling-Coaches in *France;* and they go so

* *Great Carts drawn by eight Mules, which hold eight hundred weight.*

very flowly that they would not drive round the Town in the longeſt Summer's day. The cuſtom [282] of Viſiting upon Horſe-Back, prevails here as well as in *Portugal*. The Gentlemen and Officers are dreſs'd after the *French* way; for they find the *Spaniſh* Habit unſufferable, by reaſon of the *Golilla*, or a ſort of Collar, in which the Neck is ſo lac'd up, that they can't turn or bow the Head.

The Women's Garb ſeems ridiculous to Strangers, tho' at the bottom 'tis not ſuch. I am already convinc'd that 'tis infinitely preferable to *ours*. The *Spaniſh* Women can't cover any defect of Nature; for they wear neither Hoods, Heels, nor Whale-bone Bodice. Were the *French* Ladies oblig'd to go in this faſhion, 'twould not be in their Power to deceive ſo many Men by their artificial Towers, their Shooe-Heels and their falſe Hips. 'Tis true, the *Spaniſh* Women may be cenſur'd for diſcovering their Shoulders and half their Arms: But at the ſame time, the *French* muſt not go uncheck'd for expoſing to open eye two parts that are at once more ſenſible and more tempting; for if it be alleg'd that the former give offence backwards, by the ſame juſtice it may be reply'd that the latter ſcandaliſe before. In fine, as the Women of this Country lye under reſtraints, ſo they have the ſatisfaction of being very much reſpected; for when they paſs along the Streets either in Coach or on Foot, with their Face uncover'd, every body ſtops to make 'em a Bow, which they anſwer by bowing the Head without bending the Knee. Their Gentlemen-Uſhers, who are always old Fellows paſt the reach of Suſpicion, give 'em their bare hand; for ſuch is the *Spaniſh* way: And these are the only priviledg'd Persons that have the benefit of touching their hands; for when a *Cavalier* happens accidentally to be near the *Holy Water* while a Lady offers to come to it, he [283] shakes his Beads in the Water, in order to present 'em to her. The same is the case in Dancing, which do's not happen often: For the Gentleman and the Lady come no nearer than the two ends of a Handkerchief, by which they hold; and so you may guess how Bussing would go down in this Country.

I must tell you, the *Spaniards* are not so stern and unsociable as they are represented; which you'll perceive from a slender account of their way of Entertainment. A Gentleman that I met frequently at the *Viceroy*'s, and at the *Academies*, did me the honour to Visit me; and I return'd his Compliment in the same way. When I came to return the Visit, he receiv'd me at the Stair-Head, and conducted me to a Hall, where we convers'd for half an hour; after which I ask'd how his Lady did, and he made answer, *that he believ'd she was so well as to receive us in her Chamber*. This done, the Chocolate and Biskuyts began to appear; upon which the Gentleman rose and introduc'd me to his Lady's Chamber. The Lady stood up till we made our Honours, and sate down upon her *Sofa*, while Chairs were setting for us. I told her I was infinitely oblig'd to her Husband for procuring me the honour of Saluting her. She made answer; *that he look'd upon me as a Spaniard*. After that we drank some Chocolate, and she ask'd me if I lik'd it, and whether the *French* Ladies us'd to drink it. This Interview lasted but half a quarter of an hour, for being affraid of infringing upon the *Spanish* Formalities, I rose, and after taking leave walk'd out of the Room with her Husband, who invited me to Dinner. We walk'd till Dinner time in the Garden, and after the Gentleman had shewn me his Horses, we went up again to the Hall, where the Table Cloth was laid: In [284] a moment in came the Lady, and Saluting us after her way, took her place on one side of the Table, as we did on the other. First of all, they serv'd up *Melons*, *Raisins*, *Nectarines*, and *Figs;* then every one had his Commons set before him, (like a *Monk*'s Mess) consisting of a Brest of Mutton Roasted in the first Service, a Partridge and a Pigeon Roasted in the second, and a Rabbet Pye in the third, a Fricassee of Foul in the fourth, * *Oronges* surrounded with little Trouts of the bigness of one's Finger in the fifth, and an Appricock Tart in the sixth: And after all, we had a sort of Soupe as yellow as the Saffron with which 'twas cram'd. This, Sir, was the just Bill of Fare for every one's Mess. In the mean time, we talk'd of nothing but the *French* Ladies. The Lady alleg'd that in *France*, the great Liberty allow'd to the Men in visiting the Ladies, and Playing or Walking with 'em, expos'd the Wisest and most Vertuous Women to the affronts of indiscreet and detracting Persons, who to make themselves pass for Men of happy Intrigues, defame the Ladies that resist 'em. In fine, after we had rail'd against the Husbands that tamely put up such affronts, instead of resenting 'em, we rose from

* *A sort of Mushrooms red on the upper side, and yellow underneath.*

Table: So she took leave after the usual way, and retir'd to her Chamber. When I came to take leave of the Gentleman, he walk'd before me to the Head of the Stairs, where he stop'd on the left hand, leaving me the right while I bid him Adieu. There he stood till I got at the foot of the Stairs, upon which he gave me his Hat once more, and so we lost sight of one another.

[285] I thought it proper to give you the History of this Adventure, that you may thereby know how the *Spaniards* treat their Friends. If a hundred Gentlemen had regal'd me at so many several times, there would have been no difference, unless it be as to the goodness of the Cheer; for the Ceremony is the same in one House that you have in another. So that by this description, you know all that's usual in *Spain* upon such occasions. I believe I have acquainted you that the *Spanish* Women look upon us as an indiscreet sort of People, and perhaps they are not much out in their thoughts; for all the Women of *Europe* speak of us at the same rate. I'll present you with some *Spanish* Verses that a foolish sort of a Poet made upon that Head above fifty years ago.

> *Los Discretos Espanoles*
> *A Los Maridos Zelozos*
> *Hazen en Callados Gozos*
> *Orejus de Caracoles;*
> *No san Tales les francezes*
> *Tanto no pueden Cubrir*
> *Antes Mas quieren Mil Vezes.*
> *No hazer que no desir.*

That is to say in good Prose. *The discreet Spaniards assist the Women to cuckold their Husbands by secret Imbraces; whereas the French can conceal nothing, for they'd choose a thousand times rather to be without the Adventure, than not to speak of it.*

This, Sir, is much of a piece with the Argument of that *Huron*, who alledges that we glory in requiting a Lady's Favour with a piece of Ingratitude, that tarnishes her Reputation to all intents and purposes. This caution may teach the Women not to confide in rattle brain'd Fellows. A Woman of Sense will easily find out the Character [286] of a Man, when she has a mind to give her self the trouble of inspecting his conduct. Tho' our young Sparks are Fools, yet the Ladies choose 'em before wiser Men; because Wisdom do's not take place till Nature begins to run low.

The indiscreet Tongue of a young *Cavalier*, do's a considerable injury to his Mistrifs: But at the same time, your Chamber-Maids and Confidents, are not less guilty. We have frequent instances of Women that lose themselves by neglecting a due Precaution with reference to their Domesticks. I call that Woman a Wise Woman that knows how to cover her Folly handsomely. Now, this is one of the first Accomplishments of your *Spanish* Women, who by that means oblige their Husbands very much; for tho' the Adventure makes the Cuckold, 'tis the Noise that makes the *Horns*. With this Lucky Word I conclude my Letter, intreating you would Write to me to *Bilbao*, for I design to go thither with the first opportunity. From thence I intend to Sweep (either by Sea or Land) along the *Maritime* Coaſt, as far as *Portugal*, in order to view the Ports and Havens, I have ſo often heard of. I ſhall take more pleaſure in that diſcovery, than in ſeeing the fineſt Cities of the World: And thus you ſee there's no diſputing a Man out of his reliſh.

I am,
 SIR,
  Yours, &c.

[287] A Short

DICTIONARY

Of the moſt Univerſal

LANGUAGE

OF THE

SAVAGES.

I COULD eaſily have ſent you a compleat *Dictionary* of all the Savage Words, without excepting one, and of ſeveral curious Phraſes: But I conſider'd 'twould be of no uſe to you, it being ſufficient to ſee the common Words that are every Moment in their Mouths. This is enough for any Man that deſigns for *Canada*, for if he does but learn in his Paſſage thoſe I have ſet down, he will be able to Converſe with the Savages, after frequenting their Company two or three Months.

There are but two Mother Tongues in the whole extent

Algonkin *Language.*

of *Canada*, which I confine within the Limits of *Miſſiſipi*[1]; but beyond that River there's an infinity of other Languages that few *Europeans* could yet learn, by reaſon of the little Correſpondence they have with the Savages of thoſe Parts. The two Mother Tongues I [288] ſpeak of, are the *Huron* and the *Algonkin*. The firſt is underſtood by the *Iroqueſe*, for the difference betwixt the *Huron* and the *Iroqueſe* Language is not greater than that between the *Norman* and the *French:* And ſome Savages on the Confines of *New York* ſpeak a Language that is very near the ſame. The *Andaſloguerons, Torontogueronons, Errieronons*, and ſeveral other Savage Nations whom the *Iroqueſe* have totally deſtroy'd, ſpoke likewiſe the ſame Tongue, and underſtood one another perfectly well.[2] The Second, namely the *Algonkine*, is as much eſteem'd among the Savages, as the *Greek* and *Latin* is in *Europe;* tho' 'twould ſeem that the *Algonkins*, to whom it owes its Original, diſgrace it by the thinneſs of the Nation, for their whole number does not exceed two Hundred.

---

[1] From the inception of their endeavors to convert the American tribes, the study of Indian linguistics necessarily occupied much attention on the part of the Jesuit missionaries of New France. Their narratives abound in descriptions of the native tongues, and the difficulties connected with acquiring them. They early recognized as the fundamental basis of their studies, the two stocks which Lahontan here describes. Different fathers devoted themselves to researches and compilations in each division of the great task. Brébeuf and Le Jeune, in particular, were authorities upon the Huron-Iroquois; André, upon the Algonquian tongue. In 1653 it was declared in the *Relations* that grammars and dictionaries were available for both of these linguistic types — *Jes. Rel.*, xxxix, p. 121. How far Lahontan was indebted to the Jesuits for his knowledge, and how far it was based solely on personal contact with the aborigines, is not clearly to be determined. His facility in the languages of the savages is evident throughout his narrative. — ED.

[2] For these tribes, see p. 320, note 1, *ante*. — ED.

You muft know that all the Languages of *Canada*, excepting the *Huron* and thofe which retain to it, come as near to the *Algonkine*, as the *Italian* to the *Spanifh;* and 'tis for that reafon that all the Warriours and ancient Counfellors of fo many different Nations affect to fpeak it with all manner of nicety. 'Tis fo neceffary to Travellers in that Country, that in fpeaking it one is certain of making himfelf to be underftood by all forts of Savages in whatfoever place he comes to, whether in *Acadia* or *Hudfon's Bay*, or upon the Lakes, or even among the *Iroquefe*, among whom a great many have learn'd it for Reafons of State, notwithftanding that it differs from theirs more widely than Night from Day.[1]

The *Algonkine* Language has neither *Tone* nor *Accent*, nor fuperfluous dead Letters; fo that 'tis as eafie to pronounce it as to write it. 'Tis not Copious, no more than the other Languages of *America;* for the People of that Continent are [289] Strangers to Arts and Sciences, they are unacquainted with the Laws of Ceremony and Complement, and an infinity of Words that the *Europeans* ufe to imbellifh their Difcourfe. Their Speech is only adapted to the Neceffities and Conveniences of Life, and there is not one ufelefs or fuperfluous Word in the whole Language. Farther, this Tongue makes no ufe either of F or V Confonant.[2]

---

[1] On the widespread utility of the Algonquian language, especially in its Chippewa form, which is considered the oldest and purest, see "J. Long's Voyages," in Thwaites, *Early Western Travels*, ii, pp. 28-30. — ED.

[2] For the Algonquian tongue, and the early studies thereof by English colonists, see the works of John Eliot, Roger Williams, and Jonathan Edwards as indicated in Pilling, *Bibliography of the Algonquian Languages* (Washington, 1891). — ED.

Algonkin *Language.*

To the end of the *Dictionary* I have added the four Tenses of the *Indicative* of the Verb, *I love*. The *Indicative* is form'd from the *Infinitive*, by adding the Personal Note *ni*, which signifies *me* or *I*. Thus, *Sakia* signifies *to love*, and *Nisakia*, *I love*. The same is the case with all the other Verbs.

'Tis an easie matter to conjugate the Verbs of this Language after one has learn'd the Present Tense of the Indicative Mood. To the Imperfect Tense they add *Ban*, as *Sakiaban*, *I lov'd;* to the Perfect Tense they add *ki* after the personal mark, as *ni kisakia, I have lov'd*, and to the Future *ga* in like manner, as *ni gasakia* or *nin gasakia, I shall love*. All the other Tenses of the Verb are form'd from the Present of the Indicative, for Example, *Ningasakiaban, I would love, Ninkisakiaban, I should have lov'd*. In a Word, when the Present of the Indicative, and the additional Particles for the other Tenses, are once known, the whole Language may be learn'd in a very little time. As for the Imperative 'tis form'd by prefixing *A* to the Infinitive, as *Asakia, love thou*, and the Plural, *let us love*, is form'd by subjoyning *Ta* to the Infinitive, as *Sakiata, let us love*. It remains only to shew the Personal Notes, *viz.*

[290] I or Me, *Nir*,
Thee or Thou, *Kir*,
He or Him, *Ouir*.
We, *Niraoueint*.

You, *Kiraoua*.
You and We, *Kiraoueint*.
They or Them, *Ouiraoua*.

A

ABandon or forsake, I abandon, *Packitan.*
Above, *Spimink.*
Admirable, 'tis admirable (the Savages speak it by way of Derision) *Pilaoua.*
Afterwards, *Mipidach.*
All, *Kakina.*
All of 'em, *Missoute.*
All in all, *Alouch bogo.*
Always, *Kakeli.*
Amiss, that's amiss, 'tis good for nothing, *Napitch Malatat.*
And, *Gaye* or *Mipigaye.*
Arrive, I arrive, *Takouchin.*
Ashes, Powder, Dust, *Pingoe.*
Assist or Aid, *Maouineoua.*
Ax, a great Ax, *Agackouet.*
A little Ax, *Agackouetons.*

B

Bag, a Tobacco bag, *Caspitagan.*
Ball, *Alouin.*
Barrel, *Aoyentagan.*
Beat, I beat, *Packite.*
A Bear, *Mackoua.*
A little Bear, *Makons.*
Beard, *Mischiton.*
Beaver, the Animal, *Amik.*
Beaver-Skin, *Apiminikoue.*
to Be or rest, *Tapia.*
Because, *Miouinch.*
to Believe, *Tilerima.*
Belly, *Mischimout.*
Black, *Markate.*
Blood, *Miscoue.*
Body, *Yao*
Bottle, *Chichigoue.*
Brother, *Nicanich.*
Brandy, the juice or Broth of Fire, *Scoutiouabou.*
Brave Soldier, *Simaganis.*
Bread, *Pa-bouchikan.*
Brech, *Miscoasab.*
[291] Breeches, a circumlocution for the covering of the Brech, *Kipokitie Koasab.*
Broth or Juice, *Ouabou.*
Buck, *Ouaskech.*
Buckler, *Pakakoa.*
Build, to build Vessels or Canous, *Chimanike.*

Algonkin *Language.*

C

Call, to call or name, *Tichinika.*
Candle, to fnuff the Candle, to ftir up the Fire, *Ouafacolendamaoua.*
Canou, *Chiman.*
Captain, Leader, *Okima.*
to Carry, *Pitou* or *Pita.*
Caldron, *Akik.*
Change, I change, *Mifcoutch.*
Child, little Children, *Bobilouchins.*
Coat, *Capotiouian.*
Cold, I am cold, *Kikatch.*
Come on, *Mappe.*
to Come, *Pimatcha.*
Comrade, at my Comrade's Houfe, *Nitche, Nitchikoue.*
Concern'd or difquieted, *Talimiffi.*
Corn, *Malomin.*
Covering, a white Woollen Covering, *Ouabiouian.*
Country, *Endalakian.*
Courage, I have Courage, *Tagouamiffi.*
C * *Maskimout.*
Cup made of Bark, *Oulagan.*

D

A Dab, *Malamek.*
Dance, I dance, *Nimi.*
Dance of the Savages to the Sound of Gourds, *Chichikoue.*
Dart, I dart, *Patchipaoua.*
Day, to day, *Ningom.*
One day, *Okonogat.*
Dead, *Nipouin.*
Devil, Evil Spirit, *Matchi Manitou.*
Die, I die, *Nip.*
Difh of Maple Wood, *Soule Mickoan.*
Dog, *Alim.*
Little Dog, *Alimons.*
Do, I do, *Tochiton.*
Done, 'tis done, *Chaye.*
Doubtlefs, *Antetatouba.*
Drefs Meat: I do the Kettle, (a Phrafe) *Poutaoue.*
Drink, I drink, *Minikoue.*
Drunken, a Fool, *Oufkouebi.*
Duck, *Chichip.*

E

EAch or every one, *Pepegik.*
Earth, *Acke* or *Ackouin.*

to Eat, *Ouiſſin*.
Elſewhere, *Coutadibi*.
Engliſh, *Ouatſakamink, Dachirini*.
Enough, 'tis enough, *Mimilic*.
Equal or like one another, *Tabiſcoutch*.
Eſteem, I eſteem or honour, *Napitelima*.
Eyes, *Ouskinchic*.

F

FAll, to fall, *Pankiſin*.
Far off, *Ouatſa*.
Faſt, to go faſt, *Ouelibick*.
Fat, *Pimite*.
Father, my Father, *Nouſce*.
Fatigued, I am fatigu'd, *Takouſſi*.
Few or little, *Me Mangis*.
Fields ſown, *Kitteganink*.
to Find, *Nantouneoua*.
Fire, *Scoute*.
to ſtrike Fire with a Stone, *Scoutecke*.
Firelock, *Scoutekan*.
Fish, *Kikons*.
White Fiſh, *Attikamec*.
Fork, *Naſſaouakouat*.
Formerly, *Piraouigo*.
Fort or Fortreſs, *Ouackaigan*.

Fortify, I make Forts, *Ouackaike*.
Forwards in the Wood, *Nopemenk*.
A Fowl, *Pilé*.
France, the Country of the French, *Mittigouchiouek, Endalakiank*.
The *French*, term'd Builders of Ships, *Mittigouch*.
to Freeze, *Kiſſin*.
It freezes hard, *Kiſſina Magat*.
Full, *Mouskinet*.
Fuſee, *Paskiſigan*.

G

GIrle, *Ickoueſſens*.
Give, I give, *Mila*.
Glaſs, a Looking-glaſs, *Ouabemo*.
Go by Water, *Pimiſca*.
God of Heaven, Maſter of Life; Great Spirit; the unknown Being, *Kitchimanitou*.
Good, *Kouelatch*.
Govern, I Govern, *Tiberima*.
[293] Governor General of Canada, *Kitchiokimaſi maganich*, *i. e.* great Captain of War.
Grape, *Choemin*.

Algonkin *Language*.

Great in the way of Merit, Valour, Courage, &c. *Kitchi*.
Great in Stature, *Mentitou*.
Greedy, *Safakiffi*.
Gut, *Olabich*.

H

Hair, *Liffis*.
Hair of Beafts *Piouel*.
Half, *Nabal*.
Handfome, Proper, *Safega*.
Hare, *Ouapous*.
Hart, *Micheoue*.
Hate, I Abhor, *Chinguerima*.
Have, to have, *Tindala*.
Head, *Oufticouan*.
Heaven, the upper Earth, *Spiminkakouin*.
Herb, *Mijask*.
Here, *Achonda* or *Achomanda*.
Hidden, *Kimouch*.
Home, at my Houfe, *Entayant*.
To Honour, *Mackaouala*.
Hot, *Akichatte*.
How, *Tani*.
How many, *Tanfou*, or *Tanimilik*.
Hungry, I am hungry, *Packate*.
Hunt, I hunt, *Kiouffe*.
Hurons, the People, *Nadouck*.
Hut, *Ouikiouam*.

I.

JEfuit, Black Gown, *Mackate ockola*.
Ifland, *Minis*.
Immediately, *Ouibatch*.
Impoftor, *Malatiffi*.
Indian Corn, *Mittamin*.
Intirely, *Napitch*.
Iron, *Piouabick*.
Iroquefe, in the Plural Number, *Matchinadoaek*.

K.

KEep, I keep, *Ganaouerima*.
Kettle, *Akikons*.
King of *France*, the Great Head of the *French*, *Mittigouch Kitchi Okima*.
Knife, *Mockoman*.
A Crooked Knife, *Coutagan*.
[294] Know, I know, *Kikerima*.
To know, *Kikerindan*.

L.

LAke, great Lake, *Kitchigamink*.
Lame, *Kakikatè*.
Land Carriage, *Cappatagan*.
To Laugh, *Papi*.
Lazy, *Kittimi*.

To Leave, *Packitan:*
Letter, *Mafignaygan.*
Liberal, *Oualatiſſi.*
Life, *Nouchimouin.*
Light, ſplendor, *Venclao.*
Little, *Ouabiloucheins.*
To Live, *Noutchimou.*
Long ſince, 'tis long ago, *Chachayè.*
Loſe at play, I loſe, *Packilague.*
Love, to love, *Sakia.*
To ly down, *Ouipema.*

M.

MAle, *Nape.*
Malicious, cheating, one that has an Ill Heart, *Malatchitehe.*
Man, *Aliſinape.*
March, I march, *Pimouſſe.*
Marry, I take a Woman, *Ouiouin.*
Marryed Man, *Napema.*
Meat, *Oüias.*
A Med'cine, or Potion, *Maskikik.*
To meet *Nantouneoua.*
Merchandize Goods, *Alokatchigan.*
Miſtreſs, or She-Friend, *Nirimouſens.*

Moon, the Star of the Night, *Debikat Ikizis.*
to Morrow, *Ouabank.*
The Day after to Morrow, *Ouſouabank.*
A Mortar of Wood for beating *Indian* Corn, *Poutagan.*
Much, *Nibila.*

N

NAtions, People, *Irini.*
Near, *Pechouetch.*
Needle, a ſewing Needle, *Chabonikan.*
Never, *Kaouicka.*
News, *Tepatchimou-kan.*
I bring News, *Tepatchimou.*
Night, *Debikat.*
No, *Ka.*
No body, *Kagouetch* or *Kaouia.*
Noſe, *Yach:*
Not at all, *Kamamenda* or *Kagouetch.*
Not yet, *Ka maſchi.*
Nothing, *Kakegou.*

O

OAR, *Appoue.*
Old, *Kioucheins.*
One-Eyed, *Paskingoe.*

Algonkin *Language.*

Original, Elk, *Mons.*
A young and little Elk, *Manichich.*
Other, *Coutac.*
Otter, *Nikik.*

P

PAP, or the juice of the Meal of *Indian* Corn, *Mitaminabou.*
Part, in what part, *Tanipi.*
Partridges, *Pilefioue.*
Pay, I pay, *Tipaham.*
Peace, *Peca.*
to make Peace, *Pecatechi.*
Peninsula, *Minissin.*
Persuasion, *Tirerigan.*
Pike, Fish, *Kinonge.*
Pipe, Calumet, *Poagan.*
to Piss, *Minsi.*
Pity, to take pity, *Chaouerima.*
to Play, *Packigoue.*
to Please one, I please, *Marouerindan.*
Porcelain Beads, *Aouies.*
Powder, Gunpowder, *Pingoe, Mackate.*
To pour out, *Sibikinan.*
To pray to God, *Talamia Kitchimanitou.*
Present, at present, *Nougam.*
Presently, *Ouibatch.*
Petty, *Olichichin.*
P*, *Patchagon.*
Proper, Handsome, *Safega.*
to Pursue, *Nopinala.*
I put away (a term used for a Man's putting away his Wife) *Ouebinan.*

Q.

QUickly, *Kegatch.*

R

RAin, *Kimiouan.*
Red Colour, *Mifcoue.*
Red Powder, esteemed by the Savages *Oulaman.*
to Regard, *Ouabemo.*
to Regrate, *Kouiloma.*
Relation, Kinsman, *Taouema.*
Resolve, I resolve, *Tibelindan.*
to Respect, *Tabamica.*
to Rest or Repose, *Chinkichin.*
Right, to be in the right, *Tepoa.*
A Ring, *Dibilinchibifon.*

River, *Sipim*.
Robe, *Ockola*.
Root, *Ouſtikoues*.
Row, to row, *Tapoue*.
to Run, *Pitchibat*.
Run to, I run to, *Pitchiba*.

[296] S

SAble, *Negao*.
Sack, *Maskimout*.
Sad, to be ſad, *Talimiſſi*.
Sail, I ſail, *Pimiſca*.
to Salute, *Mackaouala*.
Say, I ſay, *Tila*.
He ſays, ſays he, (a very uſual Word) *Youa*.
Sea, a great Lake without limits, *Agankitchigamink*.
To ſee, *Ouabemo*.
Seek, I ſeek, *Nantaouerima*.
Senſe, to have ſenſe, *Nabouacka*.
Ship, or Great Canow, *Kitchi Chiman*.
Shirt, *Papakiouian*.
Shooes, *Mackiſin*.
Sick, *Outineous*.
Side, on the other ſide, *Gaamink*.
Since, *Mipidach*.
To ſing, *Chichin*.
Skin, *Pachikin*.
Slave, *Ouackan*.
Sleep, *Nipa*.
Smoak, I ſmoak Tobacco, *Pentakoe*.
To make a Smoak, *Sagaſſoa*.
Softly, *Peccabogo*.
Sons, *Nitiani*.
Sorry, I am ſorry, *Iskatiſſi*.
Soldier, *Simaganich*.
To Speak, *Galoula*.
Spirit, an Intelligent Inviſible Being, *Manitou*.
Spoon, *Mickouan*.
Spring-time, *Mirockamink*.
Star, *Alank*.
To ſteal, *Kimoutin*.
Stockins, Hoſe, *Mitas*,
Stone, *Aſſin*.
Strong, firm, hard, *Maſchkaoua*.
A Strong-man, *Machkaoueſſi*.
Very ſtrong, *Magat*.
Sturgeon, Fiſh, *Lamek*.
Sun, *Kiſis*.
Sweat, to ſweat, *Matoutou*.
Sword, *Simagan*.
Surpriſing, 'tis ſurpriſing or wonderful, *Etteouè*.

T.

Tobacco, *Sema.*
Take, I take, *Takouan.*
Take hold, *Emanda.*
Teeth, *Tibit.*
That, *Maba.*
There, that way, *Mandadibi.*
There, at a distance, *Ouatsadibi.*
[297] To Think or entertain an Opinion, *Tilelindan.*
This, *Manda.*
This way, *Undach.*
On this side, *Undachdibi.*
Time, a long time ago, *Chachayè, Piraouigo.*
Together, *Mamaouè.*
Tongue, *Outan.*
Too Little, *Ossame Mangis.*
Too much, *Ossani.*
To Truck *Tataouan.*
Truly *Keket.*
A Turtle-Dove, *Mimi.*
Tyr'd, I am tyr'd, *Takonsi.*

W.

Walk, I walk, *Tija.*
Value, it is a valuable Thing, *Arimat.*
Water, *Nibi.*
War, *Nantobali.*
To make War, *Nantoubalima.*
Warriors, *Nantobalitchick.*
Way, or Road, *Mickan.*
Well, that is well, *Oüeoüelim.*
Well, well, what then? *Achindach.*
Well then, *Taninentien.*
What's that? *Ouaneouine.*
What has he? *Kekouanen.*
Whence, *Tanipi.*
Whence come ye? *Tanipi Endayenk.*
Where? *Ta.*
Where is he? *Tanipi Api.*
While, *Megaotch.*
White, *Ouabi.*
Whither do you go? *Taga Kitiga.*
Who's that? *Ouaneouine maba.*
Why? *Tanientien.*
Wicked, in speaking of the Iroquese, *Malatassi.*
Will, *Ouisch.*
Village, *Oudenanc.*
Win at play, I win, *Packitan.*
Wind, *Loutin.*
Wine, the Juice or Broath of Grapes, *Choeminabou.*
Visit, to pay a Visit, *Piametissa.*

A Dictionary of the

Winter, *Pipoun.*
I Winter, or pafs the Winter, *Pipounichi.*
To underftand, *Nifitotaoua.*
Wolf, *Mahingan.*
Woman, *Ickoue.*
Wood for Firing, *Mittik.*
Write, I write, *Mafinaike.*

Y.

Yellow, *Ouzao.*
Yes, *Mi,* or *Mincouti.*
Yes, indeed, *Ante,* or *Sankema.*
Yefterday, *Pitchilago.*
Yet, *Minaouatch.*
Young, *Ouskinekiffi.*

[298] I fhall here content my felf in giving you the four *Tenfes* of the *Indicative Mood* of one *Verb;* by a view of which you may form the Conjugation of the other *Moods.* 'Twere eafy to inlarge upon this Subject; but if I offer'd to launch out, the multiplicity of things that fall in the way, would oblige me to Write a formal *Grammar.*

To love, *Sakia.*

Prefent
I love, *Nifakia.*
Thou loveft, *Ki fakia.*
He loves, *Ou fakia.*
We love, *Ni fakiamin.*
Ye love, *Kifakiaoua.*
We and you love, *Kifakiaminaoua.*
They love, *Sakiaouak.*

Imperfect.
I loved, *Ni fakiaban.*
Thou lovd'ft, *Ki fakiaban.*
He lov'd, *Ou fakiaban.*
We lov'd, *Ni faikaiminaban.*
You lov'd, *Ki fakiaouaban.*
We and you lov'd, *Kifakiminaouaban.*
They lov'd, *Sakiabanik.*

I have lov'd, *Ni kifakia.*
Thou haft lov'd, *Ki kifakia.*
He has lov'd, *Ou kifakia.*
We have lov'd, *Ni kifakiamin.*
You have lov'd, *Ki kifakiaoua.*
We and you have lov'd, *Ki kifakiaminaoua.*
They have lov'd, *Kifakiaouak.*

Algonkin *Language*.

I shall love, *Ningasakia*.
Thou shalt love, *Ki gasakia*.
He shall love, *Ou gasakia*.
We shall love, *Nin gasakiamin*.
You shall love, *Ki gasakiaoua*.
We and you shall love, *Ki gasakiaminaoua*.
They shall love, *Gasakiaouak*.
Love thou, *Asakia*.
Let us love, *Asakiata*.

As for the *Nouns* they are not declin'd at all. The plural number is form'd by a *k*. added to a singular, ending in a *Vowel*, as *Alisinape* signifies a Man, and *Alisinapek* several Men. If the *Noun* [299] ends with a *Consonant*, the plural is form'd by the addition of *ik;* as *Minis* signifies an Isle, and *Minissik* Isles; *Paskisigan* a Fusee, and *Paskisiganik* a plurality of Fusees.

The *Algonkin* way of Counting.

One, *Pegik*.
Two, *Ninch*.
Three, *Nissoue*.
Four, *Neou*.
Five, *Naran*.
Six, *Ningoutouassou*.
Seven, *Ninchouassou*.
Eight, *Nissouassou*.
Nine, *Changassou*.
Ten, *Mittassou*.
Eleven, *Mittassou achi pegik*.
Twelve, *Mittassou achi ninch*.
Thirteen, *Mittassou achi nissoue*.
Fourteen, *Mittassou achi neou*.
Fifteen, *Mittassou achi naran*.
Sixteen, *Mittassou achi ningotouassou*.
Seventeen, *Mittassou achi ninchoassou*.
Eighteen, *Mittassou achi nissouassou*.
Nineteen, *Mittassou achi changassou*.
Twenty, *Ninchtana*.
Twenty one, *Ninchtana achi pegik*.
Twenty two, *Ninchtana achi ninch*.
Twenty three, *Nichtana achi nissoue*.

Twenty four, *Ninchtana achi neou.*
Twenty five, *Ninchtana achi naran.*
Twenty six, *Ninchtana achi ningotouaſſou.*
Twenty ſeven, *Ninchtana achi ninchoaſſou.*
Twenty eight, *Ninchtana achi niſſouaſſou.*
Twenty nine, *Ninchtana achi changaſſou.*

Thirty, *Niſſouemitana.*
Thirty one, *Niſſouemitana achi pegik, &c.*
Fourty, *Neoumitana.*
Fifty, *Naran mitana.*
Sixty, *Ningoutouaſſou mitana.*
Seventy, *Ninchouaſſou mitana.*
Eighty, *Niſſouaſſou mitana.*
Ninety, *Changaſſou mitana.*
A hundred, *Mitaſſou mitana.*
A thouſand, *Mitaſſou mitaſſou mitana.*

[300] If you can once count to a hundred, 'tis eaſy to count by tens from a thouſand to a hundred thouſand, which number is in a manner unknown to the *Savages*, and by conſequence not us'd in their Language.

You muſt take care to pronounce fully all the letters of the Words, and to reſt upon the *A*'s that come at the end. The pronunciation is very eaſy, becauſe this Language has no Guttural or Palate Letters, ſuch as the *Spaniſh J Conſonant* with their *G* and their *H*, as well as the *Engliſh th*, which puts a Foreigner's Tongue upon the rack.

I can't paſs by one curious Remark touching the Language of the *Hurons* and the *Iroqueſe;* namely, that it do's not uſe the Labial Letters, viz. *b, f, m, p*. And yet the *Huron*'s Language appears to be very pretty, and ſounds admirably well, notwithſtanding that the *Hurons* never ſhut their Lips when they ſpeak.

Commonly the *Iroqueſe* make uſe of it in their Harangues and Councils, when they enter upon a Negotiation with the

Algonkin *Language.*

French or *English*. But in their Domestick Interviews they speak their Mother Tongue.

None of the Savages of *Canada* care to speak *French*, unless they are persuaded that the force of their Words will be perfectly understood. They must be very well satisfied upon that Head before they venture to expose themselves in speaking their mind in *French;* abating for some cases of necessity, when they are in Company with the *Coureurs de Bois* that do not understand their Language.

To return to the *Huron* Language; we must consider that since neither the *Hurons* nor the *Iroquese* use the Labial Letters, 'tis impossible for [301] either of 'em to learn *French* well. I have spent four days in trying to make the *Hurons* pronounce the Labial Letters, but I could not accomplish it; nay, I am of the Opinion that in ten years time they would not learn to pronounce these Words, *Bon*, *Fils*, *Monsieur*, *Ponchartrain:* For instead of *Bon* they'd say *Ouon;* instead of *Fils*, *Rils;* instead of *Monsieur*, *Caounsieur;* and in the room of *Ponchartrain*, *Conchartrain*.

I have here added some Words of the *Huron* Language, that your curiosity may be gratified with a view of the difference between that and the *Algonkin*. The *Hurons* speak with a great deal of gravity, and almost all their Words have aspirations, the *H* being pronounc'd as strong as possible.

I do not know that the Letter *F* is usd in any of the *Savage* Languages. 'Tis true, the *Essanapes* and the *Gnacsitares* have it; but they are Seated upon the long River beyond the *Mississipi*, and consequently out of the Limits of *Canada*.

Some *Huron* Words.

To be a Man of Senſe, *Hondioun.*
Spirit, Divinity, *Ocki.*
Fire, *Tſiſta.*
Iron, *Aouiſta.*
Woman, *Ontehtian.*
Fuſee, *Ouraouenta.*
To be ſorry, *Oungaroun.*
'Tis cold, *Outoirha.*
Fat, *Skoueton.*
Man, *Onnonhoue.*
Yeſterday, *Hiorheha.*
Jeſuit, *Tſiſtatſi.*
Far, *Deherén.*
Otter, *Taouinet.*
Not, *Staa.*
Yes, *Endae.*
Pipe or Calumet, *Gannondaoua.*
Near, *Touskeinhia.*
Soldiers, *Skeuraguettè.*
To Salute, *Igonoron.*
Shooes, *Arrachiou.*
Traffick, *Attendinon.*
Altogether, *Tiaoundi.*
All of 'em, *Aouetti.*
Tobacco, *Oyngoua.*

'Tis valuable, difficult, [302] and of importance, *Gannoron.*
To be gone, *Saraskoua.*
Covetous, *Onnonſtè.*
Handſome, Proper, *Akouaſti.*
Very much, *Atoronton.*
That's well, *Andeya.*
I Drink, *Ahirrha.*
Indian Corn, *Onneha.*
Stockins, *Arrhich.*
A Bottle, *Gatſeta.*
A brave Man, *Songuitehe.*
'Tis done, *Houna.*
My Brother, *Yatſi.*
My Comrade, *Yonaro.*
Heaven, *Toendi.*
A Hutt, *Honnonchia.*
Hair, *Eonhora.*
Captain, *Otcon.*
Dog, *Agnienon.*
Softly, *Skenonha.*
Peace, *Skenon.*
I ſay, *Attatia.*
To morrow, *Achetek.*
To be, *Sackie.*

INDEX

ABE

Abenaki Indians, significance of name, 328; habitat, xxvii, 327, 328; language, 339; migrations, 90, 327, 328, 330; tribe of, 90, 328; French allies, 328; St. Castin among, 328, 329; missions for, 46-49, 328-330, 339, 340; give tidings of English fleet, 242, present numbers, 328; characterized, 339, sketch, 327, 328.

Abies canadensis, 371.

Abittibi (Tabitibi) Indians, habitat, 342; language, 342; characterized, 342; sketch, 342

Acadia, climate, 325, 326; part of Canada, 302; boundaries, 236, 323, 324; coast, 323, 324; described, 323-327; early grant of, 331; Indians, 90, 327, 328, 339, 399, 414, 734; settlement, 324, 326, 331; population, 330; capital, 330, 331; in Lahontan's lieutenancy, xxx, 281; governors of, 52, 53, 237, 288, 326, 327, 332; French officers in, 224, 236, 237; English in, 69, 227, 326; projected attack on, 274; fisheries, 324-326; fur-trade, 327, 328; missions, 329, 330; agriculture, 325; visited by bishop, 232

Acadiensis, 330

Acipenser rubicundus, 156.

Achirigouan Indians, habitat, 342; language, 342; characterized, 342; sketch, 342.

Adario (Kondiaronk, The Rat), Huron chief, characterized, xlviii, 220, 242; Denonville attempts to punish, 209, 220; French ally, 220; relations with Frontenac, 149; at Fort Frontenac, 220, 221; relations with Iroquois,

AMM

Adario (*continued*).
xxii, 149, 165, 220-225, 237, 238, 508; opposed to war, 495, 496; friend of Lahontan, xxii, 9, 165; Dialogue with Lahontan, xiv, lxi, 7, 8, 517-618; arguments, 442, 443; quoted, xliv, xlvi, 495, 496; wife, 461; funeral, 149; sketch, 149.

Adders, in Canada, 352, 357.

Africans, characteristics of, 282, 284.

Agnies Indians. *See* Mohawk Indians.

Akansas Indians. *See* Arkansa Indians.

Akouessan. *See* Longueuil.

Albany (N. Y), location, 7; raids near, 240, 262.

Alders, in Canada, 365.

Algonkin Indians, habitat, 47, 50, 51; vocabulary of language, 733-748; numbers, 733; allied with French, 51; conduct French to Iroquois country, 81, 82; Lahontan hunts with, 46, 47, 88, 89; mission for, 49; sketch, 51.

Algonquian family, tribes of, xl, 47, 77, 82, 90, 168, 174, 175, 218, 309, 317, 327, 340, 343, 398; original tribe of, 342; language, 47, 176, 297, 339, 342, 733, 734; vocabulary, 297, 736-748; name for governor of Canada, 97, 404; religious ideas of, 435

Alligator mississippiensis, 347.

Allouez, Father Claude, founds Green Bay mission, 168; monument to, 168; mentions wild rice, 175; cited, 494.

American Naturalist, 200.

Amherstburg (Ont.), Indian reservation near, 155.

Ammunition, Canadian import, 376.

AMO

Amours, Geneviève d', affair with Lahontan, xxvii, xxviii, 388–390; marriage, 391; god-daughter of Frontenac, xxviii.

—, Mathieu d', councillor at Quebec, 324, 325, 388; grants of land, 325; friend of Nelson, 389, 390.

—, Mathieu d', the younger, in New Brunswick, xxviii, 324, 325; friend of Nelson, xxviii, 389, 390.

—, Réné d', in New Brunswick, xxviii, 324, 325; defends fort, 325; friend of Nelson, xxviii, 389, 390.

Anastase, Father. *See* Douay.

Andastes Indians, identified, 320; habitat, 320, 321.

Andastogueron Indians, language, 733

André, Louis, authority on Algonquian language, 733.

Andros, Sir Edmond, uprising against, 265.

Angola, Portuguese colony, 282, 283; customs, 632; ships, 636.

Angui, Messieurs d', provision Placentia, 282.

Annapolis, site, 331; population, 331 *See also* Port Royal.

Anne, ruler of England, 3; war in reign of, 5.

Anschild (Anskoeld), Frederick, reputed discoverer, 309–311; origin of myth of, 309; *Journals*, 310

·Anse du Tonnerre. *See* Bay, Thunder.

Aoutaerobi, Indian spirit, 603.

Apache Indians, medicine men among, 468.

Appleton (Wis.), rapids at, 174.

Apple-trees, of Canada, 319, 364; fruit described, 367.

Aragon, capital, lxi, 9, 718; government, 720, 721, social classes, 724, 725; customs, 727–729; physical characteristics of people, 721; women, 722, 723, 729, 730; dress, 726; morality, 723, 724, 728–730; food,

ATT

Aragon (*continued*).
721, 728; wines, 721; inns, 721; carriages, 725, 726.

Arce, Sieur d'. *See* Isaac, baron Lahontan

Arctomys pruniosus, 111.

Arctostaphylos ura-ursa, 474

Aria *See* Viele.

Aristotle, Lahontan describes, xiv, 116, 117

Arkansa Indians, hunt buffalo, 203, 204; Lahontan meets, 203–205, 465, 466; trade with Illinois, 204; possess iron instruments, 204; La Salle among, 204; French term for Siouan tribe, 204; migrations, 204; sketch, 204.

Arkansas, Indians of, 204.

Army, troops in Canada, xi, xv, 386, 387; first troops arrive, 392; quartered, xii, xiv, 387; work for habitants, 387; in trade, 387; relations between officers and soldiers, 391; pay of officers, 383; marriage of officers, 387, 388; pay of soldiers, 383.

Arpent, French measure, defined, 35

Arrèche, Sieur d', French merchant, 655.

Arrow-heads (iron), in fur-trade, 378

Asher, George M., *Henry Hudson the Navigator*, 309.

Ash-trees, of Canada, 364.

Aspens, of Canada, 365; described, 371; food of beavers, 371, 480, 482.

Asps, in Canada, 352; poisonous, 357.

Assan-oustick, Indian word for tomahawk, 402.

Assiniboin (Assinipoual) Indians, habitat, 304, 305, 342, 343; language, 342, 343; tribe associated with, 343; migrations, 343.

Associates of Montreal, 53, 55, 233.

Astrolabe, described, 401.

Atinton Indians. *See* Teton Indians

Attikameck (Attikamégues) Indians, language, 340; habitat, 340; destroyed, 340; sketch, 340.

AUN

Aunay, Count d', escort to Lahontan, 257, 258; thanked, 259
Aunoy, Madam d', 647
Authoutantas Indians See Oto Indians.
Auvergne, commerce of, 725; mules, 633.
Aux, Chevalier Pierre d', sent on embassy to Iroquois, xxvi, 238, 239, 508; imprisoned, xxvi, 238, 239, 508; escapes, 239; brings information, 239; sketch, 239
Avaux, Count d', Lahontan's patron, 11, 12
Aveiro, Lahontan at, 619, 625, 626; harbor, 622, situation, 625; salt works, 625
Aveneau, Father Claude, chaplain at Fort St. Joseph, xx, 140, sketch, 140
Awls, in fur-trade, 377.
Axes, in fur-trade, 377
Aztec calendar, 428.

BACCALEOS, early name for Newfoundland and Labrador, 307.
Badgers, Canadian like European, 343; animal resembling, 344.
Bain, James, jr., *Henry's Travels and Adventures*, 99, 219, 309, 357, 380
Balenots, in Canada, 358, described, 360
Balzac, Jean Louis Guez de, *Letters*, 692; *Dissertations*, 692.
Bar-Haven (havre de barre), described, 622.
Bases, small fish, 358.
Baskets, of birch-bark, 370.
Basques, early American explorers, x; fisheries off New Foundland, 308
Basse-Pyrenées, Lahontan born in, ix
Bastille, French prison, 53, 265, 293, 294; Lahontan fears, xxxii.
Batteurs de faux, identified, 110, size, 351.

BAY

Bay of Biscay, fishermen at Newfoundland, 275, 305; reputation of sailors, 272; soldiers, 276, 278; aid in defence, 279, 281; captains favor Lahontan, 288; harbors in, 294.
— Chaleurs, described, 324; origin of name, 324; fishing villages, 306.
— Chequamegon, traders near, 315; French post on, 209
— Dingle, on west coast of Ireland, 302.
— Fortune, Newfoundland, 334
— Française. See Fundy.
— Fundy, 330; explored, 324; tercentenary of settlement, 324.
— Georgian, islands in, 154, 218; route through, 218, 273, north channel, 218; Indians near, 340, 488.
— Grand See Grand Traverse
— Grand Traverse (Mich.), identified, 208; early names for, 208; affluent of, 210; beaver hunting grounds, 481; described, 210
— Green, French name for, 146, 167; significance, 146; fur-trade, 146, 168; location, 167, 494; islands in, 167; Lahontan visits, xxiv, xlii, 167-173; described, 167; tides in, 168; Indian villages near, xxiv, Jesuit mission near, xviii, 168, fertility of, 168.
— Hamilton (Ganadoké, Ganaraské), 321, 322, Iroquois hunting ground, 323
— Hudson, origin of name, 311; described, 309, 314; climate, 314; discovery, 309-311, explorations, 244, 310, 312; boundary, 302; natives, 47, 308, 309, 312, 342, 734; French posts, 313; English posts, 312, 313, 316; French and English struggle for, 69, 217, 236, 244, 312-314; fur-trade, 244, 311-314.
— Irondequoit, location, 125
— James, French expelled from, 314.
— Missisaguas. See Georgian Bay

BAY

Bay Mortier, in Placentia Bay, 338; origin of name, 338.
— Noquet, 317
— Notre Dame (Newfoundland), 333.
— de l'Ours qui Dort (Sleeping Bears). *See* Grand Traverse Bay.
— Papinachois, location, 261
— Passamaquoddy, settlement, 324, 331.
— Placentia, location, 334, harbor of refuge, 335, 336, town on, 335; size, 335, harbor, 338.
— Quiberon, French harbor, 294.
— Quinté, mission at, 70, portage to, 318.
— Saginaw, size, 318; islands, 143, 318, 319; navigation, 318, 319; beaver hunting grounds, 481; Lahontan crosses, 143.
— St. Lawrence, in Placentia Bay, 338; ship-building at, 338.
— Savage, discovered by Anschild, 310.
— Seven Islands, location, 261.
— Thunder (Lake Huron), Lahontan passes, 143
— Toronto, size, 317; location, 317, 318, projected fort on, 273, 318. *See also* Georgian Bay.
— Trepassey, location, 334.
— White (Newfoundland), 308
Bayonne, port of departure for Canada, 373; brandy exported from, 375; harbor, 622; harbor improved by Lahontan, ix, xxi, 150; grant of, ix, bourgeois, ix, money seized at, xxi, 151; Lahontan at, 698.
Beads, Venetian, in fur-trade, 378.
Beans, raised by Indians, 148; at Green Bay, 168; on River Long, 187.
Bearberry *See* Sacacommis
Bearn, engineering works at, xxi, 150; justice of, 151; parlement at Pau, 150, 707; French officer from, 328, 329; Lahontan a native of, ix, reformer-general, ix; governor, x; commerce, 725; witchcraft, 696–710.

BEA

Bears, described, 115, 343, 346, 347; Polar, described, 344, 347, 348; hibernation, 115, 484; hunted, 114, 115, 346, 482–484; used for food, 115, 169, 482; near Fort St. Joseph, 484, price of skins, 380; Norwegian trade in skins, 681, not enemies of beaver, 480
Beaucourt, Josué Dubois de Berthelot, sieur de, aids in fortifying Quebec, 265, commands party against Iroquois, 266, sketch, 266.
Beaujeu, —, commander of La Salle's vessel, 335.
Beauport. *See* Juchereau.
Beaupré, origin of name, 32; location, xii, habitants of, xii, Lahontan at, xii, 34–38, sketch, 34.
Beauvais, —, commandant at Fort St. Joseph, xviii.
Beauvilliers, Paul, duke of, French courtier, sketch, 227.
Beaver-eater. *See* Carcajou.
Beavers, described, 171–173; nearly extinct, 481, 483; habitat, 319, 326, 344, 481; homes of, 170, 171, 477, 479, 480, different kinds, 343, 345, 346; amphibious, 170, 476; land-beavers, 170, 171, 482, 484, 485; habits, 171–173, 479, 480; food, 371, 480, 482; sagacity, 8, 172, 476–478; make dams, 478, 479; sentinels, 477, 478, 480; tree-felling, 477, 480, domesticated, 170, 171, enemies, 480, 485, defenses, 480; parasites, 171; hunted, 82, 143, 171, 172, 175, 319, 349, 481–485, 507, 573–575; bait for, 171, 482, 483, 485; traps, 482–485; tail used for food, 169; flesh, 173; skins in commerce, 54, 91, 122, 377, 383, 591, 609, price, 54, 91, 101, 173, 379; compared with muskrats, 110; variety of pelts, 379; method of preparing, 485, valued, 172, 280, 398, farmers-general of, 382.

BEC

Becs de scie, species of duck, 352.
Beech, in Canada, 364.
Bees, in Canada, 352, sting, 357.
Bégon, Monsieur de, courtier of Louis XIV, 254.
Belin, Lahontan at, 648.
Belle Isle, French harbor, 294.
Benedictines, in Viana, 621, 622.
Beothics, aborigines of Newfoundland, 334; hatred of whites, 334; sketch, 334.
Beray, —, sieur, Biscayan captain, 288.
Bergères, Raymond Blaise des, sieur de Rigauville, commandant at Niagara, 162; seeks reinforcements, 162; sketch, 131.
Berlin (Wis.), on Fox River, 178.
Bernon, Samuel, chief merchant of Canada, 374.
Berrien County (Mich), 208.
Berthelot, Canadian family, 39. *See also* Beauport.
Beschefer, Thierry, Jesuit missionary, starts for Canada, 259; superior at Quebec, 259; sketch, 259.
Biche, French name for elk, 103.
Bienville, Jean Baptiste le Moyne, sieur de, founds Louisiana, 74.
Biggar, H. P., *Early Trading Companies of New France*, 303.
Big Mouth. *See* Grangula.
Birch, of Canada, 364; described, 370.
Birch-bark, maps drawn on, 427; used for canoes, 63, 370; paper, 870; baskets, 370.
Bissot. *See* Jolliet, *and* Couillard.
Blackbirds, in Canada, 350.
Blueberries (bluets), in Canada, 365; described, 372, uses, 373; Indian food, 372.
Boat, —, wounded at Placentia, 279.
Boats, flat-bottomed, 85. *See also* Canoes.
Bodin (Bodinus), Jean, *Demonomanie des Sorciers*, 704.
Bois, L. E., *Isle d'Orleans*, 39.

BRA

"Bon," shipwrecked off Newfoundland, 336.
Bonaventure, Claude Denis, sieur de, announces Frontenac's restoration, 227; sketch, 227.
Bonnecamps, Father Joseph Pierre de, descends St. Lawrence, 68.
Bonrepos *See* Dusson.
Bordeaux, port of departure for Canada, 88, 373; wines exported from, 375; Lahontan at, 697.
Bossuet, —, minister of state, 150.
Boston, revolution in, 265; fort in harbor, 265, French prisoners in, xxvi, 239, 265, 330; receives information, 265; capital of New England, 330, French inhabitants near, 330; undefended, 239; fleet at, 289; editions of Lahontan in Athenæum, liii–xciii; in Public Library, liii–xciii.
Boucher, Pierre, governor of Three Rivers, 98.
— family, 98.
Boucherville, Lahontan at, xiv, 96–117; review at, 103; La Forest, 125; sketch, 98.
Bouillon, Cardinal de, Lahontan's patron, 11.
Bourbon regiment, Lahontan in, x.
Bourke, John G., "Medicine Men of the Apache," 468.
Bouteux, fishing nets, described, 401.
Bouts de Quievres, small fishing nets, 402.
Bragelonne, Claude, relative of Lahontan, xi.
— family, relatives of Lahontan, xi, 253.
Branchus, species of duck, described 355; origin of name, 355.
Brandy, imported to Canada, 373; price, 375, valuable in fur-trade, 378, 568.
Brazil, Portuguese colony, 282, 284; aborigines of, 284; customs, 632; fleet, 624, 637.

BRE

Brébeuf, Jean de, authority on Huron-Iroquois language, 733.
Breccia, on Cape Breton, 333, 334.
Bretons, early explorers and fishers, 307, 308, 324.
Brigantine, built for Frontenac, 239, 241, 242; described, 402.
Brinton, D. G , *Myths of New World*, 435, 447, 448, 468, 472, 510.
British Museum, editions of Lahontan in, liii–xciii.
Brittany, Lahontan in, 264; harbor, 294, fishers from, 324. *See also* Bretons.
Brouillon, Jacques François de, governor of Placentia, xxix, 276, 287; defends Placentia against English, xxix, 276–278; Lahontan presents himself to, 287, 288; commends Lahontan, 279; dislikes Lahontan, xxxi, 12, 287–289; attempts to prevent Lahontan's escape, 294, 297; Lahontan accuses, xxxi, 289–294, 337, 338; accuses Lahontan at court, 293, 297; unpopular, xxxi, 292–294; extortionate, 288, 290, 337, 338, wife, 291; letters, 288; sketch 287, 288.
Brulots, in Canada, 352; described, 357, 358
Bruyas, Father Jacques, Jesuit missionary, 56; superior, 56; aids in treaty of peace, 56; Indian grammar, 56; acts as interpeter, 84, sketch, 56.
Bryce, George, *Hudson's Bay Company*, 312, 314
Buffalo (Wild Beet), 343; on Mississippi, 170, 203, on River Long, 192, 197; on Missouri, 202; on Lake Erie, 320, hunted, 193, 194, 203; hunted by puma, 345; used in manufactures, 194, 213, 214; used as food, 197.
Bustards, Canadian resemble European, 351; in Wisconsin, 174; manner of hunting, 109.

CAN

Button, Sir Thomas, early English navigator, 310, 311.

CADDOAN family, tribes of, 200.
Cadillac, Antoine la Mothe, sieur de, founder of Detroit, xix, xlvi, 125, 133; secures upper country, xlvi.
California, Indian customs of, 473.
Callières-Bonnevue, Louis Hector, sieur de, governor of Montreal, 86, 88; governor of New France, 86, 129; on Denonville's expedition, 120; aids in defences of Quebec, 242; intercedes for English envoy, 246; sketch, 86.
Calumet, 58; described, 75, 76, 168, 169, 402; origin of name, 402; Indian name for, 402; uses, 75, 76, 423, 424, token of peace, 75, 77, 80, 81, 508, 509; sacred, 508; dance, 83; significance of dance, 168, 169; Foxes dance, 175; limit of authority, 189.
Camanistigoyan. *See* Kaministiquia.
Campbell, Henry C , "Radisson and Groseilliers," 312.
Canada, governor of, 153; Library of Parliament (Ottawa), editions of Lahontan in, liii–xciii; Indian department *Report*, 55; Royal Society *Proceedings*, xviii, li, 36, 37, 51, 98, 145, 151, 312; *Archives*, xviii, 87, 125, 519 *See also* New France.
Canadian Journal, 154.
Canal, Cornwall, 68.
— Grenville, 217.
— Lachine, 67.
Canibas Indians, habitat, 327, 328; language, 339; allies of French, 328; characterized, 339.
Canissee, Count, Danish envoy, 688.
Canoes, how made, 63, 64; of birchbark, 370; cedar, 63, 371; white wood, 372; skins, 106, 307, 481; gummed for water, 158; supports of,

CAN

Canoes (*continued*).
404, 406, 407; shape, 65; size, 62, 63, weight, 64; tonnage, 63; light draught, 63, 64; working of, 65, 66; unsteady, 62, 63; price, 65; Iroquois inferior, 138; used in war-parties, 501; not useful in discoveries, 211, travel in, 46, 62–65, 67, value of cargoes, 54, 64.

Cantabrian soldiers, defend Placentia, 276.

Capa y d'espada, term for councillors, 402.

Cape Diamond (Quebec), 265; place of execution, 268.

— Finisterre, Lahontan passes, 257, 258, 295, 649, 650.

— Forillon, off Gaspé, 306.

— Hurd, off Georgian Bay, 154.

— North, northern extremity of Europe, 301.

— Race, origin of name, 28; descried, 29; coast near, 334; longitude, 302.

— Ray, location, 30, 333; passage choked with ice, 325; coast near, 334.

— St Francis. *See* Long Point

— St Mary (Newfoundland), 275

— Tourmente, location, 32, 39, 261; origin of name, 32.

— West, in Iceland, 301.

Cap Rogo. *See* Cape Race.

Caps, in fur-trade, 377.

Carcajous, characterized, 344; hunted, 111.

Caribou, identified, 107; habitat, 316, 344; manner of hunting, 107; price of skins, 380.

Carignan-Saliéres, regiment de, in Canada, 35, 36, 52, 59; members perish with cold, 60; officers, 125, 328; disbanded, 328; sketch, 36.

Carolina, early explorations of coast, 303; parrots in, 354.

Carp, in Great Lakes, 359; Mississippi, 359; described, 362.

CED

Cascades, St Lawrence rapids, portage of, 67.

Carter-Brown Library, editions of Lahontan in, liii–xciii.

Cartier, Jacques, explores St Lawrence, 31, 303; gives geographical names, 31, 39, 51, 261, 324; second voyage, 67, 303; alludes to Niagara, 137; accounts of, 303; explorations, 303; sketch, 303; *Voyages*, 303.

Cartography, xxxviii, 8–10, 28, 200, 208, 376.

Casson de Dollier, François, Sulpitian superior, 55; chaplain in Mohawk campaign, 55; accompanies La Salle, 55; historian of Montreal, 55.

Castor canadensis, 345.

Castor gras d'hiver. *See* Beaver skins.

Cataracoui. *See* Fort Frontenac.

Cataract du Trou, St. Lawrence rapid, 67.

Catholic University *Bulletin*, 512.

Catlin, George, explores quarries at Pipestone, 76.

Catlinite, used for calumets, 76.

Caton, John D., *Antelope and Deer of North America*, 103.

Caudisona terguemina, 357.

Caughnawaga, mission village at, 56.

Cavelier, Abbé Jean, brother of La Salle, arrives at Mackinac, xxi, 144; Sulpitian, 145; sketch, 145.

— Jean, nephew of La Salle, at Mackinac, xxi, 144; sketch, 145.

Cayuga (Goyoguans) Indians, 77, 80; habitat, 58, 323, 341; language, 341; fishing grounds, 155, 156; chief of, 233; request missionaries, 70, English should remove, 399.

— County Historical Society, *Collections*, 127, 131.

Cedar, of Canada, 365; described, 371; two species, 371; used for canoes, 63, 371; odor of, 371.

Cedars, rapids in Fox River, 174.

CEL

Céloron, Jean Baptiste de Blainville, wife of, 391.
Cenis Indians, mission to, 145
Central America, Indian customs of, 473.
Cervus alches, 103; *canadensis*, 103; *virginianus*, 107
Chalumeau. *See* Calumet.
Chambly, Jacques de, Canadian officer, 52.
Chambly *See* Fort Chambly.
Champigny, Jean Bochart de, intendant of New France, 102, 120; advances to Fort Frontenac, 120, 121; voyage to Montreal, 239; Lahontan visits, 220; sketch, 103.
— Madam de, intercedes for Iroquois prisoners, 266, 267; mercy of, 269.
Champlain, Samuel de, gives geographical names, 32, 51, 66, 118, 325; builds Fort St. Louis, 40; controls liquor traffic, 94; hears of Niagara, 137; visits Huron, 219, founds Quebec, 303, 331; explores Bay of Fundy, 324, 331; discovery celebrated, 324, map, 325; makes enemies of Iroquois, xv.
Chaouanon, Indian slave, 156.
Chapeau Rouge, location, 334, 338.
Charles II (England), orders peace with Iroquois, 61, 79; subservient to France, 61; patronizes Radisson and Groseilliers, 313; sells part of Newfoundland, 275.
Charlevoix, Pierre François Xavier de, Jesuit historian, 42, 44, 149; describes Nipissing, 342; exposes fallacy of River Long, xxxix; *Histoire de Nouvelle France*, 149, 217, 279; *Journal Historique*, xxxix, 42.
Chateaubriand, François Auguste, vicomte de, French romanticist, xlviii.
Chauanon Indians *See* Shawnee Indians.
Chequamegon, French post on, 315.

COD

Cherries, of Canada, 364, 365; described, 366, 367.
Chestnuts, of Canada, 364; on Lake Erie, 319; in Seneca country, 131; in Illinois, 367.
Chevaliers, species of water-fowl, 351.
Chicago (Chekakou), Indians at, 340; Lahontan, 207; site described, 207; portage, xxiv, 207; canal, 207.
Chicoutimi County (Quebec), 260.
China, passage to, sought, 309.
Chipmunk, described, 348.
Chippewa (Salteur) Indians, French name for, 149, 340; habitat, 149, 152, 493; physical characteristics, 415; brave, 159, 160; courtship and marriage among, 457; war customs, 502–509; secret society among, 468; totems, 511; calendar, 427, 428; with Iroquois, xxii, 149, 153–161; capture Iroquois, 159; rescue slaves, 160; at Fort St. Joseph, 161; warn Foxes of Iroquois raid, 489, 493; war with Foxes, 489, 494; characterized, 340
Chonkasketons (Sonkaskiton) Indians, Siouan tribe, 343; significance of name, 343; habitat, 342; language, 343.
Christianity, discussion of, 517–550.
Christy, Miller, *Voyages of Captain Luke Foxe and Captain Thomas James*, 310.
Citrons. *See* Mandrake.
Citrouille, in Canada, 364; described, 369; Indian food, 148, 369
Clarke, John M., "Percé. a brief sketch of its geology," 305.
Coal, exported from Canada, 374.
Cockles, in Canada, 359, 361.
Cod, in Canada, 358; export, 374; demand for, 394, method of drying, 336.
Cod fishery, off Newfoundland, 27, 290, 305, 308, 332, 333, 336, 337; off

COD

Cod fishery (*continued*):
Gaspé, 305, 306; near St. Lawrence, 306; off Acadia, 324, 326; Tadoussac, 31; time for, 337; bait, 337, 360, 361; value, 338.
Colbert, Jean Baptiste, French minister, 118.
Colin, —, Indian interpreter, accompanies d'Aux, 238.
Collars. *See* Wampum.
Collection des Manuscrits relatifs à la Nouvelle France, 26, 124, 257.
Comitatus, among Indians, 500.
Commerce, 235; merchants at Montreal, 53, 96, 97; profits of, 54, 375–377; exchange with France, 101, 376; general view, 373–378; few exports, 373, 374, with French West Indies, 374, season for, 375; internal, 376; reform needed, 391, 392; customs tariff, 373. *See also* fur-trade.
Compagnie des Indes Occidentales, 91.
Company of Domain, 91.
— **of Merchants of London,** discoverers of North-West Passage, 312.
— **of One Hundred Associates,** xi, 34, 253.
— **of New France,** 41, 303; founded at Rouen, 303.
Compass, variation of, 403.
Conestoga Indians, Huron-Iroquois tribe, habitat, 321.
Congés. *See* Licenses for fur-trade.
Connecticut, Indians of, 90; troops to invade Canada, 240.
Conurus carolinensis, 354.
Cook, Samuel F., *Drummond Island,* 153.
Coots, Canadian resemble European, 350.
Copper, used by Indians, 195; found on Lake Superior, 316; purity of ore, 316.
Coregonus clupeiformis, 147.

COU

Corlaer, Indian title for governor of New York, 82, 84, 236; origin of term, 82.
Corlear. *See* Schenectady.
Cornaillon, — de, French officer in Danish army, 674.
Cormorants, in Canada, 351.
Costabelle, sieur Pastour de, governor of Placentia, 276; of Cape Breton, 276; envoy to English, 276, 277; sketch, 276.
Côtes of Canada, described, 34, 35.
Coues, Elliott, *Early History of Northwest,* 474; identifies River Long, xl.
Couillard, Marie, mother-in-law of Jolliet, captured by English, 243, 244; effects exchange of prisoners, 244, 249; sketch, 244.
Courbeious (bird), in Canada, 351.
Courcelles, Daniel de Rémy, sieur de, war with Mohawk, 59; recommends site of Fort Frontenac, 69; sketch, 59.
Coureurs de bois, 48, 430; term defined, 403; bravery of, 237, reliability, 477; thievery, 100, 537; prodigality, 54; in fur-trade, xviii, 54, 92, 99, 140, 153, 164, 168, 207, 315, 430, extent of ranging, 304; restricted, 99, 399; on Great Lakes, 125; Lake Superior, 315; Mackinac, 136; Maine, 236, 237; New York, 236; Sault Ste. Marie, 488, 489; Illinois, 207, commandants, 164, 165, 209, 217; protected by Perrot, 53; under Duluth, 73; enemies of English, 125–128, 209, 216, 247; garrison Fort St. Joseph, 139; repair Fort Frontenac, 232, 233; aid Lahontan, 141; captured by Iroquois, 270; robbed by Iroquois, 77.
Couttes (Ecouttes), Abbé de, uncle of Lahontan, xxvi, 253, 254.
— **Jeanne Françoise le Fascheux de,** Lahontan's mother, x.

COW

Cowper, Capt. —, English naval officer, 650.
Coyne, James H., "Exploration of Great Lakes," 484.
Crabs, in Canada, 359.
Cranes, in Canada, 350.
Cree Indians. *See* Cristinaux Indians.
Creek Cattaraugus, portage route, 155.
— Chautauqua, portage route, 155.
— Irondequoit, rendezvous for expedition, 125–127; fort at, 127.
— Mill (Pa.), identified, 155.
— Wood, rendezvous for troops, 240.
Crenger, —, ship commander, 648.
Creoles, defined, 402.
Cristinaux (Clistino, Cree, Killistinoe) Indians, Algonquian tribe, 343; habitat, 309, 342; physical traits, 415; language, 342, 343; defeat Eskimo, 308, 309, conduct French to Hudson Bay, 312; associated with Assiniboin, 343, present numbers, 309; sketch, 309.
Croche, rapids in Fox River, 174.
Crocodiles, described, 346, 347; habitat, 343, 346; capture of, 346; man-eaters, 346; Arkansa kill, 204.
Cucurbita polymorpha, 148.
Cungars, in Canada, 358.
Cutlasses, in fur-trade, 378.
Cuyler, —, early Dutch trader, 82.

Dabs (fish), described, 362; in Mississippi River, 178, 359; in Great Lakes, 362.
Dakota Indians *See* Sioux Indians.
D'Amblemont, —, commands reinforcements, 119.
Danes, discover Labrador, 307; reputed discoveries, 309, 310.
Danoncaritaoui, Seneca village, 131
Davis, John, early English navigator, 310
—, Sylvanus, narrates fall of Fort Loyal, 237.

DEN

DeCosta, Benjamin F., *Sailing Directions of Henry Hudson*, 309.
Deer, described, 348, 349; hunted in Denmark, 669; Newfoundland, 332; Canada, 343, 344; near Lake Champlain, xiv, 108, 109; Lake Huron, 317; Lake Erie, 320, 322; Lake Michigan, 210; Wisconsin, 174, 175; Illinois, 206; River Long, 183, 187; manner of hunting, 107, 113, 114; used as food, 70, 114, 122, 467, 468, 482; skins, 193, 213, 491; price, 380.
Dekanissore *See* Teganisoreu.
Denis, —, captured by Iroquois, 224.
Denmark, character of people, 669–672; government, 673; court, 667, 668, 675, 676, royal tombs, 685; society, 672, 673; cost of living, 681; army, 673, 674; pay of officers, 674, 681; navy, 679–682; laws, 675; monetary system, 682, 683; measures, 683; wines, 671; beer, 671; drunkenness, 671, 672, diseases, 676–678; horses, 684; export articles, 681; exact ship toll, 679, 680; dependencies, 664; explorers, 309, 310; Lahontan in, xxxiii, lxi, 9, 664–683.
— king of, 3, 4; character, 667; hunter, 669; marksman, 669; linguist, 667; royal residences, 666, 668, 684; natural children, 676; revenues, 673, 674; retinue, 684; Lahontan meets, 679
Denonville, Jacques René de Brisay, marquis de, governor of New France, 97; destroys Fort Frontenac, 69, 209, 225, 226, 271; fortifies Montreal, 98; reinforced from upper lakes, xviii, 73, 125, 126; arranges a review, 103; expedition against Indians, xv, 118–134; relations with intendant, 103; retains Lahontan, xvi, 118, 121; sends him to upper country, xvii, 132, 133, 151; visited

Denonville (*continued*).
by Lahontan, 219, 220; plans defense of upper lakes, xviii, 139; sends messenger to Mackinac, 144, 208; orders Lahontan to Quebec, xxii, 164; Lachine massacre, 224-226; La Tourette reports to, 136; promises reinforcements, 141; commissions officers, 164; arranges peace, xxii, 157, 162, 163, 208, 209, 221, 223; relations with Adario, 208, 209, 220-223; serves on expedition, 237; recalled to France, xxv, 227, 228, 234; last interview with Frontenac, 235; sketch, 97, 98.
— Marchioness de, 97, 98, 234; fears Iroquois, 224.
De Pere (Wis.), mission near, 168; rapids, 174.
Desnots (Hainault), —, French officer, 86, 87, 91, 98.
Des Ormeaux, Daulac (Dollard), defends Long Sault, 217.
Detroit, founded, xix, country described, 139; fruit near, 139; animals, 139; Indians, 155; projected post, 125, 133, 273.
Devonshire, William Cavendish, duke of, dedication to, 3; patron of Lahontan, xxxiv; sketch, 3.
Didelphys virginiana, 347.
Dieppe, port of departure for Canada, 373; birthplace of Longueuil, 74.
Digby (N. S.), described, 331; Gut, outlet of Port Royal basin, 331.
Dionne, —, curator of Laval University, identifies fauna, 110, 111.
— Narcisse E., bibliography of Lahontan, lii, liii; " Chouart et Radisson," 312; *Jacques Cartier*, 303; *Quebec under Two Flags*, 41.
Do, Chevalier. *See* d'Aux.
Dogs, used in hunting, 105, 111, 114, 349; for drawing sledges, 406, as carriers, 45.

Dollard. *See* Des Ormeaux.
Dongan, Thomas, governor of New York, 61, 126, 157; plans to control fur-trade, 61, 126; complains of Fort Niagara, 131; sketch, 61.
D'Opede, —, Portuguese ambassador, 628.
Dorman, Rushton M., *Origin of Primitive Superstitions among Aborigines of America*, 435, 450.
Dorsey, James Owen, "Migrations of Siouan Tribes," 200, 204; "Omaha Sociology," 499, 509.
D'Orveilliers, François Chorel, sieur de, *dit* St. Romain, commands rearguard, 127; sketch, 127.
Douay, Father Anastase, La Salle's chaplain, at Mackinac, 144, 145; founds mission to Cenis Indians, 145; sketch, 145; *Memoir*, 145.
Doughty, Arthur G., *Quebec under Two Flags*, 41.
Doves. *See* Pigeons.
Druillettes, Gabriel, Jesuit missionary, 329, 330.
Drummond, Sir Gordon, governor of Canada, 153.
Duchesneau, Jacques, sieur de la Doussinière, intendant of New France, 228; favors Jesuits, 228, 381; opposes Frontenac, 228, 381; recalled, 228; sketch, 228.
Ducks, Canadian resemble European, 350, described, 355; color, 350, 355; varieties, 351, 352, 354; on River Long, 183, 187; manner of hunting, 109; used for food, 431.
Du Creux, François. *Historiæ Canadensis seu Novæ Franciæ*, 412.
Duelling, in Hamburg, 660.
Dugmore, Arthur R., "The Outlaw; a character study of a Beaver," 477.
Du Luth (Du l'Hut, Du Lhut, Duluth), Daniel Greysolon, familiar with continental interior, xxxix, xl, 315; re-

DUL

Du Luth (*continued*).
inforcements for La Barre, 72, 73; aids Denonville, 73, 209; captures English traders, 126; posts on Lake Superior, 315, 316; among Sioux, 73; Lahontan with, xviii, 133, 140, 216; D'Ailleboust with, 233; builds fort, xviii, 136, 139; at Fort St. Joseph, xx, 139; with war party, 209; his uncle, 136; his brother, 135, 136; sketch, 73

Dumeni, —, French officer in Danish army, 674.

Durantaye, Olivier Morel de la, brings aid to Denonville, xviii, 125; captures English traders, 125; commandant at Mackinac, 144, 164, 209; commander of coureurs de bois, 164; takes possession of upper country, xviii; sketch, 125.

Du Rivau Huet, —, French officer, 86, 87, 92, 98.

Dusson, François, sieur de Bonrepaux, ambassador to Denmark, Lahontan meets, xxxiii, 665, 666, 671, 685; at Coldinck, 684; Glucstat, 688; letter to Pontchartrain, 688, 694; sketch, 665.

Du Tas (Tartre), —, Canadian officer, 68, 69, 260.

Dutch, explorations, 309; in New York, 6, 7; name for Indians, 320.

EAGLES, described, 353, 354; in Canada, 350.

Ecclesiastics, condemn Lahontan, 10; Lahontan dislikes, xv, 41, 98; interfere in private affairs, xv, 88–90, 383, 384, 391; control Canadian government, 381, 382, 385; confidence in, 383. *See also* New France.

Ecouttes. *See* Couttes.

Ectopistes migratoria, 110.

Edits et Ordonnances, 384.

ENG

Edwards, Jonathan, writings of, 734.

Eels, in Canada, 358; River St. Lawrence, 401; Great Lakes, 359; manner of catching, 49, 50, 401.

Elephant, Knights of the Order of, 675, 676, 679.

Eliot, John, writings of, 734.

Elks (Originaux), described, 104, 105; identified, 103; on St. Lawrence islands, 31; Lake Superior, 316; Lahontan hunts, xiv, 103; manner of hunting, 103–107, 112, 349, 476; skins, 106, 213, Norwegian trade in skins, 681; price of skins, 380; used as food, 468.

Elms, Canadian resemble European, 364; on Lake Erie, 319, bark used for building, 418; for canoes, 319.

Embroideries, Canadian imports of, 375.

Encyclopedists, relations with Lahontan, xlvii.

England, rulers of, 3; in War of Spanish Succession, 5; liberty in, 12; defeated in West Indies, 26, claims Great Lakes country, 127; visited by Lahontan, xxxiv, lxi.

English, in fur-trade, xviii, 78, 81, 82, 98, 125, 126, 281, 311–314, 326, 395, 398–400, furnish cheap goods, 98, 99, 281, 326, 394, 396; fleet invades Canada, 31; capture Quebec (1628), 44, (1759), 42; capture Port Royal, 244, 326, 330; to acquire Acadia, 326; revolution of 1688, 3, 217, 218; attempted capture of Canada (1690), xxvi, 240, 242–250; capture Fort Frontenac (1758), 69; capture Fort Niagara (1759), 131; imprison St. Vallier, 165; in Hudson Bay, 217, 236, 244, 311–314; allied with Iroquois, 58, 59, 237, 238; settlements in Newfoundland, 332; attack on Placentia, xxix, 275–279, 281, 287–289, 292; capture Perrot,

ENG

English (*continued*).
53; alliance with France, 218; sea-fight, 259, 260; raid into Canada, 262; attack St. John, 325; brave but ill-disciplined, 247, 248; colonists characterized, 399; privateers, 650, 651; in Maine, 236; colonial boundaries, 301, 302; explorations for Northwest Passage, 310.

Enjalran, Father Jean, wounded in Denonville's expedition, 129; at Durantaye's prise-de-possession, xviii; missionary at Mackinac, xviii; superior for upper country, xviii; sketch, 129.

Eokoros, xxxix, xlii; country of, 176; language, 185, numbers, 180, 182; characteristics, 182, 189; houses, 182; government, 182; enemies, 181; Lahontan among, xxiv, 180–182.

Erasmus, translated by Gueudeville, xlv; house at Rotterdam, 652.

Erie Indians, habitat, 320.

Errieronon Indians, language of, 733

Eskimo, described, 306, 307; habitat, 306, 309; numbers, 308, language, 342; treacherous, 308; cowardly, 308, boats, 307, 308; incursions by, 305; pursued by Cristinaux, 308, 309; cross to Newfoundland, 309, 334.

Esleich, barony of, x.

Espadon. *See* Sword-fish.

Essanape Indians, habitat, 181, 184–186; numbers, 184; language, 747; capital of, 186, 188; cacique, 186–189; superstitions, xxxix, xlii, 189; government, 186; allies, 187; enemies, 181, 182, 187; boats, 187, 188; houses, 188; unused to firearms, 188; Lahontan with, xxiv, 182–189, 197; presents to, 187.

Estrees, Abbé d', Portuguese ambassador, Lahontan with, 628, 713; befriends French, 643.

FOR

Etechemin (Quoddy) Indians, characterized, 339; habitat, 339, 340; language, 339; nomads, 339.

Explorations, early French, 303, 304; qualities needed in explorers, 210–215; methods of management, 210–215; equipment needful, 213, 214. *See also* the several explorers.

FALLEN TIMBERS, battle of, 461.

Fasting, among Jesuits, 534, 538.

Felis concolor, 345.

Fenelon, François de Salignac, Jansenist writer, 11.

Fer, Nicolas de, cartographer, 8.

Ferland, J. B. A., *Cours d'Histoire du Canada*, 304.

Ferns, maiden-hair, 365; described, 372; syrup made from, 372.

Ferrets, in Canada, 343.

Fiber zibethicus, 111

Fir, of Canada, 365; described, 371; timber made from, 371; in Wisconsin, 177; on River Long, 180.

Fish, as food, 70, 122, 431; in Great Lakes, xix, 359; River Long, 179; gold-colored in St. Lawrence, 358, 361; armed fish in Great Lakes, 359, 362; enemies, 362.

Fish-hooks, in fur-trade, 377.

Fishing, methods at Mackinac, 147, 148

Flint stones, in fur-trade, 377.

Florida, parrots in, 354.

Flying-squirrels, described, 348; in Canada, 344.

Folles-Avoine. *See* Wild Rice.

Folles-Avoines Indians. *See* Menommee Indians.

Forest, François Dauphine, sieur de la, La Salle's lieutenant, 124; brings message to Denonville, 124, 125; granted Fort St. Louis, xviii, 125, 133; at Detroit, xviii, 125, rebuilds Fort Miami, 208; sketch, 125.

FOR

Fort Abittibi, location, 342.
— Albany (Ste Anne), Iberville captures, 217; messengers from, 217
— Bougio, on River Taio, 649
— Bourbon, Radisson builds, 313; captured for English, 313.
— Chambly, location, 52; described, 90, 91; fear of attack on, 262; Lahontan at, xiii, 90, 91; trade, 90, 91
— Charles, Hudson Bay, 313.
— Crêvecœur, destroyed, 207, 208; sketch, 207
— Frontenac, 79, 323; description and sketch, 69; built, 61, 69, 70; importance of, 226, 271; La Barre at, xiii, 69; fur-trade of, 75, 83; destroyed, 69, 209, 226, 233, 395; restored, 68, 69, 233; untenable, 69, 225, 226, 271, captured by English, 69; vessels near, 395; commandant at, 73, 125, 127, 162; rendezvous for Denonville's expedition, xvi, 119-121, 126, Lahontan at, xiii, 57, 68-72, 677; peace conference at, 61, 69, 83; reinforcement sought, 134, 162; garrison supplied by Indians, 122; scurvy at, 162; suicide, 368; messenger to, 226; raid towards, 266; visited by Adario, 220
— Gratiot (Mich.), French fort on site of, 139
— Kennebec. *See* Fort Loyal.
— La Tourette, on Lake Nipigon, 136.
— Loyal (Kennebec, Maine), location, 236; French attack on, 236, English narrative of capture, 237; surrender, 237; flag of, at Quebec, 237
— Mackinac, Indians near, 73. *See also* Mackinac.
— Miami, built by La Salle, 208; destroyed, 208; rebuilt, 208.
— Nelson, attacked, 313; sketch, 313.
— Niagara, 323; built by Denonville, xvi, 131; importance of, 131, 226, 271; Lahontan at, xix, 135, 677;

FOU

Fort Niagara (*continued*).
besieged by Iroquois, 141, 142; commandants of, 131; Miamis at, 161-163, sickness, xxii, 162; pleases Indian allies, 132; abandoned, xxii, 162, 163, 226, 271; history, 131
— Pemaquid. *See* Pemaquid
— Pentagoet, location, 328
— Rémy, besieged by Iroquois, 224.
— Rolland, besieged by Iroquois, 224, Lahontan protects, 240; sketch, 240.
— Ste Anne *See* Albany
— St Joseph, site, xviii, 139, 208, 318, 320; built, xviii, 139; described, xviii, xxxvii, 139, 140, commanded by Beauvais, xviii; surrendered to Lahontan, xx, 139, 140; Lahontan winters at, xx, 140-143, 149, 484; Lahontan leaves, xx, 143; abandoned, xxii, xxiii, xli, 152, 163; revictualed, xxii, 155; Lahontan returns, xxii, 161; restored, 272, 273; Indians near, 418, 484; bears, 484.
— St Julien, Lisbon fortification, 649.
— St Louis (Ill.), site, 207; Tonty commands, 125, 133, 207, La Forest commands, xviii, 125
— St Louis (Newfoundland), 275; location, 275, 335; poorly garrisoned, 275; bombarded, 278; Lahontan flees to, 348
— St. Louis (Quebec), described, 40, 41; governor's residence, 235, 382, repaired by Frontenac, 235
— Sorel. *See* Sorel.
— Supposé, projected forts, 272, 318, 321.
— William, site of, 316
Forts, projected by Lahontan, 272, 273, 280, early French, xxxix, barriers against Iroquois, 52; near mouth of Ohio (1702), 144.
Foutereaux, described, 110, 344, identified, 111.

FOX

Fox (Outagami, Renard) Indians, characterized, 341; habitat, 34, 168, 175, 478; language, 176, 177, 341; physical traits, 415; calendar of, 427; totems, 511; village, 175, 177; relations with Sioux, 175, 176; war with Iroquois, 489-494, 502; relations with Chippewa, 489, 493, 494; relations with French, xlvi, 99, 175, 176; with Eokoros, 176; with Sauk, 175; Lahontan among, xxiv, xli, 175, 176, 179-207, 448; return to Wisconsin, 207.

Fox-Wisconsin fur-trade route, nearest to Mississippi, 168, 178; portage, described, 177, 178; Lahontan at, 177; canal at, xxiv, 177; history, 177, 178.

Foxes, habitat, 347; described, 343, 347; color, 343, 344, 347; value of skins, 347, 376, 379; Norwegian trade in skins, 681; traps for, 482-484; do not attack beaver, 480.

Franciscans. *See* Recollects.

Franquelin, J. B, cartographer, 41.

Frederick IV of Denmark, Lahontan's patron, 3, 4.

France, ministers, 5; diplomats, 12; West Indian colonies, 26; carpenters, 658; alliance with Spain, 5; at war with Spain, 191; English alliance, 217, 218; refugees in Denmark, 668; in Holland, 655

French, laws compared with savage polity, 551-570; religious and social customs compared with savage, 517-550; language spoken in Denmark, 669; diseases, 593-605; witchcraft among, 562-564, 566, drunkenness, 566; immorality, 536-538, 540-546, 566, 567; first settlement in Canada, 331; Newfoundland, 333, 334; possessions in America, 334; take possession of Northwest, 342

Frogs, in Canada, 352, 357.

FUR

Frontenac, Louis Baude, count de, arrival at Quebec, 230, 231; replaces Courcelle, 59, 60, 69; superseded by La Barre, xi, 26, 33, 381; relations with intendant, 103; restored to governorship, xxv, 227, 228; opposed by Duchesneau, 228, 381; by Jesuits, 227, 381; favors Recollects, 43, 44, 70, 413; during Phips's raid, xxvi, 237-247; relations with Iroquois, xxv, 59-61, 69, 73, 86, 124, 232-234, 266, 267; favors La Salle, 33, 69; quarrels with Perrot, 53; praises Valrennes, 226; builds Chateau St. Louis, 41, 235; builds Fort Frontenac, 69, 70, 232; fortifies Quebec, 263, 265; warmly welcomed, xxv, 228, 230, 231; relations with Lahontan, xxv-xxix, xlv, xlvi, 230, 232, 237, 250, 252, 256, 257, 262, 271, 272, 274, 280, 388-390; promotes discovery, 60; esteemed by Indians, xxv, 228; power of appointment, 257; hospitality, xxvii, 262; courtesy to English prisoners, xxviii, 265; controls sovereign council, 44, 45; issues trading licenses, 99; relations to liquor traffic, 94; visits Montreal, 231, relation to Adario, lxi, 9, 149; to Teganisoren, 222; to Oureahé, 233, 234; interview with Denonville, 234; services to New France, xxxvii, 60; sketch, 60.

— Countess de, 267.

Fruit trees, in Acadia, 325; on Lake Erie, 319, 322; on Lake St Clair, xx; in Illinois, 206.

Furs, chief article of export, 374; medium of exchange, 376; names and prices, 379, 380

Fur-trade, importance to Indians, 507; harmful to them, 577; important to Canada, 99, 280, 394; licenses for, 99-101, 384, 386; goods used in, 308, 377, 378; English goods cheap,

FUR

Fur-trade (*continued*)
59, 98, 281, 326, 394; Indians pay large prices, 59; prices of furs, 379, 380; cheating, 421, 422, illegal, 91; monopoly, 9; rivalry, 61, 326, 394; profits, 100, 101, 376, French officials in, 53, 54, 102, 326; Jesuits, 385, 386; English, 59, 61, 78, 82, 90, 91, 98, 125, 126, 131, 281, 316; coureurs de bois, 77, 92, 146, 153, 164, 168, 207, 395; in Acadia, 326, 331; Anticosti, 305, off Labrador, 307-309; Tadoussac, xxxvii, 31; Chambly, 90, 91; at Montreal, 92-95, 240; with Lake Indians, xviii, 53, 54, 60, 153, 377; Green Bay, 168; Lake Superior, 315, 316, Illinois, 207, in war-time, 241, in Norway, 681, Iroquois wish to control, 26, 59, 78, promoted by Frontenac, 60; forts to control, 131.

Fusees, in fur-trade, 377

GAGNON, Ernest, "Louis Jolliet," 244; *Le Fort et le Chateau St. Louis*, 41.
— Philéas, *Essai de Bibliographie Canadienne*, lii.

Galette, location, 86

Game, in Newfoundland, 332, wild fowl numerous in Canada, 109, 110, wood fowl used as food, 482. *See also* the several birds and animals

Gancausse, location, 122, Indian village, 121, Cayuga mission, 70

Ganondaoe, Indian word for calumet, 402

Gaspé, significance of term, 306, island near, 305; fisheries off, 305, 306; vessel from, 259; present conditions, 306; native of, 340.

Gasperots, small fish, 358; described, 360; used as bait, 360.

Gaspesian Indians, language, 339; numbers, 340; characteristics, 340; fur-trade with, 306; sketch, 340

GRE

Geese, in Canada, 350, 351; color, 350, 351; manner of hunting, 109; used for food, 431, on River Long, 183, 186.

George I of England, protector of Lahontan, xxxiii, xxxiv.

George II of England, lake named for, 91

Girouard, Désiré, *Lake St Louis*, 224, 240

Gnacsitare Indians, habitat, 187, 192, 193; language, 747, characteristics, 187, 191, 195; hospitality, 192; ignorant of calumet, 189; manner of hunting, 193; power of chief, 191, 192, 197, allies of Essanapes, 187; enemies, 187, 194, dread Spaniards, 190, 191, Lahontan among, xxiv, xxxix, 190-195.

Gnats, in Canada, 352

Gomara, François Lopez de, *Histoire Géneralle des Indes Occidentalis et Terres neuves*, 307

"Good," vessel. *See* "Bon"

Gooseberries, described, 372; in Canada, 364, 365, 369, useless, 369, 372; vinegar made from, 372

Goyogoan Indians *See* Cayuga Indians

Grand Chute, rapids in Fox River, 174
— Portage, location, 316.

Grandville, —, captured by English, 243

Grangula, Iroquois chief, 7, embassador to La Barre, 74, 75, speeches of, 79-84, dances, 84, 85, sketch, 74

Grant, —, on courtship and marriage, 457

Grape-vines, described, 368; in Canada, 364, fruit, 368, on Lake Erie, 319; in Illinois, 206

Grave, la grand, at Placentia, 336

"Great Lake," Indian term for Europe, 533

Great Lakes, Indians upon, 26, 60; discoveries of, 60, 484, navigation, 64;

GRE

Great Lakes (*continued*).
  fur-trade, 78; fish, 359, 361–363; claimed by French, 78; forts to guard, 273; Iroquois bar French from, 218. *See also* the several lakes.
— Mohawk, Iroquois chief, 239.
Green Bay (La Baie), mission at, 168.
Greenland, birds migrate from, 356.
Gregory. *See* MacGregory.
Grelans, in Canada, 351; described, 355.
Grelins episses, term explained, 260.
Grenada, French colony at, 52.
Groseilliers, Médard Chouart de, in Wisconsin, 177; visits Hudson Bay, 312; on Lake Superior, 312, 315; proposals rejected by French, 313; erects Hudson Bay post, 313, sketch, 312.
Gros-Ventre (Big-bellied) Indians, captured by Iroquois, 159; rescued by Chippewa, 160.
Ground-squirrel, described, 348.
Grouse, in Canada, 353.
Gudgeons, in Wisconsin lakes, 174, 359.
Guérin, Jeanne, wife of baron Lahontan, ix.
Gueudeville, Nicolas, Lahontan's work ascribed to, xliv, xlv; *L'Esprit des Cours de l'Europe*, xlv; *Atlas Historique*, xlv; sketch, xliv, xlv.
Guiche, Count de, sponsor for Lahontan, x.
Guiscard, Count de, Lahontan's patron, 11.
Guldenlew, — de, viceroy of Norway, 670; title, 676; Lahontan meets, 671.
Gulf of Mexico, receives Mississippi, 32; La Salle's colony upon, xii, 33, 335.
— St. Lawrence, 274; cod-fishing in, 324; islands, 324; traversed by Lahontan, 30, 31
Gull-fish, in Great Lakes, 359.
Gulo luscus, 111.

HER

Hainaut. *See* Desnots.
Hakluyt Society, *Publications*, 309, 310, 312.
Hale, Horatio, "Indian Wampum Records," 76.
Hannay, James, *Acadia*, 330.
Hanover, elector of, protects Lahontan, xxxiii, xxxiv.
Hares, in Newfoundland, 332; on St. Lawrence, 266; in Canada, 343; on River Long, 183; white, 344, 348; used as food, 105, 106, 482.
Harisse, Henry, *Découverte et Evolution cartographique de Terre-Neuve*, 28, 30, 324; *Discovery of North America*, 303; *Notes sur la Nouvelle France*, lii.
Harper's Magazine, 73, 479.
Harvard College Library, editions of Lahontan in, liii–xciii.
Havre de barre. *See* Bar Haven.
— de Grace, port of departure for Canada, 373.
Hawley, Charles, *Cayuga History*, 72; "Jesuit Missions among Senecas," 131.
"Hazardous," French man-of-war, 260.
Hazel-trees, Canadian resemble European, 364.
Hearne, Samuel, describes beavers, 480.
Heath-cocks, Canadian resemble European, 351.
Hemlock spruce (épinette), 365; described, 371.
Hennepin, Louis, dedicates book to English king, 3; at Fort Frontenac, 70; omits mention of River Long, xxxviii; Indians mentioned by, xxxix; describes falls of Niagara, xix, 137; *Description de la Louisiane*, 413; *New Discovery*, 70, 77, 131, 145, 152, 200, 413.
Henry, Alexander, *Travels*. *See* Bain (ed.).
Herns, in Canada, 351.

HER

Herring, in Canada, 358; in Newfoundland, 333; in Great Lakes, 359, used as bait, 360.
Historical Magazine, 155.
Hoffman, W. J., "Midewiwin of the Ojibwa," 468; "Native Indian Pictographs," 512.
Holland, canals of, 652; monetary system, 655, 656; weights and measures, 656; inns, 655; boats, 652, 656, 657; wines, 663; Lahontan in, 651–659.
Homer, read by Lahontan, xiv, 116, 306, 307.
Honeoye Falls (N. Y.), Indian villages near, 131.
"Honoré," vessel, Lahontan on, 257–262.
Horse-chestnuts. *See* Chestnuts of Illinois.
Hospitalières, at Quebec, 44.
"Hoy," vessel, described, 693.
Huards, described, 353; fresh-water fowl, 353; hunted, 353; in Canada, 350.
Hudson, Capt. Henry, explores for Dutch, 309; follows Danish pilot, 309, 310; discovers Hudson Bay, 310, 311; discovers New Netherlands, 311; journals of, 311; sketch, 309; *Voyages,* 309.
Hudson's Bay Company, organized, 311–313; struggle with French, 312–314; history, 313–314.
Huguenots, persecuted by Louis XIV, xlvi; banished from France, 392; useful in Canada, 392, 393; Lahontan's plan for, xlvi.
Humming birds (*Oiseau Mouche*), in Canada, 350; described, 354.
Huron (Petun, or Tobacco, Tionntate) Indians, 154, 461, English name for, 155; stock, 321; habitat, 73, 143, 153–155, 340, 418, 484; characterized, 415; clans, 461; language, 46,

ILL

Huron Indians (*continued*).
47, 339, 340, 733, 747, 748; numbers, 340; villages, 340, 418; totems, 511; burial customs, 473; inheritance, 461; cultivate fields, xx, 148; hunting grounds, 319; government, 499; calendar, 427, 428; missions to, 46, 48, 318, 340; missions destroyed, 48, 153, 155, 318; in trade, 81, 92, 241; visited by Champlain, 219; Duluth, 72; Longueuil, 74; join Denonville's expedition, xvii, 125; relations with Iroquois, 73, 140–143, 149, 153, 155, 165, 318, 340, 502; desire French fort, xvii, 132; relations with Ottawa, 146, 397; chief Adario, 9, 149; dispose of captives, 144; tribal chief, 461; at Lorette, 46, 48, 268, 269; at Gaintsouan, 484; at Mackinac, xx, 145, 147, 155; anecdote, 455; battle with Americans, 461; remnant extant, 48; sketch, 155, 340.
Huron County (Ont.), 154.
Huronia, location, 488.
Hyporcheme, compared with Indian dance, 423.

IBERVILLE, Pierre Le Moyne, sieur de, founder of Louisiana, 74, 133, 144, 145, 236; commands in Hudson Bay, 217, 313, 314; subordinates, xxxix, 227; expedition against New York, 235, 236; convoys merchantmen, 274; sketch, 236.
Iceland, discoverers from, 309.
Illinois Indians, 174; habitat, 341; described, 206; characterized, 341; physical traits, 415, 488; language, 198, 201, 204, 341; sodomy, 462; berdashes, 462, totems, 511; relations with Iroquois, 26, 77, 78, 81, 82, 198, 486–488, 502; allies of French, 78, 207; aid Lahontan,

ILL

Illinois Indians (*continued*).
207; fur-trade with French, 146, 207; with Arkansas, 204; join Denonville, 125; La Salle among, 26, 77; calendar, 427, 428, sketch, 77

Illinois, early forts, xviii, 207; La Salle in, 33, 77, 207; Lahontan, 205-207; mission, xviii; Iroquois in, 198; diseases, 465; slavery, 169; parrots, 354; chestnuts, 367.

Indian territory, tribes in, 340.

Indiana, Indians of, 341.

Indians:

Physical characteristics— in general, 282, 414, 415, 465; robust, 593-605, 415, 416, 471; stature, 415; color, 284, 285, 415; complexions, 430; unbearded, 282, 284, 414, 584, 599; longevity, 418, 592, 593.

Mental characteristics—in general, 415, 421, 423; endurance, 268, 269, 416; observation, 429; memory, 431, 438; independence, xliii, 11, 59, 82, 421, 499; intelligence, 413, 429; contentment, 421; deference to age, 431; generosity, 586; faithfulness, 452; patience, 475; politeness, 414; reasonableness, 438, 439; valor, 424; not quarrelsome, 482; not passionate, 451-453, 463; natural equity, 285; philosophy, 7, 8, 426; without jealousy, 451, 453, 460; without caste, 421; gravity, 424, 425; brevity of speech, 425, 426; without discipline, 499; superstitious, 126, 429, 467, 468; hatred, 424.

Philology— in general, 46, 47, 56, 58, 176, 733, 734; most useful, 297; vocabulary, 288, 297; picture-writing, 512-515, 590. *See also* Chippewa Indians, Algonquian, Huron-Iroquois stock.

Mythology, Folk Lore, and Religion— in general, xxxv, xliii, 435-445,

IND

Indians (*continued*).
518, 519; compared with French, 517-550; idea of God, 59, 434-437, 446; of divine justice, 436, 437; divinities of, 445-449; evil spirits, 446-448, 467, 468; animal manitous, 345, 446; solar worship, 437, 449; dualism, 446-448; belief in life after death, 435, 436, 441, 449, 450, 460, 472; in transmigration of souls, 189; in dreams, 449, 459, 460, ceremonies, 286, 448-450; sacrifices, 448-450, 501; hymn, 450, medicine men, 447, 467, 468, 563, 593, 603; influence of, 460; methods, 467, 468; difficult to christianize, 146, 413, 414, 435, 445; beliefs compared with Christianity, 517-550.

Occupations—in general, 431, 432; hunting, 82, 104-117, 319, 349, 481-485, 573-575; fishing, 147, 148; agriculture, 148, 432; map-making, 193, 427.

Food — in general, 422, 470, 471, 580-583; vegetable, 148, 175, 187, 202, 369, 372, 502; fish, 147, 148, 160, 175, 363, 431, 467; animal, 169, 170, 175, 187, 202, 431, 467; unsalted, 422, 471; no salads, 471; cooking, 470, 471; appetite the guide, 470; drinks, 170, 466, 467; avoid ice-water, 471.

Feasts—in general, 169, 170, 422, 424; political, 58, 404; feast of union, 404; wedding, 458; for sick, 467, 563, 603; funeral, 473; war, 500, 501; eat-all, 466.

Villages and Cabins— villages fortified, 417; cabins, 92, 182, 188, 454; cabins described, 417, 418.

Domestic Animals—dogs, 105, 349, 495; horses, 131; cattle, 131; fowl, 131; hogs, 131.

Utensils — cradles, 416, 417, 459; beds, 418; traps, 113, 484, 485;

IND
Indians (*continued*)
anchors, 158, for fishing, 147, 148, drums, 500; snow-shoes, 103, 104 *See also* Canoe, Calumet.

Dress—in general, 417, 581-584, unclothed, 417, 583, 607-610; cloaks, 417; caps, 417; shoes, 417; made of beaver-skins, 379; of women, 416, 609, 610, hair-dressing, 153, 416.

Warfare and Weapons — weapons in general, 155, 213, bow and arrows, 94, 115, 514; clubs, 487, 497, 498, 514; casse-tête, 402, hatchets, 512, amazed at fire-arms, 188, 203, 213; symbol of wars, 512; occasions for, 231, 232, 496; preparations, 153, 155, 500, 501, declaration, 507, 508; methods in, 128, 129, 142, 497-499, 502-508, scouting, 156, 486, 497, 498; no precautions against surprise, 485, 486, 497, 498; in forests, 70, 271, 497; fortifications, 590; seldom attacked, 237, 273, 490; ambuscades, 247, 489-493; track enemy, 498, 499, 502, take scalps, 129, 492, 493, 502, 505; personal following in, 500, private war-parties, 500; tree of peace, 407, cruelty in, 496-502; during hunting, 485-494, 498; useful to French, 237; return, 505; capture of prisoners, 503, 504; treatment of, xvi, 122-124, 137, 144, 199, 267-269, 496, 503-507; running the gauntlet, 238, 505; torture of, xlvi, 208, 268, 270, 496, 497, 504; death song of, 268, 504; adopted, 505, 506; exchanged, 194, 195, 506, 507. *See also* Slavery, below.

Slavery — in general, 94, 106, 111, 113, 420; origin of, 169, 504, 505, in Illinois, 169; treatment of slaves, 169, 432, 439, 454, 491; in declaring war, 508; enfranchisement, 474.

IND
Indians (*continued*).
Government — without laws, 7, 553, 558; in general, xxxiv, 58, 194, 424, 499, 500; authority of chief, 499, 500; under chieftains, 500, 501, council, 75, 79-85, 92-94, 422, 423; composition of, 422, 427, 431, 499, 507; functions of, 499, 505, 507; oratory in, xiii, 7, 92, 162, treaties, negotiation of, 76, 431, for peace, 506, 508, 509; alliances, 507, envoys, 509; legal institutions compared with French, 551-570

Social Customs — lack of property distinctions, xxxv, xliii, 7, 8, 282, 285, 420, 454, scorn of riches, xxxiv, 196, aversion to money, 94, 420, 421, equality, 452, 454; visits, 426; meals, 432; games, 432, 433, 594; gambling, 433, dances, 422; varieties, 423; compared with Greek, 423; occasions for, 423, 424, of the calumet, 168, 169, 423, 424, 508, 509, of war, 424, 501, 502; religious, 448, 450; of the chiefs, 168, 169, 423; gift-giving, in embassy, 84, 509, at fair, 93; in marriage, 457; for the dead, 473; articles for, 169

Sex Relations, Courtship, and Marriage — in general, 605-618; immorality, 451, 453-455, 463, 540, 541, 615, 616; unchastity, 451, 452, 540, 541, 612, 615, 616; courtship, 451, 453-457; marriage, xxxv, xliii, 605, 606; monogamous, 458; consanguineous forbidden, 606; with slaves, 613; age for, 451, 459, 541, 592; ceremonies, 456, 457, fidelity in, 453, 458, 460, 461, punishment for adultery, 416, 460, 607; divorce easy, 453, 456-458; berdashes, 462.

Women and Children — physical characteristics of women, 416, passionate, 451, 459, 475; gaiety, 453; freedom, 453, 463; occupations, 432;

Index

IND
Indians (*continued*).
assist in worship, 450; adopt prisoners, 459; prefer French, 455; widowhood, 459. 460, 462; whores, 463, 464; child-bearing, 458, 459, 606–608; purification, 458, 459; children, highly prized, 458; treatment in infancy, 459; take mother's name, 461, 462; assist in religious service, 448; training, 426, 427; of slaves, 474; of separated persons, 458.

Diseases and Remedies — diseases, in general, xxxv, 418, 465–475, 593–605; immunity from, 418, 465, 475; carelessness regarding, 465; of women, 475; pleurisy, 475; consumption, 466; pox, 465; natural remedies, 467, 468, 470; sweating, 467–469, 600–604; medicines, 161, 465–475; of roots, 466; of plant juices, 468, 471; cure of wounds, 471; avoidance of European remedies, 467–471.

Mortuary Customs—in general, 471, no mourning, 472, 473; wailing, 472; funeral orations, 472; coffins, 473; hut for dead, 473; cremation, 473; interment, 473; presents to dead, 474; resuscitation, 474; name of dead avoided, 473, 474.

Miscellaneous Customs — heraldry, 510, 511; totemism, 510; calendar, 427, 428; music, 500, 501, suicide, 368, 418, 419, 441, 459, 460, 530; hunting customs, 104-117, 349, 481-485; 573-575; hunting limits, 481, 482, 496, drunkenness, 94, 466, 568; excused, xvi, 124, 466.

Trade — articles used in, 70, 71, 377, 378; with Europeans, 574–577, 590, 591; annual fair at Montreal, 92–95; contracts recorded by wampum, 76, 431. *See also* Fur-trade.

Missions — in general, xvi, 48, 49,

IRO
Indians (*continued*).
55, 56, 59, 119, 168 *See also* Jesuits, Recollects.

Iowa, Indians in, 174, 175.

Iron, exported to Canada, 373.

Iron-ware, imported, 375.

Iroquois (Iroquese) Indians, xl; origin of name, 58; English name for, 6, 58; habitat, 26, 58, 59, 82, 323, 396, 397; numbers, 58; language, 46, 47, 56, 58, 339, 341, 733, 744; cruelty, 632, slaves, 239; feasts, 404; women commit suicide, 368; strength, 120; tribes, 58, 323, 341, government, 58, 404; in warfare, 396, 497, 498, 501, 502; name for governor-general, 80, 82, 84, 404; canoes, 138, 147; physical characteristics, 415, 488, 497; characterized, 26, 59, 339, 495–503; importance to Canada, 394, 395; relations with Europeans (general), 6, 58, 59; La Barre's expedition against, xiii, 66–86; Denonville's expedition, xv–xviii, xxiii, 118–134, 151, 162, 163, 208, 209, 221–229; Frontenac's war with, 55, 69, 231, 233, 234, 237–239; miscellaneous hostilities with French, xi, xv, xvi, xxiv, xxv, xxix, xxxvii, 6, 26, 36, 51, 52, 59–61, 74, 77, 103, 124, 136, 137, 156, 208, 218, 221, 223–227, 231, 237–240, 263, 266–273, 280, 283, 385, 485-494, 504; relations with English, 26, 58, 61, 237, 238, 262, 281; at Fort Niagara, 137, 142; wars with other tribes, xiii, xxii, 26, 51, 73, 78, 81, 86, 140-142, 147, 149, 152-161, 165, 167, 198, 199, 220–223, 317, 320, 340, 395, 485–493, 502, 503, in fur-trade, 26, 69, 78, 81, 125, 226, 395; relations to missions, xvi, 48, 55, 56, 59, 70, 121–124, 153, 155, 239, 259, 318, 339, 340; approve Adario's strategy, 225; sketch, 26, 58.

IRO

Iroquois country, described, 323; inaccessible, 80; expedition against, 149, 152–161; lacks fish and game, 323, 396

Islands, Allumettes, in Ottawa, 216.
— Anticosti, location, 30, 31, 305, history, 31; seigniory of Jolliet, 31, 243, 305; size, 305; fort, 305; trade, 305.
— Bacchus   *See* Orleans.
— Belle, 40
— Bird Rocks   *See* Island of Fowls.
— Cape Breton (Royale), origin of name, 324; described, 30, 274; governor, 276; Indians, 328; coal exported from, 374; fishery near, 324; unpeopled, 324; quarries on, 333, 334; sketch, 324.
— of Caves, identified, 154
— Charity, in Saginaw Bay, 143, 318, 319
— aux Coudres, origin of name, 31; danger off, 250; passed by Lahontan, 31, 250, 261.
— Drummond (Detour, Pontaganipy), Indian name for, 153; location, 153; sketch, 153
— Fitzwilliam, identified, 154
— of Fowls (Bird Rocks), sighted, 30, location, 31.
— Gaudeloupe, commerce with, 374; sugar-refineries, 374
— Goat (aux Chevres), in Basin of Port Royal, 331
— Hare (au Lièvres), location, 261
— Mackinac, location, 146
— Magdalen, location, 31.
— Manitoulin, described, 153; size, 317; Indians, 153, 317, 340.
— Martinique (Martinico), commerce with, 374; sugar-refineries, 374
— Mingan, seigniory of Jolliet, 244, 309.
— Miquelon, French possession, 334
— Montreal, location, 219, Indians, 119; habitants of, 96, 97; sacked by

JES

Islands, Montreal (*continued*).
Iroquois, 224, 225; fort on, 240, attempted raid on, 262.
— Orleans, location, 39, 247, described, 39, mission village on, 48, English fleet anchors off, 243; troops land near, 247.
— Percé, location, 323; described, 305; fishery off, 305, 306, 324.
— of Ré, location, 294.
— Rencontres, origin of name, 198, 199; location, 198
— Rouge (Red), location, 31, 32, 260, 261.
— St. Croix, early settlement on, 324, 331.
— St Helen, location, xv, 118; named by Champlain, 118, rendezvous for Denonville's expedition, xv, 118, 121.
— St. John (Prince Edwards), origin of name, 324, lacks harbors, 324; sketch, 324
— St Pierre, French settlement at, 334, inhabitants expelled from, 334; retroceded to France, 334, sketch, 334.
— Seven, harborage at, 261, sketch, 261.

Issati Indians, Hennepin among, xxxix; branch of, 343

Jansen, Cornelis, Dutch theologian, 383, 384, followers, 383, 384.
Jenks, Albert E., "Wild-rice Gatherers of the Upper Lakes," 175.
Jesuits, doctrines of, 518–550; accept Aristotle, xiv, 116, 117; arrival in Canada, 43, 413, mission villages of, 48, 49, 56; missionaries, 91, 129, 140, 146, 259, 345, 365, 413, 417; relations with Recollects, 43, 44, 383, 413; mission at Tadoussac, 31, 34; at Quebec, 42, 43, 259; Aben-

Index

JES

Jesuits (*continued*).
  aki mission, 48, 49, 329, 330; at Montreal, 55; Iroquois mission, 131, 259, 266, 267; among Papinchois, 340; among Gaspesians, 340; St Joseph mission, xviii, 208; Huron mission, 48, 75, 346; at Mackinac, xviii, 140, 146; at Sault Ste Marie, xviii, 149, 152, 489; at Green Bay, xviii, 168; Illinois mission, xviii; among Sioux, xviii; relations with Indians, 413, 414, 435, 437, 438, 496, 733; describe native customs, 426, 466, 468, 472; oppose brandy trade, 81, 466; preserve morals, 455, 464; in fur-trade, 385, 386; relations with government, xxvii, 6, 227, 231, 381, 384–386; as interpreters, 84, 385; as messengers, 149; rear Jolliet, 243; name Fox River, 168; Canadian superior, 56, 259; instruction condemned, 267, 268; disbelieved by Adario, 517, 518; *Relations*, xxxvi, xlvii, 26, 31, 47, 58, 68, 76, 82, 110, 124, 127, 152, 153, 165, 168, 169, 174, 175, 207, 242, 320, 330, 340, 345, 380, 382, 386, 412, 414–418, 423, 424, 431, 444, 448, 450, 457, 460, 462, 466, 468, 469, 473, 474, 479, 480, 483, 488, 512, 530, 603, 733; sketch, 413
Johnson, Sir William, names Lake George, 91.
Jogues, Isaac, Jesuit missionary, 91
"Joli," shipwrecked off Newfoundland, 335, 336; conveys La Salle to Texas, 335.
Joliet (Ill.), terminus of Chicago canal, 207.
Jolliet, Sieur de. *See* Aux.
— Claire Françoise Bissot, wife captured by English, 243, 244, 249; sketch, 244.
— Louis, seigniory at Anticosti, 31, 243, 305; explores Mississippi, 200,

KIT

Jolliet, Louis (*continued*).
  219, 243, 244; names Illinois River, 205, describes Chicago portage, 207; loses papers at Lachine rapids, 219, 244, captured by English, 243, 249; trade of, 305; in Hudson Bay, 244; in Labrador, 244; sketch, 243.
Jones, Arthur E., "Identification of St. Ignace II and of Ekarenniondi," 484.
Juchereau, Charles de St. Denis, commandant at Mackinac, 144, 165; builds Ohio post, 144; sketch, 144.
— Louis de St. Denis, expedition to New Mexico, 144
— Nicolas, Sieur de Beauport, 144.
Jutland, Lahontan in, 686.

KAKALING, Grand, location, 174; significance, 174; Lahontan passes, 173
— Little, location, 174.
Kaministiquia, French post at, 316; annoys Hudson's Bay Company, 316; fur-trade at, 316; sketch, 316.
Kansa Indians, Missouri mingle with, 200.
Kansas, Indian reservations in, 174.
Kaukauna (Wis.), location, 174; history, 174.
Kellogg, Louise Phelps, aid acknowledged, lxviii.
Kennebec Indians. *See* Canibas
Kente. *See* Quinté.
Kettles, in fur-trade, 377.
Kickapoo Indians, habitat, 174, 341; language, 341; village, 174; Lahontan meets, 174, characterized, 341; sketch, 174.
Killistinoe Indians *See* Cristinaux.
Kimberly (Wis.), rapids at, 174
Kinnikinick. *See* Indian tobacco.
Kirk, Sir David, invades Canada, 31.
Kitchi Manitou, chief Indian divinity, 445; sacrifices to, 448, 449.
— Okima, Algonquian name for governor, 93; defined, 405.

KNI

Knives, in fur-trade, 377.
Kolnus, Johannes, Polish explorer, 309.
Kondiaronk, Huron name for Adario, 149.
Kryn. *See* Great Mohawk.
Kwapa *See* Quapaw.

LA BARRE, Febre, governor of Canada, 25; supersedes Frontenac, xi, 26; in West Indies, 26; in fur-trade, 77, 91; illness, xiii, 71, 72, 81; speeches, xiii, 77–79; expedition against Indians, xi, xiii, 26, 32, 34, 46, 65–86, 72–79, 91, 97, 103, 120, 125, 226; sketch, 26.
L'Abat, —, French officer in Danish army, 674
Labrador, described, 306, 307, 309, 310; discovery, 244, 307; trade, 307–309; part of Newfoundland, 333.
Laces, Canadian import, 375.
Lachine, rapids of, 66, 67, 303; origin of name, 67; post at, 240; La Salle's embarkation, 67; canal, 67; dangerous, 219; massacre at village, xvi, 224, 225, 266.
La Fontaine, in Placentia Bay, 276, 278.
Lafontaine, L. H., "De l'esclavage en Canada," 169.
LaForest. *See* Forest.
La Galette, location, 68.
Lahontan, Isaac Lom d'Arce, baron de, father of author, ix, x, xxi, 150, 151; sketch, 151.
— Louis Armand Lom d'Arce, baron de, parents of, ix, x, 150, 151; birth, x; sponsors, x; destined for army, x; joins marine corps, x; voyages to Canada, xi, xii, 6, 25–33, 258–262; signts Quebec, xi, 32; quartered at Beaupré, xii, 34–38; ordered to Montreal, 38, 46; visits mission villages, xii, 48, 49; ascends to Montreal, xiii, 49–56; in La Barre's

LAH

Lahontan, Louis (*continued*).
expedition, xiii, 66–86, 123; returns to Montreal, xiii, 85, 88–90; quartered at Chambly, xiii, 90, 91; at Boucherville, xiv, 96–117; ordered to France, xv, 118; refused permission, xvi, 121, 132, 133; hunts with Indians, xii, xiv, 46, 88, 103–117; learns Indian languages, xii, 46, 47, 88; accompanies Denonville's expedition, xv–xviii, 121–134; at Fort Frontenac, xvi, 122–126; befriends captive Iroquois, xvi, 122–124; censured for humanity, xvi, 124; ordered to upper country, xvii, 132, 133; makes preparations, xvii, xviii, 133; journey to Fort St. Joseph, xix, xx, 135–139; describes Niagara, xix, 136, 137; arrives at fort, xx, 139; winters thereat, xx, 140–143; expects attack from Iroquois, 142; seeks provisions at Mackinac, xx, 143–151; meets survivors of La Salle's expedition, xxi, 144, 145, 347; sends letter to Seignelay, xxi, 149–151, visits Sault Ste. Marie, xxii, 152, 153; accompanies Indian war-party, xxii, 149, 152–161; revisits Fort St. Joseph, xxii, 155, 161; abandons his post, xxii, xxiii, 152, 163; retreats to Mackinac, xxiii, 163–166; ordered to Canada, xxiii, 164; postpones return till spring, xxiii, 164; embarks for discovery, xxiv, 167, visits Wisconsin, xxiv, xli, xlii, 167–178; describes Indian feast, 169, 170; among Fox Indians, 175, 176, ascends the Mississippi, xxiv, 178, 179; explores River Long, 179–197, 300; limit of journey, xxiv, 193, 197; descends the Mississippi, xxiv, 197–200, 203–205; explores the Missouri, 200–203; burns Indian village, 203; meets Arkansa Indians, 203–205, 465, 466; at mouth of Ohio, xxiv, 205, crosses

LAH

Lahontan, Louis (*continued*).
Illinois, xxiv, 205-207; meets Tonty, 207; returns to Mackinac, xxiv, 207, 208; disbands detachment, 209; returns to Canada, xxv, 216-218; encounters Ste. Hélène, 217; rescued from rapids, xxv, 219; describes Lachine massacre, 224, 225; receives furlough, xxv, 230; countermanded, xxv, 230; patronized by Frontenac, xxv, 230, 232, 237, 281; declines Iroquois embassy, xxv, 237-239; illness of, 238; on detachment, 240; sent to France with tidings, xxvi, 250; in France, xxvi, 252-257; finds estates sequestered, xxvii, xxxiii, 151, 230, 252, 253; attempts to recover, 253; receives military order, xxvi, 253, 254, 257; desires a benefice, xxvii, 254; solicits favor at court, 256; commended to Frontenac, xxix, 256, 257; appointed captain, xxvi, 257; returns to Canada, 257; arrives in Quebec, xxviii, 262, 708; marriage arranged, xxvii, 388-390; declines, xxviii, 389, 390; plans defense, xxix, xlv, 271-273, Frontenac commends, xxix, 273, 274; sent to France, xxix, 274-279; aids in defense of Placentia, xxix, 275, 276, 278, 281; praises English valor, 279; praised by English, 281, project rejected at court, 280, 281, 288; made lieutenant of Newfoundland, xxx, 281; dispute with physician, 282-286; embarks for Placentia, 287; incurs Brouillon's enmity, xxxi, 12, 287-294, 694, 695; builds house, 288, 292; entertains, 290; attempts to conciliate Brouillon, 291, 292; composes satiric song, xxxi, 293; supported by Placentians, xxxi, 292-294; in danger, xxxi, 293; escapes, xxxii, lxi, 9, 293, 294; voyage to Portugal, xxvii, 294-296; pur-

LAH

Lahontan, Louis (*continued*).
sued by pirates, xxxii, 295, 296; in disgrace at court, xxxii, 297, 298, 647, 694, 696; sent to Rochelle, 296, 297; in Portugal, xxxii, 619-626, 648-650; letter from Lisbon, 619-647; meets Abbé d'Estrées, 628; sees king of Portugal, 629; voyages to Holland, 648-650; adventures with English privateers, 650, 651; at Guernsey, 648, 650; visits Holland, xxxii, 648, 651-656, 658, 659; visits Hamburg, xxxii, 648, 657-663; attempts at reinstatement at French court, xxxii, xxxiii; letter to court, xxxii, xli; at Lubeck, 648, 662, 663; at Copenhagen, xxxiii, 663-684; meets king of Denmark, 679; patronized by, 3; journeys to Paris, 684-694; passport, 688; letter from Paris, 684-695; at Versailles, 694; adventure with German countess, 688-693; returns to native province, xxxiii, 696; letter from Bearn, 696-710; arrest ordered, xxxiii; escapes to Spain, xxxiii; at Bordeaux, 697; at Bayonne, 698; at Esperon, 698; Dax, 698-711; in Spain, 698-717; at Ortez, 710-712; letter from Huesca, 711-717; taken for Huguenot, 712-714; letter from Saragossa, 718-731; later European wanderings, xxxiii, xliii, 9, 730; in England, xxxiv, 8; at court of Hanover, xxxiii; befriended by Leibnitz, xxxiii; defends English king, xxxiv; death, xxxiii; posthumous works, xxxiv; characteristics of, xi, xlii, xliii, xlvi, xlvii; occupations, xii, xiv, xx, humanity, xlvi, 122-124, 208, 269, 270; impartiality, 299, 300; scorns criticism, 10, 11, tolerance, xlvii; obscenity, xliv; skepticism, 285, 286, 438-445, 448, dislikes ecclesiastics, xxvii, xxxvi, 42, 297; denounces

Lahontan, Louis (*continued*).
ecclesiastical tyranny, xv, 88–90, 98; belittles Jesuit missions, 329; fondness for sport, xiv, xx, study, xiv; wilderness life, xxi, xxx, xli, 7, 11, 281; knowledge of wilderness conditions, xxv, xli, 435, 452, knowledge of Indian languages, xvii, 123, 132, 176, 414, 733, beloved by Indians, 274, 281; hatred for Iroquois, 6; describes Iroquois, 57–61; satirizes civilization, xxxv–xxxvii, xlii–xliv; slanders women of Canada, 30–38, views on origin of human race, 282–286; dissertation on witchcraft, 696–710; exaggerates numbers, 237, 249, 262; keeps journals, 206, 264, 300, 370; discusses difficulties of discoveries, 210–215; describes natural history, xiv; describes beavers, 170–173, apochryphal voyage to River Long, xxiii, xxxviii–xliii, poses as a discoverer, xli, acquaintance with explorers, xli; reasons for invented journey, xxxix–xli; ignorance of Siouan country, 342, 343; skepticism concerning, xxxix; misfortunes of, xlii, xliii, extent of travels, 418; patrons, 11; foreshadows Revolution, xlvii, literary style, xxiii, xxxiv, xxxvii, xxxix, Algonquian dictionary, 732–748; memoir on Canada, 299–400; table of explanation of terms, 297, 301, 401–407, bibliography of works, xxxvi, li–xciii; *Dialogues* with Adario, 517–618; Indian participant, xliv, 9, 149; described, xliv, xlv; possible author of, xliv, xlv; style, xxxix, xlv; origin, xiv, xv, xliv, 8, 9; apology for, xli, 7, 8; published separately, xlv, borrowed from, xlviii, *Voyages*, xi; origin of, 6, motive for, xxxiv, 300; first destined to be burned, xxxiv, 5; criticized, 10, 11, copies

Lahontan, Louis (*continued*).
kept, 300; published, xxxiv; illustrations, lxii, 9, 10; correctness of maps, 300; dates, 6; vogue of, xxxiv–xxxvi; historical value, xxxvi–xxxviii; neglect accounted for, xxxviii, French editions, xxxiii, xxxiv, lii, liv–lx, lxiii–lxxiv, lxxvi, lxxxix–xci, xciii, 124, 143; translated into English, xxxiv, xliv, 8, 9; English editions, xxxiv, xlviii, lx–lxiii, lxxxii–lxxxvii, xcii; Dutch edition, lxxv, lxxxvii–lxxxix, 8; Italian editions, xcii, xciii, German editions, lxxiv–lxxxvi, xci; dedication, 3, 4, preface lxi, 5–10, *Réponse à la lettre d'un particulier*, xxxiv, *Memoir on Fur-Trade of Canada*, xxxiv.
— barony of, erected, ix; seized by creditors, x, xxi, 151, 230.
— village of, location, ix.
Lake Abittibi, French post on, 342.
— Andiatarocté. *See* Lake George.
— d'Angoulême. *See* Lake St. Peters.
— Assinipouals *See* Winnipeg.
— Champlain, Indians near, 59; affluents of, 108, outlet, 52, 90, 240; hunting near, xiv, 108–117; route from New York, 240, Iroquois hunting ground, 240; rendezvous of troops, 240.
— Chautauqua, as fur-trade route, 155
— Erie (Conti), origin of name, 320, size, 319; shores described, 319–321, 399, empties into Lake Ontario, 131, 304, 321; islands of, 321, depth, 320; navigation, 157, 158, 320; climate, 319; portage to Ontario, 321, 322, boundary of Canada, 302, trees, 319; game, 320, 322, Indians frequent, 320; projected fort on, 272, 273, 321, Lahontan coasts, xix, 138, 155, 158
— Frontenac. *See* Lake Ontario.

LAK

Lake George, origin of name, 91; Indian name for, 91; route to New York, 90.
— Grand Butte des Morts, Lahontan on, 174, 175.
— Huron, 92; shore described, 143; shape, 317; size, 316; climate, 316, 317; ice, 144, 448, navigation, 147, 317, 318; outlet, 304, portage, 322; course from Mackinac to French River, 218; islands, 153, 154, 218, 317; fish, 320; game, 317; Indians near, xvii, 154, 317, 340, 488; war-party on, xxii, 153, 154, 488, Lahontan crosses, 143, 144, 163; English traders, 125; forts, xviii, xix, 139, 272, 320.
— Machakandibi, on route to Hudson Bay, 314.
— of Malhominis. *See* Lake Grand Butte des Morts
— Michigan (Illinois), 92; described, 209, 210, 319; outlet, 143, 145, 146; affluents, 208; islands, 167; bays, 317; passage to Mississippi, 178; fish, 320; Indians adjacent, 341; Lahontan crosses, xxiv, 167, 207, 208; Lahontan familiar with, xlii.
— Nipigon (Lenemipigon), location, 304; limits of explorations, 304, 305; fort on, 136.
— Nipissing (Nepicerinis), origin of name, 218; source of French River, 317; on route to upper country, 213; Indians near, 342.
— Ontario (Frontenac), described, 322; size, 322; depth, 322; banks, 322; affluents, 322; Erie empties into, 131, 304; source of St. Lawrence, 304; portage, 318, 321, 322; route, 273; Indians near, 58, 70, 323, 341; expeditions on, xiii, 68, 126; vessels, 68, 226, 395; missions, 70.
— Pepin, French fort on, xxxix.
— St. Clair, Iroquois name for, 139; described, xx, 138, 139; beauty of,

LAP

Lake St. Clair (*continued*).
139, Indian rendezvous, xviii, 125; fort near, 418
— St Francis, in St. Lawrence, 67, 86.
— St. John, route to Hudson Bay, 244.
— St Louis, in St. Lawrence, 67, 86, 219; described, 240.
— St Peters, described, 51.
— du St. Sacrement. *See* Lake George.
— Salt, reported to Lahontan, xxiv, 194; inhabitants of, 194.
— Simcoe, described, 317, 318; river flowing from, 318; Indians near, 318, 340; Iroquois hunting grounds, 323; projected fort on, 273, 318.
— Superior (Upper), described, 315; size, 315; shores, 153; outlet, 152, 304, 316; islands, 316; climate, 316; fogs, 153; ice, 316; game, 316; fish, 316; copper mines, 316, navigation, 312, 315, 316; ports, 315; Indians, 315, 342; fur-trade, 153; trading posts, 315, 316; Duluth, 315; voyage from Hudson Bay, 314, 315.
— Temiscaming, significance of name, 342; location, 342; Indians near, 342.
— Toronto. *See* Lake Simcoe
— Trout, on Ottawa route, 219.
— of Two Mountains, in River Ottawa, 217, mission village on, 55.
— Winnebago, Indian village on, 174; currents in, 178
— Winnipeg, reports of, 304, 305; river rises near, 311.
Lalande, Jacques de, 244.
La Montagne, mission village at, 55, 339, 340.
Lampreys, in Canada, 358.
Lang, Andrew, *Myth, Ritual, and Religion*, 510.
Lapland, cape on coast of, 301; witchcraft in, 701.
La Plante, —, captured by Iroquois, 224, 266.

LAP

La Plaque, —, leads war-parties, 239, 240.
La Prairie de la Madeleine, site, 240; mission village at, 56; besieged, 226; French encamp at, 240; attacked, 240; sketch, 240.
Lapwings, in Canada, 351.
La Revue Canadienne, 244.
La Rochelle. See Rochelle.
La Salle, Réné Robert Cavelier, sieur de, as discoverer, xii, 133, 210; at Fort Frontenac, 69; embarks at La Chine, 67; at Fort Miami, 208, at Niagara, 131; accompanied by Recollects, 413; describes Chicago portage, 207; meets Shawnee, 82; in Illinois, 26, 33, 207; plundered by Iroquois, 77; discovers Mississippi, 32, 33, 88; among Arkansa, 204; envoy to Onondaga, 61; impoverished, 69; embarks for France, xii, 33; familiarity with Canada, 33; enemies, 69, 125; endorsed by Frontenac, 69; his lieutenant, 124, 125, 133; last expedition, xii, xxxii, 144, 145, 335; its survivors, xxxii, xli, 144, 145, 347; murdered, 33, 115, 145; published accounts of, xli; sketch, 33.
La Touche, Monsieur de, courtier of Louis XIV, 254.
La Tourette, Claude Greysolon de, Duluth's brother, Lahontan meets, 135, 136; at Lake Nipigon, 136; sketch, 136.
Laval, François de Montmorency, builds Basilica, 42; favors Jesuits, 43; opposes Recollects, 43; forbids liquor traffic with Indians, 94; successor of, 165; rigor, 166, establishes seminary, 386; benefices of, 383; sketch, 43.
— University (Quebec), 110; editions of Lahontan in, liii–xciii.
Law, Adario compares French and savage, 551–592; former works injustice, 555–559.

LOB

Lea, Charles Henry, *History of Inquisition*, 704.
Lead, in fur-trade, 377.
Leagues, length of, 513.
LeClercq, Christian, *Premier établissement de la foy dans la Nouvelle France*, 413; cited, 200.
Le Courrier du Livre, liii.
Legler, Henry E., "Henry de Tonty," 133.
Leibnitz, Gottfried Wilhelm, befriends Lahontan, xxxiii, xxxiv; *Epistolas ad diversos*, xxxiii.
Leisler, Jacob, rebellion of, 126
Le Jeune, Paul, Jesuit missionary, 417; describes Indian customs, 466, 472; on Huron-Iroquois language, 733.
Le Moyne. See Iberville, Bienville, Longueuil, Ste. Hélène.
Lentils, on River Long, 191.
Lepidus timidus, 348.
"Le Rocher," Illinois landmark, 207.
Léry, Chassegros, Canadian engineer, 41, 42.
Le Sueur, Pierre Charles, ascends Mississippi, xxxix.
Levasseur de Neré, —, aids in fortifying Quebec, 265.
Lewis, Meriwether, and Clark, William, describe plant, 474.
Lewiston, Niagara portage at, 136
Library of Congress, editions of Lahontan in, liii–xciii.
Licences (congés), for fur-trade, 99–101, 384, 386; reform in system, 392.
Linden, in Canada, 364.
Linen, Canadian import, 376.
Liquor-traffic, with Indians, 94.
Lisbon, described by Lahontan, lxi, 9, 297, 619–650.
Little Chute (Wis.), location, 174
— Rapids (Wis.), location, 174.
Livre, value of, 101.
Lobsters, in Canada, 333, 359, 361.

LON

Long, John, English trader, 93; *Voyages and Travels*, 93, 433, 457, 510, 734.
— Point (Lake Erie), described, 321; Lahontan portages, 138.
Longitude, former manner of reckoning, 302.
Longueuil, Charles Le Moyne, sieur de, 74; relations with Iroquois, 74, 75, 77, 81, 84, 224; ennobled, 74; governor of Montreal, 224; sketch, 74, 224; sons of, 74, 118, 236.
Lons, Marquise de, sponsor of Lahontan, x.
Lorette, mission village, 46, 48, 268, 269, 339, 340.
Loskiel, George H., *Mission of United Brethren*, 448.
Louis X, king of France, orders to governors, 290.
Louis XIV, friend of Prince von Furstemberg, 692; aids La Salle, 88; controlled by Jesuits, 384; persecutes Huguenots, xlvi; grant to Lahontan's father, ix; ministers of, 5, 254–256, 338; aids Canadian missions, 55; sends troops to Canada, 26; relations with Iroquois, 77, 280; relations with Lahontan, xxxiii, 5, 281, 298; appoints Canadian bishops, 165; chaplain, 165; recalls Denonville, 227; orders to governors, 338; receives cession of part of Newfoundland, 275; grandsons of, 227; controls king of England, 61.
Louisiana, Canadian founders of, 74, 144, 145, 235, 236; posts, 144; missions, 145; Tonty's death, 133.
Loup Indians, French name for Mohican, 90.
Louvois, François Michel le Tellier, marquis de, confers order on Lahontan, xxvi, 254; sketch, 254.
Lower Granville (N. S.), site of Port Royal, 331.

MAC

Loyalists, in Nova Scotia, 331.
Lubeck, Lahontan at, 648, 662, 663, 680.
Lucian, read by Lahontan, xiv, xv, xliv, 116.
Lude, Count de, 11.
— Duchesse de, Lahontan's patron, 11.
Lutreola vison, 111.
Lynx, in Canada, 343.

MACAULAY, Thomas Babington, *History of England*, 665.
MacGregory, Patrick, captured, 126; sketch, 126.
Machakandibi Indians, habitat, 342; language, 342; characterized, 342.
McKenney, Thomas L., *Tour of the Lakes*, 64.
Mackenzie, Alexander, *Voyages through North America*, 219.
Mackerel, in Canada, 358.
Mackinac, location, xx, 92, 145, 146; described, 145–148; latitude, 145; importance, 145, 149, 318; route thither, xxiii, 207, 208, 218, 219; Indians at, 92, 98, 143, 317, 448; neighboring villages, 144, 145, 340, 418, 429; agriculture, 144, 148; fish, 147, 148; game, 147; Jesuit mission, xviii, 129, 140, 146, 149; French settlement, 146; êntrepot of Northwest, xli, 146, security, 147; prisoners shot, 144, 222; messenger to, 144; commandants, xviii, xxiii, 125, 144, 164, 209; Duluth at, 72, 73; La Tourette, 135; Lahontan, xx, xxii–xxiv, xl, xli, 135, 143, 149, 152, 163–167, 208, 216, 300, 315, 430; survivors of La Salle's expedition, xxi, 144, 145, 347; English traders captured near, 125; map, 146, 319; sketch, 92, 146. *See also* Fort Mackinac.

McLennan, William, "Gentlemen of the King's Guard," 73; "Death of Duluth," 73; *Patriarchal Theory*, 462, 510

Macoun, John, *Catalogue of Canadian Birds*, 356

Maheu (Mahu), Jean Paul, messenger to France, 26.

Maine, Indians of, 49, 90, 126, 327, 328; St. Castin in, xi, 328, 329; French post, 327, 328, fort attacked, 236, 237, celebration by Historical Society, 324; *Collections*, 328

Maize, raised by Indians, 139, 140, 148, 502; in Acadia, 325, Green Bay, 168

Mallery, Garrick, "Picture-Writing of American Indians," 512, 514

Malomini Indians. *See* Menominee Indians

Malouins, fisheries of, 308.

Mandrake, in Canada, 364; described, 368.

Manhattan (Manathe), location, 6, route to, 91

Manitou, Indian spirits, 345, 603.

Mantet (Mantz, Manteht), Nicolas d'Ailleboust, sieur de, leads rangers to Fort Frontenac, 232, 233; with Duluth, 233, repairs Fort Frontenac, 233; raid against Schenectady, 236; sketch, 233

Manzanita, Spanish name for plant, 474.

Maples, described, 366, 367, in Canada, 364, 365; sap, 429; method of making syrup, 366, 367; drunk by Indians, 170.

Marble, varieties of, 685.

Margry, Pierre, *Découvertes et établissement des Français*, xxxii

Marine, department of, in charge of colonies, x, xi, 5, 118, 384; Lahontan in corps of, x.

Marion, Fontaine, shot as deserter, 127.

Markham, Albert H., "Voyages and works of John Davis, Navigator," 310

Marmot. *See* Whistler

Marquette, Father Jacques, companion of Jolliet, 244; discoveries of, xli, 412; establishes St. Ignace mission, 146, 154; at Fox-Wisconsin portage, 177, describes Chicago, 207; names Illinois River, 205; Ohio, 205; Missouri, 200; return route, 207; map, 200; describes berdashes, 462; michibichi, 345; calumet dance, 169, 424.

Martens, in Canada, 344; Lahontan hunts, 115; traps for, 482–484; skins of, 376; Norwegian trade in skins, 681; price, 379

Martin, Horace F., *Castorologia*, 171, 173, 346, 380, 479–481

Martinique, besieged, 288, 289

Maryland, emigrants to, 126.

Mascoutin Indians, 174, 341

Maskikik, Indian remedy, 468.

Massachusetts Historical Society, editions of Lahontan in library of, liii–xciii; *Collections*, 237.

Masson, L. R, *Bourgeois de la Compagnie du Nord-Ouest*, 417, 457, 468, 483, 500

Matchi-Manitou, evil spirits of Indians, 446–448

Mattawan, distance from Montreal, 219

Maupeau, Sieur de, accompanies Lahontan to Canada, 257, 262, preferred before Lahontan, xxix, 390

Maurault, J. A., *Histoire des Abenakis*, 328

Maya calendar, 428.

May-apples *See* Mandrake.

Melons, raised by Indians, 148

Membertou, Micmac chief, 328, 414

Membré, Father Zenobie, voyages, xli, 204

Menneval, Robineau, sieur de, governor of Acadia, 327, 330

MEN

Menominee (Malomini) Indians, habitat, xxiv, 168, 341; language, 341; village, 168, entertain Lahontan, xxiv, 168-171; French name for, 175; characterized, 341; sketch, 168.
Merles, in Canada, 358.
Merlins, in Canada, 352.
Meules, Jacques de, intendant of New France, 86; recalled, 102, 103.
Miami (Oumami) Indians, habitat, 77; migrations, 77; language, 341; physical traits, 415, 488; totems, 511, characterized, 341; mission to, xviii, 140, 208; treatment of prisoners, 504; calendar, 427, 428; fur-trade with, 146; allies of French, 78, 125; Indian allies of, 82, 486; fight Iroquois, 78, 81, 82, 157, 159-164, 208, 486-488.
Michibichi, described, 343, 345, 446.
Michigan, Indians of, 167, 174.
Michitonka, Miami chief, 161-163.
Micmac (Souriquois) Indians, habitat, 327, 328; language, 339; chief, 328, 414; devoted to French, 328; missions to, 328; characterized, 339; sketch, 328.
Mink, identified, 111.
Minnesota, boundary of, 316; *Historical Collections*, 315.
Minquas Indians, identified, 320.
Mission Indians, assist French, 119, 122, 239, 240; enumerated, 339, 340. *See also* the several missions.
Mississague Indians, habitat, 317; language, 34.
Missouri Indians, habitat, 200; characteristics, 204, 205; migrations, 200; Lahontan visits, 200-203; sketch, 200.
Mohawk (Agnies) Indians, English name for, 658, habitat, 58, 59, 341; language, 56, 339, 341; Indian enemies, 90; enemies of French, 77, 80, 238; expedition against, 55, 59, 224,

MOO

Mohawk Indians (*continued*).
missions, 56, 239, 339, 340; characterized, 339.
Mohican (Mohegan, Wolf, Fr. Loup) Indians, habitat, 90; characterized, 339; language, 339; in fur-trade, 90; wandering, 327, 328.
Molina, Luis, Jesuit theologian, 383, 384.
Monroe County (N. Y.), 125, 131.
Monsoni (Monzoni) Indians, habitat, 342; characterized, 342; language, 342; wandering, 342; at Sault Ste. Marie, 342.
Montagnais Indians, language, 339, tribes of, 261, 339, 340; at Tadoussac, 31; mission, 49; trade with Jolliet, 305.
Montmagny, Charles Huault de, governor of Canada, 40, 82.
Montmorency County, location, 34.
Montreal, founded, 52, 53, 233; location, 38; early name, 52; mountain, xxxvii, 55, 339, 513; island near, 118; described, 52-56; fortifications, 53, 88, 89, 98; government of, 52, 53, 86, 120, 144, 202, 224, 383; river transportation, 657; courts, 392; seminary of St. Sulpice, 55; Frontenac at, 231, 232; Lahontan, xiii, xxv, xxvi, 48, 52-56, 88-90, 218, 235, 239; Iroquois raid, 224, 270, 271; commerce, 96, 97, 376; fur-trade, 92-95; peace conference (1701), 149; Adario interred, 149; Denonville bound for, 103; history, 53, 55; Historical Society *Memoirs*, 169.
Monts, Pierre du Gas, sieur de, French explorer, 331.
— Notre Dame, in Canada, 274; fisheries off, 306; identified, 306.
Montortié, —, French officer, 86, 87, 92, 98.
Moor-hens. *See* Wood-hens.
Moose, identified, 103.

MOR

Moracin, Sieur de, French merchant, 655
Moravians, missions to Indians, 448.
Morgan, Lewis H., "Houses and House-Life of American Aborigines," 418; *Ancient Society*, 462.
Mortier, Corneille, cartographer, 338.
— Pierre, bay named for, 338.
Mosquitoes, torment of, 68.
Mountains, Chicchack *See* Monts Notre Dame.
— Pyrenees, Lahontan near, ix, xxi; St. Castin born near, 329; timber from, 150.
— Shickshock *See* Monts Notre Dame.
Moyacks, in Canada, 351, 355.
Mozeemlek, xxxix; habitat, 193; characteristics, xxiv, 187, 193, 195, 196; enemies, 187, 194; numbers, 187, 193, 194; houses, 194; mistaken for Spaniards, 192, 193; appearance, 193; refuse to go to Canada, 196.
Mulattoes, in Europe, 284.
Muller, Frederik, *Catalogue of Books, Maps, Plates on America*, lxxv.
Mullets, in Great Lakes, 359.
Murcey, —, French officer, 97.
Muskrats (*Fiber zibethicus*), in Canada, 343, 344; manner of hunting, 110, 111; price, 380.
Mussels, in Canada, 359; described, 361; pearls of, 361.
Myrand, Ernest, *Sir William Phips devant Quebec*, 249.

Nadouessioux Indians. *See* Sioux Indians.
Nantes, Lahontan at, 264, 279-282; brandy exported, 375; edict revoked, xlvi.
Naroutsouat (Norridgewock, Maine), French post at, 328.
Natchitoches, early French settlement, 144.

NEW

Navarre, parlement of, ix.
Nebraska, Indians in, 175.
Needles, in fur-trade, 378.
Neenah (Wis.), Indian village near, 174.
Neill, Edward D., identifies river, 315.
Nelson, John, captured by French, xviii, 265, 274; promotes Lahontan's marriage, xxviii, 389, 390; hypothetical voyage of, 311; sketch, 265.
Nemitsakouat, Duluth's post, 315.
Nepisirini Indians *See* Nipissing Indians.
New Brunswick, Indians of, 90, 327; celebration by Historical Society, 324.
— England, boundary, 323, 400; Indians, 49, 90, 126, 327, 328; early explorations, 311; English, 237, 399; forts, 236, raided by French, 236, 237; French in, 127, 330; negotiations with French, 385; Wheler in, 289; fisheries, 399, 400.
Newfoundland, 274, 275; described, xxx, xxxii, 27, 259, 287, 288, 295, 302, 305, 308, 309, 332-339, 348, 355, 374, 401; early explorations, 303, 307, 308; early name, 307; included in Canada, 302; natives, 309, 334; white population, 332, 337; English, 332; Basques, 308, 333; French, xxix, 275-279, 332, 334; officers in, 12, 266; visited by bishop, 232; by Iberville, 236; Lahontan in, xxx, xxxii, lxi, 9, 281; storms, 27, 274; trade, 282, 288; maps, lxi, 28, 30, 259.
New France, Indian name for, 93; boundaries, 301-303, 400, 414; physical characteristics, 285, 391; rivers, 64; forests, 70; mountains, 50; climate, xii, 38, 41, 45, 46, 104, 106, 249, 250; animals, 104-117, 343-349, 481; birds, 350-356, fruits, 364-372; fish and fisheries, 305, 306, 308, 358-363, 394; Indian tribes, 339-342, 710; their languages, 46,

New France (*continued*).
47; discovery by whites, 303; limits of exploration, 304; white settlement, 31, 303, 331; Indian opposition, 303; population, 304; commerce and fur-trade, 33, 54, 96, 97, 99, 101, 102, 235, 280, 326, 373–378, 382, 391, 392, 394, 657, 681; commercial companies, xi, 34, 41, 91, 253, 303, 382; agriculture, 35, 39, 55; navigation, 64, 65; travelling, 45, 46, 62–65, 70, Indian wars, 58–61; troops, 26, 36, 72, 119, 392; relations with Iroquois, 6, 26, 45, 59, 60, 92–94, 385, 397; government, xxxviii, 329, 381–393; governors, xi, 25, 26, 41, 42, 59, 97, 119, 235, 381, 384, 404 — *see also* Onontio; local governors, 51, 382, 383; intendants, 41, 42, 44, 102, 103, 239, 382, 384, 392; sovereign council, 41, 42, 44, 45, 230, 382, 385, 402; judiciary, 44, 45, 392; noblesse, 98, 260, 386; seigniories, 26, 34, 39; feudalism, 34, 36, 53, 260; land allotments, 36; luxury, 55, 97, 391, 392; Indian allies, 26, 92–95, 119, 270–272; ecclesiastics, 42, 43, 383, 386, 542–545; habitants, xii, xxxviii, 34–38, 49, 387, 391, 399, 402; manufactures, 392; invaded by Kirk, 31; Phips's expedition, 242–250, capital, 39–44, 331; histories, 412, 413.

— Holland *See* New York.
— Mexico, French exploration towards, 144; inhabitants of, 191.
— York (New Holland, New Netherlands), Indian name for, 82, 236; boundaries, 6; discovery, 311; route from Canada to, 90, 91; incite Iroquois against French, 237; Canadian raid, 235, 236; troops to invade Canada, 240; French negotiations, 385; governors, 61, 78, 79, 157,

New York (*continued*).
287; fur-trade, 126, 395–397, 399; editions of Lahontan in Public Library, liii–xciii; in Historical Society Library, liii–xciii; *Colonial Documents*, 68, 72, 74, 86, 87, 126, 131, 136, 139, 155, 157, 162, 220, 222, 236, 237, 240, 241, 262, 271, 327, 461, 486; State Paleontologist's *Report*, 305.
— York City (Manathe), name for, 6; French prisoner at, 239; easy to capture, 239; Adario in, 519.
Niagara, location, 131; fort at, 131; Lahontan leaves, xix, 135, 220; portage, xix, 136; Seneca village, 137; troops near, 73.
— Falls of, first described, xix, 136, 137; beasts and fish killed in, 137; passage under, 137.
Nicolet, Jean, French explorer, 209, 244.
Nicolas, Huron chief, revolts, 461.
Nicollet, I. N., American explorer, xl.
Nicotiana tabacum, 474; *rustica*, 474.
Nider, —, *Formicarius*, 703, 704.
Nightingales, in Canada, 350, 354.
Niles (Mich.), French fort near, 208.
Nipissing (Nepisirini) Indians, habitat, 218, 342; characterized, 342; language, 342; original Algonquians, 342, numbers, 342; sketch, 342.
Nopemen d'Achirini. *See* Achirigouans.
Noquets (Nocké) Indians, habitat, 317; language, 340.
Normans, early fisheries of, 305; early settlers, 402; founders of Canadian commerce, 373.
Norridgewock. *See* Naroutsouat.
Norsemen, early discovery of America by, 307, 309; silver miners, 681.
North America, size, xxxvi, 210, 211, 299, 300; maps, 300; explorations of coast, 303, 304, 307, 309–314.
— Sea, channels in, 658; islands, 664.

NOR

North West Company, in fur-trade, 316
Northwest (Old), not part of Canada, 302, 303; Indians of, 305; St Lusson takes possession, 342
— Passage, explorations for, 310, 312
Notre Dame du Mont Carmel, order of, 254.
— des Anges, Recollect convent, 44
Noue, Sieur de la, at Kaministiquia, 316.
Nova Scotia, bays, 330, 331; Indians, 328; Scotch, 331, Loyalists, 331; land grants, 265; Historical Society, 324 *See also* Acadia
Nut-trees, in Canada, 364, 369.

OAKS, of Acadia, 325, 326; Canada, 364; Lake Erie, 319
Oars, described, 65
Ochagach, map drawn by, 427.
Oiseau Mouche. See Humming Birds
Ojibwa, Indians. *See* Chippewa Indians
Oka, Indian mission village, 55.
Oklahoma, Indian reservations in, 174, 175, 202, 204
Old Port au Choix (Newfoundland), 308.
Old South Leaflets, 303.
Oleron, St. Castin's birthplace, xxi, 150, 151, 328.
Olier, Jean Jacques, founder of Sulpitians, 55
Omaha Indians, 499, 509.
Oneida (Onnoyoutes) Indians, habitat, 58, 323, 341, French enemies, 77, 80; to waylay English embassadors, 238
Onondaga (Onnontagues) Indians, habitat, 58, 77, 80, 81, 323, 341; language, 341, council house among, 58; embassy to, 61, 74, 77, 238, 239; orator, 74; chief, 222; Miami raid, 162; attack Miami, 163.
— French captive at, 270.
Onontio, title of governor of Canada, 80, 82, 84, 404

OTT

Onoyout Indians. *See* Oneida Indians
Ontario, boundary of, 316; Indians, 317, 342; Historical Society *Records and Papers*, 484; Archæological *Report*, 484
— County (New York), 127
Openango Indians, habitat, 90, 328; language, 339; characterized, 339; in fur-trade, 90
Opossum, described, 347; habitat, 343.
Orange. *See* Albany.
Originals. *See* Elks.
Ortolans, in Canada, 351, 356.
Ortyx virginianus, 353.
Osage Indians, habitat, 202; characteristics, 204, 205, sketch, 202.
Oshkosh (Wis.), Indian village near, 174.
Ossa. *See* Opossum.
Oswego County (New York), 72.
Oto (Otentas, Otontantas) Indians, early form of name, 200; habitat, 198–200, agriculturists, xx, 199; Missouri amalgamate with, 200; Lahontan visits, 199, 200; sketch, 200.
Otontagan Indians, Ottawa band, 153
Otréouaté. *See* Grangula.
Otsi Keta, Iroquois name for Lake St. Clair, 139.
Ottawa (Outaoua) Indians, tribes of, 153, 317, 340; habitat, 73, 92, 143, 153, 317, 340; physical traits, 415; hair dressing, 153; language, 176, 340; totems, 511; religious hymn, 449, 450; hunting grounds, 210, 317; agriculturists, 148; treatment of prisoners, 144, 504, characterized, 503; calendar, 427, 428, hunting expedition, 143; first encounter French, 153; relations to Lahontan, xvii, xxiv, xxv, 132, 165, 167, 177, 181, 184, 189, 216–218; relations with other tribes, 73, 146, 149; 153–161, 209, 317, 321, 340, 397, 503; in fur-trade, 81, 92, 95, 241,

OTT

Ottawa Indians (*continued*)
  under Duluth, 73, under Denonville, xvii, 125; cowardly, 156, 159, 160, 163, 216, 217; at Mackinac, 145-147, 317, 429; mission to, xviii, 129, 131, 140; sketch, 340
Otters, in Acadia, 326; Canada, 344; River Long, 206; enemies of, 485; attack beavers, 485; used as bait, 484; hunted, 112-114, 482; price of skins, 113, 379; Norwegian trade in, 681; varieties of pelts, 379
Ouadebaton Indians. *See* Wahpeton.
Ouiatonon Indians, habitat, 341; language, 341; characterized, 341; sketch, 341.
Oureahé (Ourehaoué), Cayuga chief, sketch, 233, 234
Outagami Indians. *See* Fox Indians.
Outchipoue Indians. *See* Chippewa Indians.

PACIFIC Ocean, rivers flowing to, 200, discovery of route to, xxxix.
Paltsits, Victor Hugo, *Bibliography of Lahontan*, xxxvi, xlviii, xlix, li-xciii; of Hennepin, xlix.
Paneasse Indians, tribe of Pawnee, 200
Panetouka Indians, tribe of Pawnee, 200.
Panimaha (Pawnee, Loup) Indians, tribe of Pawnee, 182, 199, 200.
Papinachois Indians, significance of name, 261; habitat, 261, 340; language, 339; nomads, 339, 340; trade with Jolliet, 305; missions, 340; sketch, 339, 340.
Paris, parlement of, supports Lahontan's creditors, 151, 253; members, 257; churches, 165; Lahontan in, xxvi, 252, 684-696; Adario, 536; witchcraft, 701; papers from archives, 293; editions of Lahontan in Bibliothéque Nationale, liii-xciii

PET

Parkman, Francis, 77; cites Lahontan, xxxiv, 223; *Frontenac*, 45, 77, 124, 126, 223, 234, 241, 262, 381; *Jesuits in North America*, 58, 155, 418; *La Salle*, xxxiv, 61, 136, 145, 205; *Old Regime*, 34, 37, 217, 385
— Club (Milwaukee), *Papers*, 133, 312.
Parrots (Paroquets), in Canada, 350, 354
"Partridge" (Akouessan), Indian name for Longueuil, 74, 77, 81, 84.
Partridges, described, 350, 351, 353, 355, 356, numbers, 106, 356; in Newfoundland, 332, used for Indian food, 431
Passage Courant. *See* Strait of Canso.
Passamaquoddy Indians, 328. *See also* Abenaki.
Pau, parlement of, 150, 707, 712, 713.
Pawnee Indians, sketch, 199, 200
Pearls, in St. Lawrence River, 361.
Pears, in Canada, 367.
Pease, raised by Indians, 148; at Green Bay, 168; on River Long, 187; exported, 367, 373.
Pelicans, in Canada, 350.
Peltrie, Madame de la, patroness of Ursulines, 44.
Pemaquid (Me.), birthplace of Phips, 244; projected attack on, 265, 274.
Pennsylvania, Indians of, 320.
Penobscot Indians, 328. *See also* Abenaki.
Pentagoët, French fort at, xxviii, 328
Peoria (Ill.), fort near, 207.
Percé Rock, fishing village at, 305. *See also* Isle Percé
Perch, in Mississippi River, 359.
Perrot, François Marie, governor of Montreal, 53; of Acadia, 53, 327, 330; succeeded by Callières, 86; yields to English, 327; sketch, 53
— Nicolas, French explorer, xxxix, xli; *Mémoire*, 379
Perusse-trees, 365; described, 371.
Petit Nord, fisheries, 308, 334.

PET

Petronius, Lahontan's copy mutilated, xv, 89, 90.
Petun Indians. *See* Huron Indians.
Pheasants, in Canada, 350, 353; on Lake Erie, 322; River Long, 180.
Phips, Sir William, attack on Quebec, xxvi, 242–250, captures Port Royal, 244, 327, 330; governor of Massachusetts, 244, 289; sketch, 244.
Phoca vitulina, 349.
Pickerel, in Fox River, 174.
Pigeons (wild), numerous in Canada, 109, 110, 350, 351; migration, 109, 112.
Pike, in Canada, 358; in Mississippi, 359; Wisconsin Lakes, 174.
Pilling, James Constantine, *Bibliography of Algonquian Languages*, lii, 734.
Pine trees, in Canada, 365, 370.
Pineapples, in Canada, 364.
Pingo, Captain —, commands "Tempest," 26.
Pipestone (Minn.), quarries at, 76.
Piquer de fond, 65.
Pirates, in Atlantic, 296, 327, 374.
Pirogues, on River Long, 187, 188, 193.
Placentia (Newfoundland), location, 335; harbor, 335, 336, 338; fisheries, 336, 337, 374; fortified, 275–278, 282, 288, 289, 334, 335, 348; population, 336–338; Lahontan at, xxix, xxxi, xxxii, 275–279, 287–290, 292, 294, 295, 621, 694; English attack, xxix, 275–278, 281, natives, 309; governors, xxix, 276, 292, 337; sketch, 275.
Plaice, in Canada, 358.
Platina, Bartolommeo de Sacchis, *Vitæ Pontificium*, 703, 704.
Plovers, in Canada, 351.
Plum trees, on Lake Erie, 319.
Plums, described, 367.
Plungeons, in Canada, 350, 351.
Poagan, Indian name for calumet, 402.
Podophyllum peltatum, 368.

POR

Pointe Verte, in Placentia harbor, 278, 336.
Pole-cats, in Canada, 344; price of skins, 380.
"Poli," commanded by Iberville, 274.
Pontchartrain, Jerome Phelypeaux, count de, opposes Lahontan, 5, 10, sketch, 5.
— Louis Phelypeaux, count de, opposes Lahontan, xxvi, xxx, xxxii, 5, 10, 252, 254, 273, 280, 281, 338, 647, 688, 694–696; sketch, 5.
— Madame de, xxix, 257, 390.
Pontiac, Ottawa chief, 149, 340.
Pope, Joseph, *Jacques Cartier*, 303.
Popular Science Monthly, 76.
Porcelain. *See* Wampum.
Porcupine, in Canada, 111, 112, 344.
Porphry, in Canada, 43; on Cape Breton and Newfoundland, 333.
Porpoises, described, 358, 360.
Port au Basques (Newfoundland), 333.
— Nelson, named by Button, 311.
— Ontario (New York), 72.
— Royal (Annapolis), 265; location, 330, 331; described, 330; founded, 324, 328, 330, 331; harbor, 330, 331; basin, 330, 331; poorly fortified, 327, 330; captured by Phips, 244, 327, 330; fur-trade, 331; population, 330, 331; tercentenary celebrated, 324, 331; sketch, 330.
— Royal (France), retreat of Jansenists, 384.
Portugal, described, 9; climate, 642; manners and customs, 619–647; costumes, 641, inns, 627, 628, 634; food, 627, 634, 635; wine, 635; literature, 638, 639; music, 640, 641; religion, 639, Inquisition, xlvi, 631, 632; monks, 632, 633, 639; law, 642, 643, 646, army and navy, 643–645; sailors, 650; pay of officers, 644; use of titles, 621, 629, 641; royal order, 647; weights and measures, 646; monetary system, 645,

POR

Portugal (*continued*).
646; transportation methods, 633, 634; colonies, 282, 284; women wear veils, 636; behind gratings, 634; morality of, 635-638; witchcraft in, 701; mulattoes, 284; Lahontan in, xxxii, lxi, 282-287, 294-296, 619; cartography, 376, Portuguese in Newfoundland, 333.

Porzana carolina, 110.

Pot, French liquid measure, 430.

Potawatomi (Pouteouatami, Pouteoutami) Indians, Algonquian tribe, 398; habitat, xxiv, 167, 168, 341, 398; language, 341; totems, 511; villages, 168; bay named for, 167; at war with Iroquois, 167; Lahontan with, xxiv, 168-171; sketch, 168; characterized, 341.

Portachua. *See* Old Port au Choix.

Portage (land carriage), described, 404; at Chicago, xxiv, 207; Fox-Wisconsin described, 177, 178; history, 177, 178; Lahontan at, xxiv, 177; canal, 177; Grand, 316; from Lake Erie, 155; of Toronto, 273; au Vase (Ottawa route), 219.

Portland (Me.), fort on site, 237.

Portneuf, Jacques Robineau, sieur de, leads raid into Maine, 236, 237; seigniory, 260; seigniory harborage, 261; son, 330; sketch, 237, 260.

Poterie, Le Neuf de la, Canadian noblesse, 260.

Poutrincourt, Jean de Biencourt, sieur de, French explorer, 331.

Powder, in fur-trade, 377.

Powell, John W., "Linguistic Families of North America," 47; "Mythology of North American Indians," 435; "Wyandot Government," 499, 500.

Pownall, J., quoted, 155.

Prices, of Indian products, 148.

Prince Society, *Publications*, 312.

RAC

Prowse, D. W., *History of Newfoundland*, 334.

Ptolemy, Claudius, early geographer, 302.

Pulse, in Acadia, 325.

Puma, described, 345.

Putnam, Herbert, aid acknowledged, liii.

Pyrrho, Greek philosopher, 414.

Pyrricha, compared to Indian dance, 423.

Quail, in Canada, 353.

Quapaw Indians, habitat, 204.

Quebec (Kébec), founded, 303, 331; described, xii, xiii, xxxvii, 39-45; location, 39, 40; plan of, 41; fortifications, 40, 41, 263, 265, 266; chateau, xxvii, 40-42, 235, 262; intendant's palace, 41, 42, 243, 244, 392; bishop, 42, 43, 165, 381-383, 386, 389; churches, 42, 44, 237, 386; hospitals, 44; university, 110; city hall, 43; Jesuit college, 43, 259; Recollects, 43, 44; feudalism abolished, 34; commerce, 374-378; river transportation, 657; society, xii, xxvii, 388-390; courts, 392; local governor, 383; Frontenac in, 230, 231, Lahontan, xi, xxvii, 32, 49, 216, 226, 230, 258, 261, 262, 708; Adario, 519; attacked by English, 44, 118, 242-250, letter from, 25; archives, 304; editions of Lahontan in legislative library, liii-xciii.

Queylus, Gabriel, Sulpitian superior, 55.

Quinté, Indian village, 121, 122.

Quiros, Francesco Bernado de, Spanish diplomat, 11, 12.

Quoddy Indians, English name for Openango, 90. *See also* Etechemin.

Rabbits, in Canada, 343.

Rabeyre, Lieutenant de la, burned by Iroquois, 224.

Rackets. *See* Snow-shoes.

RAD

Radisson, Pierre Esprit, in Wisconsin, 177; visits Hudson Bay, 312; on Lake Superior, 312, 315; French reject proposals, 313; goes over to English, 313; returns to French, 313; sketch, 312; *Voyages*, 312.
Rails, in Canada, 110, 350.
Raisins, on Missouri River, 202; on Illinois, 206.
Rangifer caribou, 107.
Rapids, Allumettes (Ottawa), 216.
Raspberries, in Canada, 365, 372.
Rat, Huron chief. *See* Adario.
Rattlesnakes, in Canada, 352, 357.
Ravens, in Canada, 350, 352.
Read, John M., *Historical inquiry concerning Henry Hudson*, 309.
Recollects (Récollets), Franciscan missionaries, xxxvi; early Canadian service, 31, 43, 44, 55, 70, 413, opposed by Laval, 43; by Jesuits, 43, 44, 383, 413; supported by Frontenac, 413; aid La Salle, 144, 145, relations with Lahontan, xxxi, 290-293, opinion of Indians, 413, 414; sketch, 44, 413.
Reid Transinsular Railroad, Newfoundland, 333
Reindeer. *See* Caribou.
Religion, Jesuit and savage compared, 517-550.
Rénard Indians. *See* Fox Indians.
Repentigny. Jean Paul le Gardeur, sieur de St. Pierre de, at Mackinac, 208, 209, messenger to Fort Frontenac, 226; sketch, 209.
Revenclaw, Count de, Danish minister, 670.
Ribbons, Canadian import, 375.
Richelieu, Cardinal Armand Jean du Plessis, establishes feudalism in Canada, 34.
Rigauville. *See* Bergères.
River Abittibi, located, 342.
— of Algonkins. *See* Ottawa.

RIV

River Allegheny, portages to, 155; Washington's embassy, 209.
— Arkansas, Indians of, 204.
— Aspe, valley of, 716.
— Aspree, shipping on, 660.
— Au Sable (Mich.), described, 143.
— Bagouasch, location, 315.
— Bois Brulé, Indian rendezvous, 315.
— Cannon, identified as River Long, xl.
— de la Chaudière, village on, 49.
— Chicago, drainage canal, 207.
— Condé, described, 321; identified, 155; fort, 155, 156, convenience, 399.
— Creuse (Deep), part of Ottawa, 216, 219.
— Des Moines (Otentas), identified as River Long, xl; described, 199, 200; Indians, 199, 200; fish, 363.
— Detroit, described, 161; islands, 139, 161; war-party on, 155, 161; fort, 139; Lahontan passes, 138.
— Divine. *See* Illinois.
— Du Fer, affluent of Hudson, 91.
— Ebro, Saragossa on, 719; navigable, 725.
— Elbe, mouth of, 659; tide, 659; shipping, 660; Hamburg on, 659, 660; Glucstat, 688.
— Famine, location, 72; La Barre's expedition at, xiii, 72-79; salmon, 74; Adario's ambuscade, 223.
— Fox (Puants, Renards), Lahontan describes, xxiv, xlii, 168, 173, 174; Indian villages, 168; French names for, 168; Jesuit mission, 168; fertility of banks, 168; navigation of, 174, 177, 178; beaver in, 481.
— French, origin of name, 218; described, 317; route to upper country, 218; navigation difficult, 218; fort advised, 399.
— Genessee, outlet of, 322; Seneca near, 137; vessels to visit, 395.
— Grand, near Lake Ontario, 321, 322.

RIV

River Grand (Mo.), Indian village at mouth, 200.
— Hudson (Manathe, Manhattan), location, 7; Indians upon, 90; connects with Canada, 91
— Humber, on Toronto portage route, 318.
— Illinois (Seignelay), described, 205, 206; early name for, 205; navigation, 205; game on banks, 206; fruit, 206; forts, 207; portage, 207; Lahontan at mouth, xxiv, 205-207.
— Kennebec, boundary of New England, 323; Englishman captured on, 265; French missions, 329, 330.
— Lemipisaki, identified, 315
— au Lièvre, tributary of Ottawa, 217.
— Lima, Viana on, 621.
— Lisbon (O Rey dos Rios), tide in, 641
— Loire, 279.
— Long, described, xxiv; source, 193; affluent of Mississippi, 167, 179; shores barren, 189, 190, 197; fish and game, 179, 183, 197, 206, 363; navigation, 179, 197; Lahontan's alleged journey to, xxiii, xxiv, xxxviii-xliii, 179-197, 301, 414; limits of Lahontan's voyage, xxiv, 190; regarded as fictitious, xxiii, xxxviii, xxxix; proposed identifications, xxxix, xl; on maps, xxxviii, xlv, 301.
— du Loup, location, 51.
— of Machakandibi, identified, 315; navigation, 314
— Maheu, fief upon, 26.
— Maitland (Ont.). *See* Theonontaté.
— Manathe. *See* Hudson.
— Manhattan. *See* Hudson.
— Maskinonge, location, 51.
— Mattawan, described, 216, 219
— Miami (Oumamis), Indian hunting grounds on, 486
— of Miami *See* St. Joseph.

RIV

River Michipiciton, navigation of, 314, 315
— Minnesota, identified with River Long, xxxix, xl.
— Mississippi, longitude, 302; described, 167, 178, 197, 205, 206; routes to, 168, 178, 207; islands, 178, 206, fish and game, 343, 359, 362, 363; parrots near, 354; crocodiles, 204, 205, 343; fruit, 367; Indians of, 174, 175, 203, 204, 342, 462, 747; early voyages on, 149, 200, 204, 205; Jolliet, 81; La Salle, 33, 88, 144, 145; Lahontan, xxiv, 178, 179, 197-200, 203-205; Le Sueur, xxxix; French fort, xxxix; fur-trade, 146; western boundary of Canada, 302, 414, 733; diseases, 465, 466.
— Missouri (Pekitanoui), significance of name, 200; current, 200, 203; fish and game, 200, 203, 363; Indians, 200, 205, 343; first visitors, 200; Lahontan explores, 200-203, 301, 465, 466; map, 301
— Moingona. *See* Des Moines.
— Moose, identification, 315; tributary, 342.
— Muddy. *See* de Vase.
— Nelson, described, 311; post on, 313
— Nicolet, location, 51.
— Nipigon, identified, 315.
— Nottawausaga. *See* Theonontaté
— Ohio (Ouabouskiguo), early names for, 205; depth, 205; navigable, 205; portage, 321; boundary of Canada, 302; Indians upon, 204; Lahontan at mouth, xxiv, 205; fort at mouth, 144; parrots on, 354.
— Osage, Lahontan reaches, 202.
— Oswego (Onnontagnes, Onondaga), identified, 72, 322; vessels to visit, 395.
— Otentas. *See* Des Moines.
— Ottawa, described, xxxvii, 95; rapids, 216, 270; islands, 216; tributaries,

RIV

River Ottawa (*continued*).
216, 217, 219, union with St Lawrence, 219, Indians on, 98, 323, 342; fur-trade route, 218, 219, 399; Lahontan descends, xxv, 216-218.
— Ouabache. *See* Wabash and Ohio.
— Ozao, Laruns on, 712.
— Papinachois, location, 261.
— Pekitanoui. *See* Missouri.
— Penobscot, French fort on, 328; Indians near, 339.
— Platte, Indians on, 200.
— Portneuf, location, 260.
— des Prairies. *See* Ottawa.
— Richelieu, location, 51, 90; trade route, 240.
— Rupert, post on, 313.
— Saco, Indians of, 90.
— St Charles (Quebec), 41, 42, 44, 264.
— St. Clair, described, xx; ice in, 141; fort on, xviii, 139.
— St Croix, Poutrincourt on, 331.
— St Francis, location, 51.
— St. John, described, 325, Indians near, 339; hunting upon, 325; French on xxviii; Englishman captured at, 265; posts upon, 324, 325.
— St. Joseph (Mich), Lahontan at, 207, 208, 210; La Salle's fort on, 208; later French fort, 208.
— St Lawrence, described, xxxvii, 31, 39, 264, 304; source, 304, 323; length, 304; breadth, 305; shores, 261; forests, 70; current, 304; winds, 261; becomes salt, 323; ice in, xi, 32, 38, 45, 90, 232, 249, 250, 266; navigation, 49-53, 67, 122, 261, 262, 270, 657; affluents, 49, 219, 261, 306; islands, 31, 39, 52, 118, 260, 261, 305; rapids, 67-70, 85, 122, 226, 232; lakes within, 51, 67, 219; fish, 306, 358, 360, 361, 401; harbors, 261, boats on, 239, 241, 242, 657; Indians on, 90, 221, 223, 340, early

ROC

River St Lawrence (*continued*).
explorations, 303; voyages on, 260-262, 274; naval battles off mouth, 259, 260; French captured on, 243, Canadian boundary, 302; seigniories on, 34, 260; cities on, 38.
— St Louis. *See* Illinois.
— St Mary, route to, 153.
— St. Maurice, described, 50; flows into St. Lawrence, 49, 51; Indians on, 340.
— St. Peter's. *See* Minnesota.
— Saginaw, described, 319; hunting grounds of, 143, 318, Indian murder at, 146.
— Saguenay, location, 31; Jolliet ascends, 244; vessels refuge in, 244, 249.
— Salmon, identified, 72, 322.
— Sand. *See* Au Sable.
— Seignelay. *See* Illinois.
— Taio, Lahontan on, 629, 630, 648, 649.
— Tanaouate, 322; identified, 318.
— Theonontaté (Teonontaté), in Huron country, 154, 318, 322.
— of Toronto, outlet, 322.
— Trent, portage to Lake Ontario, 318.
— of Tsonontouans *See* Genessee River and Irondequoit Creek.
— de Vase (Muddy), on Ottawa route, 219.
— Wabash (Ouabache), early name for Ohio, 205.
— Wisconsin, described, 177, 178; islands in, 177, 178, Lahontan on, xxiv, 177, 178.
— Wolf (Wis), Indian village on, 174.
— Yamaska, location, 51.
Riverside Natural History, 478.
Roach, in Canada, 358, 362.
Robineau. *See* Portneuf.
Rochelle, port of departure for Canada, xi, xxvii, 25, 26, 40, 119, 120, 145, 229, 235, 238, 373, 374, 377; La-

Rochelle (*continued*)
hontan at, 242, 252, 257, harbor, 294; merchant of, 296, 657; Adario in, 536.
Roe-bucks, in Canada, 343; Lake Erie, 320, 322; near Detroit, 139, 161; in Illinois, 206, near Lake Michigan, 210; as food, 169, 187, 367, 482; price of skins, 380.
Rolland, François le Noir, *dit*, Lachine trader, 240.
Roots, used as medicine, 161.
Rotterdam, Lahontan at, 648, 651, 652, 692.
Rouen, birthplace of Gueudeville, xliv; merchants found Quebec, 303.
Rousseau, Jean Jacques, anticipated by Lahontan, xlvii; *Discours sur l'Origine et les Fondements de l'Inégalité parmi les Hommes*, xlvii, xlviii.
Roy, Edmond, opinion as to River Long, xl, xli; "Le Baron de Lahontan," xviii, xl, lii, 37, 151, 257, 273, 279, 288, 293, 391, bibliography of Lahontan, lii
Ruche, fish implement, 406
Rupert Land, Indians of, 342.

SABIN, Joseph, *Dictionary of Books relating to America*, lii, lxxv, lxxxii.
Sabres, in fur-trade, 378.
Sacacommis, identified, 474.
Saco (Me), attacked by Indians, 90.
Saentsouan, Huron chief, 141.
Sagard-Theodat, Gabriel, *Histoire du Canada et voyages que les frères mineurs Récollets y ont faicts*, 413.
Saguenay County (Quebec), 261.
"St Albans," English man-of-war, 276, 277.
"St. Ann," Lahontan in charge of, 274.
St. Bento, Benedictine monastery in Lisbon, 630.

St. Castin, Anselm, son of Jean Vincent, influence with Indians, 328
—— Baron Jean Vincent, sketch, xi, 328, 329
St. Denis. *See* Juchereau
St. Francis de Sales, mission village, 46, 48, 49, 328.
— du Sault, mission village, 56.
— Xavier mission. *See* Green Bay.
Ste Hélène, Jacques le Moyne, sieur de, 118; leads raid against Schnectady, 236; Lahontan encounters, 217; expedition to Hudson Bay, 217; death, 248.
St Ignace, mission of, 146, 154
St John (N. B.), tercentenary celebrated, 324; attacked by English, 325
St. John de Luz, trade with Newfoundland, 282, 288; sketch, 288.
St. John de Pied de Port, roads, 716.
St. Johns (Newfoundland), described, 333
St Lazare, order of, Lahontan receives, xxvi, 253, 254; history, 254.
St. Louis, La Salle's colony in Illinois, 33
St. Lusson, Simon François Daumont, sieur de, takes possession of Northwest, 342.
St. Malo, fishers and explorers from, 308
St. Michel, —, captured by Iroquois, 270.
— order of, ix.
St. Nazaire, French harbor, 279, 281, 287.
St Pierre, Jacques le Gardeur, sieur de, receives Washington, 209.
St. Simon, Louis de Rouvroy, duc de, *Memoirs*, 227.
St. Sulpice, Parisian church, 165.
St. Vallier, Jean Baptiste de la Croix Chevrière, abbé de, bishop of Quebec, 165, 383; arrives in Canada, 232;

ST. V

St. Vallier (*continued*).
visits diocese, 232; adjusts curés, 386; intercedes for English envoy, 246; sketch, 165, 383; portrait, 165.
"Salleeman," pirate ship, 296.
Salmon, in Acadia, 324; Canada, 358; Newfoundland, 333; Famine River, 74.
Salvelinus namycush, 148.
Sandaouires, Huron Indian, 146.
Santee Indians. *See* Issati.
Sasteretsi, Huron chiefs, sketch, 461.
Sauk (Saki) Indians, habitat, xxiv, 168, 341; language, 341; village, 168; entertain Lahontan, xxiv, 168–171; amalgamate with Foxes, 175, 397, 398; sketch, 168; characterized, 341.
Sault du Buisson, St. Lawrence rapid, 67.
— des Cedres, St. Lawrence rapid, 67.
— de la Chaudiere. *See* St. Francis de Sales.
— Long (of Ottawa), defended by Dollard, 217; Lahontan passes, 217; Iroquois battle, 270.
— Long (of St. Lawrence), 67, 68.
— au Récollet, mission village, 55.
— Ste. Marie, described, 152, 153, 316; legend, 152; Indians of, 149, 152, 340, 342, 493, 494; war-party from, xxii, 153; Lahontan at, xxii, 152, 153; fort, 149, 488, 489; mission, xviii, 149; importance, 149, 152; sketch, 149.
— St. Louis origin of name, 66; described, 66, 67; mission village on, 56, 239, 339, 340; Lahontan endangered in, xxv, 219, Jolliet loses papers in, 219, 244.
Saulteur Indians. *See* Chippewa.
Saurel, Pierre de, Canadian seignior, 52.
Savary, A. W., *County of Annapolis*, 330.
Saw-mills, in Canada, 371.
Scadding, Henry, antiquarian of Toronto, 154, 155, 318; *Toronto of Old*, 318.

SHI

Schefer, John, *Lapland*, 705.
Schenectady (Corlaer), raided by French, 233, 235, 236.
Schuyler, Peter, leads raiding party, 262; "Report," 262.
Sciuropterus volucella, 348.
Scotch, in Nova Scotia, 331.
Scurvy, described, 406; causes, 676-678.
Sea of Jesso, seeking passage to, 310.
— of Saragossa, described, 9.
— Vermillion. *See* Pacific Ocean.
Sea-cows, described, 358, 361.
— parrots, described, 351, 355.
— mews, described, 351, 355.
Seals (sea-wolves), described, 349; in Acadia, 326; Canada, 344; hunted, 31, 333; skins in trade, 305, 307-309; price, 380; for canoes, 307; considered as fish, 326.
Seignelay, Jean Baptiste, marquis de, French minister, 118; Lahontan accredited to, 250-252; Lahontan's letter to, xxi, 149–152; death of, xxvi, 251, 252; successor, 252.
Seigneuries sauvage, trade stations, 325.
Seneca (Tsonontouans) Indians, habitat, 58, 127, 130, 131. 137, 323, 341; language, 341; domestic animals, 131; arms, 513, at war with Miami, 162; English should remove, 399; enemies of French, 77, 80; destroy La Salle's fort, 131; ambush Denonville, 128, country laid waste, xvi, 130, 131.
Severance, Frank H., *Old Trails on Niagara Frontier*, 131.
Seven Trumpets, 686, 704.
Shad, in Canada, 358.
Shawnee (Chauanon) Indians, sketch, 82.
Shea, John Gilmary, translator, 149, 217; "Huron Indians," 155; *Discovery and Exploration of Mississippi Valley*, 204; *Early Voyages on Mississippi*, 200.
Shell-fish, in Canada, 359, 361.
Shirts (linen), in fur-trade, 377.

SIL

Sillery, mission village, 46, 48, 49, 329, 330, 339, 340.
Silver mines, near Lake Erie, 322.
Simcoe County (Ont.), Hurons in, 154.
Siouan family, tribes of, 200, 202, 204, 305, 342, 343, 398; migrations, 200, 204.
Sioux (Nadouessioux) Indians, significance of name, 175; described, xxxix, habitat, 175, 342; language, 342, 343; totems, 511; relations with Foxes, 175, 176; enemies of, 182, 198, 199; war with Iroquois, 198, 199; Duluth among, 73; missions, xviii; Lahontan ignorant of their country, 342, 343.
Slavery, among Indians, 94, 104, 169; among French in Illinois, 169.
Sledges, described, xii, 406.
Sloops, described, 656-658; advantages of Dutch, 657, cost of passage on, 656.
Small-pox, among Indians, 595, 603.
Smelt, in Canada, 358.
Smithsonian Institution, *Reports*, 477.
Snipe, in Canada, 110, 351.
Snow-shoes, described, xii, 103, 104.
Soap, in fur-trade, 378.
Sokoki (Soccoki) Indians, habitat, 90, 328; language, 339; enemies of Mohawk, 90; wandering, 328; in fur-trade, 90; sketch, 90; characterized, 339.
Sonkaskiton Indians. *See* Choukasketon.
Sorcery, penalty for, 562, 563.
Sorel, described, 52, 90.
Souffleur, large sea-fish, 358, 360.
Souriquois Indians *See* Micmac.
South America, ships from refuge at Placentia, 335.
Southey, Robert, Lahontan memoir in library of, xxxiv.
Souza, Don John of, Portuguese governor-general, 621.
Spain, Lahontan in, xxxiii; his letter from, 718-731; war with, 5; diplomats,

SUL

Spain (*continued*).
12; treasure ships, 244; mulattoes, 284.
Spanheim, Ezekiel, *History of Cæsars*, 692.
Spaniards, Lahontan's party mistaken for, 190, 191; inhabit New Mexico, 191, 192; savages taken for, 192, 193; Lahontan inquires for, 204; fishery at Newfoundland, 308; port of, 308.
Sparrow-hawks, in Canada, 352
Spars, used in canoes, 407.
Spermophile tridecemlineatus, 348.
Squanto, Indian warrior, 90.
Squash. *See* Citrouille.
Squirrels, in Canada, 343, 344, 348.
Starlings, in Canada, 352.
Sterlets, in Canada, 351, 355.
Stockings (worsted), in fur-trade, 377.
Strait of Belle Isle, separates Newfoundland, 309, 334.
— Canso (Campceaux, Canseaux), origin of name, 325.
— of Dardanelles, 680; ceremony in passing, 29.
— Davis's, discovered, 309, 310.
— of Detour, location, 153.
— of Gibraltar, 680; ceremony in passing, 29; ship founders off, 289.
— Hudson, discovery of, 309, 310.
— of Mackinac, described, 147, 148; post on, xx.
— of Sund, ceremony in passing, 29; toll exacted at, 679, 680.
Strawberries, in Canada, 365, 372.
Sturgeon, described, 156, 361, 362; in Great Lakes, 316, 320, 359.
Sugar, scarce in Canada, 369, 374, 375.
Suicide, practised by Indians, 530.
Sulpitians, seigneurs of Montreal, 52, 55; missions of, 54, 55, 70; seminary at Montreal, 55; at Paris, 55, 165; arrive in Canada, 55; fiefs of, 55; in New World, 145; sketch, 55.

SUL

Sulte, Bénjamin, "Le Regiment de Carignan," 36; "Pierre Boucher et son Livre," 98; "Pretendues Origines des Canadiens Français," 37; "La Rivière des Trois Rivières," 51, *Histoire des Canadiens Français*, 41, 330.
Susquehannock Indians, 321.
Swallows, in Canada, 350, 352.
Swans, in Canada, 350.
Swift, Jonathan, *Gulliver's Travels*, xlii.
Sword-blades, in fur-trade, 377.
Sword-fish, struggle with whale, 30.

TABITIBI Indians. *See* Abittibi.
Tadoussac, location, 31, 261; history, 31, seigniories near, 260; fur-trade, xxxvii; English fleet off, 242, 244, 249.
Tahuglauk Indians, habitat, xxiv, 195; characteristics, 194, 196; manufactures, 194, 195; wars, 196.
Talon, Ottawa chief, 153, 317.
— Jean, intendant of New France, 42, 163; befriends Perrot, 53; successor, 228; brings back Recollects, 413.
Tanuas striatus, 348.
Tanner, Herbert B., "Early Kaukauna," 174.
Tazou, Indian measure of distance, 192.
Teals, in Canada, 109, 351.
Tecumseh, precursor of, 149.
Teganissoren, Onondaga chief, sketch, 222.
"Tempest," carries Lahontan to Canada, 26.
Temple, Sir Thomas, grantee in Nova Scotia, 265.
Tench, in Mississippi River, 359.
Temiscaming (Temiskamink) Indians, characterized, 342.

TOB

Teton (Atinton) Indians, Siouan tribe, 342, 343.
Têtu, Henri, *Palais épiscopal de Québec*, 42.
Texas, La Salle's expedition to, 145.
Thallassartos maritimus, 348.
Thegarouhies, Seneca village, 131.
Thévenot, Nicolas M., *Receuil des Voyages Curieux*, 412.
Thomas, Cyrus, "Maya Calendar," 428.
Thornbacks, in Canada, 358.
Thread, in fur-trade, 378.
Three Rivers (Lake Superior), 316.
Three Rivers (St. Lawrence), 48; described, xxxvii, 49–51; governors of, 51, 98, 131, 266, 383; fort, 239; courts of justice, 392; commerce, 376.
Thrushes, in Canada, 350.
Thwaites, Reuben G., *Down Historic Waterways*, 178; *Early Western Travels*, 93, 304, 417, 433, 457, 510, 514, 734; *Hennepin's New Discovery*, 70, 136, 137, 176, 335, 413, 460; *How George Rogers Clark Won the Northwest*, 92, 146, 315; *Original Journals of Lewis and Clark Expedition*, 343, 427, 431, 474, 483; "Story of Chequamegon," 315; "Story of Mackinac," 92, 146; *Withers's Chronicles*, 506. *See also* Jesuit Relations.
Timber, of Canada, 366, 373, 374.
Tobacco, raised by Indians, 474; Indians prize Brazilian, 140, 169, 207, 373, 377, 474; strongest known, 474, 475; Canadian resembles Spanish, 364; differs from Brazilian, 474; amount raised, 373; imported, 373; tariff on, 373; cargoes, 287, price, 373, 375; Lahontan gives as present, 169, 174, 176; boxes imported, 375.
"Toby," vessel. *See* "Joli."

TOM

Tomahawk (casse-tête), defined, 402.
Tonty, Henri de, La Salle's lieutenant, 125, 133; in Illinois, 125, 133, 207; granted Fort St. Louis, 125, 133, 207; Lahontan accompanies, xviii, 133, 207; at Detroit, 133; in Louisiana, 133; at Fort St Joseph, xx, 139; respected by Indians, 207; sketch, 133
Toronto, portage, 318. *See also* Lake Simcoe and Georgian Bay.
Torontogueronon Indians, language of, 733.
Townsend, Capt —, English naval officer, 650, 651.
"Tract Scuyt," Holland boat, described, 652.
Tracy, Alexander Prouville, marquis de, governor of New France, 52, 59.
Treaties, French shore of Newfoundland (1904), 333, 334; Ryswick, 236, 265; Utrecht, 5, 314, 334.
Trochilus colubris, 354.
Trout, in Great Lakes, 148, 316, 359; Newfoundland, 333; River Long, 190; Lake Erie, 320; size, 148, 362, 363; inferior to whitefish, 148; enemies of armed-fish, 362; manner of catching, 148, 363; used as bait, 113; as food, 467, 482, 491.
Troyes, Chevalier de, commandant at Niagara, 131, 162.
Tsonontouan Indians. *See* Seneca.
Turbots, in Canada, 358.
Turcot, —, coureur de bois, 141.
Turenne, Count de, his son, 11.
Turkey wheat, 139, 140, 199, 202.
Turkeys, furnished by mission Indians, 70; in Canada, 350; near Lake Michigan, 210, in Illinois, 206; Detroit, 161; Missouri River, 200; Lake Erie, xix, 138, 320, 322.
Turtle doves *See* Pigeons.

VIN

United States Bureau of Ethnology, editions of Lahontan in library, liii–xciii; *Bulletins*, 428; *Reports*, 47, 169, 175, 435, 468, 499, 509, 510, 512.
— Geological Survey, *Contributions to Ethnology*, 418.
Upper country (pays en haut), route to, 95, 164; Indians descend from, 241; French take possession of, xviii; project for fortifyiug, xxix, xlv, 271–273.
Ursulines, in Canada, 44.
Ursus americanus, 347.

Vaccinium canadense, 372.
Valrennes, Philippe Clément Duvault, sieur de, commandant at Fort Frontenac, 226, 233; returns to Montreal, 226; defeats English, 262, sketch, 226.
Vaudreuil, Philippe de Rigaud, marquis de, governor of Canada, 119; rescues Lahontan, xxv, 219; notified of English attack (1711), 222; pursues Iroquois, 270, 271; sketch, 119
Vaugiraud, birthplace of Sulpitian order, 55.
Vaugondy, Robert de, map of, xxxviii.
Vermillion, in fur-trade, 378
Verazzano, Giovanni da, discovers Canada, 303.
Versailles, Lahontan visits, xxvii, xxx, xxxii, xlvi, 252–257, 279, 280; court described, xxvii, 254–257.
Vetromile, Eugene, *Abenakis and their History*, 328.
Victor (N Y.), Indian village near, 127.
Viele, Arnout Cornelisse, peace messenger, 157.
Ville Marie. *See* Montreal.
Villedonné, Etienne de, captured by Iroquois, 224.
Vincennes, Jean Bissot, sieur de, 244.

VOL

Voltaire, Françoise Marie Arouet, *dit*, anticipated by Lahontan, xlvii
Vujer, John Nider de, works of, 703
Vultures, in Canada, 350, 352–354.

WAHPETON (Ouadebaton) Indians, Siouan tribe, 342, 343
Walnuts, on Lake Erie, 319; in Seneca country, 131.
Wampum, use of, 431; belts, 75, 76, 93.
Wapiti. *See* Elk
War, Frontenac's (1689–97), 55, 60, 61, 69, 70, 118, 125, 149, 209, 239, 240, 275, 328, Queen Anne's (Spanish Succession, 1702–13), 5, 12, 99; officer in, 209
Washington, Maj George, visits French on Allegheny, 209.
Watches, imported, 375.
Water-fowl, in Acadia, 331; in Newfoundland, 332, 355, 356; near Lake Champlain, xiv, 108, 109.
Watermelons, in Canada, 364, 368, 369
Waupaca County (Wis), Indian village in, 175.
Wayne, Gen. Anthony, victory over Indians, 461.
Wea Indians. *See* Ouiatonon.
Weasels, in Canada, 343, 380.
Weir, Robert Stanley, *Administration of Old Regime in Canada*, 34, 45.
Wells, H. P., "The Beaver," 479, 483.
West Indies, French possessions in, 26, 288, 289, 334, French officers in, 59, 236; death of Iberville, 236; Spanish treasure, 244, English fleet, 288, 289; commerce, 374.
Whales, struggle with sword-fish, 30, off Newfoundland, 333; in Canada, 358. *See also* Balenots
Wheler, Sir Francis, besieges Placentia, 288, 289; sketch, 289.
Whistlers (sifflers), described, 110, 111, 344

WIS

White, Andrew D , *Warfare of Science with Theology*, 704
Whitefish, at Mackinac, 147; as food, 147, 148, 169, 363, netted, 147; in Great Lakes, 316, 359.
White-wood, of Canada, 365, 371, 372
Wildcats, called "children of Devil," 344, Lahontan hunts, 115; skins, 376, 380.
Wild rice, Indian food, 174, 175
William III (Prince of Orange), king of England, 3, 217; orders attack on Placentia, 278; invades England, 12.
Williams, Commodore —, attacks Placentia, 275–279
— Roger, writings of, 734
Wines, exported to Canada, 373; made in Canada, 368; value, 375; of Aragon, 721; Denmark, 671; Germany, 663; Holland, 663.
Winnebago Indians, Siouan tribe, 398; significance of name, 146, habitat, 398; bay and river named for, 167, 168
— Rapids (Wis), 174.
Winship, George Parker, aid acknowledged, liii
Winsor, Justin, *Narrative and Critical History of America*, lii
Winthrop, Gen John, commands Canadian expedition, 240.
Wisconsin, early exploration of, 209; fertility, 168; route to Mississippi, 168, 177, 178; Indians, 77, 168, 174, 175, 341, 398, Indian wars, xlvi; Lahontan visits, 167–178, mission in, 168, territory of, 178, Historical Society, staff of, xlviii, editions of Lahontan in library of, liii–xciii; erects monument, 168 ; *Historical Collections*, 77, 82, 99, 139, 140, 146, 174, 175, 177, 312, 315, 317, 343, 460, 461, 506; *Proceedings*, 168, 174, 312.

Witchcraft, Lahontan on, 696–710; penalty for, 562–564.
Withers, Alexander, *Chronicles of Border Warfare*, 506.
Wolf Indians. *See* Loup.
Wolverine. *See* Carcajou.
Wolves, Canadian, 343; on River Long, 183; do not attack beavers, 480; traps, 483, 484; price of skins, 380.
Wood-hens, 351; as food, 105, 169; hunted, 115, 116.
Woolen cloth, Canadian import, 377.

Wrightstown (Wis.), rapids near, 174.
Wyandot Indians. *See* Huron.

YAMASKA County (Quebec), Indian mission in, 49.
Yankton Indians, Siouan tribe, 343
Yellowstone National Park, beaver-preserve in, 481.

ZENO, cited by Lahontan, 419.
Zizania aquatica, 175.